"Spirited and meticulously documented, this is a trip deep into the heart of Gaza—important for anyone who cares about the Palestinian plight, even more important for those who care about Israel."

—AMY WILENTZ, *Newsday*

"Informative, absorbing . . . Most important is that Hass makes one realize the human aspect of the Palestinian plight."

—PRUDENCE HELLER, *Baltimore Sun*

"Hass busts stereotypes."

—MATTHEW HEIMER, *Brill's Content*

"Most interesting for its analysis of the surprising contradictions of Gazan society . . . Hass is surely correct when she writes that 'the human distress of a million people is a sea of nitroglycerin.' "

—SUSIE LINFIELD, *Los Angeles Times*

"A fascinating book . . . hardly sentimental."

—CAROLYN ALESSIO, *Chicago Tribune*

"Wonderful . . . Each testimonial is a poignant vignette of eloquence and spiritual resistance, each page offers a revelation, an insight into a people who have known nothing but hard times. *Drinking the Sea at Gaza* is an appeal to our humanity."

—BILL MAXWELL, *St. Petersburg Times*

"Unique and important, Hass, 'the enemy' and a woman to boot, dropped into a war zone armed with nothing but her compassion. She brought back a powerful, compelling portrait of a tragedy."

—TOM SEGEV, author of *The Seventh Million*

"Beautiful, passionate, and profoundly disturbing, Hass's book summons up the very essence of Gaza."

—AMOS ELON, author of *Founder*

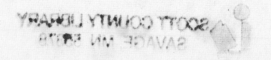

Drinking the Sea at Gaza

Drinking the Sea at Gaza

Days and Nights in a
Land Under Siege

Amira Hass
Translated by
Elana Wesley and Maxine Kaufman-Lacusta

An Owl Book
Henry Holt and Company
New York

Henry Holt and Company, LLC
Publishers since 1866
115 West 18th Street
New York, New York 10011

Henry Holt® is a registered trademark
of Henry Holt and Company, LLC.

Library of Congress Cataloging-in-Publication Data
Hass, Amira.
[Li-shetot meha-yam shel 'Azah. English]
Drinking the sea at Gaza: days and nights in a land under siege/
Amira Hass; translated by Elana Wesley and Maxine Kaufman-Lacusta.
p.   cm.
Includes bibliographical references and index.
ISBN 0-8050-5740-4
1. Gaza Strip—Politics and government.   2. Military government—
Gaza Strip.   3. Palestinian Arabs—Gaza Strip—Social life and
customs.   4. Arab-Israeli conflict—1993–   5. Hass, Amira—Journeys—
Gaza Strip.   I. Title.
DS110.G3H3713   1999   98-6103
953'.1—dc21   CIP

Henry Holt books are available for special promotions and
premiums. For details contact: Director, Special Markets.

Originally published in Israel in 1996 by Hasifriya Hahadasha,
Tel Aviv, under the title *Lishtot mehayam shel 'Aaza*
Chapter 4, "Khalid Switches Parties," has been abridged from the original.

First published in the United States in 1999
by Metropolitan Books

First Owl Books Edition 2000

Designed by Debbie Glasserman
Maps designed by Jeffrey L. Ward

Printed in the United States of America

10   9   8   7   6   5   4

To my parents—Hanna and Avraham

Contents

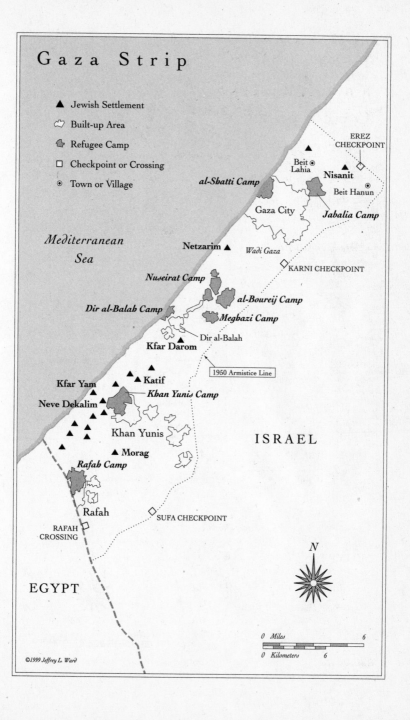

Gaza Strip

- ▲ Jewish Settlement
- ᗧ Built-up Area
- ᗧ Refugee Camp
- □ Checkpoint or Crossing
- ◉ Town or Village

*Mediterranean
Sea*

EREZ
CHECKPOINT

Beit
Lahia ◉ ▲
Nisanit ▲
Beit Hanun ◉

al-Shatti Camp

Gaza City

Jabalia Camp

Netzarim ▲ *Wadi Gaza*

◇ KARNI CHECKPOINT

Nuseirat Camp

al-Boureij Camp

Dir al-Balah Camp

Meghazi Camp

Dir al-Balah
Kfar Darom ▲

1950 Armistice Line

▲ **Katif**
Kfar Yam
Khan Yunis Camp
Neve Dekalim

ISRAEL

Khan Yunis

▲ **Morag**

Rafah Camp

SUFA CHECKPOINT

Rafah
RAFAH
CROSSING

N

EGYPT

©1999 Jeffrey L. Ward

0 *Miles* 6
0 *Kilometers* 6

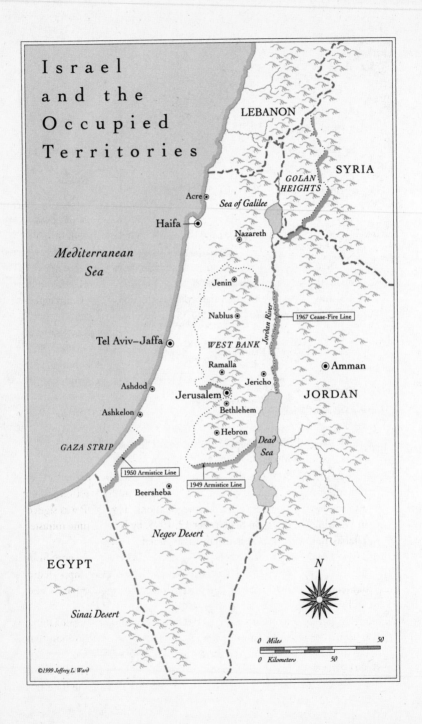

Israel
and the
Occupied
Territories

LEBANON

SYRIA

*GOLAN
HEIGHTS*

Acre

Sea of Galilee

Haifa

Nazareth

*Mediterranean
Sea*

Jenin

Nablus

Jordan River

1967 Cease-Fire Line

Tel Aviv–Jaffa

WEST BANK

Ramalla

Amman

Ashdod

Jericho

Jerusalem

JORDAN

Bethlehem

Ashkelon

Hebron

*Dead
Sea*

GAZA STRIP

1950 Armistice Line

Beersheba

1949 Armistice Line

Negev Desert

EGYPT

N

Sinai Desert

0   *Miles*   50

0   *Kilometers*   50

©1999 Jeffrey L. Ward

Glossary

Cairo Agreement: Signed in Cairo on May 4, 1994, the agreement formally initiated Palestinian self-rule and established terms for the Israeli military redeployment in Gaza and Jericho. The Cairo agreement also defined the structure of the Palestinian Authority, its relations with Israel, and the terms of Palestinian general elections. The Cairo agreement is also known as Oslo 1 and the Gaza-Jericho agreement.

Civil Administration: A separate branch of the Israeli military government in the occupied territories, set up in 1981 to handle civilian matters. The civil administration was dissolved in the Gaza Strip in 1994 but continues to function in those parts of the West Bank that remain under direct Israeli military control.

Communist Party: Established in 1919, it changed its name to the Palestinian People's Party in 1991.

Coordination and Liaison Office (CLO): The Israeli administration set this up in 1994 to replace the civil administration.

Declaration of Principles (DOP): An agreement to establish limited Palestinian self-rule in the Gaza Strip and in Jericho in the West Bank that also set down principles for further negotiations. The DOP was signed in Washington, D.C., on September 13, 1993, by Israeli prime minister Yitzhak Rabin and PLO chairman Yassir Arafat.

Democratic Front for the Liberation of Palestine (DFLP): Broke away from the PFLP in 1969; led by Naif Hawatmeh. The DFLP supported a democratic, secular state in Palestine with equal rights for Jews and Arabs; it now advocates a two-state solution.

Fatah: The largest and most influential Palestinian political organization, founded by Yassir Arafat in exile in 1959. Fatah took the position that the liberation of Palestine was primarily a Palestinian concern.

Baruch Goldstein: A Jewish doctor who lived in the West Bank settlement of Kiryat Arba, Goldstein opened fire on Moslems praying at the Ibrahimi mosque in Hebron. He killed twenty-nine Palestinians before he himself was killed. The massacre took place on February 25, 1994, during Ramadan, the Muslim month of fasting.

Hamas (the Islamic Resistance Movement): Formed at the beginning of the *intifada* in 1987 by Muslim Brotherhood leaders, among them Sheikh Ahmad Yassin and Salah Shehade. Hamas is the second largest organization in the occupied territories.

Intifada: The Palestinian popular uprising that began on December 9, 1987, in the Jabalia refugee camp in the Gaza Strip. The *intifada* ended officially in 1993 when the Letters of Mutual Recognition were exchanged between Israel and the PLO.

Islamic Jihad (Islamic Holy War): A Muslim Brotherhood breakaway group formed in the mid-1980s by Fathi Shiqaqi and Abd al-Aziz Oudeh, two refugees from Gaza. The Islamic Jihad advocates an Islamic state in all of Palestine.

Letters of Mutual Recognition: Following intense negotiations in Oslo, Yassir Arafat sent a letter to Prime Minister Yitzhak Rabin on September 9, 1993, in which the PLO recognized Israel's right to exist and renounced terrorism. In reply, Israel recognized the PLO as the representative of Palestinians in negotiations. The letters paved the way for the Oslo Accords.

Madrid Negotiations: U.S.-Soviet–sponsored Middle East peace conference in Madrid that opened in October 1991. The conference was attended by Syrian, Lebanese, Jordanian, and Israeli delegations; the Palestinians agreed to participate as members of the Jordanian delegation. Bilateral talks among the delegations continued in Washington, D.C., hosted by the U.S. State Department.

Muslim Brotherhood: Founded in Egypt in 1928 by Hasan al-Banna, a schoolteacher critical of the moral and political conduct of Arab leaders.

Oslo Accords: The umbrella term for a series of agreements signed by Israel and the PLO between September 1993 and September 1995, which includes the Declaration of Principles, the Cairo agreement, the Washington agreement, and the Paris Protocols. The accords are so called because early negotiations between the two sides were conducted in Oslo.

Palestinian Authority: The self-ruling body established in Gaza and Jericho in May 1994 as a result of the Oslo Accords; its jurisdiction was later extended to other parts of the West Bank. The Authority includes an eighty-eight-member elected legislative council, an executive branch that consists of some thirty members, and six security branches.

Palestinian Liberation Organization (PLO): Founded in Jerusalem in 1964 as a coalition of various Palestinian political factions. The PLO was tightly controlled by the Arab League until 1969, when the Fatah movement, led by Yassir Arafat, took command of the organization.

Palestine National Council (PNC): The PLO's legislative body, to which its 554 members are either nominated or elected. Seats were held vacant for residents of the occupied territories until April 1996, when all the members of the Palestinian Legislative Council joined its ranks.

Paris Protocols: Protocol on economic relations between Israel and the future Palestinian Authority, signed in Paris on April 29, 1994.

Partition Plan: In 1947 the United Nations proposed a plan to divide Palestine into two self-governing territories, one populated with Jews, the other with Arabs. The plan was accepted by the Jewish community in Palestine but rejected by most of the Arab population.

Permanent-status Negotiations: Talks on the final nature of a settlement between Israel and the Palestinians began on May 5, 1996, in Taba, a town on the Israeli-Egyptian border. These negotiations quickly broke down over Israel's delays on further redeployments in the West Bank.

Popular Front for the Liberation of Palestine (PFLP): A Marxist-Leninist organization founded in exile in 1967 by George Habash and historically the group most closely identified with the concept of armed struggle as the means to liberate Palestine.

Shabak: The Israeli intelligence agency responsible for internal security, Shabak operates within Israel and the occupied territories. *Shabak* is the Hebrew acronym for *sherut bitachon klali*, or General Security Service.

Um- and Abu-: Literally "mother of" and "father of." According to traditional Arab practice, parents adopt the name of their eldest son, who is usually named for his paternal grandfather.

United Nations Relief and Works Agency (UNRWA): Created by the United Nations General Assembly in 1949 to assist Palestinian refugees in Gaza, the West Bank, Lebanon, Syria, and Jordan.

Washington Agreement: Also called Oslo 2 or the Interim Agreement on the West Bank and the Gaza Strip, the accord was signed in Washington, D.C., on September 28, 1995. It expanded the jurisdiction of Palestinian self-rule in the West Bank for an interim period to end no later than five years after the signing of the Cairo accord, i.e., on May 4, 1999. Crucial issues, such as the status of Jerusalem, the Jewish settlements, and the Palestinian refugees were to be addressed in permanent-status negotiations.

Chronology

December 9, 1987: The *intifada* begins in the Jabalia refugee camp in the Gaza Strip and quickly spreads to refugee camps in the West Bank.

July 1989: Israel introduces "magnetic cards" in the occupied territories, an additional form of identity card that became a prerequisite for leaving the Gaza Strip and working in Israel.

January 15, 1991: The Gulf war begins. Israel revokes the general exit permit, in force since the early 1970s, which had allowed Palestinians to move freely throughout the country. In its place is a new pass system that is refined over time.

October 1991: The United States and the Soviet Union sponsor a Middle East peace conference in Madrid.

June 23, 1992: Yitzhak Rabin and the Israel Labor party win a clear election victory; after fifteen years the Likud party is out of power.

September 9, 1993: Israel and the PLO exchange letters of mutual recognition, paving the way for Palestinian self-rule.

September 13, 1993: The Declaration of Principles is signed by Israel and the PLO in Washington, D.C.

February 25, 1994: Baruch Goldstein massacres twenty-nine Palestinians in the Ibrahimi mosque in Hebron.

May 4, 1994: The Cairo agreement is signed in that city, formally initiating Palestinian self-rule in the Gaza Strip and Jericho.

May 17, 1994: Israel completes its military redeployment in the Gaza Strip; the Palestinian Authority is established.

July 1, 1994: Yassir Arafat delivers his first speech in Gaza.

February 7, 1995: The Palestinian Authority sets up the State Security Court, which quickly becomes a means to silence opposition to the Authority.

September 28, 1995: Yitzhak Rabin, Shimon Peres, and Yassir Arafat sign the Washington agreement, or the Interim agreement, on the West Bank and the Gaza Strip, which extends the jurisdiction of Palestinian self-rule.

November 4, 1995: Yigal Amir, a supporter of the Israeli religious right-wing, assassinates Yitzhak Rabin at a mass rally in Tel Aviv.

January 5, 1996: Yihye Ayash, a Hamas militant, is assassinated in the Gaza Strip.

January 20, 1996: Elections are held for the eighty-eight-member Palestinian Legislative Council.

February–March 1996: Three suicide bombings in Jerusalem and Tel Aviv leave fifty-seven Israeli civilians dead. Hamas claims responsibility.

April 22–24, 1996: The Palestine National Council convenes in Gaza and votes to repeal the clauses in the national charter that contradict the PLO's agreements with Israel.

June 29, 1996: Likud leader Benjamin Netanyahu is elected Israeli prime minister.

Drinking the Sea at Gaza

Introduction

One summer's day in 1995, I finally solved a mystery that had bothered me since childhood. Under a leafy mulberry tree in an orange grove that climbs up a gentle slope, then slowly descends toward the mosques of Gaza City that stretch out to meet the sea, I found the key to something I had read in an Israeli children's book many years ago. I have long since forgotten the book's title or the author, but I remember a boy in an orange grove swimming in a little pool. Growing up in the city, I could picture the fruit on the branches but simply could not imagine a swimming pool in the middle of an orchard.

I found my answer when friends in Gaza invited me to join them at a celebration in the orange grove of the family of Raji Sourani, an *intifada* activist and human rights lawyer. As I arrived, the orange grower was filling a large rectangular irrigation tank with water. When it was full, all the men in our group jumped in, shrieking like children at the shock of the cold water. (We women stayed out. This was conservative Gaza, after all.) And then I understood how, in my Israeli children's book, a pool came to be inside an orange grove.

It was not the first time, or the last, that I sensed echoes of my Israeli life in Gaza, whether it was in the sound of Hebrew that rang out in the refugee camps, or in the stories that old refugees would tell of their long-gone family homes in Palestine, speaking as if they had seen them only the week before, or in the darkly funny stories my friends told of their Israeli prison experiences. I had never seen my friends laugh the way they did that afternoon among the orange trees. Researchers, field-workers, and lawyers from the Gaza Center for Rights and Law, they had been among the first to introduce me to Gaza and its people; through them I got a taste of life under occupation; in their company I learned how the broad, disarming smiles of most Gazans conceal bottomless depths of sadness.

I had first come to Gaza as a volunteer for the Workers' Hot Line, an Israeli organization that represented workers from the occupied territories in their grievances against Israeli employers. Back then, in 1991, I was on the editorial staff of the daily newspaper *Ha'aretz*, and over time I began to write about the Strip, which was, in many ways, terra incognita. I made contacts: the first person to help was Tamar Peleg, an Israeli human rights lawyer who put me in touch with her former clients, all of whom she had represented during their administrative detention (a particularly odious measure that allows for indefinite imprisonment without trial) or other prison sentences. The top name on her list was Raji Sourani.

Everything else followed naturally: when the Declaration of Principles was signed in 1993, granting Palestinians limited self-rule in Gaza and in Jericho, I became the paper's correspondent in the Strip, covering the last few months of direct Israeli occupation and the transfer of authority. At that point, I decided to make my home in Gaza, at first moving from one friend's house to another's until I rented an apartment in Gaza City. Living in Gaza seemed a normal and logical step to me. How could I understand a society and write about it without actually being in the middle of it? I was, it seemed, like any other journalist sent to cover a foreign country. To most Israelis, though, my move seemed outlandish, even crazy, for they believed I was surely putting my life at risk.

Long before I actually moved to the Strip, I had discovered just how distorted the popular Israeli image of Gaza is—savage, violent, and hostile to Jews. In all the time I lived there, I made certain everyone knew that I was an Israeli and a Jew. The Hebrew speakers among my friends talked to me in my own language, without constraint—in their homes and offices, on the streets and in the markets, in the refugee camps, at a house in Khan Yunis where people had come to mourn the death of a girl shot by Israeli soldiers during a break in the curfew, at a demonstration calling for the release of prisoners, at the wedding of someone's brother. I often slept in some of their homes when Israeli-imposed curfews and army patrols still ruled the night. "What would your friends do if militants found out there was a Jewish woman staying with them?" I was asked by a man in Tel Aviv, someone with a reputation as a knowledgeable Arabist. The question took me by surprise. That my presence itself might cause trouble had never occurred to me or to my hosts, as I later confirmed. None of my friends was concerned; they opened their homes to me freely, whether in the Rafah refugee camp or in al-Shatti camp, which sprawls along the shoreline of Gaza City. Thanks to them, I learned to see Gaza through the eyes of its people, not through the windshield of an army jeep or in the interrogation rooms of the Shabak, the Israeli security service.

My experience in Gaza, the ease with which people accepted me, the natural way we talked about things and even argued, was my answer to all the Israelis who asked, "How come you're not afraid?," who wondered what on earth had possessed me. But it was in fact a partial explanation; generally I sidestepped the full story.

My parents' memories, told to me since my childhood and absorbed by me until they became my own, are the other part of the story. Holocaust survivors, Communists, southeastern European Jews living in Israel, my parents had raised me on the epics of resistance, on the struggles of a persecuted people. At my father's Romanian school in Suceava, for example, a third of the students were Jewish. It was agreed that they would come to school on Saturdays, on the Sabbath, but that no tests or other written assignments would be given. One day an anti-Semitic history teacher changed the rules and scheduled a test for a Saturday. As a child I loved hearing how my father—thirteen years old and still an orthodox Jew, deeply confident and sure of his place in the world—organized a strike of the Jewish students, even persuading the two nonobservant boys to join their classmates. The principal moved to expel him but strings were pulled (a practice known as exercising *wasta* in Arabic) and the punishment was reduced to a one-month suspension. In their appeal to a sympathetic teacher, my grandparents had argued that religious freedom and minority rights were at stake. "Nonsense!" the teacher answered. "Everyone knows the boy is a born Bolshevik." My father remained a die-hard rabble-rouser all his life.

My mother had her stories, too. She had also been accused of having Bolshevik sympathies, although under very different circumstances. In the barracks at Bergen-Belsen, to which she had been deported, the only food was a foul soup made of rotten turnips, and the person doling it out had no interest in giving equal portions. My mother and some of her friends took over the distribution and made sure everyone got the same amount. "What do you think this is?" the barracks chief yelled at her. "A Soviet?" The other women also kept watch for informers while my mother broke the rules, documenting the Nazi inferno as she wrote a diary on scraps of paper.[1] In addition, she secretly taught the children in the barracks, an infraction that put everyone's lives at risk.

A tolerant city, almost idyllic—such is the picture of Sarajevo before the Second World War that emerges from my mother's memories. The muezzin's call to prayer, the church bells, and the Sabbath psalms sung in Ladino were the melodies of her childhood. She also recalled defending that tolerance. Muslims, Christians, and Jews lived together, studied in the same classrooms, went together to university, together became atheists and joined the Communist underground. The only slap, I suspect, that my mother ever gave to anyone she delivered at that time. A fellow student, a Muslim, had made fun of the Jews and she smacked him. Later they made up.

My parents' heroes were my heroes; the scenes engraved on their memories were stored in mine. My mother talked of her math teacher—Marcel Schneider—who once, when they crossed paths, bowed to her and tipped his hat; awkward and embarrassed, she was weighed down with books and carrying her mother's freshly kneaded dough to the baker's. I too cherished his dignity and courtesy. Everyone had known his secret—that he was a Communist. During the war he joined the partisans and was captured and hanged by the Nazis. Years later, in the Jewish Museum in Belgrade, I shuddered when I saw the underground leaflet announcing his execution. My father's family was deported to the ghetto at Transnistria, where his parents died from typhus and starvation. He never forgot the pastry shop in the ghetto, where those with means and some members of the Judenrat would buy cakes while hungry children stood outside and stared with longing in their eyes. Whenever I hear the pieties of "Jewish unity," I remember that unity ended at the entrance to Transnistria.

These narratives were my parents' legacy—a history of resisting injustice, speaking out, and fighting back. But of all their memories that had become my own, one stood out beyond the others. On a summer day in 1944, my mother was herded from a cattle car along with the rest of its human cargo, which had been transported from Belgrade to the concentration camp at Bergen-Belsen. She saw a group of German women, some on foot, some on bicycles, slow down as the strange procession went by and watch with indifferent curiosity on their faces. For me, these women became a loathsome symbol of watching from the sidelines, and at an early age I decided that my place was not with the bystanders.

In the end, my desire to live in Gaza stemmed neither from adventurism nor from insanity, but from that dread of being a bystander, from my need to understand, down to the last detail, a world that is, to the best of my political and historical comprehension, a profoundly Israeli creation. To me, Gaza embodies the entire saga of the Israeli-Palestinian conflict; it represents the central contradiction of the State of Israel—democracy for some, dispossession for others; it is our exposed nerve. I needed to know the people whose lives had been forever altered by my society and my history, whose parents and grandparents, refugees, were forced from their villages in 1948.

Indeed, I quickly found that something special tied me to the refugees and the camps in which they lived; I felt at home there, in the temporary permanence, in the longing that clings to every grain of sand, in the rage that thrives in the alleyways. Only gradually, and just to a very few friends in Gaza and Israel, did I begin to explain that it was my heritage, a singular autobiographical blend passed on by my parents, that had paved my way to the Gaza Strip.

All during my childhood my parents continued pursuing their socialist vision of justice, whether through their involvement in workers' strikes and demonstrations, or their outspoken protest against the military rule over Palestinians in Israel, or their fierce opposition to David Ben-Gurion's dealings with West Germany. The police showed up on our doorstep several times, once to question my mother about distributing political leaflets, later to arrest my father for organizing illegal rallies.

I was five when I asked them why they had come to Israel; after all, they had never been Zionists. I found my answer years later, during the eighties, while studying in Amsterdam. Living there, I felt the true force of the void left after 1945, of how Europe, home to millions of Jews for hundreds of years, had simply spewed them out; how most people had collaborated with Nazi Germany's antipluralistic psychosis and accepted the gradual and final removal of the Jews with indifference. But more, I felt tormented by the ease with which Europe had accepted the emptiness that followed, had filled the void, and moved on. Today I understand that my parents' vision of a socialist utopia helped us all escape the vacuum that was left after Auschwitz. And I know too that it was the same emptiness—the familiar streets that would forever scream of the murder of family and friends and neighbors—that drove my parents, along with hundreds of thousands of other survivors, to flee, to choose a new homeland with orange trees, olive groves, and blinding white sunlight.

I do not yearn for the landscapes of their childhood. I was born to the saffron of Jerusalem, the squills on the seashore, and the dry desert wind. But in my memory there will always be my parents' backward glance, their last look at the beloved homes from which they were banished. Because of their loss, though, my parents, unlike many other Jewish newcomers, would not move into a home just vacated by other refugees—Palestinians—when they arrived in Israel in 1949.

That same lazy summer afternoon in the Souranis' orchard, July 13, 1995, was a big day for the Palestinian Authority. After years in exile, Mahmud Abbas was coming home, not to Safed—his birthplace, now in Israel—but to Gaza. Also known as Abu Mazen, this longtime leader of the Palestine Liberation Organization was one of the chief architects of the Oslo Accords, but for more than a year he had kept his distance from Yassir Arafat, dismayed at the nature of the negotiating process with Israel. His arrival in Gaza signaled a considerable improvement in his relations with Arafat; indeed, he was appointed second in command and reinstated into the inner circle of negotiators. As a journalist I was expected to stand with the army of correspondents at Arafat's headquarters and document the embrace marking the reconciliation between these two men. Instead, I had chosen to bask in the orange grove with my friends and share their celebration. I preferred to be with them in any case; it has always been my conviction that history is made more in the currents of ordinary life than it is by rulers and their ceremonies.

My friends had their own reason to be happy. Earlier that year, Raji Sourani had been removed from his position as director of the Gaza

Center for Rights and Law, which had first monitored Israeli human rights violations and later, after authority was transferred to the Palestinians, questioned the legality of Arafat's State Security Court. Most of the center's staff members resigned in protest against Sourani's dismissal. Now, after three months of suspense and uncertainty, Sourani had received permission from the Palestinian Ministry of Justice to open a new human rights office.

This gave us all hope for the chances of civil society under Palestinian self-rule and rewarded my friends' perseverance and courage. I knew of their ambivalence, too—how their lives would be consumed by work, and how tempted they were to forget the troubles of the world, to concentrate on their own needs and those of their families. But on that sun-drenched day in the Souranis' orchard (where one of my friends from the center, born in the Jabalia refugee camp, used to sneak in as a child and help himself to oranges), they put aside their misgivings and we all enjoyed ourselves for a few hours. To the east, the light stroked the fields of Beit Hanun in Gaza and the Israeli kibbutzim of Kfar Aza and Erez (once the Palestinian village of Dimra). At that distance we could see no borders slashing the brown soil, dividing the lofty cypresses or the eucalyptuses, and the shadows cast by the mulberry tree—to me so Israeli, to my friends so Palestinian—restored the soul. From the top of the hill, spread before us, was one country.

A slight turn of one's head and the view changed—it was the sea hugging the horizon. Just before signing the Oslo Accords, the late Yitzhak Rabin said of Gaza, "If only it would just sink into the sea." His harsh words reflect a widespread Israeli attitude toward the Gaza Strip and its one million inhabitants. Numerous articles by Israeli writers have used even stronger language, calling it a "hornets' nest" and a "dunghill." To Yitzhak Shamir, the former prime minister, Gaza represented the eternal untrustworthiness of Palestinians: "The sea is the same sea, the Arabs are the same Arabs," he said. The Israeli point of view is best summed up by the local variant of "Go to hell," which is, quite simply, "Go to Gaza."

Yassir Arafat also makes frequent mention of the sea at Gaza. I first heard him do so when he spoke of the Palestinian dream of an independent state with Jerusalem as its capital. "And whoever doesn't like it," he told his listeners, who were clearly enjoying his tough language, "can go drink the sea at Gaza." I needed an explanation and was told that this was a variation of the popular expression "Go drink seawater," which also means none other than "Go to hell."

When I told my friend Abu Ali from the Jabalia refugee camp that I had decided to call my book "Drinking the Sea at Gaza," the title reminded him of the Egyptian expression "to drink the waters of the Nile." It is this association that I prefer, for whoever drinks from the Nile, according to tradition, will always come back to it.

Part I

Yearning
to Be Free

Chapter 1

The Military Governor Has Moved Buildings

If the soldier in the sentry tower noticed the couple passing by down below, he apparently found nothing about them to arouse his suspicions. On that summer night in 1985, the headlights of the cars on Omar al-Mukhtar Boulevard in Gaza City and the light spilling from the building that housed the Israeli Northern Gaza Battalion illuminated a scene that seemed perfectly natural and normal: a woman in her final months of pregnancy, leaning on her short, skinny companion with the heaviness of intimacy, as, arm in arm, they sauntered along the length of the perimeter fence of an Israel Defense Forces (IDF) base in the heart of the city. The building, referred to by the people as the Majlis (Council) or al-Majlis al-Tashri'i (Legislative Council), was the seat of the Israeli military governor. It was also called al-Jundi al-Majhul (the Unknown Soldier) after the memorial erected by the Egyptians at the end of the boulevard. Of that, only the pedestal remained, since, as most Gazans recall, the statue was blown up by Israeli soldiers in June 1967.

Just a few hours before the couple took their stroll, the man, A.S., had thrown a hand grenade at the building's sentry tower. For the previous couple of days, he and two comrades had been monitoring the movements of the soldiers there. "We set the zero hour and drove by very fast. I threw the grenade. But we hadn't noticed that the top of the fence had been raised by a meter or more the very same day." The grenade hit the wire mesh and bounced back onto the sidewalk. "We kept driving and waited for the explosion. But there was no explosion. We suddenly got really scared that the soldiers would see the grenade, send it to the laboratory, find our fingerprints, and arrest us. For a couple of minutes we couldn't think straight. Our one thought was to go back, get the grenade, and hide it. Had we been thinking clearly, we'd have realized that the only thing the soldiers could do was to blow the grenade up. But we were panicking. I suggested getting B., my pregnant wife, and going back with her to look for the grenade — no one would suspect her. The others objected but I insisted."

It was then that B. first learned her husband had belonged to an armed Fatah cell for the past seven years. A.S. briefly explained the problem to her and she immediately agreed to his plan, joining the men in their car. About 200 meters from the spot, the couple got out and began to walk toward the fence. First time around, they found nothing. Fewer and fewer cars were now traveling along the boulevard. One by one the lights went out in the windows of the nearby houses, and fear gnawed at the four: where was the grenade? To the couple's relief, on their second pass B. spotted the grenade. A.S. picked it up, they walked to the waiting car, and got in.

"I wasn't afraid for myself," B. recollects. "I was afraid for A. I held on to him tightly and thought to myself that as long as I held him, the grenade wouldn't blow up." Off they drove, with A.S. holding the grenade out the window. In truth, the three men had no experience with explosives — that is, in disarming them. "We knew how to throw them," A.S. recalls ironically. In the training camp in Jordan there were no live grenades. The only thing he and his comrades had learned was how to pull out the pin. "So now our one idea was to throw the grenade into the sea. We drove to the shore and, somewhere between Gaza City and al-Shatti camp, I tossed it into the water."

A.S., today a civil servant employed by the Palestinian Authority, feels no regret for his action in 1985: he still believes that occupation by a foreign power demands countermeasures. Two days after the incident, however, he was plagued by remorse for having enlisted his wife. He suddenly grasped the danger in which he had placed her and their unborn child. "Even now I can't forgive myself," he says. His wife had not been surprised, though, to hear that for years — as he continued working by day at odd jobs in Israel — he had been involved in military activities against Israeli soldiers.

Between 1983 and 1987 — until the outbreak of the *intifada* — gunfire and grenades hurled at soldiers were a daily occurrence. "It was the usual thing," A.S. recalls. "In every Palestinian home they were struggling against the occupation," B. adds. "A.S. comes from a family of fighters. Two of his brothers were killed in the struggle, one in 1956 and the other in 1969. In my family, too, there were fighters and prisoners." And it was always understood that other family members, the women and children, were not to be let in on the secret. Nevertheless, B. had joined that particular mission without a moment's hesitation: "I told him that it was all up to fate. Even if we went to jail or died as martyrs, we still had to struggle against the occupation. But actually, I wasn't thinking about the consequences. All I cared about was protecting my husband. I was sure that he wouldn't die as long as I was with him."

A.S. was caught about one month after the abortive action. Someone had fingered him and he was sentenced to twenty-seven years in prison for throwing the grenade and on three more counts. To this day he won't speak about other operations, except to say, "They were always against soldiers." After nine years A.S. was granted early release along with a group of prisoners freed as part of the Oslo Accords. He was released in July 1994, on condition that he not leave the confines of the Gaza Strip for Israel or the West Bank. Spared eighteen years of his sentence, A.S. was still freed too late to witness the IDF evacuate al-Majlis al-Tashri'i, his grenade's target.

I go by this building almost every day, and thoughts of A.S. and his pregnant wife strolling through the quiet night are never far away. The grenade he threw would have barely dented the building's massive walls; rather his act was a symbolic protest, an act of defiance against all that the building stood for. For decades al-Majlis al-Tashri'i, the military governor's building, had served as the heart of the Israeli occupation in the Strip; it was where hundreds of men in uniform, empowered by arms and the force of their state, determined every last aspect of A.S.'s life. The men in that building vetted the schoolbooks, imposed heavy taxes and fines, hired and fired the local Palestinian civil service, decreed curfews, recruited collaborators, conducted interrogations, and sent soldiers to carry out fearsome night patrols, lethal hunts for suspects, and humiliating street searches. Day and night, outsized jeeps would come and go with engines revving, and loudspeakers would blare folksy Hebrew songs that could be heard in the distant Saja'ya neighborhood. The soldiers would shout and joke and backslap in a display of arrogance that probably hid their fear as well.

All this not only demonstrated Israel's omnipotence and military superiority but was a permanent reminder of the long history of dispossession that had begun in 1948, when more than 700,000 Palestinians (of a population of some 1.3 million) became refugees, forced to leave their land as the Jewish national home came into being. About 200,000 of them found shelter in the Gaza Strip, then controlled by Egypt, and A.S. was a child of one such refugee family, born in an impoverished and overcrowded refugee camp. Like all Palestinians, he grew up with the longing to return home and the growing desire for national independence.

In 1967 the Israeli occupation added one more painful link to the chain of deprivation, bringing as it did even greater constrictions on individual and communal freedom. For years people believed that only armed struggle against Israel would break the chain and reverse the effects of loss. For years people like A.S. and his wife dreamed only of overthrowing Israel and expelling what was to them a foreign entity. But in time, A.S. must have realized that his one hand grenade posed no real challenge to such a solid, fortified structure. He must have been aware as well of the poor, amateurish military training he and his comrades had received in the Jordanian training camps — insufficient to present a real strategic threat to the State of Israel. Perhaps in retrospect his act seems pathetic — throwing a grenade that failed to explode and then nearly getting caught. Almost as pathetic as the delusion — born of ignorance, isolation, and poor political analysis — that Israel was a passing phenomenon, easily disposed of. But A.S.'s act and all those like it carried reverberations far beyond their immediate result: this core of defiance nourished and bolstered the Palestinians' emancipatory drive, which grew as it would among any oppressed people and culminated in the popular uprising, the *intifada*, which erupted in December 1987.

A.S. has undergone a passage that is both personal and yet, to a high degree, shared and emblematic: from proud but embittered refugee to ill-equipped underground soldier; from prisoner held in Israeli jails (where, while his wife and children were taking part in the uprising, he learned to come to terms with Israel's permanence even as he clung to his desire for freedom), to civil servant employed by the Palestinian Authority, which administers the self-rule areas. This book is an attempt to chart that passage, to relate the ideological, cultural, and emotional histories that make up the human story of the Gaza Strip—histories that are bound together by the common quest for freedom.

The Egyptians, who controlled Gaza after the war in 1948, had refrained from annexing the Strip, and in 1957 al-Majlis al-Tashri'i was built as the seat of the local Egyptian governor. In 1962 it housed the very first partially elected Palestinian Legislative Council (hence the building's name in Arabic), a governing body set up by the ruling Egyptians. Although just ten of the Council's forty members were elected (ten were appointed by the governor and the rest were senior civil servants), its establishment reflected Egypt's intention to grant the Palestinians considerable freedom to administer their own civic affairs, especially in the areas of health, education, and labor relations. Palestinians welcomed the step, but their national aspirations already went well beyond both the physical boundaries of the Strip and the limitations of municipal management, and it was in the Council's sessions in this building that the idea to found a movement for Palestinian liberation was first put forward.

The Council stayed in the site for only five years. After Israel occupied the Strip in 1967, it was dissolved and the building became the base for the Israeli military governor and the IDF's Northern Gaza Battalion and remained so for almost thirty years. In all this time, while Israel referred to the structure as the military governor's building, Gazans persisted in calling it "the Council"; thus the very site itself came to represent two profoundly opposing views of government—one imposed, the other elected. Finally, in March 1996, the newly elected Palestinian Legislative Council, formed as the result of the Oslo Accords, took possession.

The building sits at the western end of Omar al-Mukhtar Boulevard, the main shopping street in Gaza City and its principal traffic artery connecting the city's densely populated, older neighborhoods—Saja'ya, Zeitun, and Darj in the east—with the modern, upscale Rimaal development, nestling on the Mediterranean shorefront in the west. The boulevard starts at the disused railway station, which once served the line that linked Haifa to Cairo and since 1995 has become a marketplace for clothes and cloth and household goods and a haven for the street stalls that once blocked the sidewalks. From the station, the boulevard climbs up Gaza Hill, the highest point in the city, before swinging down to Faras, the old market. By the time it reaches Rimaal, Omar al-Mukhtar Boulevard is lined with rows of eucalyptus trees planted in the pre-1948 days of the British mandate. Like an honor guard, they direct one's eye toward the imposing building.

On May 18, 1994, al-Majlis al-Tashri'i fulfilled its symbolic function by being the last facility in the Gaza Strip to be evacuated by Israeli troops. The soldiers' departure was the result of two agreements: first, the Declaration of Principles, signed on September 13, 1993, by two old foes—the State of Israel and the PLO—which affirmed the general terms of limited Palestinian self-rule in Gaza and the West Bank, beginning in the Strip and the West Bank city of Jericho; second, the Cairo agreement (popularly known as the first Oslo Accord or Oslo 1), signed on May 4, 1994. This document formally initiated self-rule, elaborated on the principles of mutual recognition already signed, and set forth a detailed plan for Israeli redeployment in Gaza and Jericho, in which most military bases and installations were to be evacuated and then handed over to the just-formed Palestinian police.

In the weeks following the Cairo agreement, building after building in the Gaza Strip was emptied of its hated occupants. Generally, the Israeli soldiers cleared out under cover of night during the curfew and thus people were denied the joy of watching the Israeli flag being lowered and folded for the last time. One by one, the evacuated buildings were thrown open to groups of uniformed Palestinian police—aged twenty to sixty—who came from Egypt, Yemen, and Algeria, all over the Arab world; some had been born in the diaspora and some in Jerusalem or Haifa, but each gray hair on their heads had been acquired, it seemed, in a different part of the world.

On May 11 the first group settled into the building in Dir al-Balah, south of Gaza City, formerly occupied by representatives of the Israeli civil administration. There I witnessed a meeting between a Palestinian coastguardsman returning from exile and family members he had never known. It had taken his relatives, who lived in the nearby refugee camp, only a few hours to learn, from neighbors of friends, about the new arrival who shared their name and came from the same village. They had hurried to the building to meet him. The guardsman, returning from outside the country, preferred not to malign the Israeli officers who had turned over control of the building to him and his fellow police. "Today is the day of our birth. Arafat, our commander in chief, had bidden us to speak well, to forget the past." But having lived through the occupation and the *intifada*, his newfound family could not forget so easily. "This building brings back all the painful memories of humiliation, interrogation, and beatings," one relative said bitterly. His brother summed it up: "All these buildings should have been demolished."

Then three days later, at the crack of dawn on May 14, the soldiers quietly moved out of Jabalia camp. The Jabalia refugees were especially disappointed to miss their departure—the storming of the military post in the heart of the camp had marked the beginning of the *intifada* some six years earlier. The night before their scheduled evacuation, the soldiers were still searching houses and chasing youngsters who had violated the curfew—a curfew that every evening for years had imprisoned hundreds of thousands of people in their cramped homes from dusk to daybreak. But the morning after the soldiers had gone I was there with the hundreds who trampled the wire mesh of the building's fence beneath their feet, touched the walls of the outpost as if in a dream, and raised the Palestinian flag over the sentry tower. "If only we'd been able to throw a few parting stones," a couple of boys joked.

I spent that evening with friends from the camp. They left their houses determined to stay out all night for the first time in years. Using my privileged Israeli status I had, on occasion, traveled through the dark, deserted streets of Jabalia and Gaza City and Khan Yunis and so had something to compare with this evening, and the vision was stirring. From a dusty shantytown where testy dogs barked at any shadow that dared to move and rats scuttled in the piles of garbage and junk, Jabalia was transformed overnight into a bustling Mediterranean quarter—light spilled out from every door and window; men in djelabas sat in the street on low straw chairs, sipping coffee; young married couples, some with children, made a bashful effort to be seen together in the evening outside their stifling refugee shacks. The barbershop, the furniture store, the grocery, another store that sold shutters, a makeshift garage—all were open at ten o'clock at night; even though they didn't expect customers, the shop owners just wanted to see what life was like after eight in the evening. Here and there snatches of song were piped out from a raspy tape player. Falafel and carob-juice carts decorated with colored paper or plastic flowers opened for business in the corners of alleyways, and the aroma of falafel crackling in oil seemed fresh and new.

After taking in the scene, my friends and I drove southwest from Jabalia to Gaza City, a distance of three or four kilometers. The closer we got to the city, the fewer people we saw and the darker and emptier were the streets, since the main military posts there had not yet been evacuated and the curfew was still in effect. A small number of pedestrians and a few dozen cars had dared to violate the curfew, but the soldiers—perhaps on orders—were not stopping anyone moving about in the streets. On Omar al-Mukhtar Boulevard we passed the military government building, only part of which was lit up. Several soldiers were still patrolling the unlit street; to us they looked small and frightened, clinging to their own shadows.

We got out of the car and walked around. Two soldiers on guard in a sentry tower evidently felt more secure on their elevated perch than did their fellows on foot patrol. "Just look at them strolling about," I heard one of them say, as if some physical defect had prevented Gazans from walking outdoors on past evenings.

Four nights later, on May 17, only the military governor's building remained to be evacuated by the Israeli army. The curfew had still not been lifted, but it was as if a collective decision had been made to ignore it; thousands began streaming along the boulevard to witness the exodus of the last Israeli troops. Many climbed the base of the memorial to the Unknown Soldier to get a better view. Circles of laughing, jeering people closed in on the armed but subdued and frightened soldiers, who wouldn't let anyone approach the high fence. "*Yallah,* go on, get out of here!" some kids yelled at the soldiers in army Hebrew.

The circles grew tighter and tighter, hemming in the soldiers. Some self-appointed marshals, members of Fatah, tried to come to the soldiers' aid and move people away. But around two in the morning the tension got out of hand, and suddenly there was an exchange of tear gas and stones and broken glass. It's not clear who started it—the soldiers, feeling threatened or merely wanting to make sure that no one watched their pullout, or youngsters whose fingers were itching for a little stone throwing. More than anything, this last exchange was probably a final reaction to Israeli power and the impotence it evoked, a final act of defiance and of rage over friends shot and killed, over children blinded by rubber bullets, over parents beaten and shamed in front of their families. Even moments before the evacuation, when the future seemed so promising, no order, not even from Arafat, could compel people to forget what the soldiers stood for.

The tear gas at dawn was the soldiers' parting gift. As always, it spread in all directions, seeping into the houses fronting the boulevard, forcing people to their back windows where it was less concentrated, and scattering the crowd far and wide. Teary-eyed, people fled as far as Saja'ya, coughing and covering their mouths and noses with their shirttails or kaffiyehs. Under cover of the tear gas, the IDF soldiers withdrew from the building, having turned it over to the commanders of the Palestinian police force in a brief ceremony. The police fired several joyful (and alarming) rounds to mark their takeover, and then everyone thronged back to the boulevard, climbing to the roof of the building, lifting several commanders on their shoulders, dancing and firing their rifles, and celebrating. In the midst of the noise and confusion, someone found a bunch of keys thrown in the yard and came to me to ask what was written on the Hebrew tag: "Administration Rooms: Entrance." Another wanted to know what was inside two boxes stamped "IDF" that had been left in a corner. A third, his throat still burning from the tear gas, made a path through the celebrants and asked me to translate an inscription on the walls. It was a quotation from Vegetius, the fourth-century explicator of the Roman military system: "Let him who desires peace prepare for war."

The falafel vendors showed up with their speedy carts. So did the men selling carob-juice, whose stands managed miraculously to stay upright under the mob clambering over them; to me, those carts would always represent Mediterranean color, the brightness of Gaza and its people that had for so long been dulled by the gloom of military rule. Perhaps the soldiers' departure enabled Gazans to throw off the drabness, or perhaps the gaiety was just the natural reaction of people ground down by years of resistance, mourning, and privation.

One afternoon several months earlier, I had witnessed in quick succession two sights that revealed some truth about both the weariness and helplessness bred by the occupation and, conversely, the yearning for change that it fosters, a yearning that finds expression in grand actions—clashes and demonstrations—as well as in small individual gestures. I was walking downhill on Omar al-Mukhtar Boulevard, toward the sea. The protest strike declared during the *intifada* was still being strictly observed, which meant that except for food stores all places of business were closed after one or two in the afternoon. Very few people—and no women at all—were out on the streets; there were hardly any cars either. Some schoolchildren were returning home from the morning shift while others had already begun the afternoon shift. The military governor's building loomed as menacing as ever, surrounded by a fence that during the *intifada* years had gradually eaten up wider and wider strips of the boulevard and the side streets at either end of the building. Cars were not allowed to drive around this imposing edifice and pedestrians were also kept away. An old Bedouin shepherd watched over some scraggly goats that chewed at the grass growing around the Unknown Soldier.

I passed a kiosk on the boulevard and saw that the owner had been so bold as to put out a dozen new plastic chairs of various colors, as if to say, "I'm tired of the dullness." The chairs—I checked them—were made by the Israeli plastics firm Keter, even though *intifada* directives called for a boycott of nonessential Israeli products. An act of this kind—inviting passersby to sit back and relax, to publicly enjoy their moments of leisure—couldn't have been more surprising. The sight provided a flicker of Mediterranean color peeking through the gray, of normalcy, even optimism.

I continued on my way and near a corner of the fence, in the shadow of the sentry tower, I saw two soldiers sitting on a bench. Nothing unusual about that. I walked a few more steps and noticed two young men kneeling beside the soldiers, heads bent, hands manacled behind their backs. What had they done—thrown stones? One soldier got up, walked a few steps, and nonchalantly urinated on the fence near the two Palestinians. Mesmerized, I watched this silent tableau of occupation for twenty or thirty minutes while other pedestrians walked by, showing little interest. Some children asked me if one of the young men was my son or my brother, as if only family would take the trouble to wait there and watch; anyone else would be too weary. And then the colored chairs seemed absurdly out of place—a broken plea against such routine powerlessness.

. . .

"Look at them. Why are they staring at me with such hatred?" an Israeli soldier once asked me. I have forgotten the circumstances— it might have been the soldier I chatted with one evening as he was checking people leaving the Strip or the guard who reluctantly exchanged a few words with me as he watched a building on Omar al-Mukhtar Boulevard. In any case, I was stunned by his genuine sense of victimization and persecution, undoubtedly typical of many sol- diers. Truly astounding was his ability to detach himself from the political and military context and expect the person he had stopped— to check an ID card, say—to view him as a private individual despite the threatening rifle and the uniform. And despite a catalogue of abuses, great and small: soldiers shooting at the rooftop water tanks just for fun. Soldiers chanting loud, offensive slogans while patrolling the refugee camps or pounding on the fragile tin doors to frighten the children. Soldiers confiscating identity papers for such bogus reasons as the card's frayed edges or faded type, even though it is illegal for Palestinians to be without identification. And soldiers were not the only culprits. There were also the tax officers who would take hours- long breaks, leaving people standing in the hot sun; the border guards who would kick over a vegetable stand as the desperate stall owner tried to salvage a few tomatoes; the military base that would dump its garbage in the middle of a residential neighborhood. "Break their bones," Yitzhak Rabin allegedly said when the *intifada* began, and many of the troops took him literally.

Boaz Nagar of the IDF's Golani Brigade served in the Jabalia camp in 1991. "Boy, the things we did there," he told reporter Shaul Bibi.[1] "If we caught one of them we'd make him play backgammon, and whoever won would get to beat the hell out of him." Nagar's fellow soldier Yigal stood out for his ability to catch children on the street during a curfew. "Once he caught this guy and saw in his papers that he'd been in jail, so we all really went to town." The same Yigal per- fected the practice of tearing down washing lines hanging between the houses, using his rifle to pull down the clothes. "He kept telling everyone to do it until the platoon sergeant finally asked him to stop, on orders from the company commander." The soldier was Yigal Amir, who went on to assassinate Prime Minister Yitzhak Rabin in

November 1995. In the end, Amir, who had brutalized Palestinians as
if born to it, turned his animus on Rabin, who had once given him
license to do so.

After the transfer of authority to the Palestinians in May 1994, some
positive changes were felt right away. For one thing, the soldiers were
gone from the streets, along with their guns and their noise and their
condescension. "We aren't afraid now to let the children play outside,"
people would say. "We don't run around looking for a child who's a
little bit late coming home. We've stopped having nightmares about a
son or a daughter shot in the head." Within weeks after the pullout, as
if someone had waved a magic wand, bands of small boys suddenly
materialized in Gaza City, riding bicycles in the middle of the roads,
even against the flow of traffic, thumbing their noses at the honking
cars. Beside them strode groups of chattering girls. I even began to see
girls riding bikes.

"We can finally sleep without pajamas on hot summer nights," said
S. from Rafah, who spent some three years on and off in an Israeli
detention camp. He had long dreamed of discarding his pajamas in the
summer. Even when he was briefly home between one prison term and
the next, he could not go without them in case soldiers broke in at
night. "We couldn't give them any reason to embarrass us," he said.

In addition, the afternoon siesta was reinstated. Before the soldiers
withdrew, their presence in the streets and the intrusive noise of army
jeeps induced profound anxiety. Anyone with common sense tried not
to stay outside too long, and yet people also felt trapped indoors. In the
afternoons they shut themselves inside and sank into an uneasy sleep
from which they had little desire to wake up. Now Gaza has returned
to the natural rhythm of the Mediterranean coast. Between two and
four in the afternoon a collective lethargy settles over the city and the
camps. All at once the cars and crowds disappear, the steaming streets
become empty, and for two hours the world slumbers serenely. After
the siesta, traffic once again begins to move—cars, bustling pedestrians, and people just taking a leisurely stroll. And when night falls,
lights from the stores and the vehicles give the streets an air of liveli-
ness and normalcy.

The media in Israel and throughout the world were quick to praise the changes. Gazans' trips to the beach in the evening, the crowds that filled the streets to overflowing, the lights on Omar al-Mukhtar Boulevard—all were noted enthusiastically as triumphs of the peace process. So, too, was the potential for commercial enterprise, for building and development. But in the Strip itself people were less impressed. Many were indignant at the television networks' inordinate interest in the cheery spectacle of Gazans drinking coffee by the seashore. Whoever was setting the tone in the media reports, they felt, was playing off the scenes frozen in the mind of the Israeli soldier, for whom Gaza was a dark, deserted maze of narrow, twisting alleys and its denizens the angry young men he had viewed through the sight of a gun or the windshield of a jeep.

The Palestinians, on the other hand, were making a different comparison altogether, between their lives now and before the *intifada*, between their lives in the Strip and life as they knew it in Israel. For people familiar with the beachside restaurants and enticing shop windows of Ashkelon and Tel Aviv, for people who had played a central role in Israel's construction boom, the comparison was grim. Who better than a nation of construction workers could understand the injustice of the restrictions on building and development in their own territory? And who could better understand that the frenzy of construction in the Strip that so impressed the entire world was only a belated and partial compensation for years of nondevelopment? For twenty-seven years one community had watched daily how their neighbors lived as a free people in their own country.

In the early 1960s, during Egyptian rule, the military governor's building was the site of the earliest expressions of Palestinian yearnings for national rights. Some thirty years later, in 1994, the world watched Israeli troops leave the building and believed those rights were being realized. The Israeli pullout was referred to as a "withdrawal," but mistakenly so: the IDF battalion headquarters, with the same officer in charge, simply moved north a few kilometers and set up near the Jewish settlement of Nisanit. Other Israeli military bases relocated to the vicinity of the Jewish settlements in the Katif Bloc, which effectively cuts the Strip in half. And legally and politically, the IDF continued to have the final say in the Strip.

Summarizing the terms of the Oslo Accords, Joel Singer, a former legal adviser to the Israeli Foreign Ministry and one of the legal architects of the Cairo agreement, affirmed Israel's continuing military role in an article he published in 1995:

> The nature of the regime established in the West Bank and the Gaza Strip for the duration of the transitional period is that of Palestinian autonomy under the supreme authority of the Israeli military government. Israel will continue to be responsible for, among other things, the external security as well as the external relations of the West Bank and the Gaza Strip. . . . Unlike the Civil Administration, the military government does not dissolve. Instead, it simply withdraws physically from its former location and continues to exist elsewhere as the source of authority for the Palestinian Council and the powers and responsibilities exercised in the West Bank and the Gaza Strip.[2]

In the same spirit of paternalism, Singer commented on the need for elections to the Palestinian Legislative Council, saying that Israel "recognized the importance of establishing a democratic and accountable system of self-government." Furthermore, "driven by its desire to see a fully democratic Palestinian society," Israel went beyond the provisions of the Declaration of Principles (in which the Council, as a single body, was intended to carry out legislative and executive functions alike) by agreeing to the Palestinian request for a separation between the legislative branch—the Council itself—and a committee of the Council charged with executive authority. "Such a division would ensure the existence of over-sight and accountability, two prerequisites for a democratic regime." Finally, Israel agreed to another exception, permitting "separate and simultaneous elections for the Council and for the position of Chairman [or Ra'ees in Arabic] of the Executive Authority of the Council."

Israel's willingness to accede to these changes, especially the separation of the executive and legislative branches, enabled the Palestinian political structure to move closer to the desired democratic model of a freely elected representative body. Still, the way in which the date of elections was chosen and announced was a concrete manifestation of Israel's superior decision-making role vis-à-vis the subordinate Palestinians. At a joint press conference called by Yassir Arafat and Shimon

Peres, Israel's foreign minister, in October 1995, Arafat thanked Peres for having proposed "positive initiatives," and noted that he and the foreign minister had agreed to continue their cooperation. Then, Peres, looking quizzically at his colleague, reminded him of the elections. "Ah yes," said Arafat, "the elections," and went on to announce the date: January 20, 1996.

The information came like a bolt from the blue. It seemed as if the date had been set that same day, with some moderate pushing and prodding on Peres's part. The Palestinian candidates and organizations that were to participate—including Fatah, Arafat's own movement—found themselves with just three months to prepare for the first general elections in Palestinian history.

A number of prominent Palestinians had decided not to participate in the elections or declare their candidacy, but they reversed their position when Israel agreed to allow a separate executive authority. One of those was Hayder abd al-Shafi, a surgeon by profession, who had a long background of representing his people. Elected chair of the first Palestinian Legislative Council in 1962, he received the highest number of votes of any candidate in the 1996 elections—a testament to his enduring popularity and to the high degree of respect he inspires. Palestinians trust him for his judicious manner, for his receptivity to all complaints and all views, and especially for his political stance, his outspoken criticism of the Oslo Accords and the new Palestinian Authority. Indeed, abd al-Shafi enjoys a reputation as something of a contrarian. In 1947 he was one of the few Palestinians to support the UN Partition Plan (which called for the division of Palestine into two separate states); he understood the reality of the Jewish presence in the country, a stand that was shared only by the Palestinian Communist Party. After 1967, he was one of the first to establish open political contacts with Israelis when such a step was still considered taboo. At the end of 1991, he was asked by Yassir Arafat to head the Palestinian delegation to the Madrid talks, where the Israeli delegation complained to U.S. Assistant Secretary of State Edward Djerijian that abd al-Shafi spoke in a peevish tone of voice and addressed himself only to issues of "human rights in the territories and not the substantive matters on the agenda."

Abd al-Shafi's opposition to the Oslo agreement was primarily the result of the concessions Palestinians made in regard to the Jewish settlements in the occupied territories. Allowing these to remain while establishing self-rule in other parts of the West Bank and Gaza Strip was, in his view, a fatal mistake. He disapproved of the agreement to postpone discussions on that issue until the final-status negotiations. The Palestinian people, he pointed out, would always regard the Jewish settlements—and the military presence installed to guard them—as a source of provocation and an infringement of their right to self-determination. Postponing deliberations on the settlements effectively altered the status of the West Bank and Gaza Strip from occupied territories, where Jewish settlements were illegal, to disputed ones, over which both sides possessed an equal right to bargain. And in a bargain based on might alone and not on principles, the stronger side—that is, Israel—would inevitably triumph. Even so, when Israel agreed to changes in the Council's composition, abd al-Shafi was moved to swim with the current and seek election.

"What will you be able to do for the people who elect you?" I asked him a week before the vote. "Our primary concern is that they be treated fairly, by the Palestinian Authority and by the Israelis," he said. "We won't just watch from the sidelines and keep quiet—our top priority is to put democracy into practice. We'll demand that the Executive Authority be answerable to the Legislative Council. We'll insist on our right to question it and oversee its behavior. People are already frustrated by the way the Authority acts. They complain about the Palestinian security forces, which are not subject to the law or to clearcut regulations. They resent that it takes pull to get a job. Of course they're frustrated by the economic damage caused by Israel's policy of closing Gaza's borders whenever it feels like it. And they're very angry about the free hand Israel still has in inflicting collective punishment."

Palestinians hailed the Legislative Council—an independent body of popularly elected representatives who would give voice to their needs—as a tangible, qualitative change in their lives. Although the press in Gaza barely covered the Council's fractious weekly sessions, everyone in the Strip knew within a day who had quarreled with whom, which representative had dared bring up some touchy subject that had been on everyone's mind, and which promises the Executive Authority had made and then broken. During the Council's first few months, it stood out as the only segment of the new Palestinian political system that was more than a rubber stamp, that openly and consistently opposed Arafat.[3]

But for all the Council's enthusiasm and dedication, it was quickly stymied by the most basic obstacles. Following its first session in March 1996, the Council set up eleven different committees, many of which were to meet in the West Bank. By May and June that year, however, the weekly sessions, along with the committee meetings, had been disrupted several times because the Council members required Israeli travel permits to move between Gaza and the West Bank. In mid-May, the members had been set to attend sessions in Bethlehem but their permits, good for one week, were valid only between 5:00 A.M. and 7:00 P.M. In other words, Council members would need to return to Gaza every afternoon and miss the evening sessions. Furthermore, the permits did not mention the Palestinians' parliamentary status—which would have spared them the inevitable delays at Israeli roadblocks—noting only that they were traveling for "personal reasons." The permits were sent back and new ones were issued, in which the time restrictions had been removed but the "personal" designation was still in place. The permits went back yet again and were reissued correctly—to all but three legislators: Jawad al-Tibi, a Fatah member and former prisoner, instrumental in setting up the Palestinian peace movement; Rafat al-Najjar, a member of the Popular Front for the Liberation of Palestine (PFLP), threatened with expulsion during the *intifada*; and Hayder abd al-Shafi.

This was not the first time that abd al-Shafi had been denied an exit permit. He had been prevented from leaving the Strip the previous year, and an Israeli official had explained that he was not, of course, suspected of smuggling arms, it was just that "he speaks out against the accords." The Palestinian in charge of processing exit requests was furious. "How do you expect us to become a democracy when you won't let abd al-Shafi go to the West Bank to express his opinions?"

Now only the angry intercession of Arafat himself produced the three missing permits. He gave the Israelis fifteen minutes in which to produce them or threatened to cancel the Council meetings. The permits arrived just in time. In my pre-election conversation with abd al-Shafi it had not occurred to either of us that, with all the urgent work before the Council, with the desperate needs of its constituents, legislators would be required to invest so much time and energy in securing the simple right to move freely between the West Bank and the Gaza Strip.

The army had relocated, the buildings had been evacuated, some Palestinians had returned from exile and had even cast their votes, but before they could begin to exercise their new autonomy, the first Palestinian parliamentarians were still obliged to wait for Israeli travel permits.

Chapter 2

Leaflets Among
the Diapers

The man who entered the room was visibly distraught. Wasting no time on pleasantries, he threw himself down in a chair and announced that the soldiers had gone berserk. This was in early 1994, before the Israeli pullback. Just before midnight, the man said, twenty or thirty people in the al-Boureij refugee camp had been forced out of their homes. Some of them hadn't even had a chance to put on their shoes; others complained that the soldiers had kicked and hit them. They were led to the UNRWA school (United Nations Relief and Works Agency for Palestine Refugees in the Near East) and ordered to pick up some garbage and rocks that had been strewed in the yard. Furious, the man said that someone was made to write slogans in Arabic on the wall. "Life is like a cucumber," was the worst of them. "One day in your hand, the next day up your ass."

Only later did anyone remember to introduce us: he was Marwan Kafarna, a history and geography teacher at the UNRWA school in al-Boureij. I recognized the name immediately. Instrumental in the *intifada*, he was part of the first Unified National Leadership (UNL), the revolutionary Gazan group that had prepared the ground and set the early pattern for the Palestinian uprising. The Israeli army and Shabak had worked hard to crack the UNL and arrest its members, but when they finally succeeded, a second group had sprung up in its place, and then a third and a fourth. "So," I said, "I finally get to meet you."

During the four years of the *intifada*, Kafarna had witnessed countless violent clashes and far greater indignities than those he recounted that day, but he had never managed to come to terms with any of it; he was simply unable to swallow the insult.

We became friends and then neighbors in a three-story apartment block in the Rimaal neighborhood. We exchanged keys in case one of our telephones was broken; if the water pressure in my apartment was lower than usual, I would shower at the Kafarnas', and if I ran out of coffee, I would go down to borrow some from them. We would sit together on their balcony, where the lush, fragrant honeysuckle climbed through the railing up to my own balcony above. Together we would wait, longing for the breeze that signaled the end of the scorching day—along with Kafarna's son, Azat, who clung to him in spite of the heat, and his daughter, Lana, who proudly showed her mother a picture she had drawn or a test she had passed, and both of them begging me to throw them up in the air like airplanes.

I lived above them for more than a year. In the mornings I would hear the school bus honk for Lana and another neighbor's daughter; at noon I would see her come home, her heavy schoolbag on her back. I loved to watch her managing alone in the apartment, in the kitchen, in front of the TV, until her mother and father returned from work. And in the evenings, after I had finished my daily hunt for news, I often went down to chat with Mirwat, Marwan's wife, to grumble about one thing or another, drink strong black coffee, and catch up on the local gossip.

On Friday mornings I would see Marwan come back from the market loaded down with vegetables. When he and Mirwat had a third child, Azat joined him on the Friday excursions, all but hidden from sight behind the large package of disposable diapers he carried for his father. And whenever I saw those diapers, I would think of the *intifada*, of what Marwan had told me about his days in the UNL: how he had hidden thousands of leaflets among Lana's diapers—she was then four months old—passing them on to others who would spread them throughout the Strip.

Before the *intifada*, Marwan's life was a maze of illegal activities, dissident thoughts, and subversive plans, as it was for thousands of other Palestinians; after the uprising began in December 1987, though, that number swelled to hundreds of thousands. The way the Israeli army saw it, the people of Gaza were disturbing the peace and upsetting the normal course of life. But as far as Gazans were concerned, the normal course of their lives was disturbed to begin with, subjected as they were to military rule and humiliation at every turn, random arrests, baby-faced soldiers barking illogical orders in broken Arabic, or even worse, in rapid Hebrew. All mention of Palestine was forbidden, and even one's neighbor could be working for Shabak, informing on all one's comings and goings. That was the normal state of affairs, and no one ever got used to it, not even after twenty-five years, not even when it seemed that they had.

Normal was abnormal, as my friend Abu Ali from the Jabalia camp said when he drove twenty yards against the flow of traffic, all to avoid passing an Israeli military base. "Our world is upside down. Why shouldn't we drive the wrong way as well?"

There were four of them in the first Unified National Leadership: Marwan Kafarna, Tawfiq al-Mabhuh, Ihab al-Ashqar, and Jamal Zaqut; Mabhuh, the oldest, was barely forty at the time; the youngest, Ashgar, just twenty-four; the other two were in their early thirties. Kafarna, Mabhuh, and Ashqar were arrested some two months after the uprising began and sentenced to three years in prison; Zaqut was finally captured in August 1988 and deported. In their book *Intifada* (in Israel widely considered the definitive account), journalists Ze'ev Schiff and Ehud Ya'ari mention Kafarna, Mabhuh, and Ashqar, but only in passing. According to their version of events, a unified command model had been in existence in the West Bank before the *intifada*; its members were representatives of the four principal organizations in the PLO. Schiff and Ya'ari claim that Muhammad Labadi, of the Democratic Front for the Liberation of Palestine (DFLP) in the West Bank, quickly grasped the need to channel the spontaneous protests that broke out in the Strip in December 1987 into an organized form of struggle. In close contact with his brother-in-law, Jamal Zaqut, Labadi was primarily responsible for exporting the unified command model to the Strip. So goes the Schiff-Ya'ari version.

I began to hear a different story in 1991 when I was just getting to know Gaza and the *intifada* activists. Those I spoke to argued that Schiff and Ya'ari had relied heavily on documents in Shabak's possession that gave a partial picture only and minimized the seminal role Gaza had played in the uprising. "If something doesn't start in Gaza, it just won't get off the ground," Ashqar said years later. "Whoever suffers most is always the one to force change. It took the harsh situation in Gaza to bring about the revolution." Gazans are controlled, patient, and tolerant, I would hear again and again. "We absorb one blow after another and the world thinks they don't hurt us. But there's a mountain of anger and frustration, and the big explosion always comes sooner or later." (And the characterization is as true in the post-Oslo reality, I was reminded frequently, as it was before the uprising.)

When the four men talk about the first few days of the *intifada* their accounts are sometimes contradictory and sometimes they skew the chronology—inevitable confusion nine years after the fact. But what emerges from their story of this watershed moment is a rare political and social history of the Strip during the 1980s, culminating in the combustion of long-festering feelings, years of preparation, and a string of arbitrary events that ignited the uprising. "Even if you'd asked me at the time, I couldn't really have explained quite how we started coordinating our actions and making decisions together," Kafarna admitted.

On December 9, 1987, he was teaching at al-Faluja school in Jabalia. The previous day four men from the refugee camp had been killed accidentally, hit by an Israeli truck. That night their funerals turned into angry demonstrations, which continued well into the next day, spreading through the camp. A number of Kafarna's students cut classes to protest outside the army post in the center of the camp. Then a curfew was announced and those of Kafarna's students who lived outside the camp needed a ride from him so they could get home. The streets were crawling with army jeeps and soldiers, announcing the curfew over their loudspeakers and hurrying people off the streets. "I had no idea then of what would develop from those first demonstrations," Kafarna said, "or of the role I would play."

Mabhuh, Kafarna, and Zaqut came together in the first UNL through union activity: during the months leading up to the *intifada*, they, along with Tawfiq Abu Husa, a Fatah activist, had taken part in a special committee coordinating the Strip's labor unions. The unions had recently begun to expand their activities—much to the annoyance of the Israeli military and civil authorities—recruiting more members and even electing executive committees for the first time under the occupation.

In 1965, the Palestinian Legislative Council, headed by Hayder abd al-Shafi, passed labor laws protecting the right of workers to organize—legislation al-Shafi remembers with particular pride. The

Labor Union Federation that was set up, with the approval of the Egyptian government, included six divisions: agricultural workers, truckers, tailors, metalworkers, construction workers, and public service employees. However, after Israel conquered the territories in 1967, it banned union membership and activities. Thirteen years later, in 1980, the Israeli authorities finally allowed the unions to resume, but subject to several constraints: every activity had to be reported to the civil administration; the union leaders elected in 1965 would remain in office; and the then-chairman of the federation, Abed al-Rahman Darabe, would maintain his position.

Ironically, though, in the intervening years, Darabe had become a factory owner and an employer. In fact, he had been the first Palestinian permitted to set up a plant in the Erez industrial zone at the northern end of the Strip. Then as now, the Israeli authorities used business permits to ensure good behavior and reward cooperation. With Darabe as federation chairman, the Israelis concluded, the reestablished unions would give them no trouble. One final restriction forbade new members from joining up—union activity was to be limited to members who had registered prior to 1967.

All these restrictions notwithstanding, the reconstituted unions represented a political opportunity, and the first to exploit this opportunity was, not surprisingly, the Communist Party, no stranger to workers' rights or to circumventing the authorities. Mabhuh, a longtime Communist who had worked in Israel and served several jail terms, got involved. "The construction workers' union was the first to start up again," he said. "We began signing up new members and kept two separate lists, one public and the other secret, and we told Darabe nothing." He smiled. "There were so many issues that no one was addressing: people had been working in Gaza for ten, fifteen years and could be tossed out of their jobs for no reason, with no compensation, no recourse."

Following the Communists' lead, a number of activists in the Popular Front for the Liberation of Palestine (PFLP) began to look more closely at their own organization's involvement with class issues; there was a fair amount of working-class sloganeering, but the Front had little real interest in anything other than nationalist concerns. As it happened, Kafarna had recently returned from Iraq where he had been involved with the PFLP and active in student groups. The public service employees' union seemed to him like an obvious place to get involved—traditionally it had been controlled by the al-Kumion al-Arab movement, a forerunner of the Popular Front. "First of all, we just wanted to wake up people's consciousness, get them taking part in the things going on around them, before even thinking of party politics or nationalism. At the time, hardly anyone came to the unions—they were too scared. The ones who did were courageous, because they knew they'd have trouble with the authorities."

The public service employees began to hold meetings. "We talked about politics and people started to enjoy the activities. We became a close-knit group," said Kafarna. "We started talking to the papers about union problems, about workers' problems." The union always made a point of notifying the civil administration staff officer for labor issues of any meetings. "If we didn't hear anything after two weeks, we concluded that it was all right to go ahead," Kafarna recalled. "We never did get an answer, positive or negative, so we just carried on." The ineffable name "Popular Front" was never mentioned, of course—it was an illegal organization. But everyone—even the civil administration—knew the Front was involved.

In fact, opposition came not so much from the civil administration as from the Muslim Brotherhood, which considered the "Communist infidels" a danger to Muslim society. For several years the Israeli authorities had allowed the Islamic institutions almost free rein in their social, cultural, financial, and religious activities in the hope that their influence would weaken the PLO. And the Muslim Brotherhood was in fact fairly successful in elections held by various professional associations. At the same time, it stepped up its attacks on its ideological foes, distributing leaflets against rebellious women university students and declaring open season on Communists and Popular and Democratic Front members. Some Popular Front people who had made their atheism public were physically attacked. Even the respected abd al-Shafi and the Red Crescent, a variant of the Red Cross that he headed, were targets of violence.

"Our activities and their popularity brought us into direct competition with the religious organizations," Kafarna explained, "both socially and ideologically. We started organizing self-defense patrols—they beat us up and we needed to get back at them. These things need organizing. Sometimes their attacks were even more dangerous than the occupation, and we knew we had to protect ourselves."

. . .

It was the union's self-defense efforts that earned it new respect from PFLP leaders, who had until then belittled just about any activity that couldn't be called "armed struggle." Kafarna himself had no interest in armed struggle; it was an approach "completely foreign" to his way of thinking. He couldn't see the point of it. "I just didn't see any armed struggle going on. They'd organize themselves in clandestine cells that got uncovered as soon as they tried to do anything, and then they were all sent to prison. Where's the logic in that? I wanted some kind of organization with staying power, that could really communicate with people." Kafarna takes obvious pleasure in having proven people wrong. " 'What will your union work accomplish?' they said. 'That's not resistance.'

"Until 1986 we were treated as if we weren't daring enough, but that began to change after we stood up to the Muslim Brotherhood. People began to take us seriously. The press started turning up at union events and all this made us more influential."

Simultaneously, Fatah began to look at the labor unions as a way to expand its activities beyond underground military action and to reach greater numbers of people. In his twenties, Tawfiq Abu Husa was one of the inner circle of rising young Fatah leaders in Gaza. He had become vice-chairman of the Shabiba, the Fatah youth movement, and had been successful at recruiting teenagers for Shabiba social and cultural events—all activities that were not openly identified with Fatah. It seemed only natural to extend the Shabiba experiment to other target populations.

"There was a decision to mobilize workers in a well-planned, focused way," Abu Husa said. "But our thinking, our goals, were always nationalistic." In contrast to their leftist colleagues—the Communists and Front members—Abu Husa and other Fatah activists were less concerned with the issue of workers' rights than with preventing its monopolization by other organizations. "And it was amazing," said Abu Husa, pleased with himself. "The Communists, the PFLP, the DFLP—they were working in two of the unions before we got involved, but once Fatah got started everyone came to us. From the universities, from the camps, from the villages."

For Kafarna, Ashqar, Mabhuh, and Zaqut, a personal, pragmatic decision to diversify and look beyond the constraints of the mythical armed struggle paved the way from union activism to the strategic, methodical choreography of the uprising.

To Ihab al-Ashqar, who worked with Abu Husa organizing Fatah's role in the unions, renouncing the exclusively armed struggle was linked to another significant departure from the past: the generation of Palestinians who had come of age under the occupation had begun to revolt against their leaders abroad, especially within Fatah. To the world at large and to Shabak officers in particular, the young Fatah supporters continued to insist that the PLO was the sole legitimate representative of the Palestinian people. But among themselves they rejected taking instructions from leaders who lived elsewhere. "We realized that ours was probably the only revolution in the world that wasn't actually taking place in the territories being occupied," said Ashqar. "The fight was going on in another country." In a parallel move, Fatah members were trying to throw off the authority of their local leadership as well, the *mukhtars*, who were aging and out of touch. "We came to the conclusion that we needed a new group of leaders and had to establish the PLO as active in Gaza. First of all, that meant recruiting people and then we'd figure out what to do with them. We weren't clear exactly what the next step should be, but not for a moment did we imagine that we'd get all the refugees from al-Shatti camp, give them Kalashnikovs, and then go liberate Isdud and Majdal"—now Ashdod and Ashkelon.

As a child, Ashqar had believed that military action against Israelis might lead to them "all running away," but one year in prison put an end to that illusion. In 1983, he came to the notice of Muhammad Dahlan, a more senior Fatah activist (and now head of the Authority's preventive security branch), who already had plans for a youth revolution, and intended to install members of Ashqar's generation in all the movement's institutions. "We were convinced that the old-timers didn't really want to struggle against the occupation and that they had to be pushed aside. An internal *intifada* needed to happen inside Fatah and could only begin in the Strip. Later, we thought, it would spread to the West Bank. By 1986 we'd succeeded and the young activists had taken over. We just went ahead and did what we wanted, without asking anyone's permission. We'd watched the Israelis, how they created facts on the ground, and learned from them. In every school and every neighborhood there was soon a sizable Fatah or Shabiba cell. A transformation had taken place and Dahlan was its father."

In the unions the new burst of activism led naturally to the need for a rejuvenated elected leadership, in defiance of the Israeli prohibition against replacing the aging pre-occupation officials. And in early 1987 Abed al-Rahman Darabe fell ill. His condition was not serious, but it provided a sufficient pretext for replacing him. "According to the labor law," Tawfiq al-Mabhuh explained, "no union elections could be held without notifying the authorities. So we sent a letter notifying them and set up an elections committee. The civil administration replied that elections were forbidden, but the law, which was passed during the Egyptian period but was also binding on the Israelis, only required notification, not permission."

Television crews, newspaper reporters, and Knesset members of the Communist-led Front for Democracy and Equality were alerted to the date of elections to the executive committee of the construction workers' union—February 21, 1987. In response, army troops declared the Saja'ya neighborhood where the union building is located a closed military zone. At the appointed time of the voting, Mabhuh intentionally "drew the soldiers' fire," starting an argument with the Israeli commander guarding the entrance to the building. " 'Come stand here and let's talk it over,' " Mabhuh suggested. "We moved aside and eighty or ninety workers walked in." Seven representatives were chosen for the executive committee and Mabhuh was elected chairman. A few hours later, he was arrested and ordered to declare the elections null and void—he refused.

Some six weeks later, the public service employees union followed the construction workers' lead—scheduling elections and notifying the authorities. This time, however, the army made sure to close down the union headquarters, and so a hurried unanimous vote took place in the Red Crescent building. With the agreement of those members present, a number of representatives were appointed to the committee—all of them from the Popular and Democratic Fronts. The unions' stand against the army forced those who still scoffed at workers' activities to think again. "Everyone began taking us seriously," said Kafarna. "Finally, we were on the map."

Following these successes, Fatah decided to appoint executive committees in the four other unions—agricultural workers, truckers, tailors, and metalworkers. As before, notices were sent to the civil administration, but there was no confrontation with the IDF because Fatah did not actually assemble the union members or hold elections. "We just chose the committees in our offices," said Abu Husa, seeing nothing wrong with Fatah's method. "I personally selected the committee members and appointed them, but we told the press and everybody that we'd held elections. Of course, nobody in the union dared complain. They didn't want to sound like the Israelis, who'd forbidden the elections altogether."

However, the Communists and the two Fronts did complain. "They said we were just playing a game and things shouldn't be done that way," Abu Husa recalled. "I told them they could say what they liked, but I still had those four unions in my pocket. They belonged to Fatah and still do." According to Jamal Zakut, who was affiliated with the DFLP, the metalworkers union had petitioned the civil administration, demanding elections and calling for a temporary elections committee, only days before Abu Husa's strike. "Then all of a sudden," said Zakut, "we read in the papers that we'd held elections and Fatah had won."

Mabhuh learned of Fatah's mysterious elections at the military governor's office. Just as Abu Husa was announcing the new executive committees, Mabuh was arrested (as he was sixty times in the following two or three months, detained one day and released the next). "The Israelis brought in the construction workers' whole executive and asked us why we were still holding elections. We had no idea what they were talking about until we heard of Fatah's move."

Real or staged, the elections were beginning to create tensions among the political organizations. Everyone was angry with Fatah and its methods of taking control, but the strife did not stop there. Despite the DFLP's weak presence in the Strip, it demanded representation on the public service employees' committee. In addition, the PFLP and the Communists had for some time been competing for control of the Red Crescent, the blood bank, and the UNRWA employees' committee, and this competition trickled down to the labor unions.

In light of the tension, as well as the dispute with the religious organizations, some activists began to feel the need for a coordinating committee to mediate agreements and compromises between the different movements. Thus Abu Husa, Mabhuh, Kafarna, and Zaqut found themselves working together, and their coordinating committee gradually emerged as an effective tool for cooperation and problem solving, not only on union issues but also on general concerns. A decisive factor in the committee's success was the close personal relationships that evolved, relatively free of the enmity and competition that existed among the different movements. Even people outside the unions came to see the committee as a place to go to resolve disputes.

Perhaps the harmony was strengthened by shared backgrounds: Zaqut, Abu Husa, and Mabhuh had all grown up in refugee families, among the two-thirds of Gaza's one million inhabitants who originated from Palestinian villages and towns outside the Strip. Indeed, the refugee camps accounted for a disproportionately large number of the actvists who had begun to make themselves felt in the 1980s, which was a transitional time when resistance consisted of stretching the limits of the law. The union activities created a new confrontation with the Israeli authorities, one that was more direct, overt, and popular, and this boldness was effecting a profound change among the refugees. Their feelings of discrimination and their jealousy of the *muwataneen*, the old Gazan families (literally "citizens"), converged with a kind of tribal pride in being more resilient, more daring, more forceful.

Throwing off the old guard's authority was not simply a blow against the aging leadership who, together with Yassir Arafat, had built up Fatah, but also a strike at all those Palestinians who kept their distance from the narrow, miserable alleyways of the camps. As the struggle became more popular, it was only natural that the refugees moved into key positions. Who better than they could understand the fury in the camps? The sense of injustice bit deep, and its causes were many—the national dispossession of 1948 and then the occupation, economic exploitation in Israel, and even social discrimination by other Palestinians.

In December rage finally washed over Gaza. In the first few days, it seemed the whole Strip was swept up in the protests and yet at the same time everyone felt caught unaware, as if they were watching from the sidelines, amazed by the strength of the eruption. On the second day, December 10, Marwan Kafarna, who then lived in Beit Hanun, was unable to reach his school in Jabalia as it was under curfew. Instead, most UNRWA teachers, including Kafarna, were sent to schools near their homes to fill in for colleagues trapped elsewhere by the curfews.

However, like Abu Husa and Zaqut, Kafarna made his way to the union building. Ignoring the curfew, the three made a tour of the Strip to see what was going on. Jabalia had not been calmed by the curfew; quite the contrary. "There were barricades, burning tires, and rocks everywhere. Most of the roads were blocked and people were streaming out of their homes to join in, to find out what was happening." The three met more formally, "to move the situation along," as Kafarna puts it, possibly on the third day of rioting. Mabhuh was absent—he had been arrested the day before while preparing leaflets for the Communist Party and was held for nine days. Other Communists had begun distributing leaflets in the name of "Nationalist Forces" and the rest of the organizations in the Strip were furious at their exclusion. Still, the Communist Party's lone action highlighted the need for coordinating the riots, and the central union committee, which had been operative for several months, was the obvious address.

Rigid control of the press and suppression of all political activity quickly made the one-page leaflet—cheaply produced underground and easily distributed on the streets—the Strip's popular form of mass communication. Leaflets giving instructions, declaring strikes, conveying news, and offering moral support became common; even though the authors remained anonymous and secret, people followed the instructions and received each new leaflet eagerly. The hallmark of the *intifada*, however, was that the leaflets were signed jointly by rival political organizations. However, the first to appear in the name of the Unified National Leadership was endorsed only by Fatah, the PFLP, and the DFLP; Mabhuh was in jail, so the Communist Party's imprimatur was missing.

All four men (and Ihab al-Ashqar, who joined the UNL soon after) light up when they remember those early days. Each one added something to the overall strategy. "Fatah decided not to use weapons," Abu Husa explained. "We started planning other ways to keep up the intense level of activity. We'd get our people, the Fatah supporters, out into the streets and then stand aside, move out of the picture. They were the ones who needed to act, not the usual suspects. Of course, a lot of people wanted to know why we hadn't shown our faces at the protests, but we were busy doing other things. We'd flee from the soldiers and make sure they saw us running into people's houses. Then they'd toss in some tear gas or come in, smash things, beat the family up. The idea was that there'd be someone wounded in every home — we wanted every Palestinian to be involved, to resist the soldiers, whether they were politically active or not. That way we made sure the whole Strip participated."

Tawfiq Abu Husa decided to concentrate his energies on Fatah and so brought Ashqar to the second UNL meeting to replace him. "Even before I introduced myself," said Ashqar, "I told them not to contact the PLO leaders abroad, not for anything. I gave them an ultimatum: 'If the people abroad interfere, I quit.' Tawfiq and I saw eye to eye on this. We'd come to the conclusion that whatever we managed to do here, they somehow wrecked over there." Kafarna could not have agreed more — he too disliked receiving instructions from the Popular Front abroad. Mabhuh, however, had no need of the ultimatum; the Communists' base was local. The DFLP also maintained a strong, well-coordinated leadership in Gaza and the West Bank and so Zaqut felt empowered to make decisions and act freely.

As a sop to the organizational hierarchy, UNL members sometimes wrote retroactive reports on their actions, which were passed on to contact people in their respective movements. Abu Husa, however, stayed in daily contact with Arafat's deputy, Abu Jihad, in Tunis. In one memorable conversation, Abu Husa tried to explain the scope of the demonstrations. "We've never seen anything like it," he said. "It's . . . it's," he stammered, searching for the right word. "It's an *intifada*."

In line with the seemingly spontaneous, almost anarchistic nature of the UNL, each of its leaders (who kept their roles secret) worked with his own organization's members and the UNL's decisions would trickle down invisibly. Sometimes the four men went personally to key spots in the towns and camps and handed over leaflets for distribution. "We'd make sure to get a copy into each and every house," said Ashqar. "We worked at night, stopping at every building, every apartment, every alleyway. But in the morning, at the demonstrations, we were nowhere in sight."

They would spread the word about different forms of rebellion that had succeeded elsewhere in the Strip. "In Rafah someone told us that it was hard to sneak out of the house at night and distribute leaflets, because of his family," said Ashqar. "We told him what we'd heard in al-Shatti: put the leaflets next to the mosque. Some boy will always see them and give them out." They passed on methods of making the roads impassable—by spilling oil at the intersections, for example, or using one metalworker's idea of leaving a brace of nails arranged in such a way that the sharp points were sure to puncture the IDF's tires. They would travel with the various organizations that brought food to the camps and neighborhoods under curfew, and Ashqar always carried pictures of Arafat with him to hand them out. "My generals," Arafat called them when he heard about their exploits.

All four agree that the source of the UNL's strength was their direct contact with the people. For example, Mabhuh joined in distributing vegetables at the Nuseirat refugee camp in central Gaza and saw firsthand that people were sustained by a sense of solidarity. He remembered knocking on one door, a basket of vegetables in his hand. A member of the family came out, saw the basket, and said, "Thanks a lot, but we just got vegetables five minutes ago." Mabhuh encountered such honesty again and again. Another time he was handing out leaflets to a group of workers returning from Israel. The flyer called for participation in *intifada* activities. "Give me a sack of flour for my children and I won't go to work for a month," one man said, showing Mabhuh there were limits to the demands they could make of people.

They took the same flak as everyone else, too. Ashqar recalled a meeting with some Fatah colleagues. They were sitting in a car when several soldiers suddenly appeared. " 'Turn off the engine and get out of the car, all of you,' they yelled. They ordered us to pick up all the garbage in the street and dump it inside the houses. At first we refused and they fell on us like a bunch of madmen, hitting us and anyone else who got too close." Ashqar was moved, though, by all the people who risked their safety trying to intervene. "They came out of their houses begging the soldiers. 'Leave them alone,' they said, 'we'll take care of it.' But the soldiers insisted that we had to do it."

In the months before they were caught, the four men laid the foundations for all the leadership cells that followed, and also for the UNL's relationship to Gaza's population. They refused to create an internal hierarchy, reflecting the relative strengths of their organizations and the decisive power of Fatah, and insisted on taking part in as many actions as they could. By August 1988, when Zaqut, the last of the original four, was arrested and deported, the first UNL had been replaced by a second group.

According to Jamal Zaqut's deportation order, keeping him in an Israeli prison was considered a threat to state security. As he left the country, though, Zaqut told the Shabak officers that he would return "with the peace." There was no doubt in his mind that the *intifada* would go on until it brought results. "The popular support for the uprising made me very optimistic. There was just no chance it would disappear without some gain." Breaking with the official DFLP position, Zaqut supported the Oslo Accords and participated in the negotiations; as an Israeli gesture of goodwill, he was allowed to return home in 1994.

I first met him on May 17 that year—the day the civil administration transferred responsibilities to the Authority, handing over the keys to their offices in an official ceremony. The handover took place at an Israeli base in the northern part of the Strip, where the civil administration had moved a month or two earlier, changing its name in the process to the Coordination and Liaison Office (CLO).

Elegantly turned out yet reserved, Zaqut took part in the ceremony as a member of the new Palestinian Civilian Coordination and Liaison Committee, a role he preferred to downplay. Each day he would now sit down with the same Israeli officers who had once ruled Gaza omnipotently and negotiate every conceivable issue of relevance to daily life in the Strip: how much money was owed to the Israel Electric Company; what to do with commercial contracts inherited from the civil administration, ranging from a retainer with a laundry in Ashdod to a deal with a Tel Aviv computer firm; how to manage the orderly transfer of maps and land registers; how to set criteria for entry to Israel; what to do with the dozen or so civil administration cars (did they belong to Israel or the Palestinians?); how to extricate income tax files held up by the Israelis; and how to implement the safe passage corridor between the West Bank and Gaza. Over the next few years, some of these issues would be resolved by the exhausting haggling process that came to characterize new relations between the two sides (in fact, the dynamic is hardly new: the Palestinians plead, the Israelis grant "favors," crumb by crumb and so maintain the balance of power). However, negotiations over the two concerns with the most impact on people's lives—safe passage between Gaza and the West Bank and criteria governing entry to Israel—were still pending four years later.

"We're polite to them," Zaqut told me at that first meeting. I had asked him how it was possible to have a committee of equals when on opposite sides of the table sat an Israeli officer and a Palestinian who was once compelled to obey his orders. "We look toward the future. We prefer to avoid talking about what the occupation left behind—rotten infrastructure, a useless water system, crumbling buildings, and ruined spirits. We can't accomplish everything at once but we've achieved our first demand of the *intifada*: Israel understands now that it can't make peace without the PLO. Who knows this better than me? After all, I wrote the first leaflet of the UNL."

When Zaqut reconstructs the UNL's early days, his memories are slightly different from those of the other three members. As a senior member in his organization, Zaqut had assumed the role of the group's mediator with the West Bank. He was therefore more involved than the others in establishing a UNL there. To him, the crucial date was January 8, 1988, almost a month after the outbreak of the *intifada*, when 150,000 leaflets signed by the Unified Command for the Escalation of the Intifada were distributed in the West Bank. He and his comrades in the Democratic Front had simply gone ahead and written the leaflet after the other organizations had prevaricated about setting up a UNL for the West Bank. According to Zaqut, Fatah had agreed tentatively, "but wanted to learn more about the subject. The PFLP never gave us an answer, and we hadn't managed to establish contact with the Communists."

The leaflet, similar to the first one distributed in Gaza, called for a plan of action and detailed strikes, demonstrations, and other confrontations with the IDF. To Zaqut, the massive response to the leaflet's suggestions was proof of the West Bank's desire for a single leadership. "Still, in Gaza," Zaqut said, "it took me five minutes to convince my friends to hand out the same flyer, but there it was signed with a different name—just the Unified Command of the Intifada. In Gaza we didn't need to talk about escalation."

. . .

There were no representatives of the Islamic organizations in the UNL although young religious people took part in every demonstration from the beginning. According to Schiff and Ya'ari, Sheikh Ahmad Yassin, leader of the Muslim Brotherhood in the Strip, initially balked at sanctioning participation in the events, preferring to continue his program of education and preaching. But his younger followers pleaded with him, explaining that the Brotherhood could not afford to exclude itself, and in mid-December he authorized a leaflet signed by the Islamic Resistance Movement—or Hamas—that called for intensifying the uprising.

Of course, members of the other political organizations were only too pleased to repeat Schiff and Ya'ari's account of how the Islamic movement's elders had to be prodded along by their followers. According to another version, however, the Islamic Jihad (founded in the early eighties by militant Brotherhood dissenters) had given its blessing to the *intifada* early on, and rather than see this small, competing organization score points with religious Palestinians, the Muslim Brotherhood realized its mistake in hanging back. Rumors persisted about various Jihad members having been silent partners in the UNL.

When Hamas supporters tell their version of events, the spontaneous nature of the uprising vanishes altogether. In various contexts— speeches and publications—Sheikh Yassin is claimed as the *intifada's* real instigator. At a rally in al-Shatti refugee camp days before the Palestinian Authority took over in 1994, Sheikh Ahmad Bahar, an imam, told his enthusiastic audience that "Sheikh Ahmad Yassin made the *intifada*. He took the decision and only later did the other organizations join in." According to H.N., an active and devout student at Gaza's Islamic University at the time, the Muslim Brotherhood was really the first of all the organizations to fully grasp the qualitative difference of the protests and exploit their revolutionary potential. From the outset, he says, the Brotherhood encouraged the students to join the protests and stir things up. Sheikh Salah Shehadeh, the dean (secretly responsible for the Brotherhood's underground military group, Majd) told H.N. he had personally ordered students to attend the funerals that initially sparked the uprising.

The Brotherhood's leadership—Shehadeh, Yassin, Ibrahim al-Yazuri, and Abed al-Aziz al-Rantisi—apparently met the day after the funerals to discuss the rioting. They were unhappy with the decision made that day by the university's student council encouraging students to demonstrate in the streets but not on campus. The forum decided that any protest organized by the Brotherhood had to go all out—"not just a demonstration but a war," H.N. said. At the university, students immediately began to organize for a large demonstration. "We bought iron pipes and sawed them up, a piece for every student. We thought the pipes would stop the soldiers coming into the university," H.N. recalled. "But the university's directors, who weren't part of the Brotherhood and had always enjoyed excellent relations with the civil administration, got word of the protest and closed the university."

Retrospectively, Abu Husa credits the uprising to Fatah and its excellent sense of timing (even though he was briefly part of the first UNL). And like Hamas's version, his negates the *intifada*'s popular nature and spontaneity. "Fatah Day falls on January 1," he said, "but we'd already prepared all the leaflets. The situation in 1987 just before the uprising was so tense that we'd started to think about bringing Fatah Day forward." The Fatah parade and the mounting tension would probably result in five or six fatalities, Abu Husa and his comrades estimated, sparking protests and confrontations.

Then on December 8, when the four Gazans were run down by a truck, Abu Husa had the idea of linking the accident to the death of an Israeli in the Strip the previous day, in other words casting the accident as an act of vengeance. "I'd hit on a way of making use of the accident," Abu Husa said. "I stood at the Erez checkpoint telling people it was all revenge and by the time I got back to Gaza City people were coming up to me, repeating the rumor. I remember thinking, wow! It worked! The rumor spread like wildfire—it was the lead story in *Al-Fajr* the next day.

"That night, on December 8, orders went out to our people in Jabalia to get the whole camp down to the cemetery. We decided to send Fatah activists out with the schoolkids the next day to protest at the military base. We figured that two or three people would get killed and then we'd decide what to do next."

In the scramble for political legitimacy and a share in the power, various organizations have sought to take credit for the uprising, and in each of their accounts they play up their critical role in the first few days. But in Gaza's collective memory there is no single official version of who staged the *intifada*. What all Gazans remember is the terrible strain of the weeks before the protests, and the sense of spontaneous outcry. "Many people had been killed at the roadblocks," said Jamal Zaqut. "One schoolgirl, Intissar al-Atar, was shot and killed by a settler, who was released from jail after a week. People were asking hard questions, not just about their political future but about their very existence. They were asking how much their lives were worth."

It was not by chance that Mabhuh, Kafarna, Ashqar, and Zaqut came together in the first UNL cell, even though their group was short-lived and haphazard and its role was always vaguely defined. In their characters and in their political involvement, the four men represented the sweeping change that had, over the years, taken place in the Palestinian sense of the struggle against the occupation. What drove them above all was their disillusionment with the quasi-religious conviction that small, isolated underground units would one day drive out the foreign regime with arms and explosives. The UNL stood for a different understanding—that change would only come through popular, collective action.

Nor was it by chance that the first UNL grew out of the labor unions, even though the unions themselves were hamstrung. Since 1967, more and more Gazans had been making their living as a source of cheap labor for Israeli employers, and twenty years later national oppression and economic exploitation had become virtually synonymous to most of the Strip's population. In their leftist orientation, Mabhuh, Kafarna, and Zaqut were in a minority among politically organized Palestinians, but their ideological training seemed to have led them toward the kinds of activities that made sense in their world. Gazan workers, having come to know Israel well and to grasp the limitations on the Palestinian side, had developed their own aspirations for real personal and national change. And in this fertile ground, the union activists' influence far exceeded the real size of their organizations. Moreover, their understanding of the reality in which they lived forced the four men to rise above party and sectarian differences and find ways to coordinate their actions and listen to each other—an excellent basis for the makeshift, improvisational beginnings of the *intifada*.

.   .   .

"All I wanted for myself and my children was to live like human beings, for people to treat them as human beings," said one Fatah activist who took part in a later UNL cell. In the end, any social upheaval is always a demand that the ruling power—especially one imposed on an unwilling population—pay attention when other attempts to be heard have failed. And the demand in the leaflets and slogans amounted simply to this: Palestinians wanted their own state, and the call was directed not only at Israel but also at Palestinian leaders. "In the *intifada* even little children were chanting 'a state and some peace,'" another Fatah member told me. "And that was before Arafat even knew what a state was."

"Why do you think we started the *intifada*?" Ashqar asked me one day. "Why do you think we want a state? It's not the land—no piece of land is worth the bloodshed. No, we want a state for the thing itself." The "thing" seemed so clear to him that he never thought to explain it; he had moved me, though, to keep asking what the Palestinians had really wanted, what it was that had fueled the uprising. And in countless conversations throughout the Strip and in a variety of ways, people told me what they wanted: they wanted to expand the limits of their freedom of choice, personally and nationally. In the long run, they will judge the Oslo Accords accordingly, by measuring the breadth of their freedom as a people and as human beings.

Part II

Families Just Like Us

Chapter 3

Bougainvillea and a Pile of Rubble

At first it is always hard to figure out what the heap of rubble is doing where it is—a few slabs of concrete, some rusty iron bars, and a couple of rotting wooden boards still sticking up in the middle of a street or a crowded camp alleyway. They are remnants of something almost wiped out by time. Over the years, though, my eyes grew used to the sight, and I am no longer shocked to come across what turns out to be the remains of a demolished house.

There are less of these piles than there used to be, however, since an intense wave of construction began before the Oslo Accords were signed, and cranes and hydraulic drills are now the hallmark of the new era as more and more apartment buildings reach toward the skies of Gaza and families add one floor and then another to their small, squat houses, using bare blocks of concrete that are not always rain-proof. The bulldozers gobble away at swaths of greenery, at the orange and olive trees, remnants of the bountiful groves and orchards that used to cover great stretches of the Strip. Land once occupied by Israeli army camps has been given over to housing developments for the Palestinian police and a few hundred well-off exiles who have returned to Gaza.

By contrast, the mangled heaps of rubble bear witness to the ravaged lives of Gaza's people like the rings of a tree trunk marking the passage of time. The demolished homes almost always turn out to have belonged to the families of men accused of what Israelis call acts of terror and Gazans call the struggle against the occupation. The families moved away or dispersed to the homes of relatives or lived next to the piles of rubble for a while, in a tent provided by the Red Cross, before they began to build new houses beside the ruins.

The Israeli army has always defended its policy of sealing up houses or demolishing them as a deterrent; the demolition is brutal, usually carried out a few days after the suspect's arrest, long before his guilt or innocence has been established in court. But when a family shows me the pile of ruins ten or twenty years later, I cannot detect any signs of regret for the deed that caused the demolition, not even when elderly parents and younger sisters are the ones who had to pay the price.

In al-Boureij they defiantly show me half a wall left standing and, beside it, a dazzling purple bougainvillea bush. In the end, it seems, the demolition of a family's home only served to reinforce its unity. The actual moment of destruction and the rebuilding afterward usually gave the family a sense of being a partner in the struggle. D.L. proudly tells of his parents, whose house was sealed up by the army. They stayed in a shack until one brother got together a little money and then another brother pitched in and they managed to build one room for the whole family. That one room has since mushroomed into a house several stories high, with space enough for all of them. A.R. from Khan Yunis shows me the lone room of her house that survived demolition. While her sons were in prison, the rest of the family had but one ambition—for the boys to come home to a comfortable, rebuilt house. That single room is now a storage space next to the new house where the family lives.

M.D.'s house was also enlisted in the struggle, but in a different way. His brothers and cousins helped him buy an inexpensive parcel of land off the beaten track north of Gaza City, on the road to some Jewish settlements. The price was low because there was reason to believe that the Israeli authorities intended to confiscate the land. M.D. bought it for the express purpose of "picking a fight with the occupation" and starting a legal battle should the confiscation become a reality. His family—who supported the gamble morally and financially—came out ahead. The area is no longer isolated and a spacious home has gone up with separate apartments for all his brothers, including the ones who came back from exile.

Most people, however, have not managed to extricate themselves from their run-down quarters in the overcrowded towns and refugee camps, from the potholed alleyways, furrowed by ditches and flowing with sewage. In the Gaza Strip, 1,022,207 people live crammed together in a 147-square-mile area;[1] 20 percent of that territory, where the Jewish settlements remain, is off-limits to Palestinians. In the forced togetherness imposed by the tiny space they share, Gazans suppress their longing for privacy. They might not even know what to call the constant agitation in which they live, preferring to leave its cause unnamed because, once articulated, the need for privacy becomes impossible to ignore.

In the last twenty or thirty years the communal efforts of the extended family have been directed at making sure its younger members receive an education. Abu Basel is mindful that his brother A.A.—who worked in Israel for two decades—is the only reason he and the other siblings were able to attend university. Now that A.A. cannot reach his job in Israel, the rest of the family will take care of his daughters' education. Um Haitham eagerly awaits the day when her sons can go back to work. Then, she says, "we'll send some money to Haitham [her son] in Germany for his medical studies." B.L. would love to travel for a year or two, but he knows that were he to leave, his family would be "crushed economically and emotionally." He is lucky to have work in Gaza, and his salary keeps three siblings in school, two brothers in Libya, and one sister in the Strip; he can't allow himself to think of his own needs and desires. So it is with every family I meet, and the poorer the people, the more pronounced the phenomenon: there is always one brother working hard to educate his siblings and give them the chance at a good profession and a better life.

This sense of shared responsibility for the family, so common in the Gaza Strip, defies any simple explanation. Certainly the conventional ones—the traditional nature of Arab society, the overcrowding that suppresses individualistic tendencies—seem to me inadequate. When staying with friends in the Khan Yunis or Rafah refugee camps, mixing up the names of all the offspring of all the brothers and sisters and cousins who would pop into the house from the dusty alleyway, I would watch the children as they sulked in the yard during the long days of curfew, glued to the gate, shaking it angrily and whining to be let out. Almost unaware, I was looking for another explanation for the family solidarity.

"In Gaza there's nothing but sand and children," I was told by A., a Jabalia native doing sociological research. He complained that even the younger, modern couples went on having one child after another. Along with my growing wonder at Gazans' staying power, I began to understand an underlying reason for their extraordinary familial devotion. They clung steadfastly to family, to respect for the eldest members, and to having large numbers of children as a bulwark—like religion—against the instability and lack of continuity in their lives. Since 1948, they have been subject to upheaval, to sweeping political changes over which they have no control, to economic uncertainty, and to the constant shadow of sudden, violent death, especially once the *intifada* began in 1987. Much has been said about how the *intifada* undermined adult authority, but it is also true that the crushing oppression and daily violence heightened the need to seek consolation among family members, to use the home to counterbalance the crumbling social framework outside.

The extent of the violence that accompanied the uprising can scarcely be overemphasized. During the first four years of the *intifada*, 60,706 Gazans were injured by shooting, beating, or tear gas. According to a study by the Association of Israeli and Palestinian Physicians for Human Rights (PHR), 2,285 people were shot in 1988, 7,049 were severely beaten, and 3,295 suffered ill effects from inhaling tear gas. In 1989, 6,974 people were shot, 10,774 were beaten, and 3,196 suffered the effects of tear gas (no distinction is made between live ammunition and rubber- or plastic-coated bullets).[2] According to UNRWA records, between August 1989 and August 1993, 1,085 persons treated in its clinics had been shot in the head: 302 of these were between the ages of seventeen and twenty-four, 163 of them (15%) were women, and 545 were under sixteen—of whom 97 were children under the age of six. In its study, the PHR points out that during the five years of the *intifada*, a child under the age of six was shot in the head once every two weeks—an appalling statistic.

On February 2, 1989, six-year-old Lulu Abu Dakhi from the Shabura refugee camp came home from school, asked for money for ice cream, and went out in the street with a friend. Her father remembers that there was no particular unrest in the area. "The streets were quiet. Suddenly we heard a shot. A few minutes later Lulu's friend came running back with her ice cream, shouting, 'Lulu's dead!' She said that some soldiers had come out from a side street. The girls had started running, and Lulu was shot in the head with a rubber bullet." In fact, Lulu was not dead. Seven years later, she was still hospitalized in the West Bank Recuperation Association's facility, totally dependent on those around her. The only voluntary movements she can control are blinking her eyes, chewing, and swallowing. The Israeli army opened an investigation some two and a half years after Lulu was injured—and only after the family persisted in demanding one—but then announced that the length of time that had passed since the incident made it impossible "to ascertain the relevant evidence regarding the actions of IDF forces on the date in question." The file was closed.[3]*

Rana Abu Tuwior, an eleven-year-old girl in Khan Yunis, went out to buy milk on December 19, 1992, during a forty-five-minute break in a curfew imposed to prevent demonstrations following Israel's mass deportation of Hamas and Islamic Jihad supporters. That afternoon, a jeep had driven around town announcing the break, the first in five days. People were unsure whether only women were allowed outside, as had been true the other times the curfew had been lifted temporarily. So M.S., a neighbor, asked Rana to get some milk from Abed al-Shafi Farka, who owned a citrus grove and a few cows.

Two days later, M.S. painfully described the events. He had given Rana a bottle, and she had set out excitedly for the main street. Although the curfew had been lifted, a number of soldiers and military vehicles were circulating in the neighborhood as the streets filled with people out stretching their legs. Fifteen minutes later, another neighbor, M.R., suddenly heard shooting, and he and others went to see what was happening. M.R. saw four army jeeps parked near the girls' school close to his house; some kids were throwing stones at them and the soldiers were firing in return. M.S., too, went out, and watched Rana walk toward Farka's house, about 150 yards from the soldiers. He saw her reach the gate, then fall to the ground. Like several others who witnessed what had happened, he tried to go to her but was prevented by the heavy gunfire. Only fifteen minutes later, during a lull in the shooting, were they able to rush her to the hospital, where the doctor pronounced her dead on arrival. She had been shot in the back.

The army spokesman maintained that "when the curfew was lifted, a large number of people of various ages came outside in an organized and deliberate manner, creating a disturbance and throwing rocks and bricks. A number of armed people were observed among those disturbing the peace. All shooting incidents were the result of a clear sense of danger on the part of the IDF forces present."

*Lulu Abu Dakhi died at home on December 2, 1998, her sixteenth birthday.

A ten-year-old named Ayman al-Suri was shot dead on February 5, 1994, as he went to return a book to the Jabalia library. Two days earlier, a little boy named Ayman Abu Hajar suffered a bullet wound to the head that left him a vegetable. By chance, his injury was caught on film by Marwan al-Ghul, a TV cameraman. Two military trucks had passed through Talatini Street and, as usual, schoolchildren had thrown stones. The film showed that the drivers were not in danger as their vehicles were high off the ground and moving quickly. Nevertheless, the first driver fired at the height of the children's heads, then continued on his way without actually hurting any of the children. The second driver, however, began shooting in the air even before any stones were thrown at him. Once they were, he too started firing at the level of the children's heads. The footage then shows a child in a white sweater, lying on the sidewalk in a pool of blood, his head a doughy red mass. The driver was court-martialed two years later and given a one-month suspended sentence. The entire Abu Hajar family is now caring for the half-dead child and praying for a miracle.

The extended family's mutual support system really comes into its own in the realm of material help, which no one ever thinks twice about giving. In the years I lived in Gaza, I saw just how indispensable that help is as a safety net during a time of general economic collapse. In the early nineties, Israel devised a new policy toward the Palestinians: general closure, which was fully implemented in 1991. For the first time since the 1970s, free movement between the occupied territories and Israel was denied to Palestinians, who were suddenly obliged to equip themselves with individual passes to cross from one area into another. These passes are granted only to a very small number of people, to specific segments of the population and employees whose work in Israel is considered essential. The system, which, contrary to the popular misconception, was put in place long before the Islamic movement began its mass terror attacks in Israel, has been refined over the years: since 1993, Palestinians have needed passes to enter East Jerusalem—their economic, religious, cultural, and medical capital. Again, very few passes are ever given. In 1994, with the advent of the Authority (or the Sulta, as it is called in Arabic), the physical separation of the Strip became more concrete: the electrified fence put up by

Israel, its multiple roadblocks, and sophisticated surveillance systems have blocked off any possible exit points for Gazans without permits.

The creeping process of segregation has caused profound damage to the Palestinian economy. There has been a drastic reduction in the number of workers allowed into Israel (almost the only source of livelihood available since the occupation began in 1967). Consequently, the Palestinians' per capita income fell by 7.14 percent in 1992 and 26.53 percent in 1993. Thus the collective efforts that typify Gazan families are directed less toward a long-term goal like education than toward satisfying the more urgent need for food.

Soon after the transfer of authority, I was in a bicycle shop on al-Wahda Street, in the commercial center of Gaza City. The salesman admitted to me that his brother, the owner, had him work there only so he would feel that he was earning his keep, so that he would not feel ashamed to accept his brother's financial support. Very few customers came into the store, even during the summer; in that working-class neighborhood, parents couldn't afford to indulge their children with bicycles. Next door was a modest restaurant. During the two hours I sat there, the busy period just after noon, only one person came in to buy a kebab sandwich. "I am living entirely off my brother," said the man behind the counter, echoing the bicycle salesman. "And my brother can't save anything for his own family because he spends whatever he has on me and my children."

A family structure like this, which cushions life's jolts economically and emotionally, is a blessing for any government. The Israeli military government set up in 1967, and the civil administration after it, were distinguished by their budgetary niggardliness, by a lack of provision for development, by heavier taxation than in Israel, by an education system that could not or did not try to keep up with the increasing number of schoolchildren, and by monumental neglect of Gaza's infrastructure: its roads, its water, sewage, telephone, and electricity systems. Families compensated for the neglect with their own improvisations, and the cost was shouldered by sons and daughters and siblings and in-laws. Such improvisations often included makeshift sewage systems, private water tanks, illegal wells, or even just a battery of jerricans filled with unpolluted water taken from pipes near the Jewish settlements or the Sheikh Radwan neighborhood—all to avoid the foul-tasting water in most homes and to cope with the frequent interruptions in its flow. Some families even bought their own electric generators, since an erratic electricity supply had become the bane of the Strip, especially during the last years of the *intifada*.

The Israel Electric Company, abetted by the civil administration, was in the habit of cutting off electricity to whole neighborhoods because some consumers, usually workshops or small factories, had not paid their bills or had pirated electricity by stringing illegal cables and wires. As a result, the Gazan municipalities—which, according to their contracts with the electric company, were responsible for all bill collection—would fall behind in their own payments. Like the residents, municipal officials and the Palestinian engineers they employed were hard put to understand why entire neighborhoods were left in darkness because of the debts of a few. The civil administration claimed that the wholesale electricity shutdowns were always for security and logistical reasons.

The disconnection at the local relay station would be done at night under cover of curfew, with soldiers in attendance. The mere mention of the civil administration officer who accompanied the soldiers, a Russian immigrant fluent in Arabic, terrified people. For days and sometimes weeks—even during holidays—residential neighborhoods and large businesses would have to manage without electricity. And yet, when I would visit large families during blackouts—their radios and TVs silent, their refrigerators defrosting and their food spoiling—I would see how readily they mobilized to face the ordeal.

This kind of network is a particular boon to any governing authority—national or foreign—at a time when many members of the community need assistance and rehabilitation: people disabled during the *intifada*, families of prisoners, released prisoners, families of people killed during the *intifada*, unemployed people, students who cannot finish their studies, severely traumatized children, and those suffering from malnutrition and illnesses aggravated by the absence of fundamental public health measures. After the Oslo Accords, all these people hoped for an improvement in their lives. But the 1996 budget for the Palestinian Authority allowed for no increase in the level of social services; security demands and the need to bolster the police apparatus ate up the funds that would have been required. The situation deteriorated after February 1996, when Israel sealed the Strip "hermetically": the number of the needy increased, but the priorities of the Palestinian Authority could not be changed.

Considering Gaza's chronic poverty, one might expect a high rate of crime, but a Palestinian police officer to whom I spoke observed that "we don't have much work." There are indeed problems with drug use and trafficking, but the police report little theft, murder, or rape. (Women killed for the sake of family honor are not included in the regular crime statistics and such murders are not considered to undermine public safety. I don't know the dimensions of this problem, but its omission shows the extent to which women are still associated with the domestic rather than the public sphere and are regarded as male property.)*

There is at least one clear explanation for the low crime rate: the large clusters of different families living close together in the same neighborhood or refugee camp deter individual members from yielding to the temptation to step out of line. With some one million people in Gaza's narrow strip, it still seems as if everybody knows everybody else. The knowledge that an injury to one family member is regarded as an injury to the whole extended family and could ignite an eternal feud is seemingly a deterrent in itself. Nevertheless, people do sometimes accidentally or intentionally overstep the bounds and harm a member of another family. A blanket of tension covers the neighborhood or the camp then, and respected elders on all sides are urgently summoned to calm the hotheads. I remember being in Rafah in early 1994 with a branch of the ten-thousand-strong Abu Jazar *hamula*, or clan. A week earlier, Suleiman Abu Jazar had been accidentally shot and killed by another Palestinian.

In the gray wintry day, the dull skies merged with the sand in the streets and the raw concrete buildings. Angry youths sat for hours on the shoulder of the road, as if waiting for their orders. Inside the dead man's house, people spoke in low voices, trying to control their anger. No one knew who the killer was; all anyone knew was that he had shown up in the neighborhood with some Fatah boys who had an ongoing quarrel with another family that lived nearby. Some of the Fatah boys had been masked; some had carried firearms. Suleiman

---

*In 1997 and 1998, the crime rates rose, especially serious crime. There have been several unsolved cases of murder and disputes with the Palestinian security forces that resulted in injury or even death. These have created a sense that the traditional supports, which always provided a feeling of stability, are beginning to crumble under the heavy toll of the closures, the political uncertainty, and the public's growing disaffection toward the Palestinian leadership.

Abu Jazar had tried to separate the two sides, a pistol had gone off, and Suleiman had been killed.

Without the name of a family to settle with, the Abu Jazar clan went instead to the local Fatah office, demanding that it turn the killer over to a religious court, where punishment would be based on the principle of an eye for an eye. Several Abu Jazar family members ended up setting fire to the office. Hamas then announced that the dead man was one of its members; the family confirmed that he had indeed been an observant Muslim, but they did not know whether he had belonged to Hamas. In a sermon, the most beloved imam in Rafah, Nadir al-Luqa, castigated the two organizations for their part in escalating the tension. People in Rafah expected a full-scale vendetta to break out between the two movements. But perhaps precisely because the dispute had been shifted from the familial realm to the organizational-factional level, a balance of terror was achieved that managed to prevent further hostilities.

Indeed, over the years, a second form of societal division, parallel to the traditional family structure, had evolved in Gaza. The different political organizations had come to represent another way in which society divided itself into groups of mutual responsibility and emotional attachment, each with its own unique identifying characteristics and language. These organizational "families" had come into existence during the years of direct Israeli rule, for the most part operating as underground organizations, their members under constant threat of arrest and trial. They were essentially political by nature, but found hundreds of channels for activism and influence that were not strictly political. Particularly during the *intifada*, there was a sense that the Gaza Strip had fragmented into distinct political super-*hamulas*; not everyone actually belonged to a political organization, but most people were united in their struggle against the occupation and it seemed that all were subject to its punitive measures. Consequently, everyone was allied, one way or another. Even in Israeli prisons inmates were allowed to maintain their allegiances: the authorities understood that permitting prisoners to choose their cells and tents according to ideological affiliation was a way to avoid interfactional tension. Ideological and temperamental differences, different choices of heroes, the constant struggle for the hearts and minds of new supporters—inside a prison any of these could spark arguments that might escalate to violence and spread to the general population.

Interorganizational conciliation committees were a prison tradition as well, proving their effectiveness at the beginning of the Oslo process. Indeed, on the day the Declaration of Principles was signed in September 1993, two former *shawisheen*—inmate representatives—who had become friends in jail managed to prevent clashes that seemed all but inevitable. In a funny and logical compromise, Sami Abu Samhadana of Fatah and Fakher Awad of Hamas proposed that the day be divided in two, one half to be given over to public celebration of the accords, the other half to protests by the "mourners." This affiliation of the various political organizations helped regulate the Strip in much the same way as tribal loyalties produced channels of authority and negotiation.

Some thinning clouds of tear gas in Rafah in February 1994 gave me the opportunity to move about between the homes of various activists—members of the three main super-*hamulas*. The fine but significant differences between them formed a kind of mosaic of allegiances and identities. It was during Ramadan, when observant Muslims neither eat nor drink nor smoke between dawn and dusk. In Hebron a few days earlier, a Jewish settler, Baruch Goldstein, had massacred twenty-nine Muslims at prayer, and throughout Gaza people were searching for a way to express their shock and grief. The IDF had extended the permanent night curfew to daylight hours in the northern part of the Strip; in the south a temporary curfew had been lifted, but only a few young people took to the streets, clashing sporadically with the army more out of habit than by any clear strategic design. Together with some friends, I came upon one of these clashes in Rafah: a few stones were thrown at some soldiers, there was a little shouting, and a TV camera or two stood ready for some photogenic action. More stones followed, then an answering salvo of tear gas.

The burning, choking effects of the gas were quickly dissipated by a deluge of rain, but the downpour gave us a good excuse to get out of there. We knew that the stone throwing was just a way of letting off steam for a few kids who couldn't see that people were simply too exhausted to take to the street in large numbers and vent their rage. We took refuge in the home of a Hamas activist who had been on fairly good terms with my friends when they had all been in prison together. On his walls hung a photograph of the Dome of the Rock in

Jerusalem, a poster with curlicued letters that proclaimed there is no God but Allah, and a picture of Imad Akel, a commander of the Iz al-Din al-Qassam, the Hamas military branch, who had been eluding Israeli security for years, killing eleven soldiers and a civilian along the way. Akel, a legendary military hero, and Sheikh Ahmad Yassin, the aging, wheelchair-bound founder of Hamas who was serving time in an Israeli jail for his role in the deaths of two soldiers, had become the symbols that identified supporters of the Islamic opposition. Their images were displayed at demonstrations and in people's homes, on the walls of houses, and on the banners that fluttered above several mosques, flouting both the Israeli occupation and Arafat's exclusive claim to leadership.

My friends wanted to smoke—something that was not done in broad daylight during Ramadan, and certainly not in a Hamas home. They came up with a lame excuse to move on to the house of a fellow Fatah activist whom they had also befriended in jail. Here, too, the symbols on proud display made the man's political allegiance transparently clear: the images of the Fatah triumvirate of Abu Amar (Yassir Arafat), Abu Jihad, and Abu Iyad (only one of whom had escaped assassination) smiled at one another across the wall, flanked by pictures of the Dome of the Rock—a religious-turned-national symbol—and a map of pre-1948 Palestine. "You're such infidels," he complained to my secular, left-wing friends when they lit up their cigarettes in full view of the Muslim symbol of devotion. Our host's barb was heavy with irony: for years Islamic activists had hurled this accusation at the left, inciting vicious attacks against its supporters and their institutions. Now, however, both groups—the left and the Islamic bloc—were supposedly united by their opposition to Oslo, but they remained as divided as ever. All this subtext was present in our host's sarcastic remark. As a Fatah activist, part of the Palestinian mainstream, he himself was expected to respect tradition, but he couldn't resist the temptation and broke his vow to fast. "It's because of you Israelis. You make me nervous," he said to me, as he joined the infidels in a smoke.

After a while we moved on to our third house and the symbols of the third super-*hamula*, the Popular Front for the Liberation of Palestine. Sure enough, a framed picture of George Habash, the Damascus-based leader of the Front, hung beside an even more famous emblem, an embroidered rendering of a refugee child known as Handale, the creation of Naji al-Ali, a political cartoonist. Handale stands with his hands behind his back, a patch on his shirt, and a question mark above his head; his name, the word for a bitter gourd, is an allusion to the bitterness of Palestinians' lives. His creator, a Galilee-born Palestinian refugee considered a Front supporter, was assassinated in London in 1987, probably because he did such an outstanding job of satirizing the PLO and the Arab world's big shots. Handale pendants, sometimes with a map of Palestine, became a kind of cult symbol and sign of identification with the Palestinian left. The Front's network of clinics had even made Handale key rings cast in lead, which proved to be very popular. But there must have been a flaw in the casting, because after a day or two Handale's right leg would break off and sometimes his left one, too. So Front supporters and everyone else who likes the image go around with a crippled Handale.

At this house we sat in dejected silence. It was one thing for Fatah members to make jokes and clown around—they were part of the coming regime and their political and material futures were assured. And Hamas people always radiate self-satisfaction and confidence in the future, given their sure knowledge that God is on their side and that sooner or later the entire population will follow the ways of Islam. But without the keys to paradise or to government offices, the dwindling Palestinian left had only the bleakest forecasts to offer, critical as it was of both Israel and Arafat and the Oslo Accords. So we sat together in silence, the men blowing smoke rings in the air.

Over the years, and especially since the eighties, the various Palestinian political organizations have all made a point of establishing educational, welfare, and health care institutions; they have set up groups to support prisoners and their families, women's groups, human rights groups, feminist organizations, and even their own agricultural committees and media offices. The left has been particularly effective in fostering this aspect of a proto-civil society. I was treated at one of the health clinics after I dislocated my shoulder in Shabura, a neighborhood in the Rafah refugee camp. When I cried out in the street (in Hebrew), people immediately gathered round and a taxi driver took me to a Dr. Yusuf, who was on duty at the clinic nearby.

One of a dozen run by the Popular and Democratic Fronts, it provides free or cheap medication, examinations, and preliminary treatment. Family doctors and specialists work there on a voluntary basis, in a whitewashed UNRWA building that once housed refugees, where someone on staff was tending a small, pleasant garden. Dr. Yusuf, round and smiling, popped my arm back into place in less than a minute. No one mentioned payment, including the driver.

I got some idea of the efficiency of a Hamas-affiliated Islamic institution at a kindergarten in the Khan Yunis refugee camp. The staff had prepared a meal to break the Ramadan fast for a thousand or so people who had just attended a rousing Hamas memorial rally. This was two months before the Israeli redeployment, and Hamas was still an illegal organization. But who could object to a communal meal provided by a charity? Quickly and in orderly fashion, the crowd was seated in circles on small straw chairs; in the middle of each circle was an empty chair on which was placed a huge tray filled with bowls of *kidra*, a spiced rice dish with beef, chickpeas, and fried garlic that had been cooked in massive pots in the kindergarten's yard.

From the seventies on, Israel allowed religious institutions to receive contributions from abroad unhindered, whereas nationalist organizations were reduced to subterfuge of all kinds in order to receive PLO funds, only a portion of which then went to the various welfare institutions; the discrimination still rankles many in Gaza. The political affiliations of these institutions were, of course, no secret, but the Israeli authorities made few efforts to impede their routine work as they were offering services that the occupation did not provide and that most families could not otherwise obtain. Services like the kindergartens were seen as extensions of the sphere of family responsibility, especially in the refugee camps.

The politically supported institutions were not just vehicles for discussion and ideological indoctrination; they also provided employment for members of their organizations. It seems that everyone understood and tolerated the idea of membership as a job qualification; work, after all, was a highly sought-after commodity. There were complaints, to be sure, of embezzlement and misuse of funds, but overall, the extensive network of social and civic institutions essentially constituted the legal, above-board branch of the underground political organizations; it was also in this network that political activities merged with the familial sphere. Those institutions without political identities, such as the Gaza Community Mental Health Program, also expanded the notion of shared responsibility, teaching people to take the initiative where they could instead of waiting passively for the authorities to act.

These institutions and services (that is, the schools, clinics, camps, and other facilities provided by UNRWA) helped create pockets of civil society parallel to UNRWA's quasi-government even while Gaza was under foreign rule. These pockets meant that the family was no longer the sole source of social support in Gaza, and they helped develop a new set of mutual demands and expectations, not just between the individual and the regime or between families and leaders, but also between the individual and society as a whole.

Whatever the political orientation of a super-*hamula*, three elements were essential to its public legitimacy in the years before the Oslo agreements. First there was the ideological aspect, that is, how the organization gave expression to people's national longings and gave impetus to the struggle to satisfy them. Then there was the aspect of support, both material and emotional—the organization's ability to care for people in the community in the difficult conditions of occupation and scarcity. Last—the base of the triangle, if the other two elements constituted its two sides—was the constituency, the followers who identified with the organization's position or simply felt at home in it and gave it strength and cohesion. The relative importance of each of these three elements was never fixed, but even today, under Palestinian self-rule, they continue to constitute a triangle of legitimacy.

The familial aspect of the political realm has, not surprisingly, been used by the super-*hamulas* to manipulate their supporters. At a massive rally held in al-Shatti refugee camp immediately after the Israeli army's withdrawal, for example, Hamas leaders vowed that the Palestinian people would spit out the Oslo agreements like waves spewing dead fish on the beach. Then a young boy, introduced as a "general of the stones," read a message to Arafat: "These words will be inscribed with the blood of our fathers, the tears of our mothers. . . . He who trades in the blood of our parents and the tears of our brothers speaks only for himself. . . . We expected Arafat to treat us with the feelings of a father."

A year later, I witnessed a similarly manipulative use of the family image, this time to bolster Arafat's position. A small audience had gathered in Gaza City's Yarmuk Stadium to celebrate the much-publicized arrival of a shipment of medical and sports equipment collected by Équilibre, a French humanitarian organization supported by various prominent Israelis and Palestinians. The "peace shipment" arrived in ten trucks. Heading the delegation was the Jewish French writer Marek Halter, who called on Arafat to come down hard against the opponents of peace and exhorted Gaza to become "the model of democracy and justice for the entire Arab world."

The event was sponsored by Suha Arafat, the chairman's pregnant wife, who thanked the delegation, noting that it was Palestinian Prisoners' Day and lamenting the fate of prisoners still being held in Israeli jails. Before the ceremony began, schoolgirls danced and chanted. "Ahalan wa-ahalan ya Mama Suha"—Welcome, O Mama Suha—they sang, leaping about. Later they clapped their hands at every mention of Yassir Arafat's name. Zakaria al-Agha, the minister of housing, greeted the audience in the name of chairman, who had been kept away by "circumstances"— attacks on nearby Jewish settlements, the closure, the Authority's large-scale (and illegal) arrests of Islamic supporters, among other things. Anyone wondering why it fell to the housing minister to address the audience (after all, the shipment was largely medical) needed only to remember that al-Agha was there in his capacity as head of the Fatah movement in the Strip. His presence was a sign of the Authority's desperate need to draw on Fatah's credibility. Fatah the super-hamula, Suha Arafat the mother, dancing children, nurture, and sports—all the symbols of one big happy family were on display at this much-hyped ceremony of goodwill and charity.

In their private comments and jokes, Gazans show how skeptical they are about this idyllic family image, but even then, the language they draw on evokes the family and the tribe. I once asked someone what a certain Palestinian leftist organization actually did. "Fady a mashghoula," I was told. "It's like the groom's mother." This, evidently, was an Egyptian saying for "making work": the groom's mother may have nothing to do, but she makes herself look busy. Another time I asked what had happened to a journalist who had had close ties with Fatah. "He's like the son of the first wife," was the answer; he had fallen from grace.

I thought of the expression again when all of Gaza was buzzing with rumors about the slate of Fatah candidates for the Legislative

Council. In the months leading up to the January 1996 elections, Fatah had made an effort to prepare for life in a democracy. For the first time, leaders had been chosen at party meetings and conventions rather than appointed secretly. These leaders, in turn, had selected their candidates for the Council. Most of their votes had gone to refugees, revered figures of the *intifada*, and former prisoners, along with a few respected elders. But Arafat and the movement's top leadership decided to delete a few of the names and substitute some decidedly unpopular representatives of large, well-to-do *hamulas*. "All the effendis got in," one of the replaced candidates confided to me bitterly. He too must have felt like the son of the first wife.

Quite apart from such high-handed maneuvering, the electoral system itself—the division of Gaza and the West Bank into sixteen voting districts—seemed to a number of people to encourage sectarian and *hamula* loyalties; they feared that clan allegiances and the factionalization that the leaders of the *intifada* had striven to replace with loyalty to the community would outweigh regard for the common welfare. The legislators elected under such conditions would feel they owed their seats not to the voters but to Arafat, and their own votes in the Council would be governed more likely by their loyalty to the ruler than by concern for the public. Critics warned of a revival of the old system, encouraged by the Israelis, in which the main channels of communication with government were through powerful *mukhtars*, or notables and elders. Such a development would retard the growth of civil society nurtured by the *intifada* and restore power to the family and the supreme *mukhtar*.

Hamas and the Popular and Democratic Fronts helped that process along when they decided not to run candidates and to boycott the voting. The elections were the result of the Oslo agreements, which they opposed, and they felt that their participation would mean indirect recognition of those agreements. Moreover, joining the Legislative Council, in their view, would mean playing in a game that had been fixed—by Fatah—from the outset, a game in which the constantly changing rules would be known only to Arafat. In earlier elections in his own movement, Arafat had proved his formidable ability to neutralize any independent force. The result of the opposition's boycott, though, was that it left the field open to one super-*hamula* alone— Fatah, which did in fact gain a decisive majority in the Legislative Council.

There were, however, several senior Hamas activists and a great many more members from the Popular Front who did support participation in the elections. They argued that the Oslo agreements had created a new reality, one that could not be denied, and that the opportunity to shape and influence the new circumstances should be exploited, especially in the case of a body such as the Legislative Council, which was to be elected by a popular vote.

In the end, the voters' choices vindicated this view. It is true that some Council members are indeed backed by *hamula* wealth, that several less-than-popular candidates were elected, and that there were complaints about fixed results. But most people proved that they knew how to choose the best candidates. A.K., who manned the polling station at the community center where he works, told me of an elderly lady who turned to him for help because she didn't know how to read. "You choose," she said. "Not on your life," he answered. "You have to decide for yourself." She suggested that he read her the names and he patiently went through the long list once and then a second time. She listened, thought, weighed her choices, and told him which names to mark. She ignored the representatives of wealthy families and the smooth talkers endorsed by the powerful, A.K. said. The candidates she chose were the best of the lot, the most promising, the ones most likely to act with integrity.

Several years on, though, those forces that opposed participation point to the way the Council has come to function as evidence of their wisdom: in the two years after the Council's March 1996 inaurguration, it was unable to bring the Executive Council (i.e., Yassir Arafat) to honor the separation of powers, sign laws that limit his reach, implement decisions intended to reduce the burgeoning size of the Palestinian police's many branches, or put a stop to corruption and bribery. To many, the Council is seen as little more than a debating society, in which even Fatah hotheads can voice their dismay, but at the crucial moment, when Arafat needs their votes, loyalty to the father-ruler and the family-movement takes precedence over principle. For this very reason, Hayder abd al-Shafi resigned from the Council at the end of 1997. Council members are still a conduit for local grievances of the sort that were once brought to clan leaders, who would then bring them to the authorities: an unpaved road, a broken pipe, a neighborhood conflict.

And as Council members are among the very few who are able to move freely between the Gaza Strip and the West Bank, they also function as a lifeline for family members caught on different sides of the territorial divide. What Council member could refuse a worried father who asks him to deliver a pot of soup to his daughter stuck in Ramalla? The father is prevented by Israel from visiting his daughter; the elected representative is prevented by Arafat from exercising his power. The impotent Council member is left with little to do but take his place in the chain of mutual assistance and material relief.

Chapter 4

Khalid Switches Parties

"Just don't speak to me about money," Arafat told the disabled *intifada* veterans who had come to honor him. "The Israeli occupation left us nothing but ruins," he continued. "But with your hunger and your sweat, my heroic brothers, we shall resurrect the ruins and build a glorious state."

The *intifada* veterans were only one of the many delegations, among them heads of large *hamulas* and Fatah loyalists, that daily clamored at the gates of the Falastin Hotel, where Arafat stayed after his return to the Gaza Strip in July 1994. Some came to honor him, some were just curious. Some were seeking Abu Amar's verdict in a dispute, others only wanted him to listen to their troubles, like a kind of supreme father. The supplicants stood on a sandy rise facing the hotel, enjoying the pleasant breeze from the sea, watching the battery of security personnel who encircled the hotel like handcuffs and the official cars that came and went, their windows darkened. Several military vehicles ferried groups of grim-faced men who sat in readiness around machine guns bolted to the truck bed.

Among the onlookers was a TV cameraman who looked familiar. He gave me a big smile and reminded me that he was Khalid, the grocer's son. I stopped in regularly at his father's store on Falastin Street, in the center of Gaza City, for tomatoes, guavas, a few blocks of hard, salty cheese from Nablus, ultrapasteurized milk from Israel, or whatever else I needed that day. If I happened not to have enough money with me, his father would tell me to pay next time.

"I'm lucky," Khalid told me proudly, "I've found work." He had just been released from prison, having served about four years of a six-year sentence for activity in the Popular Front. "After the Oslo Accords," he explained a bit sheepishly, "I began to support the peace process, and so I switched to Fatah in prison. If anyone tries to get me involved in politics these days, I just tell them I've switched parties again. Now I'm with my family and children instead." But he still carried the Front's favorite symbol, Handale, hanging on a key chain.

S.B., a high-ranking activist, was even clearer about the connection between supporting Fatah and finding work and economic stability. "People know that the Authority, the Sulta, will be giving out most of the new jobs," he said. "And everyone knows that Fatah is the backbone of the Sulta." S.B. felt confident the Oslo agreement would lead to a peaceful solution; he saw nothing wrong with his utilitarian optimism. In Israel, I told him, we have an expression: *"Mapainik kedainik"*—something like, "Aiming high? Join Mapai." (Mapai was David Ben-Gurion's ruling party; affiliates usually were guaranteed jobs and promotion.) S.B. grinned broadly.

Outside the Falastin Hotel I met a group of unemployed men from al-Shatti refugee camp, most of them in their midthirties or older. They had all been working in Israel for fifteen or twenty years, but had lost their jobs following the Baruch Goldstein massacre in Hebron and Israel's "hermetic" sealing of the Gaza Strip and the West Bank, a measure known as "closure." "What do you want Abu Amar to do for you?" I asked the men after they had been waiting there for two days. "You're an Israeli, right?" one said in Hebrew. "We'll ask him to convince Rabin to open the Erez checkpoint," he explained, refer- ring to the border crossing between Israel and Gaza. Not for the first time I was struck by how solidly the Gazans' expectations were rooted in practical concerns, even then, during the Authority's first days in power. It seemed that people knew, much as did Palestinian and Israeli economists, that Gazan society would not soon recover unless the tens of thousands of workers who had been deprived of their livelihoods since the 1991 Gulf war—when Israel had begun to implement its closure policy—were able to go back to work. They understood that the Oslo agreements perpetuated the hierarchi- cal relationship between the Palestinians and the Israelis, and they had no illusions about sovereignty and independence. Seven years after the beginning of the *intifada*, with all its national and emancipatory aspirations, Gazans were forced to define their goals in terms of their immediate needs: to extricate themselves from the quagmire of unem- ployment, poverty, and insecurity, which had held absolute sway, espe- cially since 1991.

At the time of the Oslo negotiations, Fatah had read people's feelings correctly: fatigue, a hunger for normalcy, a longing for peace and quiet. Fatah had also understood their hopes that Palestinian patience and forbearance would be vindicated, that the step-by-step process outlined in the agreements would lead eventually to independence and sovereignty. Given these sentiments, Fatah agreed temporarily to mortgage the explicit nationalist demands of the *intifada*. It willingly extended its own legitimacy to the Palestinian Authority, most of whose leaders had only recently come back to the country. To create conditions for peaceful negotiations with Israel and to justify its right to govern, the Authority depended on recognition of the PLO—by Israel and by the international community—as the Palestinians' representative; it relied heavily, too, on the credit the PLO had built up among Palestinians through its well-established organizational apparatus and by militant underground activity. But material needs had become pressing. Arafat's grandiose words to the *intifada* veterans notwithstanding, Fatah knew that from now on the support of men like Khalid and S.B. and thousands of others would depend on the material return, on the immediate economic recovery that everyone believed the agreement with Israel would produce.

As for Israel, the Oslo agreements gave it the power to enhance or diminish the Authority's legitimacy in the eyes of the Palestinians, because Israel's actions would determine the Authority's success. Following the agreement people expected to change its policies: to end the closure system, which had kept Palestinians in near-siege circumstances on and off since 1991; to release all Palestinian prisoners in Israeli jails, whom the Palestinians think of as POWs; to restore freedom of movement between the Gaza Strip and the West Bank; to allow access to Jerusalem, the Palestinians' economic, cultural, and religious center; to remove the remaining restrictions on economic activity; and to ensure free movement of workers and goods to and from Israel. The bargain struck between Fatah, the Authority, and the Palestinian people became directly contingent on these changes.

But not all of Gaza was party to this bargain. The leaders of the largest opposition bloc, the Islamic movement, represented by Hamas, were appalled by the accords, believing that they traded sacred Palestinian rights for paltry material gains. "Our people are simple," A.S., a senior Hamas member told me shortly before the redeployment, dismissing even those economic and general improvements that might actually be realized. "If someone's son gets out of prison early or someone else goes back to work or can open his store in the evenings, they'll support the agreements for a while. But later, when they discover that it's not the way to get back our national rights, they'll rise up a second time."

Addressing a Hamas rally soon after the Authority was set up, Ahmad Nimr, a senior member, spoke in the name of a thirteen-year-old boy who had been shot dead by Jewish settlers a few days earlier. "This is my message to the people. We condemn selling out Beit Daras, Burayr, and Barbara," he said, referring to Palestinian villages lost in 1948, "just so we can build the sewage system of Gaza." Like other Hamas leaders, he believed that the influence of any new prosperity would gradually subside and, with it, support for Fatah and the Palestinian Authority. The Islamic movement was the only one that stood to benefit from the evaporation of this support. It would benefit all the more if, instead of prosperity, there was a recession—and that is what happened. When it came, the recession was of a severity that the Strip had never known, because Israel did not open the Erez checkpoint; the Strip remained sealed up.

It is therefore no surprise that the PLO and the Authority were highly sensitive to pressure from Hamas, especially given the movement's many supporters (between 40 and 45 percent of Palestinians, at least according to Hamas), its impressive social welfare system, and its electoral strength in the professional associations. Hamas, too, could claim its part in the militant struggle. At the rally that Nimr addressed, one speaker after another praised Hamas for its seniority in the heroism department (in effect downplaying the role of the other organizations in the *intifada* and of the spontaneous rage that sparked it). Sheikh Ahmad Bahar, using the imam's traditional oratorical skills, honed by years of Friday sermons, all but hypnotized the audience, stirring them up, inciting them to action, wringing from them rhythmic chants of "Islam is the solution," then shifting to the tranquil, introspective attitude of prayer. His message? That if Rabin was in a hurry to implement the autonomy agreement, it was because he was afraid of Hamas's military arm, the Iz al-Din al-Qassam. Another speaker, Ismail Haniye, amplified the argument. The soldiers' withdrawal, he said, was not the product of the accord but a testament to the strength of Hamas and the "generals of the stones."

Despite the gulf between Hamas and the PLO, Haniye's speech

hinted at the beginning of a conflict within his movement and a softening of some members' positions: while rejecting the accords, Hamas also wanted to claim some credit. (A similar tension was inherent in the rally itself. Although it was assembled to oppose the agreement, its declared purpose was also to welcome home the new battalions of Palestinian police.) People saw the withdrawal—limited as it was—as a positive and welcome step, a reason for hope; as a mass movement, Hamas could not completely disregard their feelings. This admission was expressed in a new formula repeated by the Islamic opposition and the small leftist groups, which spoke of "participation in the building and rehabilitation of Palestinian civil society." Early on, one Hamas leader, Khalid al-Hindi, told me they might be willing to consider limited participation in manging the Strip's daily affairs if the Legislative Council proved to be elected by truly democratic means.

But right from the start, a balance of fear began to be evident between the Islamic opposition on the one hand and the Authority and Fatah on the other. Deep mutual suspicions were masked by soothing words about national unity and the shared desire to rebuild the Palestinian community. "We expect the police to afford us real security and not be used as a stick against us," Sheikh Ahmad Bahar said, expressing concern that Palestinian security forces might act arbitrarily and illegally, striking out against those who were not automatic yes-men. Others suspected influence peddling, or the exercise of *wasta*, in the Palestinian Authority. At one point, for example, Hamas distributed a leaflet outlining the expanding business ventures of Nabil Shaath, one of the senior negotiators with Israel. On this count, even Fatah members were concerned. One key Fatah activist spoke bitterly about Jamil al-Tarifi, a negotiator who, in his later position as minister for civil affairs, dealt closely with his Israeli counterparts. How could the Israelis be expected to take Tarifi's official position seriously, he complained, when they knew that his business dealings depended on Israeli goodwill? The message was clear: representatives of the Authority were letting their private interests interfere with their official roles.[1]

Although Fatah activists were critical of their leaders in the movement and in the Authority, they were no less suspicious of the Islamic movement, and doubted the truthfulness of its political wing's denial of any responsibility for the military branch and its armed actions. Fatah and the Authority feared that this declared separation was an

evasive tactic designed to enable Islamic loyalists to dance at two weddings: to act as a legitimate political opposition within a democracy,
while at the same time undermining Arafat's standing with Israel and
the Palestinian public by means of a bloody agenda.

Fatah and the Authority wondered why Hamas's military arm began
its massive attacks on Israeli civilians only after the Authority was
installed in 1994; during the *intifada*, Hamas's explicit policy was to
target only IDF soldiers and settlements. The movement's standard
reply—that attacks on civilians had begun after Baruch Goldstein's
massacre in the Ibrahimi mosque—failed to persuade its critics. One
could perhaps explain one or even two acts of revenge taken against
civilians, but the regular suicide bombings of buses full of commuters
pointed toward a strategy: to steal control, even flawed as it was, from
the PLO. Fatah was afraid that Hamas would hide its true intentions—
to destabilize the Authority and eventually take its place—by focusing
on the popular claim that the continued presence of Jewish settlements
and Israeli soldiers proved the occupation had not come to an end.

Israel itself could have bolstered Arafat's credibility, but it persisted
with its closure policy and dragged its feet on undertaking the other
measures so desperately needed by the Palestinians. Worried that
Israel's intransigence would weaken the fledging Palestinian government, the Authority began to depend more and more on "preventive
policing" to control its critics. "We, not they, are the ones who brought
this government into being, and we'll do whatever it takes to protect
this historic achievement," said Diab al-Luh, the head of the Fatah
Information Department. "Nobody gave us a present, not Israel, not
America. It was our work, our doing."

And then, in November 1994, Gaza woke up to a nightmare. The
delicate balance between the two rival forces was upset, setting in
motion a chain of events that verged on all-out civil war. The cycle
would recur again and again over the next few years, each time bringing Gaza to the brink of bloodshed. First, a central figure in one of the
Islamic organizations would be assassinated and everyone, including
Israeli observers, would hold Israel responsible. Second, a Palestinian
Muslim cell would attack Israelis in relatiation. Third, the Palestinian
Authority would respond by initiating forceful measures, including
mass arrests of opposition supporters and anyone suspected of planning attacks. Israel, meanwhile, would impose a rigid closure, sealing
off the Strip and the West Bank, add ever-harsher restrictions, and

bring suffering upon the entire Palestinian population. Finally, the Authority would silence all critics, harassing journalists, clamping down on the press, holding people in jail for extended periods of time after subjecting them to torture and humiliation. The end of the cycle would be signaled when the Authority released some of its prisoners and Israel began to ease the closure. Each time the cycle recurred, the rift in Palestinian society grew wider; even as Israeli and American leaders rushed to praise Arafat's actions as decisive steps "in the fight against terror," Palestinians felt only alienation from their leaders.

On the afternoon of November 2, 1994, I was sitting with some Gazan journalists at the end of a quiet workday. It was raining, which always meant a power failure and the temporary silencing of the telephones. We were all relieved that October was behind us, a month that had been painful for the Israelis and the Palestinian Authority alike. A Hamas terrorist attack in a Jerusalem shopping mall had been followed by the kidnapping of an Israeli soldier and a botched rescue. Worst of all had been a suicide bombing in which a West Bank Hamas loyalist had blown up a bus in the heart of Tel Aviv, killing scores of people. Suddenly the telephone came to life, and a young reporter considered sympathetic to the Islamic Jihad lifted the receiver. His smiling, friendly face turned ashen, and his eyes seemed to become moist as he said in disbelief, "Hani Aabed? Wounded? Badly?"

An hour earlier, Aabed, a physics teacher at the Technical College in Khan Yunis and an Islamic Jihad activist, had just gotten into his car when an explosive device, apparently activated from a distance, blew it up. Hani Aabed died at six that evening. His was the first assassination in the new autonomous Gaza Strip, surely carried out by Israeli agents.

Israelis intelligence sources claimed that Aabed had headed the military apparatus of the Islamic Jihad and was responsible for many of its military actions. That summer there had been random efforts to shoot at Israeli soldiers and settlers in Gaza, and the army believed that the Islamic Jihad was behind the incidents. The Jihad—a small, disciplined, and, some would say, elitist organization—did not have a mass following and, unlike the other parties and movements, did not maintain a social welfare network that it was afraid to harm by openly challenging the Authority. Consequently, its leaders felt bound by the word of God (as they interpreted it) rather than by the immediate needs of the people. Even so, they were inclined to think that few Gazans would feel opposed to the killing of soldiers.

Aabed was arrested by the Palestinian police but denied any connection to terrorist acts or to the military arm of his organization and was released after eighteen days for lack of evidence. No one in Gaza doubted that Shabak, aided by Palestinian collaborators, was responsible for Aabed's death. His car had blown up close to the Israeli settlements where Shabak agents and collaborators were based, it was believed. Similar attacks on Palestinian leaders throughout the world are engraved in Gazans' collective memory—if Israel could get at Abu Jihad in Tunis and Ghassan Kanafani in Beirut, what was to prevent their reaching a hill in Khan Yunis?

Israel had no official reaction but about the time Hani Aabed was killed, Prime Minister Yitzhak Rabin was addressing an annual memorial ceremony for fallen soldiers. "With one hand we reach out in peace to the Hashemite Kingdom of Jordan and with the other we squeeze the trigger at the murderous terrorists of Hizbollah and the Islamic Jihad," he said.

From my meeting with Hani Aabed several months earlier I remembered him as friendly and astute. He had just been released from a Palestinian jail, having been questioned about his role in the death of two Israeli soldiers at the Erez checkpoint. I understood his willingness to speak to me, an Israeli woman journalist, as a sign that the Strip was not necessarily firmly in the sway of fear and oppression.

Terror, he told me, would not further his movement's goals "by very much." As he saw it, those goals still included a state in all of Palestine, although "physical liberation of the land will come from outside, from the Islamic regimes." In his view, Jews would be able to remain in an Islamic Palestine. "We don't hate the Jews as a people," he said, "this is a political conflict." Asked about Jewish self-determination under Islam, Aabed replied, "From the moment that Muhammad, peace and blessings be upon him, accepted the religion, members of all religions were obliged to convert to Islam. Permission to remain faithful to their own religions is a favor that we bestow upon them."

The streets of Gaza darkened early the night that Hani Aabed died. A procession of cars wound its way toward his home, where mourners, protesters, and cameramen had gathered and small chairs were arranged in rows in the mourning tent. At the funeral the next day, there were several thousand followers of the Islamic Jihad and more people who had come just to watch. As cars crawled behind donkey carts, they marched to the Martyrs' cemetery four miles away, making part of the journey in heavy rain, their feet splashed with sewage and mud. They hurled insults at Yassir Arafat, whom they had refused to let pray with them, chasing him from the al-Omari mosque, where the funeral cortege had begun. And at every rally, all over the Strip, people angrily pledged revenge against Israel.

To me their faces showed something other than anger. Gaza was gripped by fear, but it was of a different quality from the fear of the occupation; the rules of the game had changed, and no one knew what was coming next. People reminded me of nothing so much as children howling in the night to mask their dread of the dark. "If Israel starts assassinating people on our territory, it will lead to the Lebanonization of Gaza. It's jeopardizing the entire peace process," said S.B., the man who had laughed at my *Mapainik kedainik* joke and who had been so full of optimism four months earlier.

Fatah protested Arafat's unceremonious ejection from the mosque, while joining the other organizations in pointing an accusing finger at Israel. The Authority's senior members were convinced that Israel was behind Aabed's assassination but felt that they could not file a formal complaint. At a press conference after a meeting with Rabin on November 9, Arafat refused to answer the question of whether he thought Israel was responsible for the attack.

The narrow, teeming Strip waited with resignation for the bloodshed that was sure to come. It did not wait long. At one of the memorial rallies for Hani Aabed, two masked men delivered a message that surprised no one: three soldiers had been killed in a suicide attack at Netzarim, a Jewish settlement inside Gaza. An Islamic Jihad leaflet said that the suicide bomber, Hisham Hamed, belonged to the Unit of the Martyr Hani Aabed and that the organization was responding in kind "to Rabin's murderous course of action." The leaflet warned that "every Zionist living in any part of the land of Palestine, from the river to the sea, is a target for our bullets. The concept of a red line is not part of our vocabulary." The Jihad promised four retaliatory attacks.

The Palestinian Authority condemned the killing of the soldiers, and the Palestinian police wasted no time arresting Islamic Jihad activists. They buried the suicide bomber's remains clandestinely, without his family present—"something that not even the Israeli occupier did," according to the Jihad and Hamas. Meanwhile, one senior Fatah member openly voiced the suspicion that the Jihad's real goal was to harm the Authority, not Israel. "Why did the Jihad attack soldiers now, after the agreements? Why didn't they take action during the negotiations and prove how important it was to evacuate the Jewish settlements?" he asked. Altogether, though, Gazans found it hard not to wonder how it was that Arafat wielded almost limitless power against a Palestinian organization, yet was all but impotent against Israel. And then the day arrived when it seemed that indeed Lebanon had come to Gaza.

On Friday, November 18, Hamas organized a procession in memory of Hisham Hamed that would leave from the Falastin mosque after the regular prayers and sermon. By 11:00 A.M., tense, silent groups of men had begun to converge on the mosque. The Palestinian police were determined to prevent the procession, claiming that no application had been submitted for a permit. Along with security forces, they spread out around the mosque even before the arrival of the worshipers, some of whom had to stand in the square outside the building because of lack of space. Before the prayers were over, the police approached a truck and confiscated its loudspeakers. According to the official version, immediately after prayers, the worshipers began waving placards with anti-Authority slogans, shouting abuse at the police, throwing stones, and shooting. The police began firing—in self-defense, they said—first into the air, then into the crowd.

Journalists who were present and worshipers, both Hamas supporters and others, said that some of the youths in attendance had begun throwing stones in reaction to the confiscation of the loudspeakers during prayers. Within a matter of seconds, the police replied with bursts of gunfire. Other worshipers then rushed the policemen, throwing stones, waving placards, and calling out slogans. The police retreated slightly but continued firing. Mahmud al-Zahar, a high-ranking Hamas figure, climbed on top of a car and pleaded with the two sides to calm down. The worshipers claim that they began to back off but the police continued shooting. When it became clear that there were casualties, the crowd's anger mounted. The sound of gunfire and the wail of ambulances terrified the entire city and brought even more young men out into the streets. Altogether thirteen men were killed at the Falastin mosque.

Twenty-three-year-old Hazem al-Dalu had gone to morning prayers dressed in the same clothes he had worn on his release from prison in Israel some months before. He had been suspected of belonging to al-Saiqa al-Islamiya, a Hamas wing that ferreted out alleged collaborators and punished them. His release had come after six months (he had not been tried) when he signed a statement renouncing terrorist activities. Dalu had been born in Gaza City and had worked as a tailor's apprentice since the age of fourteen, advancing in his trade until he opened a small tailoring shop employing four or five people.

Of the thirteen men killed at the Falastin mosque, Dalu was the first, dying in hospital of gunshot wounds. It was decided to bury him immediately, that same day. The funeral procession wound through the center of town and past the government offices—"so that everyone could see what the Palestinian police had done," Hamas loyalists said. Dalu's funeral and that of the second victim, Hamdi al-Imawi, further fueled the rage in the city. Youths heaved rocks at police headquarters and tore down the fence surrounding it. They broke into the Nasser Cinema on Omar al-Mukhtar Boulevard (whose owners had recently refurbished it and had hoped to start showing movies again) and began demolishing the furnishings. They burned tires and trashed several video rental shops, a constant target of Islamic wrath since the eighties. They ran roaring through the city like wounded animals, howling and throwing stones, without any idea of what to do next. Senior Hamas figures shuttled back and forth between Arafat's office and the police commissioners, trying to meet with someone who could order the police to stop shooting, but all doors were closed to them.

Echoes of gunfire were heard until six that evening; the police imposed a curfew and streets began to empty. The families prepared their dead for burial, and representatives of the political organizations consulted on how to halt the escalation and ensure that the next day— when another nine or ten funerals were scheduled—the situation would not degenerate into a state of war.

That night meetings went on at the home of Hayder abd al-Shafi. First came the left and then Hamas and the Islamic Jihad, followed by Fatah and, last, someone from the Palestinian Authority. Then Arafat's office phoned and the mediators went back and forth. Finally abd al-Shafi announced that the police would stay away from the funerals and rallies and that the organizers, for their part, would make sure that no one was armed. With every hour that passed quietly, there was a palpable sense of relief. More bloody confrontations had been averted and mediation efforts had expanded, but the violent hostilities of the day had revealed a society divided not only ideologically but also emotionally.

In the days following the fighting, Saturday and Sunday, I moved between two worlds—between the homes of mourners and the offices of Fatah and the Authority, between the hundreds of shocked people assembled in the mourning tents that had been set up and the energetic political activists intent on defending the new regime and its ruler, placing all blame on Hamas and the Islamic Jihad. I saw the mourners' expressions of isolation and grief as they closed ranks, a kind of grief profoundly different from the old pain when loved ones were shot by the Israeli army; I saw the frozen faces of the Fatah and Authority loyalists, who were rigid in their unqualified support for the regime. The pain seemed not to touch them; they stuck to their ironclad explanations and spoke of the stability of the government. A great deal of people's anger was focused on the police, who didn't dare show themselves in uniform. "No one enters our house wearing a uniform," one of my friends told a relative of hers who was a policeman.

Immediately after the bloody confrontation, the police and the Authority maintained that some of the dead were police officers. In a later version, eight of the dead were said to have been Fatah members. Then, for a time, the Authority stuck by the story that it was undercover Israeli agents who had opened fire; later, that it was Palestinian collaborators who had started the shooting. There was even talk of "foreign elements." Finally, the Authority declared the dead to be martyrs and joined in the mourning.

The first Fatah leaflet following the clash at the mosque stated:

"Hamas and the Islamic Jihad premeditatedly crossed the red line. . . . They knew that demonstrations and processions without permits were prohibited. They want to create the impression that they are above the law, a government within a government." But in a later statement, published in conjunction with the smaller, left-wing parties, the tone was more conciliatory. The accusing finger was now pointed at the "Israeli enemy and its spies," and the leaflet stated that only Israel stood to gain from the outbreak of civil war.

As the days passed, the threat of renewed armed conflict slowly receded, giving way to competition between the parties for the largest rallies and demonstrations, and even more to the rekindled historical contest over which group had the longest-standing credentials in the struggle against the occupation. One question was never settled: whether the police had opened fire so tragically in response to explicit orders from above (i.e., from Arafat), or as a result of inexperience and fear. A direct order could only mean that Arafat's regime was determined from the outset to draw unequivocal limits to opposition and eliminate anyone posing a threat to its authority. Intentional or not, that message was heard and understood, and over the course of the next year Islamic activists refrained from attacking Palestinian police. The few incidents that did occur were carried out by individuals and not claimed by the opposition movements. Instead, the Islamic organizations focused their attention on the ever-vulnerable target—Israeli civilians. After a month or two of relative quiet, the Jihad carried out a massive suicide bombing in Beit Lid, a busy intersection just two hours north of Gaza, killing twenty-one soldiers and one civilian. It was one more act of revenge in response to the death of Hani Aabed.

Five months later, in April 1995, the cycle of conflict was repeated in earnest with the assassination of Kamal Kheil, considered by Israeli security experts to be one of the most dangerous men in Hamas's Iz al-Din al-Qassam. Together with another member of his cell, and a three-year-old boy, he died in an explosion, at first described by the Palestinian police as a "work accident," in a house in the Sheikh Radwan neighborhood. The toddler's father died of his wounds a week later. "We call him al-majnoun, the crazy one," a Hamas friend once told me, referring to Kheil. "We wish he'd just go away." Kheil tended to act on his own initiative and senior Hamas people deplored his brutal behavior without knowing how to put a stop to it. The same friend also said that he himself felt increasingly unhappy with his movement's acts of terror. He had supported one suicide bombing in retaliation for Baruch Goldstein's massacre at the Ibrahimi mosque in Hebron, but a second attack had caused him deep misgivings. "What if you, Amira, had been on that bus?" he said.

Still, Kheil was acclaimed in eulogies, several massive rallies were held in his honor, and he was given a huge symbolic funeral (since once again the police had buried the bodies clandestinely). The police and Hamas kept their distance from each other and everyone and tried to suppress the sense that the attack was the work of the Israeli Shabak. One other person was allegedly wounded in the blast but then went missing. His disappearance added weight to the suspicion that Shabak had been involved in the explosion. This time, however, Hamas openly declared that "the possibility of cooperation between the Israeli and Palestinian security forces could not be ruled out." Later, Arafat and some of his ministers responded by accusing the Israeli extreme right of providing material assistance to Hamas and Islamic Jihad radicals.

The cycle made its relentless turn when, one week later, two Gazans from Hamas and the Islamic Jihad blew themselves up in the Strip, the first beside a bus letting off Israeli soldiers, the second next to an army jeep. The death toll: seven soldiers and an American woman, a tourist. A statement from Arafat's office condemned the attacks as "an attempt to play havoc with the security of the Strip, providing a pretext for the imposition of closure, causing workers and other inhabitants of Gaza to go hungry. This assault was directed not only against us and the peace process but also against our nation."

At the Erez checkpoint, men who had been working in Israel were hurrying back home. Some were bent over, carrying bundles on their shoulders, walking with heads lowered along the dusty corridor fenced off with barbed wire and topped by a roof of asbestos slabs. This corridor is the thread tying Gaza to Israel: at one end is the checkpoint, where the Israeli border patrol is stationed; at the other is the Palestinian guard. Only a day or two earlier, the Strip having been sealed hermetically the previous ten days, the men had gone back to work, happy to be passing through this corridor again. Now they were returning to the Strip as quickly as possible after another terror attack and before the new closure that was sure to follow. My friends from Jabalia and Shabura wore their fatigue and disappointment on their faces: this month, too, there would be no wages. I could see that they were baffled by the forces playing with their lives, by the militants who blew up buses, and by Israel, which closed the borders whether there were attacks or not. "We all know that not a single worker is involved," the men said repeatedly. "Why should we all be punished?" "Look at us," one friend said to me. "We're walking as if we're going to our own funeral."

Arafat promised Rabin vigorous efforts to combat terror, and the very next day the newly formed Palestinian State Security Court held its first session. The court became synonymous with speedy secret trials held at night before military judges with little or no legal training. Lawyers for the defendents had no advance knowledge of their clients' cases and no time to prepare their defense. The families of the defendents, meanwhile, were not kept informed of proceedings, and the accused themselves never knew where they were being taken when they were hustled out of their homes without warning in the dead of night. A friend of mine, a Fatah member, told me, "My friends from security were there at the trials. They said they'd never seen anything so horrible in their whole lives."

A psychological schism—almost a desperate schizophrenia— seemed to mark the comments of Fatah leaders as they vehemently defended the State Security Court in the same breath as they spoke bitterly of the unending hardship that Israel was imposing and the neg- ligible return of the Oslo agreements. "Forty-seven years of all kinds of struggle have made our nation a fact of life," Minister of Planning Nabil Shaath said, "but with the old methods, we haven't managed to liberate a smidgin of our land or bring back even one refugee. We're still subject to military, political, and economic occupation. We've been battling for months over safe-passage routes, a seaport, an air- field, transporting our goods. We're facing an adversary that's very hesi- tant about carrying out its own agreements. . . . Let's put Israel's sincerity to the test; don't give it any excuse to delay implementing the agreements."

As chairman of the Gaza Bar Association, Freih Abu Medein had been an outspoken critic of Israel's human rights violations. As minis- ter of justice in the Palestinian Authority, he had the task of defending the State Security Court, which was "intended to prevent a dual government," he told the East Jerusalem newspaper *Al-Nahar*. "There is one Sulta, and we will not permit another to carry out attacks and harm the interests of the Palestinian people." In an interview with me, however, he spoke more frankly. "We haven't been able to offer anything to our people. Their standard of living has actually declined; in the past year the Strip was sealed off for 172 days. People are terribly frustrated and fundamentalists gain their strength from the social situation. Why is there no safe passage to the West Bank? Why won't they let us hold elections? . . . Some of the settlements here must be evacuated. They cost too much in blood. True, we agreed to leave them in place for the time being, but the Oslo Accords are not the Quran. You Israelis wring concessions out of us because of our weakness. We're forced into an intolerable situation and the price is loss of life."

The mass arrests and the insidious workings of the State Security Court engendered further fury in the Strip and many feared that yet another violent clash was inevitable. To avert a crisis, various leaders from Fatah, Hamas, the leftist Fronts, and the Communists, along with the indefatigable Hayder abd al-Shafi, convened an emergency meeting on April 13, which lasted all night. The statement issued the following morning noted that "the ongoing Israeli occupation, the closures, and the poverty they cause are responsible for the tensions." Any efforts to calm the situation would prove worthless, the statement went on, if the forces of occupation remained in place. The statement also called on the Authority to release the detainees and on the opposition to rein in its people.

Arafat, however, was outraged by the statement and rejected any steps that seemed to him to contradict his obligations to Israel. "The PLO signed a peace agreement and is committed to it," he said. "The PLO is the sole legitimate representative of the Palestinian people, and every faction must honor its agreements." He was especially angry at Fatah, his own movement. For the first time, Arafat had openly placed the PLO returnees above the local, homegrown Palestinian leadership and especially above Fatah in the occupied territories. Exposed here was not only the growing rift between the public and the administration, but also between the "new immigrants," as Gazans called those who had returned from exile, and the locals, who knew the occupation and its ways well.

During the spring and summer of 1995, Gaza saw a continuous

stream of arrests and releases and secret summary trials. The Islamic opposition newspapers (the only ones to report on the oppressive manner of these arrests) were closed down, but then often granted permits to reopen. Someone from the Authority, meanwhile, leaked word that negotiations with the Islamic opposition on suspending attacks against Israeli targets were moving forward; all this time, Arafat was demonstrating his virtuosity in governing by exploiting disagreements and personal rivalries so as to foster divisions within the opposition.

The mass arrests conveyed a confusing message. They did not seem to have been thought out in any clear-cut way, and by all accounts they did not touch the hard-core military cells. Gazans concluded that the Authority was avoiding direct confrontation with the military activists, many of whom were free to move about almost in the open, while hundreds of Islamic rank and file party members were arrested, probably to "soften up" Hamas politically and ideologically while the regime tried to convince its members—in the interrogation rooms, if need be—to accept the Authority as the legitimate government.

Ripples of fear spread throughout the Strip, and a sense of political isolation crept into the prison cells. In all likelihood the Authority hoped those feelings would extend to the men in charge and those with their hands on the detonators. Israel had demanded that Arafat crack down on terror, but the night courts threw a much wider net, with the aim of teaching Arafat's opponents and their sympathizers who was in charge. In Hamas and Jihad circles, but not only there, it was ultimately concluded that the mass arrests of the summer of 1995 had probably facilitated the negotiations with Israel, which became convinced of the Authority's commitment and of the sincerity of Arafat's oft-repeated words, "I understand Israel's security needs."

By July it seemed that the impasse in negotiations over the second stage of the interim agreement (detailing Israeli redeployment in the West Bank) was finally beginning to ease. Arafat and Shimon Peres set a target date of July 25 for the conclusion of negotiations. In the end, the agreement was not finalized until late September. The West Bank was divided into three categories: Area A comprised the cities (with the exception of Hebron), where the Palestinians would control security and administrative matters; in Area B, Palestinians would be responsible for administration and policing, while Israel would retain control over security; and in Area C—the largest region, 70 percent of the

West Bank, containing Jewish settlements and army bases—Israel would retain full control. The boundaries between A, B, and C were temporary; land would shift from Israeli to Palestinian control in a series of three staged withdrawals to take place within eighteen months after the Legislative Council's inauguration. The exact dimensions of each deployment were left for future negotiations. (The negotiations eventually broke down precisely over this point—how much land Israel was willing to move from one category into another and when.)

Despite the frenzied news coverage, a member of the negotiating team confided to me that "in Gaza no one takes any interest in the negotiations." He was admitting the existence of yet another rift in Gazan society, between the Sulta's agenda and the people's concerns. "I know they're all just asking when the borders will be opened," he said, "whether more workers will be allowed to leave the Strip, whether there'll be wages next month. People aren't asking when there'll be redeployment in Jenin."

Overall, the Authority's efforts at intimidation seemed to achieve their end, not only through the arrests but through taking ever more brazen action against the Islamic opposition. On two occassions when the police set out to capture Hamas and Jihad activists, they made no attempt to hide the fact that they were responding to instructions from Israel. Early in 1996, the police killed two Islamic Jihad members suspected by Israel of involvement in the Beit Lid bombing and in attacks on Jewish settlements. During a six-month period, though, from September 1995 until February 1996, neither Hamas nor any of its wings carried out a single terrorist act. However, the Jihad did attempt two suicide bombings as revenge for the murder of its leader, Fathi Shiqaqi, who was killed in Malta. The reprisal miscarried and was quickly forgotten in the shock over Yitzhak Rabin's assassination on November 4, 1995, by the same Yigal Amir who had so loved to tear down the clotheslines in the alleyways of Jabalia.

Elections to the Palestinian Legislative Council were coming up, and the Authority and Hamas made vigorous efforts to keep the peace and mend the rift between them. As a goodwill gesture, the Authority released several senior Hamas leaders from prison. Then there was talk of secret meetings, although these became less and less secret, and of delegations that met with Hamas leaders abroad. No written agreement existed, but a verbal understanding was reached. Hamas pledged to refrain from acts that would embarrass the Authority—meaning attacks—and not to call for voters to boycott the elections. Hamas did not agree, however, to reverse its position on the Oslo Accords by running a slate of candidates.

And then, all of a sudden, without any consideration for internal Palestinian developments, Yihye Ayash was killed in the Gaza Strip in January 1996. Ayash, or "the Engineer," as he was known, was widely believed to be the architect of the horrific bus attacks in Israel. Israeli sources had long maintained that he was hiding in the Strip although he was a West Bank resident. At his death, official Israel said nothing; unofficially, Israel celebrated the Shabak's resourcefulness.

Once again, a cry of rage resounded through the Strip. Ayash's funeral was attended by Palestinians of all political stripes and in unprecedented numbers—some said a hundred thousand, some a quarter of a million (a wild exaggeration). Health Minister Riyad Zaanun, a moderate, came to the funeral, saying quietly, "I came to register my protest and anger at Israel's step. Ayash's way was not ours. But his killing is an alarming act of terror that came precisely when we'd reached an agreement with Hamas. It's as if this act was deliberately intended to bring the breakdown of the agreements, and it shows a lack of respect for the Palestinian Authority."

Sami Abu Samhadana, the commander of one of the Authority's many security branches and a well-known *intifada* activist, had played a role in the efforts to convince Iz al-Din al-Qassam to hold its fire during that period. He sounded incensed and utterly despondent. "If that's the way the Shabak is going to handle attacks, okay. Then I'm taking myself out of the picture. The peace and quiet we've achieved over the past five months hasn't made any impression on them. We've tried to safeguard Israeli security by persuading Hamas to become a political movement and reach an agreement with us. Shabak doesn't accept our way of doing things. But then the Israelis shouldn't be surprised when there are more attacks. Because one thing is for sure—they'll take their revenge."

The four suicide bombings in response to Ayash's death killed fifty-seven people in Israel in a space of two weeks, in February and March, 1996. (The first bombing was on February 25, the second anniversary of the Ibrahimi mosque massacre.) Whoever planned them probably drew encouragement from Arafat's condolence visits to the homes of Hamas supporters, from the salvos fired by the Palestinian police in

Ayash's honor, from the huge number of people who accompanied his body to the cemetery. But they obviously had not seen fit to go and speak with the fortunate men who, on the day of the first attack, had risen before dawn and gone to work in Israel after a chain of closures during the previous months had completely ruined the Id al-Fitr holiday.

My friend Muhammad, a subcontractor from Rafah, called me by cellular phone from a building site in Tel Aviv as soon as he heard the news. His two brothers had been killed in the *intifada* and he had never been a booster of the Oslo Accords. "But that doesn't make these attacks okay," he said. "All forty of us working on this site are stuck. I feel like crying. I feel like screaming. I talked to guys from Hamas. I told them, okay, so don't agree that this is peace. Let's just say it's a cease-fire. Give people a chance to live for two or three years in peace and quiet. The police came at ten in the morning and told us to stop working and get out, but where are we going to get a bus? The workers are afraid of being lynched by furious Israelis, so they went and hid in the cellar while I called for a bus. You hear these guys behind me? They're cursing Hamas and the Jihad. Why did Hamas have to wait until we went back to work? Such big heroes, they couldn't have done it during the closure? I've always been against these things. Who rides the bus in the morning? Women, children, old people. You hear? Now they're saying good-bye to us, our employers, like they don't know when they'll see us again. The day after tomorrow they've got thirty workers from Romania coming to replace us."

The rift in Gaza now split wide open with a fresh wave of arrests. Hundreds, if not thousands, of families of Islamic sympathizers began living in constant fear—of being followed, of informers reporting on their conversations in the mosques and in private, of detention. A whole layer of Gazan society—people who had no connection to the terrorist attacks—worried that their houses might be broken into and a brother, or even a wife or sister, arrested if the wanted person was not at home; they knew of the brutal, humiliating interrogations.

People were held for two, three, four months or more, without seeing a lawyer, without being tried, without charges being brought against them, without being told their offense, without seeing members of their families. No one believed that these hundreds of people were involved in terrorism. I heard of beatings, of prisoners being burned with plastic pipes, being forced to stand for hours in painful contorted positions, having their heads covered with filthy sacks for days at a time.

Unlike in the West Bank, where students and prisoners' families held massive demonstrations protesting the detentions in areas recently transferred to the Palestinian Authority, in Gaza there were almost no attempts to protest the arbitrary arrests. It soon became clear that the tens of thousands who had turned out for Ayash's funeral had been transformed from a threatening multitude to intimidated and isolated individuals. The strength that Hamas had demonstrated at the funeral quickly dissipated; from the very beginning it might have been only an illusion, deluding all sides.

From time to time, political representatives of the Palestinian factions tried to warn Arafat that the mass arrests would backfire on the government. Members of the newly elected Legislative Council spent evenings trying to track down various prisoners: their constituents had appealed to them in desperation, hoping to find out where their sons, husbands, or fathers were being held. Families used all the *wasta* they had ever accumulated to locate and make contact with their loved ones. In Council sessions and committee meetings, the legislators tried to bring up the fate of the prisoners but four who dared to hold a press conference in response to reports of torture were nearly stripped of their parliamentary immunity. The Council ordered that students being held without evidence be released so they could take their exams, but the order was ignored.

It was not the carnage of the suicide bombings that moved the Hamas leadership to try to stem the tide of attacks. It was the wave of arrests, the dread of closures, and the public's consequent dismay. Senior Hamas political figures issued pleas to the movement's military wing to halt its actions; in the process, they revealed their loss of control over the situation and the nameless men offering themselves up for sacrifice: a few days later there was another suicide attack.

Hani Aabed, Kamal Kheil, Yihye Ayash—in Gaza, as in Israel, no one doubted Shabak's hand in these killings. The assassinations exploited internal divisions and conflicts in Palestinian society, even brought it to the brink of civil war, yet they failed to prevent further acts of terror. From Israel's point of view, the interim agreement put the Palestinians on probation, asking as it did that they prove they could stop violence and terror. The assassinations took place because Israel concluded that the Palestinians as a whole—the Authority, Hamas, the Islamic Jihad, the people—had not passed muster. But for the Palestinians, Israel had also been on trial: the Jewish state was expected to abandon its long-standing roles of master and spy, to grasp that violence and terror are not self-generating but nourished by enmity, and finally to stop its reflexive tendency to impose collective punishment on all Palestinians. Israel also failed the test, and throughout that period—from the IDF redeployment in May 1994 until the Palestinian elections in January 1996—the Authority and Fatah's hopes of convincing their people that the Oslo Accords were worthwhile were repeatedly dashed. The Authority was unable to point to any tangible improvement in employment conditions or in the general economy as an encouraging sign of things to come. Thus the Authority lost its principal weapon against the Islamic factions obsessed with terror and turned instead, with growing fervor, to repression and intimidation.

The second anniversary of Palestinian self-rule, May 17, 1996, came and went without anyone paying much attention. Divided Gaza was united by its shared worries: how to put food on the table, how many exit permits would be allowed that week, how much longer Israel would keep the Strip closed.

Chapter 5

As It Is Written in the Quran

The first time anyone suggested I become a Muslim was two years after I had moved to Gaza. The idea came from the mother of a friend, who made her proposal with warmth and affection and out of genuine concern for my well-being. This was a refugee family, veteran Fatah supporters long familiar with prisons and curfews and beatings and now supportive of reconciliation with Israel. "The Quran is the final and definitive book of revelation," the mother pleaded with me, "the one true book that overrides the Torah and the New Testament. But of course," she went on, "we do recognize the Prophet Musa—Moses—and the Prophet Isa—Jesus—peace and blessings be upon them."

We were all sitting on mattresses on the floor, my friends and their children, along with an acquaintance from Nablus, a teacher visiting from Saudi Arabia, and one son serving with the Palestinian police in the West Bank who had come home for a quick visit and was now stuck in the Strip, blocked by Israel from returning to his unit. At some point we were joined by a sister and her husband, or maybe it was a brother and his wife. The talk was relaxed and noisy, and moved effortlessly from old prison stories to jokes to the problem of an uncle having trouble with his eyes who couldn't get an exit permit to visit the opthalmic hospital in East Jerusalem.

I don't remember how we arrived at the subject of faith and apostasy, but suddenly the mother launched into a spirited retelling of the exodus from Egypt and the miracles witnessed by the children of Israel as they wandered in the desert—as they had come to her by way of the Quran. She described the parting of the Red Sea with drama and feeling, as if she had been there herself. At the climactic moment when the pharaoh's army drowned, she squeezed my hand. In a voice filled with indignation and sorrow, she related all the troubles that Musa, "peace and blessings be upon him," had had with the children of Israel. She sighed with relief, as if from a terrible thirst, when she described how Musa struck the rock and released a stream of water.

At the end of her story, she shifted to the inevitable fate of infidels and her desire to spare me, her hope that along with all believing Muslims, I too would reach paradise. After a short theological debate among the family, one daughter explained that the Quran explicitly states (in the *surah*, or chapter, of the Cow, as I learned later) that "infidels are destined to receive humiliating punishment because when they are told to 'believe in what Allah has revealed,' they respond, 'We believe in what was revealed to *us*.'" They "deny what has since been revealed," the passage continues, "although it is the truth, corroborating their own scripture" (2:91).[1] The daughter's tone, while not aggressive, lacked her mother's care and concern; the word "infidels" dropped from her lips laced with distaste, the displeasure of a woman who believes in the literal truth of the holy word.

The holy word is ubiquitous in Gaza, but it is not, as some pious Muslims and Israeli observers would claim, monolithic, inflexible, pointing inevitably to a single—murderous—meaning. Quranic parables and allusions and Islamic historical allegories are as much part of the Strip as the fine grains of sand hanging in the air and just as profuse, but they are pliable, too, changing shape and meaning from speaker to speaker, often in line with his or her political affiliation.

My friend Abu Basel, for example, is a devoted advocate of Palestinian workers' rights and tends to cite passages that both reflect his left-wing outlook and speak to the pain and despair of living in the Gaza of the present. On a gray fall day in October 1995, following the assassination of Islamic Jihad leader Fathi Shiqaqi, Abu Basel and I were walking in Rafah, close to the mourning tent set up by the dead man's brother. By now, I was sick of the mourning tents and the loudspeakers calling the faithful to battle while people's eyes and bearing showed nothing but the exhaustion in their hearts. The sun was hiding behind heavy, grimy clouds and the air was taut with the anticipation of retaliatory attacks on Israel and the rigid closure that would surely follow. Abu Basel abruptly broke the silence. "The Quran says that the Jews love life, but I think that's wrong. When I look at us, I see that we love life more than you."

His reference, also from the *surah* of the Cow, was by now familiar to me: "Indeed, you will find they love this life more than other men: more than the pagans do. Each one of them would love to live a thousand years. But even if their lives were indeed prolonged, that will surely not save them from Our scourge. Allah is watching all their actions" (2:96–97).[2] I'd first seen the passage in a less forgiving context, in a leaflet circulated by Hamas's military wing, the Iz al-Din al-Qassam, which promised further attacks on Israel. The author claimed that the Jews love life too much and are prepared to sacrifice much of their self-respect and human dignity to keep on living. "You are afraid to die," the author wrote, "and so our threats of suicide attacks and other actions achieve their purpose."

A straight line leading from the Quran to suicide bombings is, in the Israeli imagination, the epitome of Muslim devotion and Gazan religiosity in particular. But here was gentle Abu Basel, himself not a believer, drawing on the same source to express not power but impotence, not certitude but despair; in his sad comment, he took issue with the Quran, too, questioning its words and meaning. The specific and concrete circumstances of Abu Basel's life, unique to him, had shaped his Muslim awareness. And there are, of course, as many shades of Muslim awareness, understanding, and practice as there are strands of Gazan life—sometimes contradictory and unclear but always nuanced and varied, and only fathomable from within the reality of the Strip.

On the same walk, Abu Basel began to talk about Muhammad's successor, the second caliph, Omar ibn al-Khattab. As if to prove the suppleness of religious allusion and the importance of context, ibn al-Khattab was then mentioned to me no less than three times in the same week, to vastly different purposes. Ibn al-Khattab, a frequent hero of the sermons in the mosques, ruled between 634–44 A.D. In his conquests, he laid the foundations for the Muslim empire and even captured Jerusalem. He instituted a hierarchical system of pensions for his occupation army, but non-Arab Muslim soldiers were excluded from the plan. Despite this inequality, Abu Basel chose to remember an act of compassion. "He never punished people who stole during a drought," he said, telling us more about Abu Basel than about the caliph himself.

In a typically Gazan coincidence, I heard about ibn al-Khattab again only hours after leaving Abu Basel, this time in the home of

Ismail Faqawi, a secular teacher from Khan Yunis camp. During the *intifada*, Faqawi had been arrested at home, at 3:00 in the morning, blindfolded, handcuffed, and then taken to Ansar II, a large prison camp in Gaza City; on the way, he had been beaten on his knees and shoulders with nightsticks. Once he reached the camp, Faqawi was forced to kneel in a large outdoor plaza as he waited his turn in the interrogation room. Questioning began many hours later, and when Faqawi refused to confess to false charges of organizing demonstrations he was sent back outside, handcuffed and blindfolded, to kneel throughout the night.

In the isolation and the cold, he suddenly heard a friendly voice. The guard watching him had noticed that Faqawi had not once asked to drink some water or visit the bathroom. In caring, compassionate tones, he invited Faqawi into his tent, where he removed the handcuffs and blindfold and handed him cigarettes. The guard, it turned out, was a Druze, a member of a religion that had broken away from Islam in the eleventh century. (The Druze of Israel, unlike other Arab Israeli citizens, are conscripted to serve in the IDF.) "Aren't you afraid of being punished?" Faqawi asked him. "We have a system," the guard said. "If we hear a Jew approaching," referring to his fellow soldiers, "one of us calls out, 'Who wants to smoke?' as a warning."

The act of kindness inspired Faqawi to talk about the history he shared with the Druze guard. "Omar ibn al-Khattab brought your ancestors, the most courageous of warriors, from the Arabian peninsula to Syria and Lebanon to fight against Byzantium and secure the northern borders." In that moment, ibn al-Khattab, prince of the Muslim believers, represented the shared fate and origins of prisoner and jailer. To Faqawi, this remote history explained why the guard had dared to defy orders and offer not only the comfort of a cigarette but the warmth of solidarity.

Despite his historical allusion, though, Faqawi is not generally known for religious sympathies. For one thing, he uses Marxist theories to explain the spread of Islam in his society; for another, he's had his own clash with vigilant Muslims for refusing to remove secular books from the library he ran, an act for which he was labeled an "enemy of the people." Faqawi joined other "infidels" on a list published by the Muslim Brotherhood in the early 1980s and became a target for threats and harassment, which culminated in two thugs throwing acid in his face. After the acid attack, Faqawi agreed to make a token visit to the mosque, which helped calm the strife.

Omar ibn al-Khattab turned up for a third time that week—in a sermon given by Hamas leader Sheikh Ahmad Bahar at the Falastin mosque. The sermon came soon after Bahar was released from a three-month period of detention in a Palestinian prison. The suspicions against him were vague, but he was a key figure in the Islamic movement and his arrest had been noted by Israel as step in the Palestinian Authority's "struggle against terror." And when high-ranking members of the Islamic opposition are released from detention, their public statements are always scrutinized with special attention by all sides. Have they been softened or broken? Would they now tone down their criticism of the Authority? Indeed, after the multiple arrests and extended detentions of many Hamas activists, their sermons did in fact become more coded and less explicitly pertinent to current events.

But to believers the Quran is eternal, and any mention of the caliphs—immortal and metahistorical as they are—is always pertinent and direct. At the time of Bahar's sermon, in the fall of 1995, Hamas and the Authority were making efforts to renew their dialogue, and the sheikh's words gave his attentive listeners Islamic reinforcement for Hamas's positions. The second caliph, the sheikh explained, had wanted to set the bride price a man was required to pay the family of his betrothed. As he proclaimed his intention, a woman in the crowd stood up. "You want to fix what even Allah has not determined," she called out. The caliph heard her words and acknowledged his error in front of the entire congregation, withdrawing the proposal. Islam, Sheikh Bahar seemed to be saying, applauds and encourages free expression, even the right to criticize a ruler's position. He inferred that true dialogue could only take place and mistakes be prevented when people are able to speak freely, when their wisdom is heard. The reference to the Authority was clear. (Bahar and others are quick to defend their faith against the demands of democracy and feminism. The sheikh also seemed to be implying that Islam makes room for a woman's opinions. People hastened to tell me that in the days of the Prophet Muhammad, peace and blessings be upon him, women sat behind the men during prayers; only later were partitions and then a separate women's section introduced. But the women were always listened to, I was told. They even fought in wars and took equal part in making decisions.)

In the same sermon, Bahar went on to speak about Abu Sufyan, whose son governed Syria during the second caliph's reign. One day ibn al-Khattab encountered Abu Sufyan returning from a visit to his son and the man's caravan was laden with goods. "Where did all this come from?" the caliph asked. "I am a merchant," said Abu Sufyan, "and my son has been helping me." Ibn al-Khattab was furious. "I sent your son to be a governor, not a merchant," he said, and confiscated the goods, transferring them to the state treasury.

No one in the Falastin mosque needed an explanation. Woe unto those in the ruling class who exploit their positions to line their own pockets—and all the worshipers knew exactly who they were, the people in the ruling class. No secret is ever safe in Gaza. If someone snores in Saja'ya, according to the local joke, everyone in Palestine wakes up. The police officer who just bought a luxury apartment far beyond the reach of his salary, the minister doing a little business on the side—the Palestinian press might not cover such details but they are common knowledge in the Strip. The unspoken text of Sheikh Bahar's sermon was that a strong leader would put a stop to his officials' corruption. Judging by the number of Islamic preachers arrested by the Authority's police, those same officials seemed to feel at least as threatened by the preachers' social and political censure as by the Islamic movement's potential to carry out armed attacks.

The various PLO factions (Fatah, the PFLP, the DFLP—usually referred to as the "nationalists"), which compete with the Islamic movement for followers, complain that the ostentatious piety of Hamas preachers is a tool to help the party gain power and control over Palestinian society in general and government institutions in particular. In truth, Hamas supporters make no secret of their hope and belief that a Palestinian state will one day be ruled by Islamic law, but insist this can only come about through people's will and conviction, not through coercion. (The same supporters prefer to forget the campaigns of intimidation waged against leftists in Gaza, especially in the early 1980s. The violence began in 1980 with attacks on Hayder abd al-Shafi and the Gaza branch of the Red Crescent that he headed.) In their view, religion and state are inseparable; Islam is a way of life that does not make distinctions between the private and the public spheres.

Whatever the motives of the Islamic organizations, the vast crowds of men that flock to Friday midday prayers, especially to the mosques where the preachers are renowned for their oratory, attest to the powerful draw of prayer and the accompanying sermons. And the more a sermon speaks directly to the worshipers' lives and experience, the more it provokes them to engage in all kinds of discussions—religious, ideological, political, and social. The boundaries are fluid.

One result of the mosques' popularity is that Authority leaders feel compelled to take part in the worship as well. Ever since Yassir Arafat set up his office in Gaza in July 1994, he has made a point of praying at a different mosque every Friday, always flanked by an entourage of police officers and senior aides. Palestinian television comes as well, to immortalize Arafat's participation in the prayer service and his attention to the sermon, "like any ordinary person." On the third Friday after his arrival, Arafat prayed at the oldest mosque in Gaza City, the large al-Omari mosque. That day, the imam, Yassin Jamusi, who is politically nonaffiliated, gave an outstanding demonstration of a sermon's power to erase the boundaries of time and create a connection between the most current events and the distant roots of Islam.

The imam began, his voice resonating through the loudspeakers past the congregation and out into the city beyond. "The Prophet Muhammad, peace and blessings be upon him, succeeded in establishing a state on a plot of land smaller than the Gaza Strip and Jericho," Jamusi said, referring to the limits of the self-rule area first governed by Arafat. "His successors extended the territory's borders and founded a magnificent civilization, stretching far out to the east and the west," the imam went on. "We are inspired with hope," he proclaimed, "that our state will also expand until we have restored to ourselves all of our land and all of our rights." Unequivocally, the imam was stating his support for the most important congregant present and for the "Gaza and Jericho First" agreement he had signed; Jamusi was countering the voices of opposition that claimed the Oslo deal was headed inevitably toward an impasse. "The most important thing," he concluded, dispelling any last doubts as to where he stood, "is that we preserve the unity of the people and act together with the authorities for the sake of our common goal."

Arafat's arrival prompted imams in mosques all over Gaza to

place special emphasis on the quality of Muhammad's relationship with his followers in their highly contemporary sermons. Nadir al-Luqa, the most popular imam in Rafah refugee camp—also politically nonaffiliated—devoted much of his sermon in the Bilal mosque to the prophet's flight, his *hijra*, from Mecca and his eventual return to that city. Luqa was less concerned with Muhammad's territorial conquests than with his spirit. The prophet had fled, he said, to protect his principles. Only when he had managed to raise a strong army did he return as a victor, proudly, without a trace of humiliation. Whether Luqa meant to imply a similarity between Arafat's and Muhammad's returns or the vast difference between the two was left to his listeners to decide. However, he did point out, either as advice or a plea, that Muhammad had behaved graciously toward his people in Mecca. "Rejoice in the return of your brother," the imam said, "but do not offend our morals," he added, as if addressing the many diaspora Palestinians returning with Arafat. On a final note, Luqa threw in word of reproach for local municipal bigwigs: "I'd hoped Arafat would come sooner," he said, "so the city would have cleaned up our streets a little quicker."

From national pride and humiliation to garbage disposal, the imam knew what bothered his people and showed that their grievances were his grievances too. Nestled among the sand dunes in the bright noonday sun, the Bilal mosque, built shekel by shekel with the meager savings of refugees, echoed with the harmony of ancient prayers, stories of the prophet, and subtle censure of the leaders of the day. To the congregation, refugees and the sons of refugees, the imam's blend of words, his mix of all these elements, was taken for granted, wholly natural, part and parcel of all their aspirations, national and spiritual.

Of course, Yassir Arafat also understands the power of sprinkling his messages and patriotic speeches with familiar Islamic references. On the day after his arrival in Gaza, Arafat addressed a rally in Jabalia camp. The event was held in the Faluja schoolyard (where the *intifada* began), which was jammed with a massive crowd. "Whoever fights for the homeland is fighting for Allah!" Arafat began, and the words could just as easily have been spoken by an Islamic Jihad leader. Squeezed together in the Faluja schoolyard, hanging from balconies and rooftops, the people responded in one voice, "*Allahu akbar*, Allah is great!" Bodies pressed against bodies, the crowd surged forward, and a few Fatah men joined hands to create a protective circle around me and another woman journalist to stop any men from accidentally brushing up against us.

"I am not the only one who says that our people are strong, a people of Jabarin," he continued. "The Quran says so, too." The Jabarin, I was told, lived in Canaan before the Children of Israel conquered it; they were a godless people, idol worshipers, and also remarkably strong. Usually, devout Muslims do not appreciate being compared to Jabarin, but the context of Arafat's speech gave his words an ironic twist. "Oh Moses!" begins the relevant passage in the Quran, in the *surah* of the Table, "a race of giants dwells in this land. We will not set foot in it till they are gone. As soon as they are gone we will enter" (5:22).[3] The speakers in the passage are the Children of Israel; the people of whom they speak are the Jabarin, that is, the indigenous inhabitants of the land. Thus Arafat had managed to make the point that the Palestinians are the true inhabitants of Palestine. Through his poetic play on words, Arafat sought to establish that the Quran is not the exclusive property of the Islamic opposition, and he was rewarded by the audience's knowing smiles.

(Poetic license can easily twist a negative Islamic reference into a positive one, or even make it funny. Abu Ali Shahin, a veteran Fatah hero, once got into an elevator with me and a friend of his. "I am Satan," he declared as the doors closed. I could tell he was fooling around but I still didn't get the joke. Seeing my puzzled face, he attempted an explanation. "You're a woman and he's a man," Shahin said, pointing to his friend. "The Quran tells us that when a man and a woman are left alone Satan comes between them. So," he concluded with a flourish, "I am Satan!")

The Authority's efforts to curry favor with its devout constituents also leads to importing Islamic language into the political realm. Behind the speaker's podium in the Palestinian Legislative Council hangs a large banner bearing the words, "Let there be *shura*," a term from the Quran meaning "consultation." (One PLO official who had returned from Tunis was having trouble adjusting to the religious etiquette newly adopted by the Authority. "If we're supposed to pray five times a day, then we do it six times," he joked.) For pious Muslims, though, the sign only reinforces their argument that the Quran contains built-in democratic principles.

Borrowing language is a two-way activity, however, and believing

Muslims sometimes need to adopt terms from outside their tradition. For years, I was told, the Islamic bloc objected to the term *democracy* as a Western concept, claiming that Islam contains its own version of the idea—*shura*. But the Quran does not explain how this consultation should be applied to decision making, and the concept of *shura* lacks both the dimension of sovereignty deriving from the will of the people and the idea of representation. Without language to describe these principles, Islamic resistance to using "democracy" has eroded over time, and the devout will now sprinkle their conversation with the word, even citing it as a more desirable system than that practiced by many Arab regimes.

At the time of Arafat's return optimism was in the air, and as a result, outward demonstrations of piety seemed to be on the wane. I had seen this dynamic at work before, in 1991, during the multilateral Madrid negotiations. As everyone's hopes were running high, the self-imposed prohibitions from the *intifada* slackened and the soldiers were behaving less aggressively. One indication of the mood, a friend told me excitedly, was that people had started playing soccer again; the men were leaving the mosques to cheer at the soccer field. During the uprising, mosques were the only safe places for meetings and discussions; public events were banned and youth and sports clubs were closed, hence the popularity of religious services.

Three years later, in 1994, the same dynamic was in evidence: for the first time in years, more worshipers were attending the Fatah-affiliated mosques in Rafah than the mosque identified with Hamas. The implication was that even those who were unwilling to relax their religious practices were choosing to associate with the movement that offered more worldly, immediate promise. In another turn of events, the sale of hair-care products suddenly went up. Everyone in Gaza knew how to read the phenomenon: women were planning to dispense with the religious edict to cover their heads, enforced successfully during the *intifada*, and expose their hair. The expectation of change had had the immediate result of undermining the coercive power of Islamic stalwarts, and women simply felt freer to make their own decisions about their appearance. Today, though, most women in Gaza, especially in the camps and poorer neighborhoods, continue to cover their hair, either because their hopes dwindled as the days of closure piled up and husbands stayed at home, idle, or because of the deep-rooted power of tradition.

Hamas supporters are not unaware of the symbiotic relationship between hope and religious observance. Several months after Arafat's return I went with a Hamas friend to watch a Fatah rally celebrating the movement's founding. Thousands crowded into the Yarmuk Stadium in Gaza City waiting for Arafat's appearance and speech. There weren't enough seats to go around and people stood on tiptoe to catch a glimpse of the stage. As we looked around, my friend and I suddenly registered a shocking fact: men and women were sitting together. Whoever had organized the rally hadn't arranged separate seating for the women, the usual arrangement at public meetings, and everyone was mingling quite happily. "Will Hamas try to stop this from happening again?" I asked, trying not to sound too pleased. "We don't want to impose our will when we clearly can't succeed," my friend answered. "People are thinking in a very different direction at the moment."

Nowhere was this clearer than at the beach, which in those early days quickly became the most reliable indicator of Hamas's power—or lack of it—to control Gaza's behavior. Once the IDF withdrew, night curfews became a thing of the past. Right away, thousands of Gazans began to converge on the beach every evening after work, delighting in the sea, a novel source of pleasure and relaxation. As if by magic, small huts sprung up for use as changing rooms, and stalls selling falafel and corn-on-the-cob appeared along the shorefront. Fast-moving entrepreneurs set out chairs for a fee and parents sat and watched the evening tide, keeping an eye on their children collecting shells and jumping the waves. On Fridays, the regular day off, people started taking dips in the morning—young men and children, of course, but women too, who waded into the sea with their skirts billowing above the water's surface like giant mushrooms. And at sunset, dating couples were spotted strolling along the shore—a really revolutionary sight.

At first, Hamas tried to put a stop to the nightly beach carnival. Leaflets were passed around that contained lurid descriptions of sordid activities: men and women together, alcohol, all kinds of licentiousness. But the leaflets were ignored and Gazans laughed. "As if we need an occupation to keep us moral," they said. "Where else are we supposed to take a break, have some fun, breathe fresh air, if we can't do it at the beach?" Faiz from al-Boureij put an end to the discussion. "Hamas people come here too," he said, and the frivolity by the sea went on. The shorefront was eventually taken over by a string of expensive (but mediocre) restaurants that cater to Authority types and foreign visitors—too costly for my friends, most of them refugees.

To a devout Muslim like Kh., the beauty of the sea invokes nothing so much as the immanence of God. "The world was not created by accident," he said, explaining his faith. "Man's achievements lie only in uncovering the laws that Allah created. Airplanes, agriculture, buildings—they are all based on divine laws. We are free to organize the practical aspects of our lives however we like, but we must cleave to the principles of faith." Kh. does not remember how long he has known that there is a God. "From the youngest age we tell our children about Allah, and about hell and paradise. This is a natural part of our society."

Natural. How could Islam not seem natural when the call of the muezzin five times a day rations out portions of the day and night, as punctual and powerful as the sun and the moon? Five times a day he summons the faithful to prayer, interrupting their sleep, their work, their play. Prayer is forbidden at sunrise or sunset, so as not to be interpreted as sun worship. Thus an hour and a half before the first hint of daylight, the darkness is broken by the muezzin's amplified cry. The stillness of the night carries the call wafting from several mosques at once, the one next door and the one in the next neighborhood, and the deep, warm chant of verses from the Quran floats over the silent air, stealing into homes and dreams.

Five times a day even nonbelievers are tempted to take pause as the muezzin defines time much as the leaves on the trees define the seasons. The cyclical call of the muezzin stops time too, its dependable continuity merging the past with the present. In Gaza, even an atheist like myself can understand how secure this cycle feels—an anchor— to people who have lost their past and have so little control over their present. Indeed, one woman, W., told me that religion gives her back control and flexibility and choice, since each person can be devout in his own way. As an adolescent, W. was drawn to the Popular Front and its message of equality, although her father was religious. "But during the *intifada*," she said, "I began to believe in God. I started to talk to Him. And during the uprising, that made it easier for us to go out on the streets and face the soldiers, to see one of us get killed. We had faith that this was not death, that the dead were going to paradise."

Imad Akel, commander of Hamas's military wing, was known to have killed eleven IDF soldiers during the *intifada* and one Israeli civilian. In the uprising, eight people were killed in the Jabalia alleyway where his family lived. The children from his camp would throw stones at the soldiers and shout, "We are all Imad, we are all Imad!" When the army finally tracked Imad down, he died of multiple bullet wounds. "But they didn't hurt him at all," his brother Adel said. "Imad appeared in several people's dreams and told them he'd only felt nips. 'Where are you?' they asked him. 'Are you really in paradise with Muhammad? With Salah al-Din?' 'Yes,' he answered. 'It's true.' At the funeral, I just knew he was looking down at us and telling us not to cry. We know that he lives," Adel concluded. "It is written in the Quran."

Imad had been devout since the age of twelve or thirteen; Adel, however, belonged to Fatah and had spent several months in jail every year since 1982 for burning tires, flying the Palestinian flag, and writing slogans on walls. "Why are you praying and fasting and reading the Quran?" he asked Imad. "Why do you bother with all this nonsense?" In 1988, at the beginning of the uprising, both brothers were arrested and sent to the Ansar III detention camp for eighteen months. During that time, Adel began to change and went over to Hamas. "I began to see that we were fighting and dying in the *intifada*, but no one cared, no one helped. So I gave myself over to God—only God promises and delivers."

In hard times, Gazans put ever greater trust in God's deliverance. During the long, harsh closures, when Palestinians were cut off from doctors and hospitals in Israel, Islamic healers, who treat all kinds of disorders, began to flourish as never before. My initial encounter with Islamic or Quranic treatment was at a clinic run by Ziad al-Tatar in the poverty-stricken Saja'ya neighborhood. First he tries to establish whether the patient is suffering from a physiological affliction. If he concludes that the patient has been invaded by an evil spirit, a jinn, he calls on the power of Allah and he sets out to banish the demon. To diagnose the problem, al-Tatar asks his patients to stretch out on a low examining table. He sits at the head, places earphones on the patient, and plays taped verses from the Quran. If the pain remains in one spot on the patient's body, Tatar concludes that its source is physiological, in which case he recites holy passages over a container of olive oil and spreads the oil on the area that hurts. Reciting passages for twenty or thirty minutes repeatedly over a two-month period will often cure the pain, he explains, depending on the patient and the problem. "It is not the oil that heals," Tatar insists, "but Allah, and the application of the Quran is His ammunition."

If the patient has been invaded by a jinn, then the same taped verses played through the earphones will cause it to jump around in the patient's body and the pain will move accordingly. For believing Muslims, there are two worlds: one of human beings ("the children of Adam") and one of demons ("the children of Satan"). As Tatar explained it, God has barred the demons from entering a human, but sometimes they simply disobey his orders and do so anyway. Quranic verses confuse the jinn, which begins to jump around like a mouse trapped in a hole. The jinn scurries back and forth, looking for an escape; in turn, the pain hops about from one spot to another. First, it might lodge in the heel, for example, and then leap to the shoulder. The symptoms will vary according to the strength of the demon. In especially stubborn cases, Tatar might inject a patient with an infusion, having declaimed Quranic passages over the solution; the Quran enters the bloodstream with the infusion and so banishes the jinn that way. After the treatment, the patient often remembers nothing.

Sometimes a patient might begin to tremble and the demon may even start to speak. "Where are you from?" Tatar might ask, or "Why are you here?" The most common reasons are the evil eye and weak moments when the patient is afraid, angry, or has an uncontrollable impulse. A jinn could even invade a fetus in its mother's womb and lie dormant for many years. "According to the Prophet Muhammad, peace and blessings be upon him, the evil eye is an arrow in Satan's quiver," I was told. The jinn enters the body at the spot where the evil eye settles. Demons are also motivated by vengeance. Some Muslims believe that they live in the sewers and are accidentally killed when people use water. In such a case, a demon's son will seek revenge. Finally, the same jinn might well turn up in several different people.

Ziad al-Tatar's family has lived in Gaza for generations, descended, he claims, from the Tartars. He worked in Israel as an electrician until 1993, when he first watched a Quranic healing cure a friend's sister of various aches and pains. Impressed by the method, he then opened his own clinic. A healer needs a strong and fearless heart—any weakness could attract the jinn—and unshakable faith in God; the patient must simply be a believer, regardless of religion. Tatar is willing to treat Muslims, Christians, and Jews, and claims that he could heal by using the Torah as well—it's the faith that counts.

He sees some fifteen to twenty people daily and cures 60 percent of his cases. In various printed testimonials one man claims to have been cured of headaches after seven years of suffering, another was rid of his ulcer, someone else was finally free of epileptic seizures that began after a severe beating by soldiers.

On the day of my visit to the clinic, a short, skinny woman came in, smiling cheerfully. She had come alone, and Tatar would have turned her away had I not been there, forbidden as men are from being alone with a woman. She had already received four months of treatment after conventional medicine had failed to rid her of a tenacious urinary tract infection and stabilize her diabetes. Tatar was convinced a jinn had taken up residence, although it had not yet spoken. Before starting the tape recorder, he placed his hand on the woman's forehead. "With God's help, get out, you spirit, get out," he intoned. When the woman heard the first Quranic verses, she felt prickles and heat in her feet and the palms of her hands—a sure sign the demon was trying to run from the holy words. Yet again, though, it failed to speak, and the treatments would have to continue.

During the *intifada*, the UNL called a halt to the fairly widespread use of healers and exorcists, especially those who charged for their services. The UNL was convinced that the pains treated by such healers were primarily psychosomatic, the result of the occupation and its many frustrations. Quranic healing only diverted attention from the real problem and the real solution: fighting the soldiers, shaking off passivity and fruitless messianic faith, and taking the initiative.

It was no surprise that M.S., a secular Gazan, part of the Palestinian left, a refugee who had studied in the West Bank and worked in Israel, agreed with the UNL's position. Yet even he swore that he had once witnessed a successful treatment. His sister-in-law had been invaded by a jinn and seemed to be losing her mind. One elderly uncle, who limited his healings to family members, agreed to treat her. M.S., his father, and his brother all heard the woman speak, but in a voice that was not her own. They were stunned. "To this day, we just can't believe what we saw," he said.

The uncle ordered the demon to leave her body. "Get out!" he said. "I don't want to," the demon replied. "Then I'm going to hit you," announced the uncle and landed a blow. The demon jumped to another part of the woman's body and M.S. and his father were asked to join in the beating. After hesitating, M.S. also walloped the demon until his uncle placed a bottle next to the sister-in-law's big toe. "And suddenly, her toenail flew off and plugged the bottle," he said, laughing with astonishment. The woman woke up, remembering nothing; only the nail in the bottle remained as proof.

By 1996, the Quranic clinics were booming as people flocked to them with headaches and hard-to-treat ailments. "The air is probably just swimming with demons," M.S. said wryly, and began to tell a story about a different kind of wonder cure, a magic fish. "Once upon a time," he said, "a fisherman caught a strange fish. It was square and flat and brightly colored. As he reeled in his catch, the fish began to speak in a high, clear voice. 'Fisherman, fisherman, don't kill me—I can cure all your illnesses,' the fish said. The magic fish then tripled, and each new fish tripled as well. And as the fisherman learned, drinking the water where the fish swims heals all pain."

M.S. paused, and when he continued I understood that the rest of the story was no fable. "Some say that the fish was caught in Yemen and the Palestinian police who came back here brought it with them," he said. "But I've also heard that it originally came from Libya and was caught in the Strip, off the coast of Rafah. People swear they've seen the fish swimming in bowls in some houses here, and everyone's trying to get one of their own. Me," he concluded, "I'll settle for vodka."

No sooner had I left M.S. than I ran into a large crowd of people clustered around a Sulta building near the sea. They must be looking for the fish, I thought as I saw a few policemen trying to impose order. As it turned out, I wasn't far off—the crowd had come in search of a different salvation, one that was no less fantastical. And little wonder: the Strip was sealed tight; unemployment was running at 60 or 70 percent; cupboards were bare; men were fleeing their homes to escape the whine of hungry children; women were wringing their hands, wondering by what miracle they'd manage to put food on the table.

"What are they doing here?" I asked one of the policemen, who, with frantic hand motions, was trying to move several women from the middle of the road. "They say the Sulta is giving out 150 shekels to each person who brings a photocopy of their identity card." The word had spread like wildfire and people had walked miles to save the fare money, a half-shekel, which was needed for the photocopy. They were all turned back, disappointed; there was no money to be had, no magic fish to cure all pain.

Over time I learned to adapt to many things in Gaza—to the sand that coats every book, chair, and plate, and crunches between my teeth; to the biting winter cold, unrelieved by indoor heating; to taking off my shoes at the entrance to people's homes; to eating most food with my hands, wiping it up with a piece of pita; to accepting such effusive greetings as "Hi! Where've you been? I've missed you!" as routine rather than personal; to the half-hour visit that always lasts for two or three hours; even to the abrupt bursts of gunfire in the night, which I now shrug off as some quarrel between two security forces.

But I have never gotten used to the way most conversations end when we're talking about the Strip: "With God's help it'll all be okay," "Thank God for this and every other situation." The sighs are long and the words are passive, heavy with the expectation of a miracle. Contrary to every stereotype, the people of Gaza are not hotheaded, but patient and slow to anger; their powers of endurance border on apathy and they easily put their faith in fantasies. "We go on until we explode," I'd often heard, and no one can ever predict the moment of explosion. Of course, the passivity only makes the outbreak of the *intifada* all the more remarkable: the popular uprising succeeded in defining a set of political goals precisely and realistically. Through the UNL's organization and preparation, its members were able to transform Palestinian rage into initiative and to translate the hope for heaven-sent salvation into deliberate, coordinated action.

Once real hope for improvements faded, though, Gaza rededicated itself to historic myths and visions, which are utterly divorced from the here and now. Desperate people conjure up the glorious victories of Islam's beginnings and sustain themselves with the fantasy of a triumphant Islamic return in our day. Thus support for the Islamic movement is closely tied to a sense of Palestinian impotence, and Hamas people recognize this. "If Israel had recognized the PLO after it declared Palestinian independence in 1988 and had worked for a two-state solution," one Hamas activist told me, "there wouldn't be any Hamas." Which is one way of saying that religious affiliation does not necessarily imply unconditional acceptance of the most extreme of Hamas's political and military positions (such as an Islamic state in all of Palestine, armed struggle, and *jihad*, holy war).

Few events demonstrated the interdependence of Palestinian powerlessness and support for Islamic politics as well as the funeral procession following Hamas militant Yihye Ayash's assassination. The tens of thousands who marched, the thundering cries of *"Allahu Akbar!,"* God is great, the clenched fists stabbing at the air, and the masked men firing volleys—all gave the impression that the entire Strip had embraced radical fundamentalism. But the religious crowd was joined by numerous secular Palestinians and Fatah people who had simply felt the need to express their feelings of injury. "If Ayash had been killed carrying out a military operation, I wouldn't have bothered to come," said A.M., an old Popular Front secularist who had once happily exchanged blows with the Muslim Brotherhood. "But with his assassination, I felt as if thieves had broken into my house." Z., a woman also close to the Front, said Ayash's death made her feel "stripped naked." The Arabic term she used conveyed an Islamic notion of shame and dishonor.

Affiliation with the Islamic bloc might also express defiance and opposition to the establishment, the Authority, rather than an endorsement of the militant aspects of the Islamic program. In May 1996, the Islamic slate swept to victory in the UNRWA employees' elections for the UN agency's executive committee. Gazans understood the vote more as a revolt against the competing Fatah–Popular Front slate (the "Nationals") and, by extension, against the Authority, than as an outburst of religious fervor. It is worth noting that many Hamas votes came from the professional elite—doctors and teachers—while Fatah's votes came mostly from people employed in the service sectors, poorer people whose families had more to lose from the closures.

The vote for Hamas was clearly a protest aimed at the regime—the only kind possible at a time of growing fear and increasingly rigid repression by the Sulta. (Accordingly, news of the victory was suppressed by the Palestinian press, which regularly claimed that Hamas had been crushed by the spate of detentions and interrogations and by popular rage against the movement, given its responsibility for the endless closures.)

Even so, a fair number of votes were still cast for the Fatah-Front slate (six Islamic representatives and three Nationals were elected by 5,500 UNRWA employees). A UNRWA janitor who was always an unsparing critic of the PA nevertheless backed the Nationals, explaining that "the Islamic followers always know best what Allah wants and we're left with no say. You can be sure there'd be no democracy if they came to power."

The janitor had put his finger on a problem that Hamas circles were acutely aware of, namely the conflict between a rigid interpretation of religious injunctions, on the one hand, and the effort to respond to the needs and desires of the Palestinian constituency, on the other. One Hamas supporter told me that "everyone in the movement subscribes to the armed struggle, *jihad*, until the final liberation of all Palestine. But most people aren't ready to pay the price for their faith." It seemed to me, though, that five or six hard-liners were causing everyone to pay the price, in arrests, torture, and the closures. To Hamas and Islamic Jihad activists, their reading of the Quran offered justification for suicide bombings against Israel; for the majority of Palestinians, however, suicide bombings were linked more to the closures than to Islam.

This conflict was particularly intense in 1994, when the Palestinian Authority was installed. How was Hamas to respond to the new, post-Oslo situation? The struggle between the Islamic bloc and the secular Authority would have to center on relations with Israel, forces within that bloc argued. Military operations would have to continue. If the struggle were to be limited to the domestic arena only, then the PA would surely begin to remove Hamas and Jihad leaders from their positions of influence in the mosques, or so their supporters feared. (Indeed, this began to happen in 1996.) Palestinians would support the Authority over such an issue, Hamas people explained to me; it would seem to be acting within its rights as the ruling party. However, exposing the Authority as a servant of Israel's security interests, acting at the expense of the Palestinian people, would serve the Islamic bloc better. "Stopping the operations against Israel just because of the crumbs generated by employment would be the easy way out," I was told. "We can't transform a holy principle into a solely material issue."

Hamas was faced with the contradiction between strict adherence to the Quran and its desire—or pretension—to serve and represent Palestinians better than their internationally recognized representatives. I can well imagine that UNRWA janitor's response to the conundrum. "I'm afraid of you when you cut yourselves off from the people and the reality of their lives," he probably would have said, "when you insist on only your own interpretation of the Quran. You're not interested in our opinions or our feelings because you have the holy word, the final say."

In the dispute over the one true meaning of the holy word, nationalists and the Islamic opposition are not the only contenders. There is a third interested party as well: Israel's self-appointed experts on Arafat and the PLO, ex-intelligence officers who learned what they know of Palestinians in the interrogation rooms and from deciphering the Arabic media, who have also shown some skill in wresting Quranic passages from their historical context and applying them to present use. Arafat's speeches are scrutinized and routinely lambasted for provocative citations from the Quran, especially for his liberal use of the word *jihad*.

In a speech given to a Muslim audience in South Africa in May 1994, shortly before he put his signature to the Gaza-Jericho agreement, Arafat assured his listeners of the ongoing *jihad* until the liberation of Jerusalem. He went on to compare the agreement to the Sulh Hudaibia, the ten-year nonaggression pact that the Prophet Muhammad signed with the Quraysh tribe. Israeli Arabists stress that Muhammad broke the treaty two years later when his army had grown strong enough to conquer Mecca. In response, Moshe Sharon, a Middle East scholar, was reported as saying, "Words have value in the Middle East. A word can move the masses and whoever doubts this should just remember the massacres (in Hebron and elsewhere) of 1929, which began in the wake of the Mufti's provocative speeches."

Sharon went on, "Arafat's insinuations and explicit comments in Johannesburg should not be taken lightly. Whoever dismisses his words as a flight of the oriental imagination is making a very grave mistake."

Sharon's remarks, reported in *Ha'aretz*, were taken from a speech given at a right-wing conference, although Sharon insisted that he attended as a Middle East expert, not as a supporter of the right. According to Muhammad, Sharon noted, the Quraysh treaty was violated because "treaties and wars are undertaken for the good of Islam. Then it was good for Islam to enter into the treaty, today it is good for Islam to terminate it."[4] To Sharon, Arafat was saying that he attached no more importance to the agreement with Israel than the Prophet Muhammad attached to his treaty with the Quraysh tribe.[5]

In Gaza, however, in the Palestinian context, Arafat's speech was seen in a very different light, even by the most devout of Muslims. After all, the agreement to which Arafat had just put his name allowed all the Jewish settlements in the West Bank and Gaza Strip to remain in place (removing the settlers from Hebron, a must for Palestinians after the Baruch Goldstein massacre, was never even raised as a demand); failed to secure the release of all Palestinian prisoners held in Israel (whom Palestinians view as POWs); perpetuated the Palestinians' chronic economic dependence on Israel; avoided all mention of restitution from Israel for the harm done by the occupation; and did not secure an Israeli promise to halt construction in East Jerusalem. To his listeners in Gaza, Arafat's need to dip into the Islamic lexicon only exposed his weakness—having signed away almost every Palestinian grievance, Arafat was clearly going to great lengths to offer some comforting quasi-historical comparisons that would perhaps help to sweeten his people's bitter sense of impotence and frustration.

In Gaza, similar speeches might be greeted enthusiastically, but for much the same reason that so many Gazans embrace the idea of Quranic healing and magic fish. Arafat's illusory use of language connotes strength where there is so little. "The more extreme and abrasive his language, the more his people rely on the most militant quotes from the Quran, the more alarmed we become," Hamas supporters have told me. "This kind of talk only means that the Sulta has made even more concessions to Israel and is even weaker."

Shimon Peres and Yossi Beilin, former deputy foreign minister, pressed Arafat to stop using the word *jihad* in his speeches because Israelis hear the term as a call for their destruction. Altogether, Israeli commentators and policy makers tend to hear ideas and quotations from the Quran and believe they are picking up on some kind of well-calculated battle plan, a strategic blueprint. Meanwhile, Palestinians hear the same words and wring their hands at their leaders' incompetent handling of such grave negotiations and at the domestic rivalries that only serve the other side. They might even counter with different quotes or examples from the Quran, ones that disclose both a sincere desire for peace and an urgent sense of the need for it.

Israel's misreading of Palestinian intentions is rooted in its own illusions, in Israeli society's skewed grasp of reality whereby it fails to recognize its clear superiority in every sphere: military, economic, educational, and technological. Inherited and manipulated fear, the perception of oneself as the perennial victim, and the primordial Jewish dread of the gentile are projected onto the other people who live in the same country. In this light, all Palestinian behavior is explained in terms of past Jewish experience, and Islamic religious texts and manifestations are interpreted accordingly, as the expression of fanatics only.

Visiting the mourning tents, I've often thought of those same Israeli experts and their blindness to the nuances, even contradictions, of Palestinian religious life. Families grieving over a son or father killed in the *intifada* or in a suicide attack on Israel are supposed to be happy—their loved one has fallen as a martyr and is "not dead." And in fact the parents and wives and children do proclaim their happiness in front of the television cameras and also serve sweet juice as a sign of celebration. Up close, though, you can see the telltale puffiness around the eyes and hear the weeping behind closed doors. "The scriptures are one thing," N., a religious man admitted, "and feelings are another. At the home of a *shaheed*, a martyr, I always drink the juice and it always sticks in my throat."

The tangled web of politics and piety, the sleight of hand that turns weakness into strength, the impossible act of balancing hard reality with Islamic fantasy—all these came together in a joke that was making the rounds of the Strip and the West Bank in early 1994, a time of intense negotiations and agreements. "Abu Amar," people said to Arafat. "What will happen with Jerusalem?"

"You'll see," said Arafat. "It'll be fine. Every Friday I'll go to the holy city, to Jerusalem, and pray at al-Aqsa mosque."

"But Abu Amar," asked one man, "how will you get past the Israeli checkpoint? How will you get an exit permit?"

"No problem," said Arafat. "Have you forgotten that I'm over forty?"[6]

JUST A PIECE OF PAPER

Unlike the Quran, which is given to interpretation and subject to a range of different understandings, the Palestinian National Covenant, devised in 1964 when the PLO was founded and revised in 1968 by the Palestinian National Council (PNC), is clear in its meaning. In its time the defining statement of the Palestinian liberation movement, the covenant states:

> Armed struggle is the only way to liberate Palestine. Therefore it is the overall strategy, not merely a tactical phase.... Commando action constitutes the nucleus of the Palestinian popular liberation war.... [Every Palestinian] must be prepared for the armed struggle and ready to sacrifice his wealth and his life in order to win back his homeland.... Claims of historical or religious ties of Jews to Palestine are incompatible with the facts of history and the true conception of what constitutes statehood. Judaism, being a religion, is not an independent nationality. Nor do Jews constitute a single nation with an identity of its own....[7]

As part of the Oslo negotiations, Arafat had promised Yitzhak Rabin to convene the full membership of the PNC (which included a number of men wanted by Israel who were barred from entering Israeli or occupied territory) for the purpose of repealing those parts of the covenant that call for eternal war against Zionism, refer to it as imperialist or racist, and deny Jewish nationhood. In January 1996, the election of the Legislative Council established the Palestinian government and so opened the door to convening the PNC in April that year. "Repealing the covenant" quickly became a key phrase in regional politics and the focus of intense speculation.

In fact, the majority of Palestinians, even former prisoners and *intifada* activists, had never even read the covenant, a long-outdated document in which an independent state is never even mentioned. In response to popular demand, the press published the text and many Palestinians saw the subject of dispute and of such loaded symbolism for the very first time. The phrase "armed struggle," however, which derived from the covenant, had entered the Palestinian language, adopted as a kind of liberating mantra long before Hamas and the Islamic Jihad began building their homemade weapons. "When I threw a grenade, I felt as if I was liberating the whole of Palestine," said A.S. Like many thousands of others, though, he realized that the ultimate goal of the "armed struggle" was a fantasy, that the true balance of forces made nonsense of the notion of eradicating Israel. Still, people clung to the phrase as shorthand for independence and liberty and the right to fight for them.

As a bargaining chip, the covenant was a dud card, an empty concession, said Salah Tamari, a longtime Fatah hero, at the PNC session that convened on April 22, 1996. Israel seemed to see the text as a strategic threat but to Tamari the covenant was "just a piece of paper, which anyone can tear up." The Palestinian presence, on the other hand, is a nonnegotiable fact on the ground, he concluded. "Our struggle has not ended, but it involves different methods"—the struggle he spoke of was clearly the effort to gain an independent state, not the liberation of all of Palestine.

Not all the delegates were quite so sanguine about revoking the covenant, though. True, it was only a bargaining chip, but one for which the Palestinians should receive something in exchange. As those delegates saw it, the Oslo process and its implementation were dominated by Israel and its demands. Palestinian leverage lay in holding on even to outmoded national symbols, trading them only for far-reaching and fundamental changes in the other side's attitude. The covenant could not be repealed, they argued, until Israel recognized the Palestinian people's right to self-determination and a state. Even Hayder abd al-Shafi, who had accepted the Partition Plan back in 1947, supported this uncompromising position.

The PNC session—also an emotional reunion for old comrades in exile who had not seen each other for many years—opened with statements by Arafat and his deputy Abu Mazen in which they presented the covenant as a document that had already been radically altered, in spirit if not in the letter, by a succession of PLO resolutions beginning in 1969. Abu Mazen pointed out that the resolution adopted that year to solve the conflict with a "secular, democratic state in which

Muslims, Christians, and Jews would live together in absolute equality" in fact contradicted articles of the covenant. In 1974, the PNC resolved to establish a Palestinian state "in every bit of Palestinian territory that is liberated,"[8] and the PNC declaration of independence in 1988 certainly inferred recognition of Israel, as did the Letters of Mutual Recognition, exchanged in September 1993, and the Declaration of Principles.

A compromise was reached between those who would repeal the covenant and those who preferred to retain it. The resolution's wording, approved on April 25 by a resounding majority of 504 to 54, was indeed clumsy and bewildering: "It is hereby resolved to amend the declaration by repealing all articles that contradict what is written in the Letters of Mutual Recognition exchanged by Arafat and Rabin." Of course, a substanial group of Israeli detractors and Arafatologists waiting in the wings quickly pounced on the vague and muddy wording, citing the lack of mention of specific articles and the PNC's failure to propose a new covenant. (The current covenant essentially remained in force while the PNC empowered a committee to formulate a new one.) To those Israelis, the compromise only provided further evidence of the enemy's wily, duplicitous nature.

At the time, I was listening to Israel Radio—which largely agreed that the PNC had outfoxed Israel by resorting to contorted legalese to avoid canceling the covenant—and reporting from the PNC session at the Shawa Center in Gaza, where one got an entirely different impression of the process. Several members of the committee charged with drafting the proposal remained in constant touch with the Israeli Foreign Ministry, consulting with legal advisor Joel Singer and Director General Uri Savir. Some members had suggested replacing the obsolete text with the 1988 declaration of independence. "The covenant says that as long as Palestine is not liberated every Palestinian lacks self-respect, pride, and freedom," said one delegate derisively. "Are we really supposed to stick with this? I've never felt that I have no pride or self-respect."

Word came back that Israel would not accept the 1988 declaration in lieu of the covenant. PNC members heard that its position was backed up by a letter signed by 100 American senators and representatives stating that formal adoption of the declaration would likely cause the collapse of the Oslo process. In fact, people on the drafting committee told me that Israel, or more precisely, the Labor Party, had begged the PLO not to formulate a new text—which would no doubt include language involving an independent state and Jerusalem, creating yet another controversy within Israel.

Yet any text that spoke of anything less than a state had no chance of Palestinian acceptance. Moreover, had the compromise wording in fact listed all the covenant's articles that contradicted the Letters of Mutual Recognition, the only item remaining, some quipped, would have been Article 33, which states that any amendment requires a two-thirds majority. A slight exaggeration, perhaps, but the PNC was motivated by the need to leave the Palestinian people with a text that was not totally emasculated. What for many Israelis was proof of subterfuge and insincerity was in fact a nimble, even elegant, way to conceal weakness. And in the end, Israel's government and its security apparatus and the White House finally confirmed that the PNC resolution fulfilled Arafat's commitment to repeal the offending articles.*

As the special PNC session ended and Israeli right-wingers and Middle East experts deliberated over the new proposal, weighing whether the Palestinian threat of annihilation had finally been defanged, a dozen trucks attempting to transport oranges from the Strip to the port of Ashdod stood idle at the Erez checkpoint. The drivers had spent the night in the cabin of their vehicles, stranded since the previous day. There were not enough IDF soldiers available to inspect the increased traffic at the checkpoint, despite the long-scheduled conclusion of the PNC session and the oncoming Id al-Adha festival, both of which meant an inevitable increase of pressure at the checkpoint, which could have been taken into account.

A convoy of cars, containing various Palestinian VIPs, foreign observers, and myself, was kept waiting in the heat of the day for some four hours as the soldiers changed shifts, took a lunch break, and went about their work indifferent to the clamor and discomfort. At three in the afternoon, the citrus trucks turned around and headed back toward Gaza City—Ashdod port would be closed soon anyway. The oranges would be ruined.

*Subsequent claims by the Likud party that the PNC had failed to fulfill its obligations with regard to the covenant are disingenuous, in light of Israel's orchestration of the special session—from setting its date and permitting entrance and exit passes to exiled PNC members to formulating the resolution's text.

"Some holiday," said one truck driver as dozens of PNC members, many of them elderly, one on crutches, hobbled the distance to the crossing on foot, loaded down with suitcases. Their restricted travel documents did not permit even the briefest of visits to family in Israel or the West Bank, or the quickest of glimpses of their former villages. "You want to know what I think about changing the covenant?" said a man from the West Bank. "I'm one of the lucky ones." He had only managed to see his family in the Strip by stealing in as the chauffeur of a PNC delegate. "The Israelis can keep me from joining my family, yet they're still afraid of some piece of paper."

Part III

Loss

Chapter 6

A *Tax on Being Alive*

One morning in 1991, when Israeli troops still patrolled the Strip, I was sitting with friends in their office at the busy junction of Nasser and al-Wahda Streets. The traffic outside had been flowing as usual, then we heard it freeze abruptly. Even behind our thick glass windows and the closed door we could sense the blanket of fear that had fallen over the street outside. It turned out that a group of soldiers had stationed themselves at the crossing, some aiming their rifles at the stream of cars. Two soldiers were stopping the vehicles, one after another, looking them over, checking papers, and waving them on their way. Eventually, a van drove up and the driver extended his hand out the window, holding his papers; one of the soldiers examined the documents, said a few words, and the driver got out of the van. In a flash, the soldiers had jumped inside the van and zoomed off, leaving the driver standing in the street. The traffic immediately resumed its flow and everyone went back to their own affairs.

My friends explained quickly: the soldiers would hand the van over to other soldiers working under cover and disguised as local Palestinians. They would use the vehicle for two or three days to ambush some wanted man or ferry a collaborator from one destination to another. Meanwhile, the driver would run around, feverishly searching for his van; if he was lucky, he would eventually find it at one of the military bases where Shabak was located, with a smashed headlight or side mirror, a few scratches, and covered with mud. Everyone in Gaza was familiar with the procedure; confiscation of people's vehicles was just one of the abuses of property practiced by the occupation.

There was another kind of abuse, more widespread and far more traumatic. On three occasions I was in different people's homes just after the Israeli army had finished searching for wanted men. The pattern was similar in hundreds of other homes and had nothing to do with the suspect's political affiliation or the gravity of his purported act. A large group of soldiers, possibly accompanied by a Shabak officer or two, would break into the house, usually in the middle of the night but sometimes even in daylight, and let loose an orgy of shooting and destruction, emptying wardrobes and tearing them apart (conceivably weapons might be hidden inside), spraying the thin walls and ceilings with gunfire (there could be a double ceiling), and ripping open mattresses (ammunition might be concealed in the stuffing). The one thing I never could understand, though, was the ritual destruction of televisions, radios, chairs, beds, and dressing tables, all smashed beyond repair, the mirrors splintered in rage, the telephone wires torn out of the walls with what seemed like infinite hatred.

A.'s home in Shabura had suffered this kind of rampage; I saw A.'s family stepping around the havoc in a daze. Like so many other Palestinians whose homes had been wrecked in this way, A.'s family had no direct involvement in the events that brought the soldiers to their home. In A.'s case, a Fatah man named Salim Muafi, had been shot by a group of undercover soldiers close by. Bleeding heavily, he had fled for his life, banging on people's doors, pleading for them to let him in. When the soldiers had caught up with him they had fired again and killed him. Then they had broken into houses in the area, looking for friends of his. (According to the army, Muafi had refused to surrender and opened fire on the soldiers first, but this version contradicted eyewitness reports given to Fatah people and human rights field workers.)

Even those whose homes remained undisturbed had suffered from routine disrespect for Palestinian property. During the *intifada*, soldiers were frequently stationed deep in the heart of heavily populated areas as a way of suppressing the uprising. They often set up observation posts on the roofs of people's homes and there were constantly stories of their smashing the solar heating panels on the rooftops, defecating on the stairs, and making horrendous noise. As a matter of course, the neighborhood children threw stones up at the soldiers, more often breaking windows than hitting their targets. (To this day my friends in Khan Yunis fondly remember the soldier who came down from his post on the roof, leaving his gun behind, and asked to speak to the children. "Look," he said, "I don't like being here. And I want you to know that I'll never shoot at you. But it's a shame to keep throwing stones and breaking your neighbors' windows.")

However the army explained its rules of engagement, whatever justifications it offered for the ruins it left behind, there is no way to account for the smashed television, often the main source of comfort for a family penned up every night in its cramped corner of the refugee camp. The wreckage of the double bed and dresser and mirror are engraved in the family's memory as yet one more gratuitous act of harm to its home and well-being. Children who have watched soldiers use their rifle butts to smash the only sink in the house are unlikely to feel remorse when Jewish possessions go up in flames. Sons and daughters who have seen soldiers confiscate their father's car probably have little respect altogether for the middle-class notion of private property and its sanctity—especially if it belongs to Israelis. Possibly they have even grown indifferent to the sight of Palestinian property being destroyed.

In Gaza soldiers' vandalism was only one aspect of Israel's disregard for Palestinian welfare; systematic abuse of property and resources began with the soldier on patrol but was practiced in one form or another by officials from the civil administration, the customs collector and tax man, all the way up to the Israeli finance and defense ministers. In response, economic crimes such as tax evasion, tax fraud, and theft were seen as a legitimate reaction, even an essential form of pain relief—part of the informal economy that develops under any occupation or autocratic regime. And the ruinous effects of Israeli policy in the Strip did not end with the Oslo agreements; in fact, today's stalled economic development in the occupied territories is largely a product of that policy. The effects of thirty years of erosion could not be corrected instantly on May 17, 1994, when the keys were handed over to the Palestinian Authority. Israel was simply relieved of responsibility for the consequences of its neglect and for the necessary rehabilitation.

The greatest economic hardship was taxation. I remember a taxi driver who took me around Gaza on one of my first trips in 1991, complaining bitterly about the burden of taxes. On the verge of tears, he asked me—as if I represented the occupation—how he was supposed to pay full taxes when there were curfews and strikes and closures. He pulled out of his pocket a sheaf of forms covered with unintelligible computer symbols. Somewhere in all the hieroglyphics was a sum that represented the taxes he owed, but neither he nor I could figure it out.

At the time, the lowest taxable monthly income in the Gaza Strip was approximately 500 new Israeli shekels ($200 at the 1991 rate of exchange), compared with NIS 1,200 ($480) in Israel. A civil administration official defended the discrepancy thus: "A whole crate of tomatoes is cheaper in Gaza than a pound in Israel. The cost of living here is much lower." His response involved a unique application of inverse discrimination: he had conveniently ignored all the essential goods and services that cost Gazans exactly the same as they did Israelis, sometimes even more in the absence of the government subsidies on water and electricity that Israelis received. Gasoline cost the same, as did dairy products, most kinds of fruit, electrical appliances, automobiles, cement, to list just a few basics. The value-added tax (VAT) applied equally to Gazans and Israelis. Over the years, Israeli officials offered an alternative explanation for the high tax rate: "We have poured a lot of Israeli money into Gaza," they said. Figures issued by the World Bank tell a different story, showing negative investment in the Strip. But even without such hard, authoritative evidence, one look at Gaza's rotting infrastructure—the lack of clean running water, paved streets, reliable electricity, and modern sewage systems—belies the claims of massive investment.

During the peace talks in Madrid in 1991 and later in Washington, World Bank experts were asked to analyze the economic concerns and "developmental challenges facing the Middle East," especially in the Gaza Strip and the West Bank, and to define the region's fiscal needs and prospects in a peacetime economy. The World Bank's study, laid out in 1993 in five hefty volumes, was then handed over to the Palestinian Authority as a development proposal. Using language that is notable for its courtesy, detachment, and brevity, the World Bank chronicled the occupied territories' history of economic erosion as a result of Israeli policies.

In one dispassionate summary, the World Bank addresses the different taxation levels for Israelis and Palestinians:

> A wage earner in Israel with a nonworking wife and three children, with an annual income of NIS 12,000 ($4,800) pays no income tax, while in the Occupied Territories he pays NIS 464 ($185.60), or

about four percent of salary. On an annual salary of NIS 30,000 ($12,000), the Israeli taxpayer pays NIS 1,999 ($799), or about seven percent of salary, while in the Occupied Territories, he pays NIS 5,088 ($2,035), or 17 percent of salary.[1]

The World Bank enjoyed a more receptive hearing than Palestinians who had been complaining for years about discriminatory taxation.

Had the Israeli authorities been willing to listen to these complaints, it would not have had to look very far for reliable corroboration. In 1991, the civil administration asked an economist, Ezra Sadan, to propose solutions for the crisis that gripped the Strip following the Gulf war and the six-week curfew that accompanied it. (Many Palestinians had lost their jobs in Kuwait and Saudi Arabia as a result of Yassir Arafat's support for Saddam Hussein. Their wages often had been the sole source of income for whole families in Gaza.) The civil administration was looking ahead, too; while Sadan was unaware that closure was about to become permanent policy, the administration certainly knew. As it happened, Sadan was a member of the right-wing, prosettlement Tehiya Party, but his political orientation did not lessen his disapproval of the high rates at which Palestinians were being taxed. In his dry, uninflected report he writes:

> In addition to the relative burden of the tax, it creates unnecessary friction and adds fuel to the fire of the hatred, the motives for which are national, that is fed by day-to-day hardships. Furthermore, the collection method in practice is based to a significant degree on the issuance of non-tax liability documents that are required for receipt of entry permits to Israel. From the point of view of businessmen, this is an onerous collection method, oppressive and arbitrary, and does not jibe at all with any kind of relations of confidence between the government and the entrepreneurial level of society in the Strip.[2]

When the Palestinian Authority took over the treasury in 1994, it promised the sponsors of the Oslo process and the various donor nations bolstering the Authority with considerable financial help that it would improve tax collection in order to cover its ever-expanding operating budget. That budget, formulated with the help and oversight of the World Bank, is hardly populist; in fact, the treasury said candidly that there was no foreseeable possibility of raising the level of social services. Nevertheless, the treasury has managed since 1995 to reduce the level of taxes substantially—further proof of the unreasonable burden previously imposed by Israel.

Based on a monthly wage of NIS 1,000, table 1 shows the changes enacted by the treasury.

TABLE 1. TAXES WITHHELD AT SOURCE (IN NIS)

MARITAL STATUS	1993	1994	1995
SINGLE	58.20	53.44	27.50
MARRIED	35.40	33.36	12.00
MARRIED + 1	33.60	31.36	8.50
MARRIED + 2	31.80	29.36	5.00
MARRIED + 3	29.90	27.36	1.50
MARRIED + 4	28.10	25.36	0

While Sadan's report indicates a willingness on the part of some Israeli officials to address the economic crisis in the occupied territories, in 1991 the civil administration applied ever-more nonsensical criteria in its calculation of tax liability, with the result that ordinary Palestinians ended up owing astronomical amounts. When I first heard Gazans talk about a "life tax," I thought some degree of Oriental exaggeration was at work; eventually I learned that "life tax" was the nickname given to a sum "assessed," in the official jargon, "according to the best judgment possible in the absence of a tax return." To understand the aptness of the term, one need only take the example of Feisal. His magnetic card was due to expire in June 1991 and without it he could not enter Israel and find work. A supplementary form of identification introduced in Gaza in 1989, the card gave access by means of a computerized magnetic strip to the same information as the standard ID (dates of arrests, prison records, and political affiliations) but was distributed only to "clean" Palestinians. Thus its ostensible purpose was to weed out *intifada* and political activists, people considered potential security risks, and prevent their entry into Israel, but over time, receiving a magnetic card—or renewing one, as Feisal was doing—became conditional on clearing one's outstanding taxes and debts. In other words, Feisal's right to work was in the hands of the civil administration's finance division. An overdue electric bill of, say, NIS 243 (about $97) could prevent a person from receiving his magnetic card, without which he could not leave the Strip, or get paid, or rid himself of the debt, which would accumulate interest and late charges like mold growing on damp walls.

It turned out, however, that Feisal owed far more than his outstanding electric bill. At the civil administration office where he went to renew his magnetic card, Feisal received a so-called debtors' form, a convoluted Hebrew notice telling him to settle his affairs with the income tax office and the Shabak. Feisal got a clean bill of health from the Shabak but at the income tax office he felt as if the sky had fallen in. The computer spewed out a page of indecipherable symbols but the numbers at the end of the column were clear enough: Feisal owed a whopping NIS 66,872 (about $27,000) in back taxes on estimated income of NIS 130,000 ($52,000) in 1987. "How on earth could I ever have earned that much?" he asked in utter astonishment. "I'm the son of refugees, a menial worker who's been paid by the day for the last twenty-five years," he said. "You're self-employed, a subcontractor," the clerk answered and pointed to the appropriate code on the computer printout. "Me? A subcontractor? I wish!" said Feisal. "All I do is go to the junction and wait for someone to pick me up for a day's work. I work on construction sites for fifty shekels a day." In response, the tax clerk scolded him for not filing a tax return and then suggested a compromise: NIS 1,600 ($640). Feisal was lucky; most people in his situation were offered settlements of NIS 3,000 ($1,200).

In the years following the Gulf war, the Palestinian Labor Union and Gaza's Accountants Association were flooded with hundreds of desperate complaints. Many workers had lost their jobs (and their back pay) after the war and the long period of closure that followed it. Even more lost their magnetic cards, especially those whose Israeli employers had avoided paying taxes on their behalf and those like Feisal, itinerant workers who had always been paid in cash. In addition, the procedures governing entry into Israel and access to jobs there became stricter after the war, and workers not only had to carry ID and magnetic cards but separate work permits and proof of registration with the Israeli Office of Employment.

A worker would begin his bureaucratic quest for the new papers only to run into a tax file showing a huge debt, based on the false or mistaken information that he was self-employed but had failed to submit a tax return. (In Israel, taxes are deducted at the source and only the self-employed are obligated to file tax returns.) In some cases, the Israeli employer had declared that the Palestinian worker was a subcontractor as a way to avoid paying taxes for him. But primarily, "life tax" was an opportunity for the civil administration to step up revenue collection, a process that had intensified with the beginning of the *intifada*.

I discovered that this mysterious tax, "assessed according to the best judgment possible in the absence of a tax return," is occasionally applied within Israel to prevent tax evasion. But in Gaza, the tax office knew it was not dealing with delinquents and tax evaders, hence its instant willingness to drop its full demands and slash a debt of NIS 60,000 to 1,600. After all, self-employed Gazans—shopkeepers, small-scale manufacturers, and taxi owners—had been filing tax returns for years. It was precisely the tens of thousands of itinerant workers and Palestinians with steady jobs who were unaware of the life tax, just as most Israeli wage earners had never heard of it.

Israeli law stipulates that litigation over tax payments can take place only when the tax office has issued a formal assessment and an official bill. But many Gazans came to bargain with the authorities bearing nothing but a computer printout. The assessment could be contested, but only in writing, within thirty days, and most Gazans never received formal notice of their alleged debt. However, some laborers who suddenly found themselves transformed into subcontractors began receiving little booklets of tax prepayment coupons in the mail, with attached notes stating specifically that appeals could be made only in person. Gazan accountants who nevertheless sent letters of appeal received no replies. In the end, the worker was usually forced to argue his case in person with the tax clerk, who was in an obvious position of strength and who never thought to inform the supplicant that compromise sums, once reached, could not be appealed.

Gazans were stunned by the twisted logic at work, that a man who was unemployed could be taxed on a hypothetical income. "I'm unemployed," the worker would tell the tax clerk. "So what are you living on?" the clerk would ask (as if unaware of the Strip's familial support system) before slapping a tax on the laid-off worker. The man would leave the office with the bizarre exchange ringing in his ears: "What are you living on? Nothing? So pay!" The occupation, people said, made them pay "just for being alive." The phrase *life tax* crept into the language, adopted—oddly enough—even by some Israeli officials.

To me, the life tax exemplified the way civil administration staff made Palestinians' everyday existence as burdensome as the behavior of the soldiers did: rigid, arbitrary policies were set at the highest levels of the Israeli government, then capriciously and arrogantly enforced. One Palestinian laborer recounted his meeting with the tax authorities. "You've got to pay for the air you breathe," he was told. And his experience was by no means unique.

Gazan accountants complained to the civil administration about the arbitrary way in which tax officials arrived at compromise sums. Clearly, no uniform criteria were being applied and no consideration was being given to prevailing conditions in the Strip. Instead, the putative back taxes and the compromise figures were consequences of a given clerk's mood and of some overriding objective that had been set elsewhere—in the distant halls of the Israeli ministries. When the same accountants met with chief tax officials to dispute the legality of imposing "a tax in the absence of a tax return," given the massive extent of unemployment in the Strip, they were told: "There's just no choice. We have to raise a fixed sum"—that is, the sum needed to cover the civil administration's budget.

Moreover, the civil administration's disingenuous response completely ignored the political context: in the first year of the *intifada*, Palestinians had launched a tax revolt on orders from the Unified National Leadership to protest the heavy tax burden and Israel's illegal distribution of the revenues raised. (Palestinians had long contended that the taxes collected were not being used in full for the benefit of the local population, as stipulated by international law; the World Bank substantiated their claim.) Israel had retaliated by enforcing tax collection even more aggressively. With military escorts, civil administration officials began to seize property and confiscate the identity cards of delinquent taxpayers and their relatives. I suspect that the life tax was one more instrument of repressive taxation.

. . .

Gross injustices in tax matters did not stop with individuals. In his 1991 report, Ezra Sadan highlighted the choke hold that Israeli authorities maintained on Gazan business and industrial development:

> Conditions for development will not be created if there is no repeal of various administrative restrictions and red tape, intended to *inconvenience* [my italics] the development of initiatives and business in the Gaza Strip, especially those that compete with initiatives and business operating in Israel.[3]

It seems that Sadan understood that the negative effects of Israeli interference derived not only from government policy but also from the whimsical power of individual Israeli officers:

> Likewise, conditions for development will not be created if there is no assurance of the prevention of red tape and the avoidance of intentional hardships that cause red tape on tax issues; thus, it will be necessary to avoid (generally) involvement with issues of indirect taxation (VAT, duty) in the assessment and collection processes for direct taxes.[4]

One form of Israeli procrastination that hobbled Gazan businesses was the civil administration's failure to refund VAT monies. In June 1994—some months before the Palestinian Authority took over taxation—several Gaza City accountants complained that various production and commercial firms were not receiving VAT refunds on the purchase of supplies. I was showed a list of seven companies waiting for refunds that ranged from NIS 16,000 ($5,000 according to the 1994 rate) to NIS 487,000 ($152,187). Two construction firms had been forced to borrow money from the bank to cover the outstanding sums and could not accept large orders on credit until their refunds came in. Nor could they buy additional supplies. They needed cash. According to Israeli law, VAT must be refunded within forty days of application or else interest must be paid and the amount owing adjusted in relation to the shekel's fluctuating dollar exchange rate (a procedure known as linkage). "We're so happy when VAT finally comes in," the accountants said, "that no one ever thinks about interest and linkage." Until January 1994, they added, there had been few problems other than delays in obtaining VAT refunds, but several months before the Palestinian Authority was due to take over, the money was suddenly stuck in the civil administration's VAT office.

The accountants could see what was coming: they feared that the moment the Palestinians received the office keys the VAT files would fall through the cracks and Israel would abdicate responsibility. During the two weeks preceding the transfer of authority, they met with several civil administration officers to plead their case. The head of the administration made notes and promised to take care of the matter but, according to the accountants, the VAT officer said, "I don't have the funds now. Anyway, you owe lots of money," referring to the whole Strip. "The electric company, for example." In addition, the civil administration maintained that some of the companies listed were new, and it was therefore necessary for officials to visit their sites before approving VAT refunds; these visits, however, had been postponed for security reasons. Some of the refund requests, moreover, had arrived only three or four days before the Palestinian Authority took over. The accountants argued that one of the new companies was not a manufacturer, so a photocopy of its vehicle permit should have sufficed, as it always had in the past; as for the "security reasons," the two other new companies were both located on a route the administration staff traveled every day. With regard to the refund requests that arrived late, the civil administration had closed its office a month before the transfer of authority, moved to its new base, but then failed to send out application forms. Nevertheless, the accountants noted, the civil administration had continued to collect money right up until the last minute. Somehow, though, it was unable to process the refunds.

Three months later, in September 1994, an Israeli spokesman issued a predictable response:

> Now that the Accords have been signed, the Israeli VAT office has no authority to deal directly with the Palestinian companies, except following an official request by the Palestinian VAT office and after the Israeli VAT office's examination of the files in its possession.... Once the Israeli VAT office has reviewed the Palestinian Authority's requests, each refund will be dealt with on its own merits. As of today, no request has yet been received from the Palestinian Authority VAT office.

As the accountants had predicted, the VAT files, like much other bureaucratic paperwork, had fallen through the cracks. Their seeming disappearance has, of course, spawned a thousand excuses: "The matter is being held up by the Palestinians," or "The Authority hasn't sent us the applications yet," or "They haven't consulted us on this matter." True, there is one significant improvement: now, at least, Palestinians are spared direct encounters with Israeli officials. All requests are communicated through the Palestinian Civilian Liaison Committee, which since May 1994 has been meeting with Gazans and then transmitting their needs—VAT refunds, exit permits, travel documents—to the Israelis. However, trying to track down the cause for delays or refusals is a detective job that challenges one's faith in the honesty of both sides. And, incidentally, the seven companies are still awaiting their VAT refunds.

Then there is what the economists call a "fiscal leak," the surreptitious disappearance of monies—the Palestinian public service employees' pension fund, for example. In 1991—again, before the transfer of authority to the Palestinians—the Committee of Retired Civil Administration Employees approached a prominent businessman from a well-to-do *muwataneen* family, Mansur al-Shawwa, to represent it. The committee hoped that Shawa, the son of Gaza's former mayor, would present a persuasive face to the Israeli authorities. "About three billion shekels have accumulated in the pension fund," Shawwa told me. "It would have made more sense for the money to stay in Gaza, but it's invested in Israel. The pensioners asked me to convince the Israeli government to transfer part of the pension fund to Gaza and deduct a proportional amount from their monthly pensions. They wanted about $300,000 to establish some sort of industry here, set up factories, create jobs. One after another we went to the civil administration, but nothing helped." The UNRWA workers' pension fund is also invested elsewhere, in Vienna. "It's worth more than one and a half billion dollars," Shawwa explained. "If that fund were brought to Gaza and the West Bank, together with the funds that Israel has stolen from us—or borrowed from us, if you prefer—we wouldn't need donations from outside. We could manage by ourselves."

Long before the Israeli redeployment, I began to notice another fiscal leak, a virtual flood, in fact. At the grocery store on Falastin Street I saw that goods imported from abroad—coffee, tea, chocolate, crackers, cleaning supplies, cosmetics, dishes, and pots—bore an importer's stamp on which the broker's address appeared, and the broker was always Israeli. Once when I was about to purchase an electrical appliance I was astonished to find that the duty on it was as high for Palestinians as for Israelis (usually 50 to 100 percent of the appliance's cost). Thus Palestinians were augmenting Israeli customs revenues as well. "But of course," the salesman told me with a resigned smile. "After all, we're one country."

After 1967 the Gaza Strip and the West Bank were subjected to an involuntary one-way customs union with Israel: there was unrestricted commerce in one direction only—from Israel to the occupied territories. Foreign goods and raw materials such as gasoline reached the territories via Israel and were subject to Israeli customs duty, taxes, and surcharges. The duties paid on most imported products purchased in the territories, however, were not transferred to the civil administration (i.e., for the benefit of the Palestinian population) but went straight to the Israeli treasury. What counted was not the consumer's location but the point of entry of the product. The only duties transferred to the civil administration were those paid on the small amount of merchandise entering the occupied territories from Jordan or Egypt. Some Palestinian companies were able to import goods directly, but these were very few; for the most part, Israel imposed a myriad of administrative restrictions on trade, forcing Palestinian businesses into some form of cooperation with Israeli firms, which could operate free of such limitations.

Complaints about these fiscal leaks—and the dependency they have generated—have been echoed by numerous Palestinian economists and analysts. They argue that long-term reliance on donor nations, the World Bank, and the International Monetary Fund could have been avoided. A more resolute negotiating stance toward Israel, one that dealt with the details exhaustively, would have addressed compensation for economic damage caused during the occupation or, at the very least, repayment of debts incurred by the Israeli government in the form of taxes collected but not plowed back into the territories. The Oslo Accords make no mention of these long-standing grievances and only serve, therefore, to close the account.

Negative investment in the Gaza Strip was, of course, hardly the result of one official's whim or even of crippling red tape. It was the outcome of a systematic Israeli policy that, since 1967, had allocated a minimal budget to the occupied territories' administration or, more precisely, to the needs of the Palestinian population. The sections of the budget devoted to the calculation of revenue never included a record of the huge sums paid by the Palestinians in taxes that have disappeared forever into the coffers of the Israeli treasury. "There is some evidence," write the economists at the World Bank in their dry style, "that not all of the tax revenues collected by the Israeli authorities from residents of the Occupied Territories have been made available to the Civil Administration."[5] The extensive physical neglect in the areas populated by Palestinians is perhaps the most tangible evidence of these missing funds. And the woeful lack of development, or even of basic infrastructure maintenance, stands in glaring contrast to the rapid and highly noticeable construction taking place wherever land was expropriated for Jewish settlers (who were not governed by the civil administration's budget and enjoyed subsidies on taxes, building costs, and the price of water that were denied to their Palestinian neighbors).

According to an estimate of the Palestine Economic Policy Research Institute (considered low by its authors), between 110 and 224 million dollars annually were lost to the occupied territories' budget from 1979 to 1987, in taxes, import duties, and other payments on commodities consumed by Palestinians—all of which funds remained in the Israeli treasury.[6] The World Bank also addresses the issue: "First we will try to estimate the magnitude of the taxes paid by the residents of the Occupied Territories and which do not accrue to the budget of the Civil Administration." The report arrives at a figure of NIS 400 million for the year 1991.[7]

Then the report presents Israel's response to these claims: "Second, we present the estimates by the Israeli authorities of the benefits accruing to the Palestinian residents of the Occupied Territories from interaction with Israel." The lion's share of those benefits—some NIS 1.676 billion annually—falls under the rubric "Expenditures on Security."

According to the Israelis, under international law, the occupying power may require the local population to defray the cost of governing it. Since the Intifada, the costs of security operations have increased sharply. The expenses incurred by the Israeli army in connection with the uprising amounted to NIS 600 million annually. Additional expenses not associated with the uprising and expenses incurred by other security organizations have brought the total security expenditures to about NIS 1 billion annually in recent years.

In other words, Israel claimed that the Palestinians benefited from money spent to suppress the uprising but were not being asked to bear the cost themselves—or, as it was ironically observed in the Strip, "Our taxes are paying for the bullets and the tear gas."

Additional benefits to Palestinians in the occupied territories are listed thus:

> Use of Roads. There are 150 kilometers of roads in the Occupied Territories whose construction has been financed by the Israeli budget at a cost of NIS 500 million. The annual cost of capital is 8 percent and the volume of traffic of Palestinians using them is estimated at 80 percent of total use. The value of their annual use by Palestinians is estimated at about NIS 30 million. Using the same methodology, the annual value of the use by Palestinians of Israel's road network of 15,000 kilometers had been estimated at NIS 180 million (assuming Palestinian use is about 5 percent of total use).

> Movement of Manpower. Each day about 120,000 workers from the territories enter Israel and about 80,000 of them are employed on a regular basis. According to the Israelis, in effect, the export of labor services from the territories represents the import of unemployment into Israel. Assuming the rate of substitution of workers from the territories for Israelis is two to one, payment of unemployment benefit to some 60,000 persons arises from the export of unemployment from the territories into Israel. The resulting cost to the Israeli budget is NIS 90 million annually.

The Israeli response failed to weigh these expenditures against the profits made by Israeli employers from the use of cheap Palestinian labor. Indeed, the new source of cheap labor was one of the primary components in the massive economic boom Israel experienced throughout the 1970s and 1980s. This analysis also ignored the fact that Israeli workers have generally refused to do the kind of menial jobs assigned Palestinians. Last, the Israeli government itself made the decision to open its borders to workers from the occupied territories; its objective was to create an economic dependence that would forestall the territories' eventual political separation from Israel.

There is more:

> Benefits from Israeli-subsidized Goods. Goods that are subsidized by Israel are also available to the residents of the Occupied Territories. Subsidies on basic commodities and agricultural produce amount to about NIS 1.2 billion annually in Israel. Assuming that the residents of the Occupied Territories consume about 5 percent of such goods the benefits accruing to them are estimated at NIS 60 million annually.

Note, too, that the occupied territories constitute the second-largest market for Israeli products.

> Technology and Know-how. Expenditures on research and development in Israel are estimated at NIS 1.2 billion annually, and the benefits to the residents of the Occupied Territories from Israeli R&D was estimated at NIS 40 million annually.

The report summarizes various other benefits that Israel included in its calculations: subsidized health services, use of sea and airports for international trade, agricultural subsidies, and income tax credit point entitlements. This section of the report concludes that the direct, nonsecurity-related transfers of revenue to the occupied territories amounted to 2 percent of the Palestinian GDP, while lost revenues— those that remained in Israel—amounted to 8 percent of the GDP.

The economist Samir Abdallah, a resident of the West Bank, participated in the Oslo negotiations and went on to head PECDAR (the Palestinian Economic Council for Development and Reconstruction), among whose tasks was the coordination of economic rehabilitation under Palestinian self-rule. Reviewing the figures, he found that between 1967 and 1994 Israel had invested an average of $15 per capita annually in the Strip's infrastructure. The corresponding sum within Israel: $1,000 per capita.

The civil administration's expenses were largely funded by taxes collected from the local population—at least 70 percent of its budget, in fact. The rest was financed by transfers from the state treasury, drawing on a small percentage of the monies drained off through various fiscal leaks, not all of which have been mentioned here. The budget itself covered only the administration's operating costs and the salaries of the 200 or so Israelis and 7,000 Palestinians employed mainly in education and health care; it was hardly sufficient to prevent the disintegration of what little infrastructure existed, let alone to finance development or expansion. Ephraim Kleiman, a Hebrew University economist who specializes in the occupied territories, attests that "Israel has invested almost no money of its own in the development of the economic infrastructure in the territories in general and in Gaza in particular. Any investments have been financed from the local population's tax revenues and put into building institutions, not physical infrastructure."[8]

Living in Gaza I had firsthand experience of the real-life implications of Samir Abdallah's statistics and Ephraim Kleiman's observations: the endless power outages when the temperature outside soared over a hundred, the trickle that passed for a shower, and the foul-tasting water from the kitchen tap. Like every other Gazan, I learned the negligible place of the individual in the occupation's thinking. But unlike other Gazans, I had my weekly return to Tel Aviv, where such luxuries as bountiful running water, paved sidewalks, and a telephone that did not suddenly die for no reason gave me a standard of comparison they lacked.

In 1996, just before the first Palestinian elections—for me a time of frantic reporting—I had two days' grace when my telephone began working again after months of silence. For two glorious days I savored the pleasure of making calls from home. But on the third day, I woke up to the wind tapping on my windows and a dead telephone line. Of the eight months that I lived in this particular Rimaal apartment, four were spent without a working telephone, one more daily reminder of the paltry dollars-per-capita expenditure on infrastructure in Gaza. If it was not the rain that was at fault, it was an expensive cable that had been damaged, and there was no money to buy a new one from Israel. When the telephone was working, the connection was staticky and noisy. The great technological advances touted by Israel in the World Bank report did not seem to have improved telephone service in the

Strip: the antiquated manual switchboards were replaced only in 1992, and to this day, one sees exposed wires hanging overhead, the scant cables dangling in the streets. Just try to get a line during morning hours.

Still, I had it easy. My friends in Jabalia ordered a telephone in 1982 and were still waiting fourteen years later. In 1991, Israel had one telephone for every two people; in Gaza there was one for every fifty.[9] By the beginning of 1995, there were 22,000 telephone lines in Gaza (serving a population of one million). As for trying to do business, 1,040 out of the 1,909 commercial firms in the Strip (54%) were without telephone service at the end of 1992.[10]

Like everyone else in Gaza, I learned to manage without a telephone and even to accept the breakdowns with a patience bordering on apathy, to trust fatalistically that, one way or another, things would work out. As long as I had a car, I could get to a working telephone—that is, if I remembered to watch out for the craters in the roads, the puddles that were too deep to navigate. I kept track of who among my friends had a functioning telephone and which of them I had not bothered too much recently: could I go to the taxi station in Jabalia or should I call on the woman who was at home on maternity leave? I rotated among my friends at the human rights center, people I knew at the Information Ministry, and another woman journalist, when her phone was working. My forced expeditions served at least one good purpose: my car and I, especially the tires and exhaust pipe, became intimately familiar with the condition of Gaza's roads.

When Gaza City's chief municipal engineer, Zaher Kheil, was appointed to his post in August 1995, he found that not one section of the city's four hundred kilometers of roads, major thoroughfares, and side streets was in good repair. By the winter of 1996 the municipality had completed basic restoration of a mere fifteen kilometers of road, a laborious task that included installing a new sewage system and storm sewers, laying pipes, paving the road, and constructing sidewalks. The multiple potholes in the roads had accelerated the wear and tear on the infrastructure and on the vehicles that traveled those roads. After years without upkeep, the system was ruined. The World Bank states:

> The physical condition of the roads serving the Palestinian population has deteriorated to the point where the assets will be lost unless

immediate attention is taken to rehabilitate them. . . . In terms of the ratio of the length of the road network to population (a standard comparative indicator for determining the degree of access provided by the existing road facilities), the accessibility of the road network in the Occupied Territories (1.2 km per 1,000 population) is less than elsewhere in the region, with the exception of Egypt—1.4 for Jordan, 2.0 for Syria and 0.6 for Egypt. By comparison, Israel, which has a greater per capita GDP, has nearly two and a half times the road network of the OT per 1,000 population—2.75 km compared to 1.2 km.[11]

On the day before the Palestinian elections I had resigned myself to the idea of covering the event without a telephone, when my car would not start. I had parked it outside the Rashad al-Shawwa Cultural Center, where Jimmy Carter—the most prestigious observer flown in to oversee the elections—was holding a press conference. When I came back to the car, the motor refused to turn over. I groaned, remembering the huge puddle by the YMCA, two streets from my house. It had looked shallow enough until I was halfway through it.

With the help of passersby I managed to get the car to a gas station on the edge of al-Shatti refugee camp. The men at the gas station were engrossed in their election pool, but they offered me coffee and immediately switched to Hebrew when they learned I was Israeli. "So, how are things over there?" they asked (all of them had once worked in Israel). "What do you think of the peace? Will they open up Erez so we can leave the Strip like normal people?" Within thirty minutes the gas station crew had mobilized what seemed like half the refugee camp, including an electrician and some mechanics. The one good thing to come out of the budgetary inequities and lack of development in Gaza was that everyone had become a garage mechanic.

The rain fell steadily in the darkness, but by the light of a neon lamp brought over by one of the station crew, the electrician fixed the problem in my car. Fifteen minutes later, the car was moving and a crowd of refugees was waving me good-bye. "See you soon, all the best," they called out in Hebrew. All that day, Israeli radio had broadcast dire warnings: any Israeli traveling in the territories on election day was taking his life in his hands.

Had I been driving on a "Jewish" road, one leading to the settlements, my car would not have broken down in the first place. As a rule, the settlement roads are of much higher quality than others in the Strip. Over several years, however, the few sections of these roads that were open to Palestinians had gradually been forbidden to them in response to attacks on settlers and soldiers, so the local population was forced to resort to back routes that were all but impassable. From the World Bank:

> Since 1967, investments in transport infrastructure have been primarily designed to: (i) increase Israeli security; and (ii) incorporate the Israeli settlements in the OT with the Israeli economic and social structure. These policy objectives have resulted in the construction of modern and high-standard roads linking the settlements with major centers in Israel, often bypassing the Palestinian cities, towns, and villages. On the other hand, the road networks serving solely the Arab population have been largely neglected. As a result, two weakly connected road networks have emerged serving two sets of distinct transport demands. Even though the roads linking the settlements can also be used by all, those used exclusively by the Palestinians . . . are inadequate to meet the needs of the OT's economic development efforts.[12]

Although the Israeli government ignored Gaza's need for telephones and usable roads, it did introduce indoor plumbing and electricity grids to much of the Strip. In the refugee camps people still speak of this act appreciatively. Nevertheless, Gaza remains dependent on the Israel Electric Company for its electricity, which the company supplies in bulk to the municipalities and other governing authorities; they, in turn, collect payment from the consumers. But the system is woefully inadequate. Instead of an electricity grid capable of supplying more than 3,500 kilowatt hours per capita annually, as in Israel, 400 kilowatt hours per capita annually is a representative figure for the electricity supplied in the Strip, according to Ezra Sadan.[13] Frequent power outages, the absence of transformers, and the lack of a high-voltage system mean operating on anywhere from 120 to 180 volts rather than the standard 220—a problem especially for factories dependent on a steady flow of electricity. Two years after Sadan's report, the World Bank calculated the average annual electricity supply per capita for Gaza and the West Bank at 679 kilowatt hours, which it ranked as "low compared to countries of similar income levels: Egypt 815, Columbia 1198, Jordan 1054, Tunisia 615, Syria

699, Turkey 893, and Zimbabwe 891." The World Bank offered this explanation:

> The basic reason for the poor state of the infrastructure sectors and the inadequacy of the services provided is related to the governance of the OT. First, the institutional structure to formulate, implement, and manage investments is inadequate, and Palestinians are only weakly involved in the decision-making process. The lack of an effective mechanism for responding to the wishes of the population has resulted in formulation of policies and investments that do not serve the needs of the OT well.[14]

Of all the inadequacies of Gaza's infrastructure, perhaps the worst is the poor quality and irregular supply of running water. "Oh, there's no sweet water," my friends would say, offering coffee instead of tea. At first I was nonplussed but within a year I was saying the same thing. The tap water in most Gazan homes is salty and the bad taste is more noticeable in tea. Even the "sweet" water, though, is contaminated with sewage—causing, at the very least, intestinal trouble. Anyone who can afford a substitute finds one.

Foreigners with sensitive palates and stomachs—diplomats, UN staff members, American and European economic advisers—buy bottled mineral water. Local people, however, are happy just to find sweet water and often travel to relatives or friends supplied from wells where the water table has not yet fallen below sea level and the water is free of sea salt. In 1996 the Gaza City municipality installed public taps in several neighborhoods, including one at the corner of my street. These taps deliver salt-free water, and all the neighborhood children are sent to them, the small ones carrying large plastic bottles, the big ones lugging yellow or green jerricans; they fill the containers and return home with water that is good for brewing tea. Families that don't have lucky relatives or public taps in their neighborhoods or that can't afford special trips to a source of sweet water—that is, most families— risk the unsanitary water from their taps or drink very little (the reason, I think, why so many people in Gaza have constant headaches). A report compiled by the European Community found that the amount of chloride in Gaza's water exceeds 200 milligrams per liter (the upper limit permissible in drinking water) throughout most of the Strip. The chloride levels range between 200 and 1,000 milligrams per liter, and in the eastern part of the Strip they exceed 1,000.

Israel explains the problem thus: when it occupied the Gaza Strip in 1967, it found a water delivery system that was already in a state of deterioration. After 1948, when the tide of refugees coming into Gaza more than tripled the Strip's population, the Egyptian authorities were in the habit of overpumping from the Gazan section of the coastal aquifer, the Strip's only source of water. The quantity of water that replenishes the aquifer yearly is estimated at 50 to 70 million cubic meters, not enough to replace the quantity used; since 1948, the deficit has increased yearly by some 30 million cubic meters. After 1967, Israel maintained Gaza's traditional system of private ownership of water rights but instituted a series of prohibitions on well owners— municipalities, local authorities, and private individuals. Much water is wasted because of poor maintenance of the pipes, inadequate storm sewers, and seepage of sewage, but attending to these matters has always been the responsibility of the local authorities, meaning the Palestinians' responsibility. In late 1993, Israel set up a desalination plant in one Gaza town to provide 20 percent of the safe drinking water required by the region.

The World Bank presents an alternative picture, one that more closely resembles the Palestinian view: the failure to deliver adequate services was rooted, among other causes, in "a complex amalgam of several legislative systems, amended by military orders, that is not transparent to all parties, and gives extensive discretion over the application and interpretation of laws and regulations to the CA." Second, "local governments have very limited control over resources, transfer utility revenues to subsidize other services, and have difficulty in collecting revenues in the context of current governing arrangements." Finally, "procedures for selecting investments or external funding by the CA are neither transparent nor predictable, and there is a general unwillingness among the Palestinians to cooperate with the CA." The World Bank is subtly hinting at the civil administration's practice of allowing foreign contributions and investments into Gaza only in exchange for "good behavior." The cumulative effect of the paltry budget and lack of investment has been to cause 40 to 60 percent of the running water in most municipalities to be lost.[15]

I found a more direct formulation in the work of Zaher Kheil and two other Gaza City municipal engineers, who, in 1995, compiled a comprehensive survey of the city's most urgent needs.[16] "Gaza City's development was severely suppressed under the Israeli occupation," they write. "The Gaza City municipal government provided only the most basic services, such as the collection of garbage and payment for water and electricity. It was not allowed to undertake any municipal planning or to contribute to the development of the local economy." Clearly detailed in the same thick volume is a five-year plan for all twelve areas of the city, as well as specific projects for urban renewal and construction, listed in order of urgency: the water and sewage systems, roads, the electricity system, public parks, public buildings. The total cost of the proposed projects is $137 million, "even though real rehabilitation (for Gaza City alone) would require one billion dollars. This is just small change," says Kheil.

The low price tag on many of the projects only reinforces the claims of long-standing neglect. For example, a $35,000 generator would solve the problem at the Sheikh Radwan pumping station, where the water supply is interrupted with every power outage. And $50,000 would buy the Rimaal and Tufah neighborhoods filters to eliminate sand from the drinking water; $21,000 would pay for a 450-meter sewage pipe for the main road connecting Gaza City with Jabalia and would stop the regular sewage floods. Seven different projects, at a total cost of $2.3 million, would significantly improve the city's storm sewer system.

Again, the quality and plentitude of the water increases as one approaches the Jewish settlements. The statistics speak for themselves: Palestinians in the occupied territories receive an average of 93 liters per day per capita (101 liters in Gaza and 85 in the West Bank); Israelis living in the territories receive 280 liters per day. Israeli spokespeople rationalize the gap as the natural outcome of cultural disparities and differences in levels of income. But in Tunisia the daily level of supply and consumption of water is 115 liters, in Jordan 142, in Egypt 230.[17] According to the World Bank, demand in the occupied territories exceeds current consumption levels but is held in check by prohibitions and restrictions on pumping that do not affect the Jews who live there. Nor have Palestinians ever enjoyed the benefit of the water subsidies available to Israelis in general and settlers in particular.

The Palestinians claim that the Strip's settlements are robbing them of a significant portion of their territory's groundwater, but Israel maintains that it has compensated Gaza by transferring a similar quantity of water from Mekorot, the national water carrier. The Palestinians also charge that Israel diverts most of the surface water that flows in Wadi Gaza for its own use even before the water enters the Strip. In addition, Israel has dug wells adjacent to the 1967 borders (commonly known as "the green line"), redirecting water that would otherwise join the stores of groundwater in the Strip.[18]

Israel has denied these accusations, and the World Bank reports seem to accept its denials. But one fact is clear: Israel has always regarded the Strip's water system as an autarkic, or self-sufficient, entity. The situation is analogous, say, to that of the Negev desert— were that dry, barren region obliged to subsist on the groundwater found there without additional water's being brought in from the Galilee, an area with greater water resources. At no time, either under direct Israeli rule or during the interim period, when the Palestinian Authority was set up, were the Arab residents of the Gaza Strip perceived as part of the general Palestinian population entitled, at the very least, to water resources located in the West Bank. Yet the Declaration of Principles signed in 1993 explicitly states that both sides view the West Bank and Gaza Strip as a single territorial unit in which the Palestinian community lives. By contrast, Jewish settlers in Gaza (like those in the West Bank) enjoy the water from shared Palestinian-Israeli sources located throughout the entire country: the mountain aquifer, which is mainly supplied by rainfall from the West Bank that flows into Israeli territory; the Jordan River; and the ground and surface water of the Gaza Strip. While the aquifers of the West Bank and Israel supply an estimated 580 to 830 million cubic meters annually, West Bank Palestinians consume between 110 and 133 million cubic meters of that water, or only 15 to 20 percent of the supply originating in the region.[19] The rest is transferred to Jewish settlers and residents in Israel. In other words, the whole country's water supply is considered a common, shared resource for Israelis, but when Palestinian consumption is at issue, the 1967 borders are suddenly reinstated and those same common resources are off-limits to Gazans, who are expected to subsist on the limited supply from the local acquifer.[20]

The inequitable standards of water allocation were governed by the same logic that was applied to the territories' working budget. On the one hand, the West Bank and Gaza Strip were seen as separate, self-contained units that had to finance their ongoing expenses and development independently, out of "internal" revenues; that is, Israel recognized the 1967 borders when it came to Palestinian needs. On the other hand, the borders dissolved and the occupied territories became an integral part of Israel when Israeli—or rather, Jewish—needs were at issue: "outgoing" resources and monies such as customs, duties, VAT, and income tax flowed straight into the Israeli treasury. From the Palestinian point of view, this logic was at work too when Israel opened up the occupied territories to Jewish settlements. The settlements demonstrated to the Palestinians that the land on which they lived was a common resource that Jews were permitted to exploit at will but that they themselves were not free to develop. Conversely, land under Israel's sovereign legal jurisdiction—within the 1967 borders—was a resource belonging to Israelis alone.

After the transfer of authority in 1994, some of these distortions were eliminated: the Palestinian Authority's budget was based in part on taxes and duties that had previously gone to Israel. But in regard to water resources and land reserves—two substantive issues directly affecting the future development of Palestinian society—Israel changed its basic approach not at all, and the discriminatory logic remains in force. The past is the present for the million Gazans living in the narrow strip of land allotted them by history. Resolving the land and water disputes has been left to the negotiating committees, and any final agreement will reflect the relative strengths of the negotiators, not the application of universal justice.

By virtue of their very existence, the eighteen Jewish settlements in the heart of the Strip perpetuate all the forms of dispossession and discrimination Palestinians have experienced daily since 1948. The five to six thousand Jewish settlers, living in affluent homes—well-tended, spacious, and lush—a stone's throw from the cramped, dismal refugee camps, only serve to intensify the continuing sense of injustice and the longing for land lost in 1948. Moreover, they embody every aspect of Israel's policy of separation in their separate budgets, roads, water, laws, and historical rights. A Fatah loyalist from the Khan Yunis refugee camp, whose family was expelled from Beit Daras village (today the Israeli Beit Ezra), once asked me, "How is it that I don't have the right to return to my parents' land while a French Jew can come and live right here, beside me?"

The settlements are concentrated in two main areas: in the northern

Strip near the 1967 border and in the Mawassi area (the Katif Bloc, to Israelis), a lovely place of sand dunes, rich in water and perhaps the most beautiful spot in the Strip. Three isolated settlements outside these blocs—Morag in the south, Kfar Darom in the center, and Netzarim, just south of Gaza City—have compelled the Israeli government to build new bypass roads through Palestinian agricultural areas or to limit Palestinian traffic on the existing roads. Each of these settlements has no more than two hundred occupants.

Altogether, the settlements and Israeli roads cover twenty-eight square miles—19.36 percent of the total area.[21] In other words, a fifth of the Gaza Strip is restricted, in this post-Oslo era, to one-half percent of the people who live within its borders. Put differently, one-fifth of the land is designated for the use of Jews only.

Many is the time I have seen the scattered, glittering lights of Mawassi from the cramped home of refugee friends. Sometimes when the power has been shut down we have sat shrouded in darkness, and the sense of discrimination has become as tangible and powerful as night and day. Several hundred Palestinian families have long lived in the Katif Bloc area and earn their livings from agriculture. Even today they are forbidden to hook up to the electric grid and are obliged to make do with private generators or candlelight. Once, when Palestinian vehicles were still allowed on the settlement roads, I drove to the Neve Dekalim settlement after staying with friends in Khan Yunis. My friends had no running water during the day; at night the family would turn on a noisy generator and fill up the tank on the roof—with salty water, which often gave out in the afternoon or slowed to a thin trickle. As soon as I reached Neve Dekalim, I ran to the Regional Council rest room and let the cool, plentiful water run over my hands and face. Sweet and refreshing, the free-flowing water still had an aftertaste, the bitter flavor—I couldn't help but imagine—of apartheid.

Chapter 7

We Are from
the Same Village

Driving along the main market street of Jabalia village, we were forced
to slow to the speed of the rickety donkey cart ahead of us, an assem-
blage of rough wooden boards nailed together and tied to a lopsided
undercarriage. Two or three children wearing shabby coats were sitting at the back facing us, their legs dangling over the edge, swinging
in tempo with the cart, which lurched wildly whenever it rolled
through an especially deep puddle of rainwater or sewage (it was hard
to tell which) or managed to work its way out of a pothole, splashing
mud in all directions. Each bump was accompanied by the shrieking
of the children, who could make anything into a game. They looked at
us and giggled, clearly enjoying their cart's triumph over our car.
Behind the wheel, Abu Ali forgot for a moment that he himself was no
longer a child and set out to pass the plodding cart and its driver, a
stooped, ageless figure wrapped in a djelaba and kaffiyeh, who was
conveying several black-clad women as well, on their way to the city to
sell the sacks of oranges that lay beside them.

The Israeli army still maintained a presence in the densely populated areas but during the daylight hours withdrew from the refugee
camps, so there was a semblance of normalcy. A light drizzle obscured
Abu Ali's field of vision, but even if he'd seen the car coming at us
from the opposite direction, he still wouldn't have been able to resist
gunning his engine, swinging his steering wheel, and forcing his way
up the left side of the narrow street, if only to show the giggling children a thing or two. He was, after all, a thirty-one-year-old man with
two and a half years of prison behind him.

And, of course, the inevitable happened: the two cars screeched to
a halt, bumper to bumper. Behind each of us stretched a long trail of

cars trying in vain to pass the other cars and donkey carts—all because my friend had played the child. Several storekeepers who'd been huddled in their shops because of the rain and the mud came out to help. They weren't very busy anyhow, since few people were buying their wares or the meat that hung from giant hooks in the doorways of the butcher shops. Each shopkeeper offered different advice on how to undo the bottleneck, until one voice rose above the others and above the rising cacophony of car horns. Patiently, one of the men directed us an inch to the right, the other driver an inch back, us two inches more to avoid a bump in the age-worn asphalt, until finally Abu Ali's left hand was almost touching the hand of the driver whose path we'd blocked.

I was ready for a lively shouting match but instead saw the driver and his three passengers grinning from ear to ear. "Where're you from?" he asked Abu Ali, as if to say, "Where were you born that you drive like such a jackass?" "From Simsim," Abu Ali responded, referring to the village where Kibbutz Gvaram now stands. I was confused, since I knew Abu Ali was from a village called Burayr, where Kibbutz Bror Hayil is today. That is, his family was from Burayr; he himself was born in the Jabalia refugee camp but had assimilated all his parents' memories, down to the colors of the wheat and corn, the sight of the plums and oranges and grapes, the smell of the fertile earth. My confusion reminded Abu Ali that I wasn't a native of the camp, where every one of the 80,000 residents knew everyone else, and he explained, "That's Ashraf, and he's from Simsim—that is, his parents are from Simsim, the next village over from ours—and I was laughing at him just as people from Burayr always laugh at people from Simsim, and vice versa. He was trying to say that I drive like an idiot because I'm from Burayr, and I basically told him that only a jackass from Simsim would drive like that."

But Abu Ali was saying something else, too. He was saying, We Gazans continue to hold on to our allegiances to villages we no longer possess, each of us to his own village and to our neighbors in the next village a good mile or two down the road, even if we've been living huddled together in this sea of gray buildings and sandy alleys for fifty years now, forced to stretch our necks for a little bit of open space, for a glimpse of sky.

Later, I'd hear more of the jokes they tell about the people of

Burayr—a southern village near the Negev desert—who speak with a singsong accent. Burayr villagers, in turn, ridicule the Simsim folk, who have always been—they claim—notorious thieves, although they would never dare to steal from Burayr. And everyone grumbles about the city folk from Majdal (now Ashkelon), who still look down their noses at the villagers, all because the Majdalites were businessmen and merchants and had cash on hand at the time of the *hijra*, the flight to Gaza.

Abu Ali and I must have planned a visit to Burayr, his village, at least ten times. Together, we wanted to see if we could piece together the mosaic of memory, the remembrance of houses and fields he'd inherited from his family, and match it with the fields of present-day Bror Hayil. Another trip I'd planned time and again was with Abu Basel and his father, Abu Aouni, who was eighteen when he heard the guns of the oncoming Jewish army and fled Burayr. We wanted to visit the sites of the dozens of Arab villages that once filled the region south of Jaffa. The older man was able to name every last one of them: which village had sat atop that green hill now stripped of all remains or in this innocent field of sunflowers, near that deserted house— so Palestinian-looking—standing alone at a junction, dignified in its desolation.

Gradually my trips to and from Gaza became journeys of discovery, opportunities to chart the invisible map of the southern coast and inland plain. As I met more and more people, my itinerary began to swell with the many place-names that had been wiped entirely off the map of Israel. A second road map began to form in my mind: looking out over the lush hills that draw the eye to distant horizons, I learned to see the vanished landscape of my friends who for half a century now have been packed into the refugee camps of the Gaza Strip.

Burayr was the first of the villages whose loss I personally grasped. It was late March 1993, and I was spending the week with friends in Shabura. One day a sudden curfew caught me at the home of Abu Aouni and his family. We sat in a little yard with an asbestos roof and a concrete floor; a makeshift kitchen, a toilet, and four bedrooms surrounded it, home to Abu Aouni and his four sons, two daughters-in-law, and six grandchildren. An Israeli helicopter circled above us with a relentless, frenzied whirring sound that intensified our feeling of being caged in.

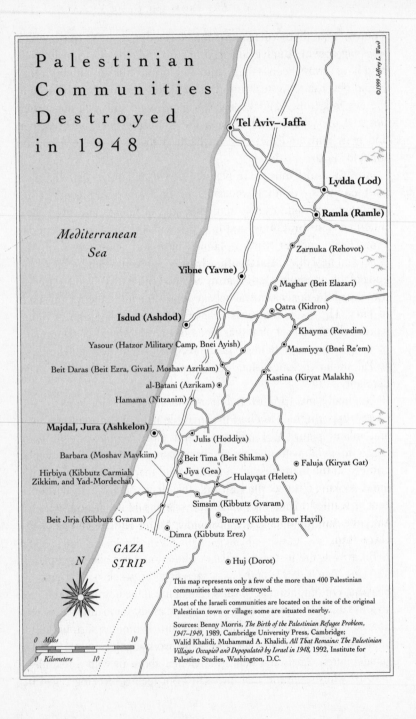

Palestinian Communities Destroyed in 1948

©1999 Jeffrey L. Ward

Mediterranean Sea

Tel Aviv–Jaffa

Lydda (Lod)

Ramla (Ramle)

Zarnuka (Rehovot)

Yibne (Yavne)

Maghar (Beit Elazari)

Qatra (Kidron)

Isdud (Ashdod)

Khayma (Revadim)

Yasour (Hatzor Military Camp, Bnei Ayish)

Masmiyya (Bnei Re'em)

Beit Daras (Beit Ezra, Givati, Moshav Azrikam)

Kastina (Kiryat Malakhi)

al-Batani (Azrikam)

Hamama (Nitzanim)

Majdal, Jura (Ashkelon)

Julis (Hoddiya)

Barbara (Moshav Mavkiim)

Beit Tima (Beit Shikma)

Faluja (Kiryat Gat)

Hirbiya (Kibbutz Carmiah, Zikkim, and Yad-Mordechai)

Jiya (Gea)

Hulayqat (Heletz)

Simsim (Kibbutz Gvaram)

Beit Jirja (Kibbutz Gvaram)

Burayr (Kibbutz Bror Hayil)

Dimra (Kibbutz Erez)

GAZA STRIP

Huj (Dorot)

N

This map represents only a few of the more than 400 Palestinian communities that were destroyed.

Most of the Israeli communities are located on the site of the original Palestinian town or village; some are situated nearby.

Sources: Benny Morris, *The Birth of the Palestinian Refugee Problem, 1947–1949*, 1989, Cambridge University Press, Cambridge; Walid Khalidi, Muhammad A. Khalidi, *All That Remains: The Palestinian Villages Occupied and Depopulated by Israel in 1948*, 1992, Institute for Palestine Studies, Washington, D.C.

0 Miles 10

0 Kilometers 10

So we found an escape of a different sort and talked about the Arab-Israeli wars of 1948, 1956, and 1967.

Abu Aouni was sixty-three years old. Like all the Burayr refugees I've met since, he was tall. At one point in the conversation, he suddenly jumped up from the mattress on which he'd been sitting cross-legged and, his hand to his chest, declared, "The corn we raised was so high it came up to here, I swear it, no kidding." And I remembered: "This high, up to here, no exaggeration," was how my father described the wheat he harvested in his family's fields in Romania before the fascist government confiscated their land, before they were deported to the ghettos of Transnistria. The raindrops beating on the asbestos roof in Shabura reminded Abu Aouni of his rain-drenched land, even now, forty-six years after he'd been cut off from it. His fingers crumbled imaginary clods of earth, and his yearning for the smell of the land meshed with my own memories of my father's stories of his heavy, moist soil.

A year or two later I would meet Ahmad G.'s grandfather, then ninety-three years old, who had owned a fabric store on the main street of Burayr, where the weekly market drew villagers from all over the area to buy and sell. While he was telling his story, I saw in his place my maternal grandfather, sitting in his own fabric shop in the market of Sarajevo wearing his red tarboosh, talking in Ladino with his Jewish neighbors and in Serbo-Croatian with the Muslim, Orthodox, and Catholic customers who were feeling the rolls of cloth or had just stopped by to exchange pleasantries.

"Once the *mukhtar* of Dorot, the nearby kibbutz, came to visit," Ahmad's grandmother told me proudly. Dorot had been built right next to Huj, a friendly Arab village whose friendliness did not prevent the expulsion of its residents in May, 1948. "The man forgot his satchel in the store," she went on. "He came back the next day to get it, without even bothering to look inside." Such was the relationship of trust between us, she seemed to be saying. Her memory, too, blended with my own family memory, that of my grandfather and his sense of integrity, my grandfather who perished in Nazi-occupied Sarajevo: during a period of economic crisis, when the collapse of the banks was bankrupting small merchants like him, he meticulously paid his debts off to the last penny and to the last cotton thread. Once a week, Ahmad's grandfather would ride by mule or camel to the big city, Gaza, and he can still recall the names of the villages he passed along the way—Najd, Dimra, Beit Hanun—just as my father could, to his last day, list the names of the villages he passed as he rode his horse to the regional capital at Suceava.

My parents' sense of longing and loss was passed on to me early in my childhood, and in Gaza their stories seemed echoed in the pain of the Palestinians—in the stubborn way the refugees clung to their lost villages, in the whiff of rusticity that hung even over people born long after the expulsion and the flight. On my way south from Tel Aviv to Gaza, the moshavim and kibbutzim that I passed became markers for the vanished villages that had stood in their place. I would see the destroyed buildings that are still scattered across the landscape and wish for one of my friends who could tell me whom they had belonged to, which village, which family. Three years after moving to Gaza, I was still discovering new villages, the many Palestinian communities that had dotted the country, their inhabitants working the land, making the desert bloom.

The road to Gaza takes me past the turnoff for Yavne, which reminds me of Wijdan's father, who took her there once to show her the site of the old marketplace where he used to go to sell produce. He remembered an immense tree on which the proprietors of some of the stalls would hang their wares—brightly colored scarves and necklaces. Sure enough, the tree was still standing, a nail or two embedded in its trunk. Wijdan's father had once bought a necklace there for her mother, who had died young, leaving Wijdan doubly deprived, an orphan and a refugee both.

A little further south, near Ashdod (or Isdud), is where the village of Hamama once stood. My friend Souad's father came from Hamama, which was famed for its many romances. He once told Souad that the fields and orchards of Hamama (Arabic for *turtledove*) were thickly planted to keep the sands from shifting; there were bountiful olive trees, apricot trees, almond trees, fig trees—and daring lovers would hold hands under the cover of the foliage. Souad herself lived in al-Shatti camp, in a concrete forest with improvised tin fences and alleyways riven by ditches running with sewage. There is no fruit in al-Shatti—most fruit is imported from Israel and is too expensive—but when Souad remembers her parents, I, too, can picture the juicy figs and the apricots, round and golden.

Several miles on and a sign for Ashkelon, once Majdal, comes into view. I think of M., who told me that the Majdalites are terrible chatterboxes. "But my sister-in-law," she said, introducing a young woman of nineteen, "isn't like that. She's more like us from Hamama." I realized that she was right, that all the Majdalites I know—Majdi and his brothers, Um Yusuf and her husband, all born in the camps— were fast talkers, never lost for words, never caught in an awkward silence.

The twinkling lights of Ashkelon are plainly visible from Um and Abu Yusuf's apartment high up in the outskirts of Beit Lahia. "There's our Majdal," they say, pointing to the town of their parents, for they themselves were born and raised in al-Shatti refugee camp. Abu Jamil, only thirty-three, also speaks of himself as a Majdalite. "We were always called the Jews of Palestine because we were so learned. We all finished high school, and students came to Majdal from all over, from Burayr and Barbara and Beit Daras"—which no longer exist. "There was also an agricultural school, and we had no problems with money because we were businessmen." "And you talked a lot," I added.

Where the road narrows, I pass Moshav Mavkiim's general store and roadside restaurant, where we can stop and freshen up. The same building once housed a school, which Ihab al-Ashqar's father, from Barbara, attended. The father was especially proud of the top-quality grapes grown in his village—everyone knew of Barbara grapes, he said, even in Tel Aviv. He also remembered the trees that were planted at the village entrance, eucalyptus and olive trees that grew tall and majestic. "If I could take you there, I could tell you who owns each plot of land," he said, "just from looking at the sabra plants." The road to Gaza is lined with clumps of sabras, standing against a backdrop of tall cypresses or stately palms. For the handful of Gazans who can still travel this road to and from their work in Israel, the sabra plants are an enduring memorial to the Palestinians' presence. After 1967, according to one story, some village elders made the twelve-mile trek from Gaza to their village for the first time since the *hijra*. They returned to al-Shatti and died of broken hearts.

On one of those happy days when Abu Basel could still get an entrance permit to Israel, we made the return trip from Tel Aviv down to Gaza together, on the bus designated for Gazan workers, the only form of transportation they were allowed to use in Israel. Just south of the Bnei Darom junction I noticed a change in his face and his expression turned serious. I asked him what was wrong, but in a way I already knew the answer. "That big tree we just passed, it must've been there long before 1948. My father and the other old people probably walked past it who knows how many times. They might even have played under it. And now the sign says Beit Ezra and Givati. Over there, that used to be Beit Daras. We just passed some Israeli workers walking home through the fields, and it made me think of the people who used to walk home to Burayr through the fields. They must've gotten really tired walking all that way home."

Many years ago, Ismail Saleh's father begged his son to take him back to their village of Hulayqat. The British-Iraqi Petroleum Company had once drilled nearby, looking for oil. In his meager refugee house, Ismail joked with me: "They actually found some oil on our land. Imagine, we could have been rich."

Ismail hired a cab and went to Hulayqat with his father. "It was the first time I'd gone there," he said. "I didn't even know where Hulayqat was. They told me it was east of Ashkelon, but I didn't know the place. My father said, 'When we get there, I'll know it. I'll know where our house used to be.' And then, in the middle of nowhere, he told the driver to stop and we got out of the cab. I took his hand and we walked for fifteen or twenty minutes. All of a sudden he said, 'The gate to our house was right here.' I looked around and saw nothing, only rocks and clumps of sabras in the distance. 'How do you know?' I asked him. He pointed to a tree stump and said, 'That's the mulberry tree that was next to the house. It was three yards from the gate. When the English ran the oil pipeline through here, I got some cement from the site and built the gate.' I saw nothing but he just knew it was there. He felt it. He dug around a little and, sure enough, there was the concrete post. At that moment I felt as if I'd lived there, too. We went to where the house had stood and he showed me. 'This is where we used to receive guests, this is where I married your mother, and over here your brother almost stabbed your sister. They were about eight or nine at the time.' He showed me my cousin's house, not far from ours. He found the main street, pointing out the different places and describing them to me. There was nothing left, but together we walked around the whole village. It had all gone. There were just rocks and tree stumps. But he knew the whole place, just from the stumps."

Driving along the road from Tel Aviv to Gaza, I gradually became aware of the great void where a thriving community had once flourished, but discovered a facsimile of that community, preserved and nurtured in the narrow Gaza Strip. After the expulsion and flight in 1948, the map of the southern coast and inland—with all its towns and villages—was compressed and transferred in its entirety to the Strip. A little replica of Palestine emerged, and the fact that Gaza was not annexed to Egypt between 1948 and 1967 preserved its refugee character and its people's permanent sense of rootlessness.

Being a refugee, in Gaza as in Syria, Lebanon, and Jordan, means longing to go back home. But being a refugee in Gaza involves several particular elements that make it the most extreme example of Palestinian experience. For one thing, this smallest of territories houses the largest concentration of refugees in the Palestinian diaspora, making it the most densely populated area—more than one million people live in less than 150 square miles. Not even in the West Bank is there comparable overcrowding. Second, the refugees far outnumber the Strip's original inhabitants and their descendents.

As in the West Bank, the people in Gaza became refugees in their own country—some living as close as fifteen miles from the ruins of their homes—and many people say that is harder than being a refugee in a foreign country. But the Hashemite Kingdom's annexation of the West Bank in 1950 made the Palestinians there Jordanian citizens, while Egypt's refusal to annex Gaza rendered the refugees there stateless. This limbo extended to the old families as well—the *muwataneen*, who had been living in Gaza before 1948—casting the whole Strip into legally imposed obscurity.

The tiny ribbon of land was marked not only by the longing for return but also by private and general mourning for the material loss, as well as the spiritual. Along with the grief came poverty, unemployment, and total dependence on the assistance of the United Nations Relief and Works Agency for Palestine Refugees in the Near East

(UNRWA). Rightly or wrongly, the refugees also felt the contempt of the *muwataneen,* which only intensified their sense of alienation. The Israeli conquest in 1967, with its provisions for the occupation of Gaza and the West Bank, isolated them from their people in the other Arab countries. One result was that, even as they continued to yearn for a homeland, they gained a different perception of the Israelis. "We were the first to have normalization with Israel—before any of the Arab states," Ihab al-Ashqar said. For Palestinians in Gaza and the West Bank, Israelis gradually became three-dimensional and human, in contrast to the undifferentiated monstrous image held by Palestinians abroad.

Beginning in May 1948, some 200,000 people living in the south of Palestine had found themselves running to keep ahead of the approaching Israeli army, seeking shelter from its gunfire as it took village after village. They were fleeing from the unknown, convinced nevertheless that in two or three months they would be able to return to their wheat fields, their vines, and their storerooms of flour. Reaching Gaza, they joined its 70,000 inhabitants. By March 1996, UNRWA figures showed the number of refugees and their descendants as having reached 700,789 out of a total population of just over one million.

According to Israeli historian Benny Morris, each village acted as an autonomous unit in 1948.[1] The village as a whole either chose to fight the Jewish army or to attempt to keep the peace with its Jewish neighbors. The village's solidarity was a source of strength but of vulnerability as well, for each village felt isolated in its panic as the war came nearer and rumors spread of a massacre in Dir Yassin and the military might of the Jews.

Everyone who remembers or has heard about the frantic flight paints the same picture. Mothers carried babies, while grandmothers held the other children. Whoever could manage hauled a sack of flour on his back or the remains of that day's bread. Although each community seemed to be making a careful, autonomous choice when the villagers fled to the hills or to Majdal and other areas under Egyptian control, they were in fact all bit players in a much larger political and military endgame, one over which they had no control. Morris notes that the villagers in the south fled their homes only after they or their neighbors were attacked; moreover, the army never hid its intention to drive the inhabitants out, and on a few occasions they were expelled by force.

With their characteristic tenacity and dedication, the villagers sought one another out in the tent camps of the Strip, until the old neighborhood took shape in their new location, reproducing the same divisions and loyalties as before: here was Zarnuka, and there Yavne, and over there Bir Salam and Burayr, lasting memorials to the places that once bore those names. Thus hundreds of villages defied their destruction long after the Israelis had demolished the inhabitants' empty houses or settled Jews in them, harvested the crops or set them on fire to prevent the refugees from returning to reclaim their land.

Hirbiya is now Kibbutz Yad-Mordecai, Kibbutz Zikkim, and Kibbutz Carmiah; Dimra is Erez; Huj, Dorot; Nabi Rubin, Palmahim; al-Hima, Revadim; Najd, Sderot and Or Haner. Al-Batani is next to the Azrikam and Beit Ezra moshavim; Jura has been swallowed up by Ashkelon; Yasour is the Hatzor army camp. That is to list just a few of the names that come up in the course of ordinary conversation. Even if most Gazan refugees are now ready to accept the political consequences of losing their land, emotionally they will always see the villages as home.

Not everyone, though, has reconciled themselves to those political consequences. For example, forty-year-old Um Saber is an enthusiastic Fatah supporter who nevertheless has conflicting feelings about the Oslo Accords. For her, the pain of being uprooted is exacerbated by the proximity of her village, Burayr: "The village is right there before our eyes, but we can't go and see it. How would you feel in such a situation?" She went on, "In my soul I always hoped to go back. We grew up knowing that we had property there. And here we had nothing. Of course, we were always thinking about liberating Palestine because we are Palestinians, not Gazans and not West Bankers. Gaza is a city in Palestine. So is Majdal. Isdud, Faluja, Burayr, Beit Daras—they're all Palestine. Israel is Palestine. Tel Aviv isn't really called Tel Aviv. There isn't a single Israeli who's really Palestinian; they all came from Germany, from Europe, or from Sarajevo, like you. We're Palestinians and have to think of liberating all of our country. Look, we held out our hands in peace, we want to live in peace. But Israel refused. Israel's the one dragging its feet. It won't let the prisoners go." By peace, Um Saber meant establishing a state in Gaza and the West

Bank, a state alongside Israel. But in her heart, she is unable to give up on all of Palestine. "I don't buy this peace," she said. "This situation has been forced on us." Um Saber's younger brother joined in. "When I was able to work in Israel, I always went past our fields, and I'd think to myself, What did we do to deserve this?"

When Ismail Saleh spoke of visiting Hulayqat, he said, "I felt as if I belonged there, in a place where I never lived. It's a strange feeling, as if I have no place here. When I was abroad, I didn't think about our village. I always thought about Gaza and the children and the family. Politically I've made my peace with what's happening today and hope there'll be two states that will coexist." I asked him how he felt about one state for both peoples. "I hope for it, but I know the Israelis and I can't imagine that they would share a state with us."

The enduring sense of connection to the village and the family home cuts across all political divisions and affiliations. Hamas and Fatah members alike identify with their villages of origin. Ismail Haniye, a Hamas man—from Jura—planned to tell his children all about their land as soon as they were old enough to understand. But a fellow Hamas activist, Said al-Siam, whose family is from the same village, is less resolute. Neither he nor his father has talked to his children about their land "because it is the past," Siam said. "There are things that are gone and will never be again." When I asked him whether he hoped to return to his village, his father waved away the idea as a lost cause.

In the years that I've lived in Gaza, not a day has gone by without someone mentioning his house or the number of acres that his family had or the size of his village. In Barbara, 2,500 people lived on 3,500 acres; 2,750 lived in Beit Daras, which was spread over 4,000 acres; Burayr was the largest, with 11,500 acres for about 2,800 people; the smallest village, Dimra, had 2,125 acres for 520 persons. While I cannot remember whether the bearded young fieldworker at the local health center is a Hamas member, I do know that he is from Beit Jirja, because that is how he introduced himself, testing me, even though I found nothing offensive in his steadfastness and loyalty.

In the Palestinian elections, candidates mobilized their fellow villagers on their behalf. I heard a blacksmith say that he was going to vote for Marwan Kanfani "because he's one of ours." I was surprised, because the blacksmith came from Jaffa while Kanfani's family came from Acre. No matter—there was no community of ex-Acre people in the Strip but there were many former Jaffaites, and Kanfani's father had often done business in Jaffa. On the other hand, a candidate from Burayr, S.B., the optimistic *Mapainik kedainik*, went around sullen and ill-tempered because the other Burayr villagers had not rallied behind him.

In time, I learned to connect family names with specific villages. I said, "You're from Beit Daras, aren't you?" when I met Fayez Abu Shamalla, a founder of the Palestinian peace movement and now deputy mayor of Khan Yunis. He answered with a glimmer in his eye. I discovered that Kastina and Masmiyya and Julis are more than just the names of highway junctions in Israel. It turned out that the Mohana family, whom I had come to know, once owned the gas station in Masmiyya, where I sometimes stopped. Today several of the sons own a successful contracting firm in Gaza.

I once overheard a conversation between a commander in the new Palestinian security force and a civilian clerk who recorded goods entering and leaving the Strip. "Where are you from?" the officer asked the clerk. "From Dimra," he replied, even though he actually lived in the Jabalia refugee camp. "And you?" the clerk asked the officer. "Al-Batani," he answered, even though he lived in the al-Boureij camp. Both the men were born in the Gaza Strip and knew of the villages only from their parents and grandparents. But in mentioning the names, the two took their place in an essential human chain that challenges history and defies the passage of time with an individual and collective inner truth that refuses to die.

One autumn afternoon, while resting on Abu Aouni's roof, I learned how family traditions, transferred from the fields of a farm to a concrete rooftop, help preserve the flavor of the village, pass on an agricultural heritage, and halt the passage of time. I was woken from my siesta by the sound of little feet dancing on the bare concrete steps that climbed up from the floor below. The children wanted me to get up, jumping on me with delight, thinking they had finally found someone to play with them. But then the rooftop began to fill with adults as, one by one, they came up the staircase. Someone carried a large roll of plastic sheeting, someone else brought two big containers, a younger brother hauled up two pails of olives, and eight-year-old Maha had the honor of bringing salt and an egg, the purpose of which I was about to learn. The entire family had come to take part in the ritual of pickling the olives. Traditionally, olive pickling is a time when Abu Aouni's married daughters come to visit their father and brothers and he can boast about his daughters' beauty. The ceremony is one of the threads on which memories of the village are strung like beads. Each memory represents another longing, another tale of loss and adjustment.

With the children running around us, Abu Aouni, three sons, two daughters-in-law, and I sat down around the edge of the plastic sheet. Muein poured the olives onto the sheet and we all began to pound them with stones and wooden mallets, talking about this and that as we pounded. Meanwhile, Aouni, the eldest son, filled a container with boiling water, added salt, took the egg that Maha was holding so carefully, and launched it into the liquid. The egg sank, then began to circle around an invisible axis. As Aouni added salt, the egg continued to circle but also began to rise toward the surface. "My mother taught me this," he said, in answer to the puzzled look on my face. "When the egg floats to the top, the amount of salt is just right." A lot of chili peppers, garlic, and slices of lime were added to the water, and each container filled with enough olives to last for six months. Once a year the olives were harvested, usually at the beginning of autumn, just after mid-September. In the village, of course, people picked their olives. In Gaza they buy them but pound and pickle them at home. In the village, the work was done in the yard; here at least there was a roof.

Religious customs, family ties, and women's work in the home—all these are bulwarks against the passage of time. And unlike the men's jobs, the women's household chores were never interrupted by curfews or closures or shooting in the streets. Even the rural rhythms of the day have survived the village. In the early evenings, after prayers, the older men—and many of the younger ones who are out of work—go out to the alleyways dressed in white or gray djelabas and, depending on the season, look for a sunny or shady spot. They sit together or alone, on the sand or on a folded mat, and boil tea or coffee on coals burning in a sooty grate. Grandchildren join them for a moment or two and then run off to play. People pass, nodding their heads in greeting, stopping to exchange a word or two: women coming back from market or going to hang the laundry; bored kids on their way to or from a soccer game, mumbling their greetings; schoolchildren on their way back from late classes, bent beneath huge knapsacks. Taking the afternoon rest in public creates an intimacy that is redolent of the village. Cut off from the villages as children, these men still have in their blood the rhythms and cycles of working the land, and for two or three hours a day they elude history and take a rest as if from a hard morning's work in the vineyards and orchards.

I would watch the men gazing into space, at the fine grains hovering in the air, and see in their eyes a near-mystical expectation—a passive hope of external political change that might transform the shape of their lives. It is hard to fathom the source of their passivity—whether it is their religious convictions or their experiences as refugees—but it affects the younger people, too. "I knew the hope of returning wasn't realistic," said Abu Ali, talking of his fantasies of going back to the village. "But it gave me an alternative, a way out of our situation."

Even the architecture of the refugees' world speaks of transience. Their tacked-together, makeshift homes offer little in the way of comforts or improvements. Where space is scarce, however, there is at least room for memory and there are no limits to the dimension of time; the past might be real or beautified, the future more illusory than realistic, but both have the power to transport the refugees out of the present. I made a practice of asking old people what they remember most from the village. In the end, their almost stock reply said more about the present and their hopes for the future than about the past: "Freedom," they said. "Life without fear."

There are those who suggest that UNRWA, the United Nations Relief and Works Agency, has played a part in fostering the passivity that has come to characterize so many Gazans. Established in late 1949 to provide assistance to the Palestinian refugees, it originally operated on the assumption that most of them would soon return to their homes, while others would move to neighboring Arab countries. But circumstances proved otherwise and UNRWA's role steadily expanded from providing basic food and emergency medical care to setting up schools, youth clubs, and regular health services. Gradually UNRWA became the largest employer in the Strip after the Egyptian administration, but its workforce was still not large enough to ease Gaza's unemployment problem significantly.

Following UNRWA a second agency began to function in the camps, the UN Development Program, which invested in infrastructure. The blue UN symbol and the UNRWA buildings, with their turquoise windows and doors surrounded by oleander, honeysuckle, and other well-kept greenery, have become an integral part of the Strip's landscape, as have the UN Citroëns, which dart among the camps, and the several dozen more-or-less devoted foreigners who run the UN's various departments.

It may be that UNRWA's very existence has enabled Israel to avoid complying with the UN Security Council's Resolution 194 of December 1948, calling for the refugees to be either repatriated or compensated for their loss. At the same time, it has perhaps allowed the Arab countries to exploit the refugees' misery in political maneuvering that has led nowhere. Finally, the aid provided by UNRWA may have accustomed people in Gaza both to dependency and to subsistence on the bare minimum compatible with self-respect.

"What should we have done? Let them starve to death?" UN General Commissioner Alter Turkman said angrily in response to my raising these issues. There was some justification for his anger. The Palestinians' natural social fabric, which had evolved over hundreds of years, was destroyed within months of their expulsion. The UNRWA program may indeed have been the only possible way to help traumatized people pick up the broken pieces of their lives and build anew as they underwent one metamorphosis after another: from farmers (for the most part) to unemployed dependents in the period from 1948 to 1967, then to day laborers from 1967 to 1991, and back again to unemployed thereafter. Throughout these changes, UNRWA helped set up youth clubs, sport clubs, clinics, libraries, summer camps, study groups, and soccer teams—all to keep the individual from being forgotten.

First, there was the tent set up by the UN Relief Agency (the precursor of UNRWA) in November 1948. The old people remember head lice and sickness and tramping through puddles. Then came the mud-and-clay huts, followed by grim concrete blocks, and eventually a few rose bushes and some bougainvillea, their rich red and purple blossoms a striking contrast to the endless poverty and grayness.

Under the Egyptians most Gazans were jobless; people passed the time waiting for the miracle that would take them back to their homes, quarreling over UNRWA jobs, finding seasonal farmwork in the Strip. The children went to UNRWA schools and Egyptian high schools free of charge, then on to university in Egypt, also free, where students received living stipends as well. At some point the growing family would add a room, then a makeshift shower in the covered yard, which had been fenced in to create a little privacy. Thus the pathways between the rows of concrete buildings became narrow, claustrophobic alleys.

Early in the seventies, with the Israeli occupation, large numbers of refugee houses were demolished, opening up spacious plazas in the camps. Ariel Sharon, then general of the Israeli Southern Command, had ordered the demolitions to help the army search for wanted men from the Palestine Liberation Army. Sharon succeeded in suppressing that early flutter of resistance, but at the cost of destroying some two thousand houses in August 1971 alone, leaving sixteen thousand refugees homeless, uprooted for a second time.[2] Jamal Zaqut's home in al-Shatti was demolished during that time. The army proposed that his family move to a house in Kalkilya, in the West Bank, that had belonged to wanted men whose families had been exiled to the Sinai desert. Zaqut told me, "My father said to the officer who made the offer, 'Okay, it's a nice place, but I'll move there only on condition that you provide me with fourteen soldiers on guard round-the-clock, because if someone took over my house I'd kill him.' "

There is another roof on which I like to relax, at Ihyam's home in Jabalia (though through the memories of her parents it is in Burayr, too). Even in the summer there is a pleasant breeze. From the flat concrete rooftop, only the tips of two tall eucalyptuses and the minaret of the mosque are visible. Once, though, we saw a Bedouin shepherd woman dressed in black walking down below, leading several wizened goats, probably on their way back from the green open spaces in Beit Lahia. The sight sparked a chain of memories for Ihyam's parents, who had been five or six years old in May 1948 when their village was attacked.

"It was morning," Ihyam's mother began. "My mother woke me up because of the shooting. We had a big house made of clay, and the goats in the yard began to run around like crazy, back and forth. My father was out working in the citrus groves, and we children stayed inside with my mother. We didn't know what to do. We didn't know what was happening outside, we just heard a lot of noise. We didn't know whether other people were running away. Suddenly my father came back, breathless. He said something to my mother and let the goats out the yard. My mother lifted us little girls under her arms and followed Father outside. We all started walking with the goats toward Beit Tima, probably because there were men there from the Palestinian militia who were trying to defend the village. We left all our things in the house—our clothes, pots and pans, and all the wheat. Once we were settled in Beit Tima, my mother and oldest sister went back to Burayr at night to get the sacks of wheat. During the day my father and the boys went out to pasture with the goats, and my mother and we girls would sit and grind the wheat with a mortar and pestle. After two months or maybe less, the Jews came to Beit Tima and attacked us over and over again. Some people died and whoever was left fled to Majdal, where the Egyptians were."

"There were so many Egyptian soldiers in Majdal," Ihyam's father joined in, "they could have reached Tel Aviv without firing a single shot had they wanted to."

"We were in Majdal for about five months," Ihyam's mother continued. "People kept going back to Burayr. Some of them had hidden gold and went to get it. But we were hungry more often than not, and that's how it was until they attacked Majdal."

Ihyam's father told about the attacks, which began in October 1948. "They went after civilian places so that people would flee. After a week the Egyptians retreated along the coastal road in their vehicles and we followed them on foot, each family with its children and old people, in the direction of Gaza. Some of the people from Burayr had gone straight to Gaza even when the Egyptians were holding Majdal."

"In Majdal, we lived next to a citrus orchard," Ihyam's mother said. "Once a shell landed there and the shrapnel hit the house. A pregnant women was killed on the spot. I saw her die with my own eyes. I couldn't stop crying. All our clothes were burned. My father was praying in the mosque and my mother took me over there and yelled at him. 'What are you doing?' she said. 'You're praying while the house burns down.' We left that same day. We had nothing. Some of the goats had already died from hunger. We took the ones that were left."

Ihyam's uncle Fauzi added his own memory. "Our parents always talked about one aunt whose husband wouldn't leave Burayr. She decided to go back and look for him, but someone from Majdal told her that he'd been killed. She went anyway, taking a big hoe and her younger brother and they walked all the way to Burayr. They found her dead husband and dragged him in a sack to the village cemetery, where she buried him. The Jews saw them and began to shoot. When her father heard what had happened, he swore at her. 'Your husband wasn't the only one who was killed,' he said, 'and you took my only son with you. Why? So that he would be killed, too?'"

Ihyam's mother told how, once in Gaza, she and her family first went to the Khan Yunis camp. Then, when there was a cease-fire in February 1949, they moved to Jabalia, to the *jorn*, an open space where the villagers brought their wheat for threshing. It is now covered with refugee shacks. "We were the first family there and they gave us a tent. Some of our goats died and we sold the rest. After that, each family began to look for relatives so they could all move into the same tents."

"The small tents, about two yards by two yards, were called parachutes," Ihyam's father said. "They were for the small families. Bigger families were given a *jaras*, about four by four. The largest families lived together in a tent called a *kuch*, three and a half by seven for three families. It made no difference whether they were related or not."

"We got two tents," Ihyam's mother said, "until we could start to build. The UN gave us flour. We children didn't understand what was happening. But we heard the adults saying, 'Tomorrow, *inshallah*—God willing—we'll go back to our village. Tomorrow, *inshallah*, we'll go home.'"

"And ever since, their lives have been one long wait for something that gets farther and farther away," Basaam, a son, interjected.

Ihyam's father continued. "At first the adults in the camp would sell their land in Burayr to one another. Whoever had money bought land from someone else. That's also how they arranged marriages: they sold a plot of land so there'd be a bride price, and everyone understood exactly which plot they were talking about."

"Our families bought land just before they fled from Burayr." Ghassan, one of the sons, was speaking. "Mother had five acres and father seventy-five. We were rich, like the effendis here in Gaza."

"In winter, when the wind came up, the tent would blow away," his father said. "We'd find ourselves out in the rain, getting wet and drowning in the puddles."

Uncle Fauzi was born in Jabalia. "After 1967 our oldest brother wanted to go and see Burayr. I was small at the time," he said. "We went together to look for the house. It was the only one made of concrete in the whole village, because our father was an only son and had inherited all his parents' land; they didn't need to divide it up among lots of brothers. So he could lease plots to other villagers and make money. That's how he built a house out of concrete and not clay and mud. In 1974 we took an iron doorpost from the ruins of our house and brought it to Jabalia. We used it for our door here."

The family stayed in the same run-down UNRWA structure for forty years, until 1994; four rooms were joined together in a row like railroad cars, with only one small window to let in a little air. The space was too small for the growing family and their various needs — privacy being one of them — but they only began to break down the walls and dig a foundation for their new three-story house on May 17, 1994 — the very same day the Palestinian Authority took over in Gaza.

There was no money for a professional contractor and construction workers. So the entire Jabalia branch of the Popular Front — friends of the sons and daughters — was recruited for the job, pouring concrete, building scaffolds, moving mattresses and closets and papers from one room to another, building the first new wall, putting up rafters for the ceiling, hacking out openings for the windows, installing the electrical wiring. After all, they had all worked in construction in Israel at some time or other and were now all but jobless. Every time Israel imposed a closure — and who could keep track of how often that had happened — work on the house would stop for a month or two as Fauzi and Ghassan lost their incomes from their jobs in Kastina (Kiryat Malakhi to Israelis). Once there was no money for the doors and windows; another time they couldn't pay for the floor tiles or the electrical wiring.

"Why did you wait until 1994 to begin enlarging the house?" I asked the family. The brothers had been working in Israel for several years and could surely have saved some money. The father's answer was accompanied by bitter laughter. "It took the Oslo agreements to finally convince me that we won't be going back to our village."

Ihyam's father was too young to remember how the men of Burayr tried to fight the Jewish army. But Abu Aouni talked about his village's resistance with pride: "We had weapons in the village, of course; some people had sold their land to buy them. We shot at the Jewish army

convoys that went by on the main road, carrying food to the Negev settlements. Of course we did. They were forced to use a less convenient
route. When the army finally surrounded the village, they left two
escape routes open, to the west and to the south, so that we would flee.
I came back one night a few days later to get some clothes. The road
was covered with bodies and I buried them. I know of forty-five people
who were killed in the battle for the village."

Almost fifty years have passed, but my friend Ahmad's grandmother
still chooses her words carefully. "Our people only shot at the army
jeeps that kept coming to the center of the village. Their engines made
an annoying noise, dr-r-rum, dr-r-rum, dr-r-rum. The soldiers always
had weapons and stopped beside our well. So we shot at them."
Ahmad's grandfather recalls, "On the day they took the village, the Jews
closed in on us on three sides. They left an escape route open to the
south. They wanted us to go that way."

In retrospect, their behavior in 1948 seems absurd to many of the
refugees, and the Zakut family hero is the one uncle who obstinately
stayed in his home, refusing to flee from Isdud. The Israelis forced
him to move to Ashkelon and then to Ramle, where he was put under
house arrest until 1972. "But he is there and we are here." And to this
day S.'s father from Baseet does not understand why he left. "We
should have stood fast," he says, "held on, not given up."

Many Gazans remember the dates of events according to the crops
that were in season. Abu Aouni remembers that the problems started
in Salame (south of Tel Aviv) during the orange season, in December
1947. He left Burayr in the spring, just as the days were getting longer
and the wheat was ready for harvesting. Even though the date of the
attack on Burayr is documented as May 12 or 13, 1948, Ihyam's father
is convinced that his family fled on May 17, the date of the transfer of
authority forty-six years later. His memory has made a mythical connection between times and events, between disaster and disappointment, like the cyclic rhythms of nature.

Certain words, too, have been turned around and become weighted
with significance. The word *hijra*, used to describe the expulsion and
flight from the villages, is also the word for the prophet Muhammad's
journey from Mecca to Medina. According to the historian Albert
Hourani, "The word has not simply the negative meaning of a flight
from Mecca, but the positive one of seeking protection by settling in a

place other than one's own. In later Islamic periods, it would be used to mean the abandonment of a pagan or wicked community for one living in accordance with the moral teaching of Islam."³ But in deeply Islamic Gaza, ironically, the word *hijra* has no positive connotations, except to the extent that it spares the Israeli listener the loaded word *nakba*, or catastrophe, which Palestinians use when talking about 1948.

The word *inside* has also been upended. The land within Israel's 1967 borders, including all the Palestinian cities and villages, is referred to as "inside," partly as a way to avoid saying Israel's name but also because of the geopolitical fact that up until 1967 all the refugees from inside the borders lived outside them. But "inside" remained in use after 1967 and is still the common term, even since the practice of sealing up the Strip became regular policy in 1991. People ask, "When are you going back inside?" or "When are you leaving for inside?" or even "I'd love to get out and go inside with you." In a 147-square-mile ribbon of land with no exit, "inside" has become synonymous with wide-open spaces.

The morning sounds in the camp, too, seem to invert time and events—the muezzin's call to prayer is accompanied by an orchestra of village noises: cocks crow, birds twitter in the few trees that someone planted in his homesickness, doves coo, and as daylight starts to lighten the streets, donkeys bray and wheels clatter over the stones. But when one opens one's door, the sight of the outside world shatters the pastoral illusion. Everywhere is gray: the concrete houses and asbestos huts and crowded tin-roofed shanties, fenced off with whatever junk is at hand. Concrete blocks and other objects are strewn across the tin roofs, sometimes for lack of storage but usually to keep the roofs from blowing away. Narrow alleys seem to buckle beneath the weight of the buildings heaped up on either side; they spill onto the main road, which is clogged with street vendors and old, smoking cars, crowds of pedestrians, ramshackle stands offering inferior fruit and vegetables, peddlers frying falafel for half a shekel, a few grocery stores selling canned goods and cookies.

In many places water flows through the pipes only six hours a day or less—brackish water, in a weak stream and with a strong odor of chlorine. In 1996, only 27 percent of the camps' houses were connected to sewage systems, compared with 40 percent outside the camps. But everyone pays great attention to keeping the camps clean. It is

UNRWA's job to collect the garbage and the alleyways are swept spot-
less, as are people's yards. Little wonder—without some order the
camps' overcrowding would be intolerable: approximately half the
refugees in the camps live three or more to a room.

There are eight camps in the Gaza Strip, and some 393,000 human
beings, 55 percent of the refugees, make their homes in them. The rest
of the refugees, about 320,000 people, have been scattered throughout
Gaza's old and new residential neighborhoods. In al-Shatti camp on
the outskirts of Gaza City, 186 acres house 66,000 human beings.
Al-Boureij, in the center of the Strip, used to be a British army camp.
In 1948, some of the 13,000 refugees who gathered there were housed
in old army huts, while the rest lived in tents near the camp, on a total
of 132 acres. Today, that number has swelled to 27,000 refugees. The
smallest of the camps is Dir al-Balah, where 18,000 people live in a
tiny area near a town of the same name. The Jabalia camp is the
largest, with 86,000 people on 350 acres. The 52,000 inhabitants of
the Khan Yunis camp live on 137 acres west of the city of Khan Yunis,
which until 1948 was an important commercial center on the trade
route from Egypt to Palestine, Lebanon, and Syria. There are 18,000
people living in the 150-acre Meghazi camp in the central part of the
Strip. In the neighboring Nuseirat camp, 50,000 people are crowded
onto 147 acres. In 1948 the largest group of refugees—41,000—fled to
Rafah, the southernmost point away from the fighting. Today there are
76,000 refugees living in the Rafah camp (which includes the Shabura
neighborhood).

The camps were located next to existing cities and villages, but
close at hand today are astonishing seas of green fields planted with
vineyards and orchards, where generously spreading mulberry trees
invite one to enjoy their shade. These green areas are the only spaces
left, except for the seashore, that offer respite and solace for the eye
and the soul, but most of them belong to a small number of old Gaza
families and are off-limits to the refugees, who pine for the outdoors.
Basaam made his mother, from Qatra (Kidron to Israelis), very happy
when he bought her a small plot of land from one of the Gaza City
landowners. The plot was in a citrus orchard that was no longer profitable. The owner had uprooted the trees and sold plots to people who
had managed to save a bit. Basaam's parents travel there every other
day and lovingly raise fodder, peppers, eggplant, and squash and keep

a few hens that his mother enjoys watching as they peck at the earth—real earth. "This is the first time I've felt happy since we were forced from the village," she says.

With all this, the grimness of camp life seems temporarily suspended when I visit my friends in Jabalia or Khan Yunis or Rafah. In one camp, a friend's little girl loudly announces my arrival and I am instantly surrounded by children, some of whom hang on my car as I try to park it between a heavily laden clothesline and an electric pole tangled with wires. One boy tries to count in Hebrew to impress me; a girl tries to extract a promise from me that I'll spend the night at her house; another child begs me to at least drive her to the seashore.

I quickly forget the oppressive dinginess of the Khan Yunis camp when the older children somehow find a space—at the table, on the floor, leaning over a chair—to concentrate on their books even as the adults' conversation swirls around them. They are not distracted by talk of the elections and campaigns, about a particular candidate's rally where people asked difficult questions. They ignore their parents' boasting about their good grades. The poverty seems far away when Kauthar, having taught school all day, nursed her infant son, fed her other two children, and baked thirty-seven pitas, sits down to pore over *Hamlet* for a course at the Islamic University, "because life cannot be just food and children." Or when Y. talks candidly about how he and others like him who joined the Authority security forces are losing their sensitivity. Or when M. tells me about her frustration with her sisters-in-law, who are satisfied doing housework and waiting on their husbands and children and don't understand that they have to get out and develop their talents. Or when Khalid plays the oud and reads a poem he wrote, the fragrance of coffee filling the air as his elderly father enters the room with a loaded tray, ready to serve his children's guests. How can I think of the sewage flowing through Shabura when Khalid S., an editor of the Gazan literary journal *Al-Ashtar*, tells excitedly about the unpublished stories and poems the journal has received from Iraq, not one of which is written on regular paper? International sanctions have caused such widespread scarcity and poverty there, he reports, that everything came in tiny, cramped, handwritten scribbles on scraps of cigarette packages, doctors' receipts, electric bills.

When the younger refugees talk about their shared upbringing, the uniformity of their experiences reminds me, in many ways, of the stories kibbutz children tell about growing up together. But these children knew they were refugees even before they understood the meaning of the word and before they knew how other people lived. Only refugee children had to go to the communal showers. Until the camps were connected to the water mains and the electrical grid (an Israeli improvement that everyone appreciated), the children would shower in the UNRWA center every Thursday right after school. "There was one Jewish woman there," Fayez from al-Boureij told me, "Um Muhammad, who was married to a Palestinian. She'd scrub us down, all three hundred of us children. She was strong. Afterwards we ate lunch there. And as we left, someone checked to make sure we hadn't stolen anything. I always hid a piece of pita in my sock, a cucumber in my back pocket, a tomato up my sleeve. Um Muhammad pretended she didn't see, but there was another one, a real bitch, who always caught me and pulled my ear."

But the refugees are united by more than hardship and memories. "I'm proud of the refugees," Ihab al-Ashqar declared. "We have a saying, 'I am the shepherd and it is my hand that lifts me up.' It means that I'm independent. Our poverty has made us strong, given us experience, so that nothing can budge us. Remember that we started the *intifada*." Abu Ali also reminded me: "We revolted against the Israeli occupation immediately after 1967." And Fayez Abu Shamalla from Beit Daras, who was the head of the refugee committee in the Khan Yunis camp, the first of its kind, told me, "When I was in prison, I looked into it—only 5 percent of the prisoners weren't refugees. All the rest of us were. The daily poverty turned us into fighters." When Abu Taher introduced his friend N., he was quick to compliment him: "His family's from Gaza, but he thinks and feels exactly like a refugee."

"Where do you get your self-confidence?" I asked my younger refugee friends, those who had been born and bred in the misery of the camps. "I'll explain," said Abu Jamil, the Majdalite, whose middle name is confidence. "My mother always told me that from the very beginning the refugees understood that they'd lost everything and should invest whatever they could in their children's education. And Egyptian policy made it possible. The Egyptians put nothing into infrastructure and most people had no work, but education was free, including the universities. So we were well educated. That began to change in the seventies, when teenage boys went to work in Israel, but then their wages gave them a different kind of confidence and our parents carried on seeing that the other children still got an education."

Jamal Zaqut studied at the Falastin High School in Gaza City with the children of well-to-do established Gazan families. "I was always comparing myself with them and, along with our tough living conditions, that gave me the incentive to do well. The Egyptians wouldn't let us build toilets and bathrooms in our homes, and I still remember lining up to use the communal facilities in al-Shatti camp. It was that kind of thing that made me feel I had to be the best at everything. I'll never forget how the rain leaked through the roof. I'd wake up every night with my pillow soaked. So I decided to do whatever I could to live like a human being. I always tried to wear nice clothes, and I remember my father, who worked for UNRWA, had his own austerity program. For half the year he'd stop smoking so he could buy us new clothes for school. He wanted us to feel we were as good as our classmates."

Basaam's mother raised seven children in two rented rooms that were leaky and cold in winter and sweltering in summer. "We invested in the children," she said proudly. "The children are our house." Now one of her sons is a doctor, her daughter is a poet, and her youngest son is interested in sociology. S. was the first girl from Rafah to study law in Egypt. Her father insisted on her right to do so, even though everyone around him thought she should just get married. In the 1940s he used to leave Baseet, his village, to work in Jewish-owned citrus groves, and he could still repeat in Hebrew what his employers told him back then: "What a pity. Being an Arab doesn't suit you." I sensed that he said this with a mixture of sorrow for the patronizing attitude and pride at having distanced himself from some of his society's constraints and allowed his daughter to develop her talents.

"Thirty years ago there was nothing in the Khan Yunis camp but sand, not even a tree. We went barefoot because there was no money for shoes, and the hot sand burned the soles of our feet," recalled Fayez Abu Shamalla. "Today, despite the crowding and the thin trickle of tap water, every house has a tree, a mint plant, something growing. Until 1955, my two uncles and their wives all lived in one tent, with only a blanket for a partition. Just imagine. And then in the sixties the children left home to study or work. One sent money from the Persian Gulf; another one worked with UNRWA and shared his income."

Ihab al-Ashqar mentioned his uncle who barely managed to graduate from high school and now has business dealings around the globe.

His uncle, he said, was a peasant and a refugee. "These people had nothing, and they built themselves up. What's so hard about becoming a doctor or a lawyer if your father owns land in Khan Yunis? But someone whose father had nothing and who still becomes a doctor or an important businessman—that's an independent person."

"The absence of basic human rights," summed up Ismail from Khan Yunis camp—and from Jaffa—"made every one of us thoughtful, serious, a person who holds out for change."

Other emotions, of deprivation and regret, accompanied the refugees' feelings of self-confidence and pride and their sense of mission. "I don't feel that I had a childhood," thirty-three-year-old Ashraf from the Jabalia camp, a member of a Bedouin family from Beersheba, once told me. "We never really laughed, we didn't really play, we didn't just live like children are supposed to. And after 1967 many of us boys started working in the summers in the Tel Aviv or Beersheba markets or in the fields of the moshavim." Saber remembers asking his parents when he was twelve, "Why did you have me? It would've been better if I'd never been born." At university, Basaam from Saja'ya liked to read Nietzsche with other refugee students. "He suits our situation. He's so full of despair." Ihab al-Ashqar's mother assured me that, no matter how much I wrote, I wouldn't have enough words to describe the refugees' pain. "We always have the sense of having lost something," said H., a twenty-nine-year-old mathematics teacher from Lod, an observant Muslim who was born and raised in al-Boureij. "We lost our self-confidence," she explained, though my impression had been otherwise. But the refugees always compare themselves with the native Gazans, the *muwataneen*. "They just haven't been through the same losses that we live with all the time," said H.

Abu Majed's home is in Gaza City's Nasser neighborhood, where refugees and *muwataneen* live side by side. Four years ago, his daughter reached school age and was about to start at the UNRWA school for refugees. "We'll be able to walk to school together," she told a friend happily. The friend, the daughter of *muwataneen*, replied haughtily, "No, we won't. You're a *mehajera*, a refugee. You have to go to school in the camp." "That was the first time she'd heard the word," Abu Majed said, "and she came to ask me what it meant. She thought the girl was cursing at her. I told her that it's an honor to be called a refugee. It means that we left, but we have land in Beersheba and her grandfather and parents used to live there. I'd always hoped that I wouldn't have to tell her and now she keeps asking me when I'll take her to Beersheba. Sometimes we feel like the Gypsies in Europe, like people without respect. If one of us wants to marry a Gazan girl, the first thing they say is that he's a refugee. That hurts."

Thirty-year-old M. grew up in the Khan Yunis camp. "Whenever I went to the market with my mother, she'd point out the border between the camp and the city." At the government high school, where refugees and Gazans studied together, M. really began to feel the differences. "We'd go out to demonstrate against the soldiers, but the *muwataneen* kids wouldn't join us. And when we ran into the orange groves to get away from the soldiers, the *muwataneen* chased us away because they were afraid. So I started to think that the city kids were on good terms with the occupation. I developed a prejudice against them, and it was only at university that I found out they felt the same resentment as we did."

During the *intifada*, B. from Jabalia camp (and Burayr) hid illegal leaflets in his house, running out during curfews to distribute them, risking arrest. He remembers how his father would look at him indulgently and sigh when he used to open his door to youngsters who had thrown stones and were fleeing from the soldiers. "Why are you doing all this?" his father would ask. "You know that even if there's any change they'll be the only ones to benefit." B. knew whom his father meant—the *muwataneen*, the landowners, people with property.

One day Fayez from al-Boureij phoned me and poured his heart out. Here was a man who had worked in Israel for twenty years; he had even lived in Tel Aviv for a while. Now he was working for the Palestinian Authority and couldn't get along with a certain high-ranking colleague, one of the *muwataneen*. "I tell you, Amira," he said, "it's anti-Semitism. The way the Gazans treat us refugees, it's just anti-Semitism."

Some of the young *muwataneen* bristled defensively when I asked them about the refugees' feelings. I heard facile nationalistic slogans, especially from landowners and children of the well-off old families. "We're all Palestinians, we all feel the same," they said. "We didn't cause their loss, we're not responsible." But in the same breath, they admitted to never having set foot in any corner of al-Shatti camp, only ten minutes' walk from their comfortable homes in the shade of the poinciana trees.

A friend of mine, one of the established Gazans, spent time in prison with Z., a refugee. "I've never seen anyone eat so much," my friend said derisively, describing how Z. would polish off his cellmates' portions. Later, when I met Z., I asked him to tell me his most potent childhood memory. "The hunger," he said without hesitation. "In the morning we'd be lucky to get a glass of tea. We'd divide up the pitas and dunk them in the tea. At lunchtime my grandmother would cook onion and water and oil and we'd have it with some bread." I felt ashamed of the thoughts I'd had about him.

M.K.'s mother was a refugee, but through family connections M.K. grew up with the village children of Beit Hanun and was spared the refugee experience. She wasn't even aware of the refugees' feelings of discrimination and only began to think about the subject after I kept asking questions. "Imagine," she told me in disbelief, "one of my friends just admitted that until her first year of university she was physically unable to eat or drink anything in refugees' houses. She'd always been told that refugees were thieves and were dirty, not like us."

Poorer Gazans from the older, run-down parts of the city also react defensively. They point out, for example, that the UNRWA schools were much better than the government schools. "We live in poverty and it's overcrowded here too, and we don't have any citrus groves either," said H., a Hamas activist. "But there's no discrimination in our movement, not at any level."

Gaza's marriage statistics, however, confirm the society's segregation of the refugees: the percentage of "mixed" marriages—between refugees and old Gazans—is minuscule. In 1995, there were 8,788 marriages, according to the records.[4] Of those, 45.8 percent represented *muwataneen* couples and 45 percent refugee couples; only 5.1 percent were marriages between refugee men and *muwataneen* women and 4.1 percent between refugee women and male *muwataneen*. And that year actually showed an increase in intermarriage over previous years. In 1992, for example, there were 7,280 marriages and only 6.1 percent of those were mixed.

"We were like peasants," said my friend Abu Basel from Rafah, referring to the fact that the camp was never connected to the Egyptian electrical system. Al-Boureij camp did not have electricity and running water until 1978. "The first day we had electricity we danced under the lightbulb as if it were the sun god," recalls Fayez, who was a teenager at the time. I asked Abu Basel why these modern necessities were so late in coming. "Because there was no money, but mostly because we were idiots," he replied, half in jest and half in self-reproach. In addition to the other privations, the Egyptians did not allow the camps' growing populations to expand beyond the camp's boundaries, lest that be considered a political concession to Israel, an admission of the refugees' permanent status and therefore a relinquishment of their claim to their villages. "Today we curse them and ourselves. The whole area west of Khan Yunis, for example, has been settled by Jews," Abu Basel told me.

During the fifties and sixties the Egyptians even prohibited UNRWA from putting up buildings that could be construed as permanent: concrete foundations and roofs were forbidden, and all construction was limited to single-story structures. Thus the only possibility for expansion was horizontal, toward the street. The refugees themselves opposed any resettlement plan—in Sinai, for example, under Egyptian rule—afraid they would lose the right to return home. Basaam's grandfather, for example, refused to buy land in the Gaza Strip even though he had a little money; he rented an apartment instead. Until his death he remained faithful to the land he had left behind, and thus his family was denied the opportunity to build a real home while they still could, before the price of land skyrocketed. In the end, though, most refugees made some improvements to their homes as the force of events and their own material needs eventually proved more powerful than emotional restraint or the political restrictions dictated by the surrounding Arab countries.

After Israel occupied the Strip in 1967, the idea of going home became more remote, and the refugees' temporary world seemed to be more permanent. As the Israeli borders opened and the Palestinians were sucked into an expanding market for cheap labor, the land they had lost was reachable once more yet less attainable than ever. The unemployed multitude of refugees underwent a process of proletarianization; their wages were at the bottom of the Israeli pay scale and they were exploited more than any other segment of the workforce. But as a growing number of Palestinians became salaried workers, they were able to make more tangible demands not only for the future but also for the present: they could install private showers, hook up electricity, buy refrigerators. At the same time, without seeing any contradiction, they supported the armed struggle, thereby backing the effort to recoup the past.

The Israeli authorities in fact encouraged refugees to move out of the camps to new neighborhoods. Their offer of better living conditions came, however, with a high political price; Israel's clear intention was to wipe out the past. Those who registered for government housing were required to sign a declaration relinquishing their refugee status and any claims that might derive from it. They had to demolish their homes in the camps or pay a fine. In all, the Israeli authorities built twenty new neighborhoods and some 10 percent of the refugees had moved to them by 1989.[5]

Although seeking to lessen the refugees' misery, the Israeli authorities also had other expectations from the new neighborhoods. I remember a briefing that the Israeli civil administration held in the spring of 1992. "Look, we built them the Sheikh Radwan neighborhood and they still turned against us with their *intifada*, they still threw stones at us," a senior official said, with more than a little irritation at the Palestinians' ingratitude. The spokesman had articulated the widespread Israeli assumption that material improvements—limited as they were, relative to the Israeli standard of living—would blunt, if not eliminate, Palestinian national aspirations. Defense Minister Moshe Dayan had been guided by the same assumption—among other considerations—when he opened the borders and the Israeli labor market.

Israel's profound need to rewrite Palestinian history was also evident in the identity cards issued to refugees born before 1948. If the card holder was born in the Gaza Strip, then the space for "Place of Birth" was filled in with the name of a specific town or village, such as Khan Yunis or Jabalia. But if the card holder was born within the borders of what had since become the new Israeli state, then only one word appeared in that space: "Israel." The refugee's place of birth had been erased not only physically but also in the workings of the Israeli bureaucracy. (The new identity cards issued jointly by the Palestinian Authority and Israel replicate this information. Only two elements of the document have changed: the Palestinian national colors have been added, and the Hebrew wording now appears beneath the Arabic.)

According to his identity card, Abu Aouni, who comes from Burayr and lives in Shabura, was born in 1930 in "Israel," a state that did not yet exist. The PLO leader Abu Mazen was born in Safed in 1933; he too was born in "Israel." With a few taps on the keyboard, the Israeli Interior Ministry can enlist every Palestinian refugee in a process that manages to place Israel outside historical time and to divest him of his own history.

In the end, though, it was not political considerations that kept people from moving to the new neighborhoods; experience had taught them to ignore pieces of paper and empty slogans. Relocating simply cost more than most refugees could afford. Refurbishing their current homes was the only option. Legally, the land in the camps was owned or leased by UNRWA, but substantial structural changes in a house required an Israeli permit, and in the early years of the occupation, such permits were rarely given.[6] During the *intifada* years and especially after the 1991 Gulf war, the situation gradually began to change. Some refugees even took the bold step of putting up permanent homes without applying for permits—large, spacious houses, two or three stories high, that stand out as striking exceptions in the landscape of the camps. I do not believe that money alone enabled those few to change their circumstances, while so many refugees seem caught in a time warp.

One day toward the end of the *intifada*, I accompanied Abu Basel on an errand to the civil administration building in Rafah. There were two entrances: one a shady front gate for soldiers and local officials, the other a revolving back door, cordoned off by barbed wire and guarded by an armed soldier, for all other Palestinians. Abu Basel and I went in through the front gate: I didn't know then that there was a back entrance and Abu Basel figured that, if I could do it, so could he. We must have walked in looking quite assured because the soldier on guard did not stop us.

We took our place on one of the benches along with the two dozen other people who had come to take care of bureaucratic business. Armed soldiers paced back and forth outside the administration offices, which overlooked the waiting area. We were obviously in for a

long wait, the usual couple of hours at least. Suddenly someone—a
soldier or one of the clerks—noticed that I looked different from the
other women, dressed as they were in their black djelabas and gauzy
white head scarves, and he came over to check on me. I told him in
Hebrew that I had just come along with a friend and all hell broke
loose. The man ran to an office and hissed whispers at someone
inside. An army officer who had been standing guard, his legs planted
firmly apart, called me over. "There's a problem," he said. "I'm not
sure you're allowed to just wander around Rafah. You should be careful. Now let's see what's happening with your friend's permit." Then
he phoned the army spokesman and was told that I was in fact allowed
to wander around Rafah. "But you're not allowed in here without
clearing it first," he concluded. "Only the locals come in here. And he
should've come through the back door." Still, the officer did let us
leave through the front gate and they took care of Abu Basel's business
in a matter of minutes.

We walked in silence, crossing a plaza swarming with Israeli soldiers and police. Then we reached the Rafah junction and turned
toward the camp's Yavne section, passing a Dumpster overflowing with
stinking garbage on one side, an unidentifiable mound of earth and
stones on the other. An old man was barely dragging his legs across the
broken, cracked asphalt. Abruptly Abu Basel broke the silence. "Don't
think that you're really seeing us. We're just a picture. Inside everything's empty."

I kept turning that sentence over and over; for me it seemed the key
to understanding the complex and often baffling Gazan character. It
explained the contradictions in so many of the people, who were
impulsive yet passive, warm but inscrutable; it explained their sense of
being separate and other and the way they shifted from pride to
despair and vulnerability, from helplessness to faith. Our trip to the
civil administration and Abu Basel's throwaway sentence had shown
me how easily and with what little regard an officer of the occupation
could decide whether one spent an hour or eight hours or three days
waiting for permission to do some ordinary thing. I saw how accepting
the two entrances and complying with all the other rules kindles rage
that has to be suppressed because what matters is getting the permit,
getting a signature from the soldier in charge. I understood how one
never gets used to the barbed wire, never forgets the quiet tremble that

slips into one's voice when one talks to Israelis in uniform. A refugee learns to tolerate greater vulnerability and more suffering so that the lack of autonomy does not paralyze his life and stop him from doing the everyday things that preserve a sense of normalcy: putting the children to bed and checking their bags before school, making sure there is enough flour in the house in case the Israelis impose a curfew or seal off the Strip, taking food to a sick aunt.

I began to see how, consciously or otherwise, Gazans perceive the rifles, the khaki uniforms, and the bulge of pistols in the officers' belts as links in a chain that began with the loss of their villages, the expulsion, and the flight and continued with hunger, poverty, and death. And again and again I found that even people born and raised in the harrowing conditions of the camps, people who have never known anything else, are aware that they are being deprived. It enrages them. "We can endure and even forget our past suffering if we feel that will lead to hope for our future," Jamal Zaqut said when we talked about the Oslo Accords and the widespread Palestinian feeling that the agreement was unjust. Said al-Siam of Hamas could not say that he has accepted the idea of the State of Israel, but he has adjusted to reality. "I don't hate the Israelis as Israelis or as Jews but because they've treated us so badly, because of what the occupation has done to us." Siam felt that Israel first had to recognize that the Palestinians have been wronged. Whether the wrongdoing began in 1948 or in 1967 was not a pressing question for him. "You people still don't acknowledge that the West Bank and the Gaza Strip are occupied and that we have rights. The first condition for change is that you have to recognize the injustice done to us." "We must look for a solution that will stand up to history," said Fayez Abu Shamalla, "a solution that will help us root out the hatred that has piled up in our hearts since the expulsion."

Abu Shamalla and others like him are worried: more than any other element of the confict, the refugee camps embody all the contradictions that demand resolution. But the Oslo Accords were designed to postpone discussion of the most difficult, substantive questions—the fate of the settlements, the refugees, and Jerusalem, the questions of borders and sovereignty. The idea was to approach them gradually, one step at a time, after creating channels of dialogue and understanding. First, confidence would have to be built; Palestinian security forces, for one, would need to prevent terror.

In the wake of the agreements, the Israeli army redeployed in the Gaza Strip and withdrew from heavily populated Palestinian areas; the civil administration gave up direct control over people's lives. These steps were intended to create a conciliatory atmosphere that would help the talks proceed and provide the Palestinians with some training in managing their internal affairs. But in Gazan terms, the first purpose of the process was to resolve the most burning issues, especially economic ones. For most refugees, this meant two things: work—first and foremost in Israel, "as it used to be" before the Gulf war—and freedom of movement, a freedom that was revoked in 1991.

But so far almost every improvement has taken place outside the refugee camps. The reason is clear: their future is an essential part of the negotiations for a permanent solution. The Palestinian Authority's intention was always to link the question of the camps to UN Security Council Resolution 194, which calls for repatriation or compensation for the refugees. But it is highly doubtful that it is within the Authority's power to achieve this, and the Authority may in effect have already waived the demand. At any rate, sweeping renovations of the camps might provide Israel with a pretext for claiming that the problem had been solved. Likewise, it would hardly be worthwhile to spend millions to fix the camps when the only logical step is to raze them to the ground and rebuild from scratch.

Some of the old Gazan families have proposed relocating refugees to the West Bank as a way of solving the intolerable overcrowding in the Strip. (Among those making that proposal are owners of the land on which some of the camps stand.) Transferring refugees to the West Bank will depend, however, on the amount of territory the Palestinians ultimately control, whether that territory is contiguous or broken up into isolated enclaves by Jewish settlements and Israeli roads, whether Israel agrees to such a move, and, of course, whether the people themselves agree to being uprooted yet again.

Even were the Palestinian Authority to decide to keep all the refugees in the Gaza Strip and build new towns from the ground up, the Jewish settlements—which occupy 20 percent of the land—would still pose a problem. And while al-Shatti camp, for example, could have expanded to the north, the Authority chose to use that precious government land to build a luxury hotel. Meanwhile, the freeze on any real rehabilitation of the camps only underscores the differences between the *muwataneen* and the refugees. The terrible hardship that results from sealing off the Strip does affect the poorer *muwataneen* in the towns, but the problem is felt most acutely in the camps, where the joblessness and poverty are far more pressing and widespread.

Very few refugees can afford the $45,000-to-$60,000 apartments available in Gaza City's new towers. The apartments of high-ranking Authority officials cost considerably more—their prices are spoken in whispers. Some 1,500 apartment units that were built with donations from abroad were meant to be sold under convenient mortgage terms, but they cannot solve the general housing problem. Of necessity, they are earmarked for overseas Palestinians moving back to Gaza, tens of thousands of whom are urgently in need of roofs over their heads. And a large portion of the donations and the construction and renovation efforts have been directed at Gaza City, where the Authority's institutions and personnel are concentrated and where diplomats and journalists drop in for a day and are duly impressed by the pace of development.

In the summer of 1996 a few hundred refugees met in a hall at the Jabalia sports club. In public meetings like this all over the Strip, people have begun to voice their frustration and impatience at the unresolved contradictions in their lives. "We don't want *mukhtars* and VIPs here. We want ordinary people to come," one organizer said. And as the complaints burst forth I heard the kinds of frank, insightful words that one cannot find in the Palestinian press but that fill the streets: "The truth is that we're just refugees on paper; everyone knows we won't be going back to our villages. We're just pawns, that's all, and we're being treated like circus exhibits. They bring the donors through the camps so they'll be shocked, and then all the money goes to Rimaal. Why don't they pave our streets? Why don't they plant a few trees? Why shouldn't we have a little shade? Why are there electric wires dangling all over the place where they can hurt the children? Why don't they build parks for our kids? Why can't we use the beach? It's the only place where we can get out, forget a little. They're putting up a hotel over here and an officers' club over there, and smack in the middle is somewhere for Arafat. The north and the south, that's all that's left, and you know what's there? The settlements."

Chapter 8

Missing in Action

The simple room was adorned with a gallery of photographs showing the men of the family. I was in the house of supporters of the Popular Front, once considered the vanguard of Palestinian secularism. The daughter-in-law who entered the room was in an advanced stage of pregnancy, held an infant in her arms, and was all of eighteen years old. "Why are there no pictures of women on the wall?" I asked her later. "That's the custom," she said. "It would be a disgrace to show their faces," she explained. "After all, men come to visit, you know."

In my years in Gaza, I almost never wrote about women's inferior position in Palestinian society and its emotional and intellectual consequences. I was hitched to the tireless hunt for breaking news, and the newsmakers were men. The IDF redeployment, Arafat's arrival — these were decidedly male events. The organization heads I interviewed were men; the military and religious leaders, the unionists, the politicians, the economists were almost exclusively men. Even most of the journalists, photographers, sources, and drivers were men. Like a skulk of foxes, we would streak after the male architects of the day's headlines and events. In the pursuit I failed to report on a compelling dynamic: in a patriarchal society such as the Gaza Strip, women's absence from public life becomes a motivational force in itself. Hidden away at home, cut off even from one another, women began to organize themselves; openly, timidly, they had begun to confront their domestic oppression, forcing it into the public and political spheres, bringing it into the light. Feminist developments and expressions had been especially prominent during the *intifada*. Women's committees, for example, set up learning centers offering classes in reading and writing and courses in sewing, juice making, and other ways to support a family. Centers like these, coupled with the sudden transformation of many women into household heads while their husbands were in jail, encouraged women to speak out, come forward, and make demands of society and the men who dominated it. Unfortunately for me, a woman journalist, I arrived in the Strip at a time when this dynamic was on the wane.

I learned that the distinction between the public and private domains was carefully observed, even within people's homes. As a guest, I often felt like a *jasusa*, a collaborator, when, with a wave of his hand, a husband or a brother would order the women to make me coffee or when I, the Israeli guest, joined in a conversation about politics or work while the women were excluded. Or when I sat on the men's side of a length of cloth separating us from the women's area, or when the woman preparing the refreshments would call to her husband to pull himself away from the clouds of cigarette smoke and come get the tray, or when we'd all troop out to visit some interesting people and the women would stay behind to take care of the many children. Every so often, I'd say something about how the men sat around at home during curfew or when they were unable to work, not lifting a finger while the women did all the household chores.

In Gaza, women's absence from public life is as conspicuous and tangible as their presence at home. As a journalist, I lived most of my life outside, in the world, and realized that I actually knew very few women. Those I knew well, those who had talked to me about their lives, were awake to women's inferior status in Gaza and were part of the effort to remedy it. I would like to believe that their awareness and protest was emblematic, that Palestinian women everywhere were chafing at their constraints, but I had too few such conversations to be able to generalize.

M.H. from the Khan Yunis camp is a determined feminist active in the Popular Front. A thirty-five-year-old mother of four, she lost her job in a kindergarten when it ran out of money to pay her. M.H. grapples with her simultaneous absence and presence in public life. She is clearheaded and vocal about her pain and anger. I once heard a story about a woman who tried to make a match between her engineer son and M.H., a traditional match in which the engaged couple would not meet until their wedding. M.H. was staunchly opposed to arranged marriages but still turned the mother down politely and pleasantly.

When the mother refused to give up, M.H. picked up a table, according to her delighted friends, and dropped it at the startled woman's feet. The mother fled and with her all other potential matchmakers.

At the Islamic University, where M.H. studied biology in 1985, she and her girlfriends organized a Popular Front rally commemorating the massacre at Dir Yassin in 1948. But the Islamic distaste for Communists proved stronger than the national cause and M.H. and her friends were denied permission. The rally went ahead in spite of the university's opposition, and M.H. was eventually expelled.

M.H.

As a child I dreamed of being a fighter like my father and brothers. At ten years old I already had a brother in an Israeli jail, one of the first men to be imprisoned in the seventies. My father was an officer in the Egyptian police intelligence. When the Israelis took over in 1967, they insisted that he continue working in intelligence, but he refused along with eleven other men, preferring to stay at home even though he had no work. Now they're all working for the Palestinian Authority.

So the role models were the men in my family. My mother was shut up inside the house all the time, which might be why I felt I had to resist, to get out, although I didn't really analyze things at the time. I just knew that something was wrong. Whenever my brother went outside, my mother would say that I was a girl and had to stay at home. It was always like that, all the way through school. Once I graduated and went to university, it became a little easier, though. But I was the only one of my sisters to behave this way. They said I was strange, aggressive, stubborn. I'd fight with my mother to let me join in the protests, to let me go out in the street with other kids and demonstrate.

In a way, fighting the occupation led to feminism. It also taught me to not just obey blindly. I watch my sisters obeying orders and I see their lives, which are so difficult. On the other hand, maybe it's easier for them because they don't know what it's like outside, they don't know what they're missing. Still, they're jealous of me sometimes. They ask their husbands why I can make decisions when they're not allowed to. And they ask me why our men make all the decisions. They always tell me that I'm strong but my answer is that we all possess strength.

For example, my sister complains that her husband gives all his wages to his parents. If she needs money she has to get it from them. So my sister is oppressed by her husband and her mother-in-law. Lots of women have to get permission from their in-laws as well as their husbands when they want to visit their families.

Things began to change with the intifada. During curfews the women instead of the men went out to bring home food. When the soldiers tried to grab at the children, the older women would argue with them, even fight with them. Traditionally women are not allowed to open the door, but during the intifada it was the women who opened the door to the soldiers. So our society began to get used to behavior that had always been considered improper. Also, the men weren't bringing in as much money so the women were encouraged to go out and look for work, to grasp more freedom for themselves.

And this affected relations in the family. When I was working at the kindergarten, I felt I had more of a role, that I was in a stronger position, I was listened to more. Now I'm not earning anything and my role is weaker. When I want to buy something I have to explain it to S., my husband, because he hands out the money. Now I can't make my own economic decisions and I feel ashamed and angry. S. is relatively okay, but his Middle Eastern way of dealing with things sometimes really irritates me and it makes me rebellious. If we have a decision to make, he always wins because he's the man. When I agreed to marry him, he promised that I could go on studying, that he'd share the chores at home, and that I could carry on being active in the Women's Committee. Now he complains when I'm away from the house and I have to keep reminding him of his promises. Sometimes he apologizes. Still, his attitude is different from that of most men and it's really noticeable. My mother and grandmother told me their husbands always treated them badly and stopped them from doing all kinds of things. Now I understand that my mother was always depressed, especially when she had to live with her husband's parents. They constantly meddled in the way we were brought up.

I began to think about my needs maybe after I got married. Actually, when I thought about myself before that—beyond activism at the university—I realized that I had to get married, the demands of my society made it unavoidable. I wasn't crazy about it—S. asked me three times before I finally agreed at the age of twenty-two, which is considered late.

Most of my friends waited like me, but my sister got married at sixteen. Even now, her husband overrules her on everything. He treats her like a little girl whose only job is to bring children into the world. Getting married so young means the man can remake the woman, actually brainwash her. Sometimes my sister's husband really bullies her and she runs away to our parents.

One time when she was staying at our parents' house, I convinced her not to go back home before our father spoke with her husband. Since our father's signature is on the marriage agreement, all the problems are brought to him. He was angry at her the first time she ran away and sided with her husband, ordering her to go back to him. But when her husband began hitting her, our father took her part. S. and I argued about it. He tried to rationalize the way my brother-in-law behaved, saying that the economic difficulties were making him act badly. This really upset me and we kept arguing until he got fed up and said, "Okay, your sister's not wrong and neither is her husband."

Since Oslo, the atmosphere has changed a little. There's some encouragement for women to work outside the home, but mostly in the towns, not in the refugee camps. Nothing has changed in the family, though. In fact, we've even lost ground. There's no work for men, so they escape the house, the children, and the wife. It's hard for them to deal with the family's demands when they can't even help support the household. At the same time, we women feel that we can't complain or make demands either, given the situation.

Now my one dream is to live in a house by ourselves—me and my husband and the children, without the rest of the family. That's all I want. I suppress any other dreams I might have had. When I let myself think about it I feel terribly sad that I'm satisfied to just dream about a house, not about something really for me. And then I just feel the whole sadness of our society pressing down on me and I can't think about myself.

M.H. and I left her house to walk among the tin huts and cinder-block shanties of Khan Yunis camp and she quickly covered her head with a *mandeel*, a scarf. At the university she covered herself up to the eyeballs, she told me. "Here, even if I go out covered with long pants and a long-sleeved blouse, people still call me a *safra*, a barefaced woman disobeying Islamic law, so I certainly can't go without the *mandeel*. I don't really care enough to fight for the right not to wrap up. Actually, it bothers me that people on both sides think it's so important. If the social pressure dies down, then I'll take it off."

I met H. and A. at a friend's house. H. teaches mathematics and A. works in a kindergarten run by a Hamas-affiliated charity. My friend and I waited in the doorway, watching the street. "Here they come," my friend said, spying two women sheathed from head to toe in veils and traditional dresses that thoroughly blurred the outlines of their bodies. Once inside the house, after making sure that no man could see them, the women began to peel off the layers: first they removed the veils covering their faces. I caught myself staring at their slanting eyes and long eyelashes, at their full, round mouths and smiling lips. Then they removed their gloves, pulling them from their wrists, until long, delicate fingers were exposed. When the women sat down I saw their ankles revealed beneath perfectly ordinary jeans. Perversely, in the very act of stripping off their gloves, the two women radiated sensuality and sexual self-awareness.

H.

We cover ourselves up because that's what's written in the Quran. Allah commanded the Prophet Muhammad to order his wives and the wives of his companions to wrap themselves in their clothes and cover their faces so no one would harm them. I've dressed like this since my wedding. Until then I wore only the mandeel, *but later, out of inner conviction, I decided to cover my whole body.*

It's not that men are so dangerous but that woman is a temptress by nature, liable to seduce a man and spoil his marital relations if she's more beautiful than his wife. So Islam commands women to conceal themselves. Also, uncovered women might encourage prostitution, because unmarried men would be tempted and feel the urge to go with women in exchange for money.

It's a fact that family relations in the West are a shambles. Families that don't observe the ways of Islam are not secure. True, not all men are weak, we can't generalize; but this prohibition is meant to protect those who are. I myself feel safer. I know that my clothing immediately sets limits for a man. I'm not angry at women who dress differently, but I hope God will guide them to behave according to Islamic doctrine.

During the *intifada*, our hostess—a secular woman—was attacked by a group of young men because she was in the street without a head covering. The incident took place far from her own neighborhood, where no one would have dared attack her, she says, "because we all know one another." The young men called her a *jasusa*, a collaborator, and demanded to look inside her purse. She refused and the enraged men began hitting her and yelling hysterically. Fortunately, a friend of her brother's happened to pass by and immediately summoned help. Word of that incident and others spread quickly, making it clear to every woman that she would be better off covering her head. When I met with H., though, she denied all knowledge of such tactics. "I haven't heard of physical coercion," she said. "I know that leaflets and graffiti spread the idea that women should dress according to the laws of Islam."

Like other devout Muslims, H. believes there is nothing to prevent a woman from entering public life—joining demonstrations, working, or studying at a university—as long as she wears traditional clothing. And there is nothing to stop a woman from working outside the home as long as she doesn't neglect her family duties. Covering her face and body, though, is a way to increase a woman's absence from public life, even when she is taking part in it. Some women consider this a source of power: they can see without being seen; strangers cannot know their identity.

H.

When I was young, I dreamed of having my own Islamic family, and I've done it. I did once think of being a doctor, but there are no medical universities here and my father didn't want me to travel abroad. I accepted his position and gave in, and I'm satisfied with my life. It's natural for every woman, when she becomes an adult, to want a good marriage. I wanted a Muslim husband because I believe in the words of the Prophet Muhammad, peace and blessings be upon him: every Muslim man who loves his wife is to treat her with generosity and graciousness. Even the Muslim man who doesn't love his wife must treat her justly. I hear of many problems in other families and am convinced that a man who is truly a Muslim will not hurt his wife. According to the Prophet Muhammad, the best Muslim is judged on the basis of his family and marital relations. The fact is that my husband irons and helps with the housework.

As for permission to leave the house, it's only natural. The Prophet Muhammad said that the wife who goes out without her husband's permission will be cursed by the angels until she returns home. When my husband was in prison, I told him I needed to leave the house to take care of all kinds of things and he gave me blanket permission to go out as long as he was in jail.

At the time of our conversation, A.'s husband was being held in a Palestinian jail with other Hamas and Islamic Jihad detainees. A. is his second wife. She agreed to marry him only after reciting the *istikhara*, the prayer of choice, in which Allah guides the supplicant toward the correct decision. "Marriage had been proposed to me once before," she said, "and I had felt a choking sensation. I didn't know what to decide. I recited this special prayer but still felt a kind of suffocation, so I said no. On the other hand, with the man I married, I also said this prayer and immediately felt serene and tranquil even though he was already married." A. recounted that it was her husband's first wife who suggested she marry him. "But why?" A. asked, and was told that the wife was ill. After a month of marriage, A. discovered that the first wife was beautiful, well-groomed, and attentive to her children. "I was angry, and my husband felt it," A. said. "I asked him why he'd married me if his wife was healthy, and he said time would tell. The truth is that in time I saw the first wife was irritable and restless and didn't care about her husband."

A young woman—a second wife—came into J.'s yard in al-Shatti camp, seeking the advice of her older neighbor. Her husband's first wife had a young son who had married a sixteen-year-old girl. One month into the marriage, the couple were unhappy and the son wanted to marry a new wife and kick the girl out of the house.

Fifty-five-year-old J. listened politely, concealing her annoyance at the interruption. "*Ya ukhti*, my sister," she said to the young woman, who kept smoothing her hair and rearranging her *mandeel* as she talked, telling us how hard it was to share the house with her husband's son and his unhappy wife. "*Ya ukhti*," J. said again. "You can't undo one mistake by making another. You were wrong to marry him off at such an early age. And to a girl so young. Don't add to your mistakes by sending her away."

The suffering of women who marry young is reflected in the divorce statistics: in 1995 approximately 39 percent of women getting divorced were between fifteen and twenty years old. Their proportion of the divorce rate has been stable for years, even as the numbers of women marrying in that age group have declined from some 30 percent in 1992 to 25 percent in 1995. On the other hand, the overall ratio of divorces to marriages has risen steadily since 1991: from 9.7 percent in 1991 to 14.2 percent in 1995, or 1,239 couples getting divorced while 8,698 couples got married.[1]

Very young women and older women alike must cope with the demands of a society in which large families are the norm. On a routine day when I visited one of the refugee camps' UNRWA clinics, eight women had come in to ask the family-planning nurse about contraception. A few, though only twenty-two or twenty-three, already had three or four children and wanted a rest. Sometimes, the nurse told me, the women are older, forty or so, and want to stop getting pregnant because of health problems. One of that morning's patients had five daughters and no sons. The nurse was surprised. "Your husband agrees to using contraception?" The woman explained: "Yesterday we all felt bad, me and the girls. Some of them simply lay about whimpering. I announced that I'd had enough, that I was exhausted, and my husband agreed I could stop getting pregnant. So I came straight over. If his mother found out, she'd never agree." The day had been set aside for counseling only, not for fitting diaphragms, but the nurse was willing to take care of the woman right away.

"It's a problem," the nurse told me. "There's a general understanding that having too many children doesn't make sense. But the mothers-in-law insist on keeping to the old ways. The more children there are, the more secure they feel in their old age. They think there'll be someone to take care of them. And the women are afraid their husbands will take another wife if they don't have a child every year." Other family-planning departments report a growing number of inquiries about contraception. One such department is at the Women's Health

Center in al-Boureij camp, the first center of its kind, offering a range of services related to women's health, from exercise classes to psychological counseling.

More than a few couples learn the hard way that having many children is not a guarantee of security in old age. There are very few places to turn in Gaza for the many children with genetic defects—marriage between first cousins is fairly common in the Strip. For children suffering from hereditary mental retardation, there are, however, the Forget Me Not Centers, a rare source of support and the brainchild of Naama al-Hilu, a groundbreaking woman who ran as a candidate of the Palestinian Democratic Union (FIDA) in the elections.

Hilu was one of fourteen women candidates. She was not elected, but two Gazan women were, out of thirty-seven representatives. In the course of her campaign, Hilu met hundreds of women and found that their chief concerns were the low level of general education among women (I know two school principals whose wives are illiterate) and polygyny. "The women demanded that we pass a law prohibiting marriage to a second wife. They demanded that we take action against the practice of forcing girls into marriage, and they complained that educated women can't find work." But the Legislative Council is unwilling to challenge the religious authorization of polygyny. As the Council begins to debate the Palestinian constitution, it apparently will not intervene in Islamic matrimonial law.*

A founder of the Democratic Front in the Strip (and of its pro-Oslo breakaway faction, FIDA), Hilu was imprisoned four times in Israeli jails for a total of fourteen years. Everyone in her office proudly reminds me that she was one of the first women to join the armed struggle: in 1970 she threw a grenade at an IDF unit beside her refugee camp home. In the explosion and the ensuing gunfire she lost

---

*In 1996, Palestinian feminists set up a model parliament that debates issues related to women's status and equality. The same group organized consciousness-raising groups throughout Gaza and the West Bank and, in its parliamentary "sessions," drew up "bills" to be presented as working proposals to Palestinian lawmakers. The Gaza branch of the model parliament (closures frequently prevented joint sessions with West Bank members) drew considerable anger from religious figures when it posited that Islamic law, the sharia, is only one source of legislation among other systems, which include universal principles and international conventions. In another vote, a decisive majority of the eighty-eight members (men from various grass-roots organizations also participate) "approved" a law forbidding polygyny.

her right hand and an eye. Early in the *intifada* she was placed on the Israelis' wanted list and eventually sentenced to four years in prison. In the two years before she was captured, though, she set up the Strip's first nursery school for mentally challenged children. Later she established an elementary school for these children and a vocational school. Her educational venture expanded, and now there are twenty-five kindergartens under her direction and thirty classes for women. At one of her campaign rallies, Yassir Abed Rabbo, a FIDA leader, spoke of Hilu's experience in the Palestinian struggle: "She has given her life for her people. Instead of being a mother, she has sacrificed herself." Even among political activists, Hilu's choice to remove herself from domestic life and not to marry is considered a sacrifice.

Motherhood is the main calling in the life of D. from al-Shatti camp. Thirty-four, she has been separated from her husband for twelve years now and has brought up her children alone. To make some money, she opened a kindergarten in her house, but during 1996 the number of children attending plummeted—the long months of closure meant that few parents could affort the NIS 20 ($6) monthly fee. I met D. at the home of her sister S., who coaxed her to speak to me without fear.

D.

Look, nothing good has happened to me in my life. Nothing good my whole life. The best thing that ever happened was when my father was allowed back into Gaza. He left the country before the war in 1967 when I was in elementary school, and then the Israelis wouldn't let him come back. He finally got a permit from Israel, but that was after my brother was killed.

I'm laughing, but it's because of the sadness of my life. Because of my tragedy. I have to bear all the responsibility for my children. This is my fate. I believe in fate. And I do have bright, healthy children. Everything comes from God, but I am suffering a great deal. I have to be mother and father to my children. It's not worth getting divorced officially. What for? Marriage is only for having children, and I have them.

When I was a child I just wanted to study. My parents destroyed my dream when they arranged my marriage. I was the best in my class, but

*my father decided to marry me off and my mother was too weak to
object. Then I understood what a big difference there is between sons
and daughters. For my own daughters I wish that they finish school and
that they have good husbands and marriages, because that's what
brings happiness in life.*

*Our society shackles our dreams. I dream of visiting London by
myself, but our society would never let me do that. But I do have one
dream. I'd like to own a plot of land where I'd build a model kindergarten. There'd be lots of kindergarten teachers and I'd be in charge.*

S., D.'s SISTER

*The whole time we were growing up we saw our mother sacrificing her-
self. Her life is joyless, even today. Her big mistake was to raise us for the
same kind of life. But now I'm beginning to learn how to take things for
myself. I've signed up for a video course. And I can see that our daughters are different.*

J., age fifty-five, was forced by her father to marry young and then
swore she wouldn't rush her daughters into marriage. Today, one
daughter is thirty and single, and J. is consumed with regret and worry.
"Maybe I made a mistake. Maybe she was taken over by a jinn, a
demon. Do you believe in demons?" M., a twenty-eight-year-old engineer, has called off three engagements. "Maybe a jinn got into me,"
she wondered. "Do you believe in demons?"

UM AHMAD

*I was signed up for the ninth grade. I'd paid twenty-five liras, I remem-
ber. It was at the end of the summer and I was working in the fields. My
brother-in-law has a plot of land and we were working there. I told my
father I had to go to school the next day and I would only be able to
work on weekends. He said no, that I was a young woman and had to
bring home a little money. All that night I cried, I was so angry. It's been
twenty years and I'm still angry. That's why the one thing I care about
is my children's education. Look at my neighbors. One of them had a
thirteen-year-old girl and wanted her to help in the house and get mar-*

ried. Another neighbor has a nineteen-year-old daughter who has been helping in the house since the sixth grade. Her other girl stays home when she should be in junior high. I'm angry at these people. When I sit with them, I always talk about these things, education and marriage, but they say that a twelve- or thirteen-year-old girl is only going to be a housewife anyway, so she might as well start early.

Still, our lives have improved a bit, in spite of everything. Twenty years ago, you couldn't find a mop or a bottle of bleach in the whole village—we had to kneel on the floor to wash it by hand, with a rag. Today there are lots of courses for women, so they can learn to read and write. We've got young women here who've never been to school—can you imagine? A twenty-year-old woman who doesn't know how to read and write? UNRWA organizes the courses. Sometimes we used to go to brush up a little. I'd knock on all the doors to convince the other women to come with me.

And now we've got a proper sewage system. It's much easier for women when there's a better standard of cleanliness. We didn't use to have plumbing in the house, before my husband went to prison. We didn't have a bathtub or a toilet. Sometimes I'd cook over an open fire from wood that I'd brought in from outside. My husband was constantly talking about wanting to move to another house, but it was always tomorrow, never now. When he was in prison, though, I fixed up this room and I put in a bathtub over there. I didn't ask him. I saved up the money and consulted with friends. We couldn't live like that, it was impossible. I had money from sewing that I took in and UNRWA helped us with flour and things like that.

My husband is the one who decides things. I'm not ashamed to say it. When he was in prison he told me to do whatever I thought needed doing. But now that he's out, he decides what I do. I have to take his mother to the clinic, even though he's not working. I don't argue. I'm used to not arguing. He believes he's doing the right thing when he makes decisions for me, and I do too. One day he decided I should stop smoking and I obeyed him. That was good. He still smokes, but I can't decide for him what he should do. That's the way it'll always be among Arabs—the man decides. But my husband wants our daughters to study. He's not like my father. He'd give anything for me to keep on studying. He gave me money to learn to drive, and I got my driver's license just as they took his away. During the intifada I'd drive into Gaza City and

*bring home fresh vegetables for the whole neighborhood. I bought corn
on the cob and cooked it. Everyone would wait for me to get home
because I bought good produce and didn't take too big a profit. It felt
good to be doing something.*

*A while ago I was visiting some family in Israel. They have four sons
and a daughter and they're very rich. The youngest boy had fallen out of
bed and broken his arm. When he fell out of bed a second time and
cracked his head, a social worker came round. They thought the parents
were abusing him. I thought they should come to Gaza and see how
people behave. There are women who hit their children really hard. But
it's the pressure. The mothers are under so much pressure—from the economic situation and the daily grind, but mainly from their husbands
and their mothers-in-law. My mother-in-law decides for all of us and I
don't dare argue. What I dream of is privacy in a home of my own. My
oldest son says one day he'll bring home some dynamite and blow up the
house. Then we'll build a new one.*

The percentage of women working outside the home is lower in the
Strip than in the West Bank. A 1992 study by FAFO, a Norwegian
research center, found that some 8 percent of the Strip's workforce were women, compared with 19 percent in the West Bank.
The Palestinian Ministry of Planning puts the figures even lower,
probably because, unlike the FAFO study, its findings do not include
women who work as cleaning ladies outside their homes or as seamstresses at home.[2] One way or the other, the low percentage results
from a combination of factors: the traditional inclination to see a
woman's proper place as in the home, household chores that make it
hard for women to take on other work, chronic unemployment in
the Strip, which prevents them from entering the workforce or rele-
gates them to unskilled jobs, and fundamental doubts about women's
capabilities.

In 1995, according to Planning Ministry figures, a workforce of
131,000 included 6,200 women, or 4.7 percent, but this was an
improvement over previous years: in 1991, 2,900 women worked outside their homes out of a total workforce of 107,700, 2.7 percent.[3] At
the beginning of 1995 there had been a general drop in the number of
civilian wage earners in the Gaza Strip (that is, those working in Israel,

in the Strip, or for UNRWA, but not for the Palestinian security establishment); by the end of the year the number of employed persons had increased within the Strip as a whole and in the Palestinian Authority's ministries in particular, and the percentage of women had doubled. For one thing, following the advent of Palestinian self-rule, educated and well-trained women had returned from abroad. The number of clerical jobs increased, as did those in the public sector, especially in the education and health ministries. Moreover, the Palestinian Authority intentionally sought to promote women's employment. Some saw this encouragement as a welcome aspect of the struggle between the Authority—or the secular tradition of the PLO—and the Islamic opposition.*

Late in 1995 the Palestinian Ministry of the Interior issued a regulation requiring that a woman's request for a travel permit be signed by her husband, her father, or some other male guardian. Possibly the Authority hoped to appease its Islamic rivals with the new regulation (and Hamas was pleased by the legislation), although it also confirmed how deeply ingrained patriarchy is in Gazan society, even as the Authority appeared to encourage women's participation in public life. Women's organizations and female candidates for election protested. "Why didn't we need men's permission when we struggled against the occupation? Why maintain the pretense of democracy while discriminating against women?" demanded one leaflet distributed a week before the Legislative Council elections. Although increasingly disregarded after the elections, the regulation is still enforced ad hoc according to each clerk's disposition.

Ashraf, a religious man turned secular, returned to Gaza after ten years in jail and was shocked at the regression in women's status. "The women, poor things, that's not living when you can't make your own decisions." He quickly noticed how much stronger the institution of the family had become in his absence. Research findings of the Jerusalem Media and Communication Center concur:

*In subsequent years, women's employment fell in tandem with the Strip's overall lack of employment due to the closures.

Deprived of their land and the right to live independently and freely, the Palestinian family has become one of the few institutions in which the Palestinians have been able to live and act as they were accustomed to doing. The family has thus gained an enormous importance as a protector of national identity and as a maintainer of the Palestinian culture.

The home and the family, "the inner circle" and domain of women, has become the only arena where men have been able freely to enforce their otherwise restricted possibilities of control and domination. The home has also become, even more than formerly, the place where the menfolks could seek shelter from psychological wounds and where they would be taken care of by the women members of the family.

A big family also has meant a stronger family and a stronger community, thus the bearing of children has become a national duty which women carry out proudly.

On the one hand the Israeli occupation has reinforced the traditional duties of women, while on the other hand it has led, ironically also, to the development and change of their position in society, by confronting them with situations and circumstances which women in orderly conservative patriarchal societies, such as the normal Palestinian one, would usually not have to face.[4]

FAFO offered statistical confirmation of a conservative trend among younger women:

Perhaps the most interesting comparison is the regular difference in attitudes between the age groups 15–19 and 20–29 year olds. On every issue, the youngest age group of women is consistently more conservative than women in their twenties. The important point lies not so much in the degree of differences but in the consistency of the differences. This suggests that there might be a larger set of inter-related ideas about women's correct role in society that has had an impact on the young women who came of age during the last few years of the *intifada*. Stated more directly, the data seems to vindicate observations that there has been a general social retrenchment during the *intifada*, with women in their teens being most affected by new conservative ideologies.[5]

Affirmative responses to the question of whether it was "acceptable for women to work outside the home" were divided as follows: 71 percent of females between the ages of 15 and 19 answered yes; in the 20–29 age group many more—87 percent—responded in the affirmative, as did 66 percent in the 30–39 age group and 77 percent of those between 40 and 49. And to the question of whether it was "acceptable for women to send their children to day care centers," 46 percent of the youngest females, 15–19, 59 percent of those between the ages of 20 and 29, and 58 percent of those between 30 and 39 answered yes.

Um Saber and Abu Saber are both forty years old, and their views have been influenced by emancipatory ideas, both personal and national. They live in the Nasser neighborhood of Gaza City with their seven children. Abu Majed, a friend, dropped by to talk while I was visiting them.

UM SABER: When I was a girl I dreamed of being an airline hostess or a journalist. Without a passport there was no chance of being an airline hostess, so that left journalism. Before I knew it, though, I'd signed up for advanced classes in husband, home, and children. I got married when I was fifteen years old, just a child.

ABU SABER: That was because I asked for her hand. I saw her, we met, we married, and that was it for her.

UM SABER: Thanks be to God, I'm satisfied with my life. I'm active in the Fatah Women's Committee and work to help women recognize their strength. Women should be able to say no to anything they don't like at home, instead of saying *khader*—at your service—all the time. We talk about the role of women in society, about how to educate children so they'll value peace and know right from wrong. But we still don't have a permanent place to meet and bring women together.

ABU SABER: The movement still hasn't found somewhere for the Women's Committee. I know Um Saber has been fighting for that. She wanted to build on the land near our house, but they haven't agreed yet.

UM SABER: During the elections we campaigned for the Fatah slate. We wanted the good people to get voted in, the ones Abu Amar chose. We went from house to house, explaining how the elections worked. But we didn't campaign for the independent women candidates. We didn't know them. We hadn't heard of them, people like Rawya al-Shawwa, nor her newspaper articles. In Palestinian society, we women are cut off from what's going on outside. We're uncultured. We don't know one another.

There are things I've gotten used to. Studies are a lost cause. That was finished when I married Abu Saber. I was a girl, and there's no room in your head for learning when you're taking care of children all the time. Now I want to give my children the things I missed out on. I want my daughters to go to university, and I push them harder than I push my sons. I'm satisfied with my life, but I was angry that they married me off so early. When Abu Saber was arrested, I could have done more for the children if I'd had a profession, had a diploma.

ABU SABER: Do you know how hard it is for a woman on her own, without money and without a profession?

ABU MAJED: My wife managed. We've got a big family. When I was arrested they took care of her, but I saw with my friends how hard it was for their families. Some women worked as seamstresses while their husbands were in prison. By the time the husbands came home, their wives couldn't see, their eyes were so tired. They'd worked day and night to bring in a little money.

ABU SABER: When I got out of prison a year ago I had friends whose wives had changed so much they wanted to take a second wife. It took me six months to understand the changes Um Saber had gone through. When I was arrested, I left behind an inexperienced woman. I used to do everything at home. The new situation had made her strong, more masculine. Before 1985 she wouldn't go to the market by herself. We'd go together and we'd shop together and come back home. Now she goes out. She'd been to Egypt and Jordan while I was in jail. Living without me let her think for herself. It strengthened her opinions.

UM SABER: During the *intifada* I had to see to the children's education, make sure they didn't get arrested, make sure they didn't get hurt, that they came home before the curfew, that there was something for them to eat in the house.

ABU SABER: While I was in jail she could do things that would have been considered improper at any other time. She gained a lot of self-confidence, which helped her do things without people finding fault. Now she goes out of the house without even telling me, and I've gotten used to it. If a woman lived alone during that time, then she learned how to manage just by living. If she lived with the *hamula*, the clan, then everything stayed the same.

ABU MAJED: It's bad for a family when one of the daughters-in-law has to go out to work to bring home food. In our house, my father takes care of everything. But the women are treated with respect. We don't sit in judgment over them. When I was in prison and the children needed their inoculations, my father took them to the clinic. Now that I'm home I let my wife go out with them. My father's not happy with the situation, but he coddled her too much.

UM SABER: Look, character doesn't just come out of nowhere. It comes from experience. In our society a woman who comes home late at night is a bad woman. But her personality develops through her husband if he gives her the opportunity, if he prods her, if he supports her efforts. A woman needs her husband's support to be independent. Consensus at home is very important, but if a woman's not convinced by her husband's opinions then she should cling to her own.

ABU SABER: She always said that I gave her a free hand to do everything, even to discuss things with me.

ABU MAJED: Thank God my wife isn't like that.

On windy days my friend M. likes to drive to the shore early in the morning when the beach is empty and she can find a secluded spot. Far from people, she turns her face to the sea and screams into the wind.

Z., A PSYCHOLOGIST

We're not used to crying and yelling, showing our feelings. We can't, because everyone lives so close together. I'm sure the men want to scream too, but they can't let go. Not long ago I started praying. We women have no strength, but I've found that praying gives me strength. It calms me down, like drinking beer does for other people. A woman whose husband beat her asked me where she could go. Who would have her afterward if she went back to her parents' home? I told her to wait until her children grew up and then Allah would solve the problem. If we lived somewhere else I would tell her to leave him. But it's hard for a woman to get a divorce here and I mustn't make her situation worse, especially

*with the closures, when we're falling apart economically. This crisis has
taken over every part of our lives. It's our major battle now, just struggling to get by. Women and men are in the same battle, and as long as it
controls our lives we can't fight for the other causes. Like that of most
other oppressed peoples, our women's thinking has gotten distorted.
They'll need time to take up their place in history, not just be driven by
it. That was the great achievement of the* intifada *that we miss so much:
women took part in the struggle. Women made decisions.*

AN ASIDE

"You mean, you're Jewish?" the women would say, lowering their
voices and swallowing the last syllable. With their limited experience of Israel and Israelis, it was the women of Gaza who tended
toward surprise and discomfort when they realized that yes, I was in
fact Jewish. Sometimes they would direct the question to my friend
or my host, whoever had brought me into their circle. "You mean,
she's Jewish?" Their gaze would drop and their tone would fal-
ter, confused and uncertain, and the word "Jewish" would come out
in a whisper, mostly from good manners, I felt, from a wish not
to offend with a probing, delicate question, in much the same way
that many Israelis tend to clear their throats and hesitate before saying "Arab."

Early on in Gaza I decided to confront the touchy question head
on and told people right away that I was both Israeli and Jewish. Reactions ranged from hushed embarrassment to an open and direct
response that dispelled any awkwardness. As it happened, those who
rose to the occasion with humor and ease usually turned out to be
Popular Front supporters. At one home in Khan Yunis I was sitting
with a group of aunts, sisters, and grandmothers shelling peas. "And I
thought you were Italian," one aunt said when I told her that I came
from Tel Aviv. "Hey!" she called out. "We've got a Jew here!" Then
she moved toward me in a self-mocking pantomime of the violent
Palestinian and we all laughed. At a vegetable stall in the Faras Market
the young man serving me asked the inevitable question. I remember
the day was particularly tense—Israeli forces had assassinated an
Islamic Jihad man and retaliatory attacks had followed. To make
things worse, a bout of cholera had broken out in the Strip, meaning

even more restrictions on exporting produce. When I answered the man he grinned and with lavish parody yelled to his friends, "Quick, quick, she's a Jew, bring a knife!"

There were always a few Gazans, though, who seemed to have internalized the Israeli image of the bloodthirsty Palestinian and would warn me never to reveal my identity—for my own safety, they said. (One turned out to be a minor collaborator; another was mentally ill, with the papers to prove it.) To all those who worried for my safety, I'd tell about my friend Aouni in Shabura, where I often stayed overnight. "Isn't she scared?" his neighbors once asked. "Why, are we so scary?" he said. I'd also mention the many people who readily and publicly spoke to me in my own language, calling out Hebrew greetings in the markets and refugee camps (and still do, even now, when the IDF soldiers are gone from the streets). "Proof positive that there's nothing to be afraid of in Gaza," said Diab al-Luh, a Fatah leader. "Too bad Israelis don't understand that it's nothing unusual, that if they treat us normally then they'll get a normal response in return."

Skewed perceptions are held on both sides, however. At one of my stays in Aouni's home in Shabura, his children, who were all born during the *intifada*, pointed to the TV screen where UN soldiers were driving around Sarajevo. "Jews, Jews," they cried out. Their mother apologized, explaining that the children say the same thing about Egyptian soldiers as well. Until May 1994, at least, uniforms, guns, death, and shooting were all associated with Israelis—Jews—and the occupation. "If you're a Jew," said ten-year-old Yihye, "where's your gun?" and added, "If you get an exit permit, will you take me to see my grandmother?"

The negative associations of the word *Jew* are not limited to the occupation and expulsion, though. "The Quran teaches us that Jews don't honor their agreements," Hamas people told me more than once in connection with the Oslo agreements. "The Quran teaches us that the Jews are our worst enemy."

Mild versions of the same mistrust and antipathy creep into the language of secular Palestinians, too. Once I promised my avowedly secular friend M.S. to sell my car to him if I had to stop driving it in the Strip. Later I began to regret my promise and backed out of our arrangement. "I made two big mistakes in my life," he said with bitter humor. "The first was being born and the second was making a deal with a Jew." When I told R.S., another friend, about some personal worry, he responded, "May it fall not on your head but on the heads of the Jews," and then laughed immediately when he heard himself using the folksy Palestinian saying (which he doesn't agree with) out of concern for me. R.S. is always careful to point out that the Palestinian confrontation is not with Jews but with Israeli society.

At least until the occupation in 1967, Jews were simply strange and other. R.N. was ten when the IDF briefly occupied the Strip in 1956. He remembers running after every Israeli soldier on the street staring intently at his behind. "What on earth are you doing?" his father asked. "Looking for his tail," the child explained. I've heard similar stories from other Gazans who were taught from Egyptian textbooks and who came to feel pretty silly for believing the information. And despite the present familiarity with Israelis, some anti-Semitic myths persist. M.S. tried to explain to me that Jews are a dominant force in the world because they are wealthy. He was taken aback when I reminded him that these assertions (which appear in the Hamas charter) are in fact drawn from writings published in the decadent West).

Ismail Haniye, a leading Hamas activist, attributed the anti-Semitic parts of the charter to the Palestinians' bitter experience with Jews since 1947, to a defense of the weak against the strong. From Abu Taher, a Hamas friend, I learned that "Jews' money" means something plentiful that may be freely wasted. "What do you think this is, Jews' money?" he scolded his son for leaving meat on the plate. Once or twice, when I visited Abu Taher's family I made a point of bringing fruit or chocolate and mentioned that the gift was Jews' money.

In the end, most reactions to my being Israeli and Jewish simply give yet more proof of how well Gazans know Israel. "Really?" they say. "You're from Tel Aviv?" Then the waiter or policeman or student reels off a string of Tel Aviv garages or restaurants or building sites where he worked, the names of his employers, the one who invited him to a family bar mitzvah, the one who came to his wedding, and the one who did his military service in the Strip.

So many of the feelings Gazans have about Jews are tempered by personal experience and their knowledge of individuals. Every day I'd be reminded that for more than twenty years the Strip was, in effect, an Israeli bedroom community, and that Gazans know there are many different Israels: the ultra-Orthodox world of yeshiva students, the slums of the unemployed where Palestinians workers slept illegally, the haute-bourgeois suburbs where they swept the streets. And I'd be reminded too that while the women of Gaza were fighting their battles at home, the men were learning what they know of Israel, if not in its stores and factories then in its jails.

Chapter 9

Bring Home the POWs

Abu Jamil and Abu Nader liked to sit over a plate of hummus at one of
the string of beachfront restaurants that had opened in the last few
years. Their restaurant of choice was a favorite of mine too, in spite of
the food—it was one of the few places a woman could sit alone without people staring. The seashore offered a rare corner of escape where
one could watch the fishing boats set sail for the twelve nautical miles
open to Gazan fishermen and turn one's back on the old Israeli military court building and the police headquarters circled by concrete
blocks and ugly reels of barbed wire. And now, after the IDF pullback,
the restaurant stayed open past 7:00 P.M. and was blissfully quiet, free
of the incessant noise from the police loudspeaker, which had blasted
Hebrew songs and soldiers' duty schedules throughout Rimaal and
al-Shatti refugee camp.

The entrepreneurs had built the restaurant, one of the first along
the shore, with a loan from a Palestinian investment and development
agency, confident that the chronic shortage of places for leisure and
relaxation, coupled with the needs of Palestinians returning from
exile, young people resuming studies, and ex-prisoners who were picking up the threads of their lives, would make the venture a sure success. On a mound rising up from the shore, the owners had laid tiles
for a patio and set up large beach umbrellas; one balmy summer day
in 1995 I shared a table with Abu Jamil and Abu Nader. The view had
changed: several beachfront hotels had sprung up, the military court
had been transformed into a Palestinian fire station, and the old police
headquarters, stripped of the concrete and barbed wire, now housed
"Arafat's orphans," children whose parents had fallen in the pursuit of
the PLO cause and whom the chairman had "adopted."

Abu Nader picked at his hummus while Abu Jamil sipped a bowl of lentil soup. For a long minute Abu Jamil held the spoon in the air as his eyes took on a glazed, contemplative look. "This reminds me of the soup in Ansar," he said suddenly, talking about the mass detention camp Israel had set up in the Negev desert to deal with the popular uprising. I was taken aback by the nostalgia in his voice, a tone I had heard from other ex-prisoners as well. I remembered the time that Jalal, a taxi driver, had picked me up at the Erez checkpoint. As we drove to Gaza City, we discussed the dangerous rift that had opened between Hamas and the Palestinian Authority. Jalal, a four-term detainee and dyed-in-the-wool Fatah man, interrupted our talk to point out the new sidewalks (paved with flagstones from Gaza) and praise a park near the Unknown Soldier monument, laid out with bushes and palm trees and benches. "Look how nice it is," he said. "*Inshallah*, God willing, there'll be plenty more parks like this." He spoke of Abu Amar—Arafat—with love and reverence and talked of his hopes that all these developments pointed to the emergence of a Palestinian state. Then abruptly, without warning, his tone shifted. "How I miss prison!" he cried. "In prison everything was clear. We knew when to eat, what was right, and what was wrong. We knew who was good and who was bad and when our sentences would be over."

Jalal probably did not know it, but he was heir to a long tradition of postrevolutionary disappointment. His feelings were amplified by Ihab al-Ashqar, a leader in the Unified National Leadership of the *intifada*. "A few days ago," he told me, "I went past the prison. I don't know why, but all of a sudden I remembered the smell of my cell in solitary, the moldy smell it had, and I missed it. It's strange, missing a jail cell, but those were our best moments, when we really felt we were paying the price for defending other people."

I have since heard many prison memories, often full of pride, nostalgia, and even affection, but I am no longer tempted to romanticize the Israeli prison experience. True, most prisoners learned excellent Hebrew and many acquired English as well; some men finished their high school education and a few even registered with the Open University for correspondence courses on such things as anti-Semitism and modern European Jewish history. One seasoned prisoner had earned a reputation throughout the Strip for comforting younger men serving their first sentences. A young prisoner had made his name overnight when he managed to smuggle a dozen transistor radios into the prison tent compound. Rousing as these stories are, I soon learned that they only thinly disguise profound regret and sorrow—for lost time, lost opportunities, and years of deprivation.

Once, while waiting to interview a senior member of the Palestinian Authority's security forces, I chatted with the man's bodyguards. "I know Israel very well," one said, "I've been all over its prisons." In the course of some ten years of incarceration, he had been shuttled from one prison to another, seven in all, and the list read like a map of the country: Gaza, Ashkelon, Ramle, Beersheba, Nafha, Tel Mond, and Ayalon. His colleague chimed in, telling me that he had served six years. "Only six?" I asked, without thinking. "What do you mean, only six?" he said. "I remember every day of my life that I lost in prison." A similar lapse occurred when I spoke to Fayez Abu Shamalla, who was one of the prisoners released early under the terms of the Oslo agreements, having served half his eighteen-year sentence. "So you gained nine years," I said, immediately wanting to bite my tongue. "On the contrary," he said. "I lost nine years."

For Palestinians, serving time has played much the same role as the Palmach, the Jewish combat corps of prestatehood days, did in Israeli society: a grueling shared rite of passage that forged lifelong bonds among a sizable number of Palestinians. By and large, prison has been a male experience that has accentuated the traditional, religion-based separation of the sexes. At the same time, though, it has enlisted and united entire families in support of their absent kin; indeed it is hard to find a family in the Strip that has not lived through the detention or imprisonment of at least one of its members. Every day I meet someone else who has experienced late-night arrest, interrogation by Shabak, detention without trial, or long periods in solitary confinement. Since 1967, 280,000 Gazans have passed through Israeli prisons, detention cells, and interrogation rooms; 80,000 during the *intifada*, according to the Association of Veteran Palestinian Fighters and Prisoners. In Gaza ex-prisoners rub shoulders with each other all the time, at every public and private venue. Prison memories, prison gossip, and prison slang crop up in every conversation. In time I came to learn which men had shared a cell, who had gone on hunger strike with whom, which of the prisoners' representatives had abused their powers, who had jumped ahead in the bathroom line, and which men had refused to share their food parcels from home.

For all the talk of jail, however, most ex-prisoners say little about the legacy of trauma, precisely because the experience is so common and widespread, and also because Gazans rarely talk about the emotional aspects of their hardships. Palestinians who have spent years with twelve other men in a tiny cell or a leaky tent in the Ansar detention camp are rarely willing to talk about the damage to their spirits, taking pride instead in their maturity and fortitude, in the unity of their group. In conversation, they quickly move on to their new lives, saying how pleased they are to be working. Only very few men will acknowledge the disparity between their successful reintegration into public life and their haunted personal lives, their difficult adjustment to a world that went on without them.

"You're not the man I married," Ibrahim Abu Nada's wife told him three days after he was released from jail. "The words were like a knife in my soul," Abu Nada confided, but they alerted him to the crisis among his fellow ex-prisoners and their families. "If there are one thousand prisoners, then there are one thousand wives who have been hurt," Abu Nada said. He spent a year in an Israeli jail; many Gazans have been imprisoned for much longer. Some men yell at their wives, some hit them. Some express their alienation and isolation in long silences. Many spend nights with their friends, away from home; their quick tempers are ignited by the children, who find it hard to get along with their fathers. "My son doesn't come to me for money. He goes to his mother, because that's what he did when I was in prison," S. told me with a bitter smile.

A male nurse, Abu Nada works at the Gaza Community Mental Health Center, where he monitored an experiment in group therapy with some twenty ex-prisoners. The center hopes to expand the project to reach hundreds of men, and the promise of more prisoners' returning home as a result of the Oslo agreements has forced its head, Eyad al-Sarraj, to speed up its efforts. Beyond offering counseling services, the center works to explain to the Palestinian community that the jail experience does not end with the prisoner's release and that psychological help is no less important than physical rehabilitation.

The program's first step is to get people to speak out, to shed their embarrassment and talk, publicly, about their ordeal. The tendency of most prisoners is to stifle their broken sense of themselves, a feeling that haunts them all. The house search is the initial act of intrusion to leave its mark, whether an arrest is made or not: when a dozen soldiers break in at night, destroy the furniture, humiliate family members in front of an elderly mother or terrified children, shame and trauma result. After the search, one develops an acute sensitivity to noise, but worse is the erosion of trust. People begin to suspect colleagues and neighbors who might have given names to the Shabak. There must have been a collaborator involved, they feel sure. How else could the soldiers have found their way through the camp's labyrinth of alleyways?

Then there is the arrest. Tawfiq al-Mabhuh of the Unified National Leadership recalls his arrest in 1988. It was not the first time, but no less traumatic for that. "My wife was just about to give birth. Throughout the early months of the *intifada* the soldiers kept coming to the neighborhood and breaking into the house, looking for me, but my family didn't want me to turn myself in. Then one night the soldiers came again at midnight. They threw tear gas into the house, they hit my wife and children and my mother too, and said they'd wipe us out if I didn't turn myself in. My wife inhaled a lot of gas, and they took her unconscious to Shifa Hospital. Someone who knew where I was hiding called me to the hospital. When I got there my wife had given birth to a boy, Shafiq, but she was still unconscious. I waited for an hour or so until she came to. 'Now I want you to turn yourself in,' she said. I'd broken in my replacement in the UNL and I'd just written two new leaflets, so I left everything in order."

Mabhuh presented himself at Gaza prison. "The Shabak guy in charge of Jabalia camp only makes the arrest, he doesn't do the interrogation. So he put a blindfold over my eyes and sent me with two soldiers to the *maslakh*, the waiting room." There the Shabak holds the men brought in for interrogation, their hands cuffed behind their backs, their heads in sacks. The men are forced to sit for hours on low chairs tilted backward in positions that cause unbearable pain. "When they took off my blindfold," Mabhuh continued, "I saw how wide-eyed the officers were. They said, 'Oh good, you're here.' " Like most other prisoners, Mabhuh stopped short of talking about the interrogation itself.

I learned a little more about interrogations from A.I., who was arrested in 1985 on suspicion of fighting with Palestinian forces during the Lebanon war (he had in fact been a student in Eastern Europe then). "They covered my head with a sack," he told me, "and tied my hands behind my back. Sometimes they'd tie my hands to a pipe behind me. Sometimes they'd tie me up and leave me lying on the floor for hours, even for days and nights. Once or twice a day they'd take me in for interrogation, hit me, twist my testicles, tighten the handcuffs, pour ice water on my back. They kept saying how they knew everything about me but now I had to tell them what I'd done. They actually let on very little about what they really knew. It was a game of cat and mouse." Diab al-Luh, a Fatah member, was held for days with his hands bound behind him. After his release his friends fed him because he could not move his hands. The several hundred ex-prisoners treated at Eyad al-Sarraj's mental health center and the questionnaires they filled out all indicated that interrogation leaves wounds that continue to rankle, even ten years after the event. Thousands of other former inmates have described a similar pattern of abuse that didn't vary with the severity of the alleged offense, and that testifies to a policy of interrogation rather than isolated incidents. The mental health center's Abu Nada described the procedure:

> Four Shabak agents lay the prisoner on his back. One jumps on his legs, the second on his chest, the third on his genitals; the fourth covers the prisoner's mouth and nose so he can't breathe. Someone keeps track of the time. A doctor may also be present, overseeing the session. Then they cover the prisoner's head with a stinking sack. The prisoner can't see a thing, can't tell day from night. He spends days without sleep and without enough food and without being allowed to go to the bathroom. After this softening up or at the same time, they begin the questioning, which is always accompanied by psychological humiliation in addition to the physical torture: "You won't be a man by the time we pull you out of here, you won't be able to have children; we'll bring your wife and your mother and fuck them right in front of you." Sometimes they make homosexual threats. Men who have restrained themselves for days so as not to urinate or defecate in their pants develop physical ailments like kidney stones. Those who couldn't hold back feel a sense of humiliation and a loss of self-respect for a long time afterward. The sexual degradation can cause sexual dysfunction years later. Some men become sterile because of injury to their sexual organs.

A prisoner later interrogated by the Palestinian security forces noted the efficiency of the Shabak's methods: "choking, blows to the genitals, pressure on the chest—they have them down pat. They don't leave evidence. Not like the injuries our people inflict, when they have to put you in a cell for a few weeks until the marks disappear."

Ghazi Abu Jiab, a Popular Front activist, was sentenced to several life terms in 1969, at age seventeen, but was released in a prisoner exchange after sixteen years. He generally volunteers little about his time in prison. But we were talking in passing about the Shabak when something reminded him of the night during the *intifada* when he was among a group of detainees being guarded by regular army troops. The Shabak officers had gone for a rest. There were about twenty detainees in the room, their heads covered with sacks. The soldiers, who seemed to be looking for entertainment, ordered each prisoner to announce his name and then say, "I'm queer and Arafat is a son of a bitch," or something similar. Abu Jiab was the third or fourth in line. From beneath his moldy sack he raised his voice so all the room would hear and said, "You must be dreaming if you think I'll say that." Although his Hebrew was fluent he spoke in Arabic for the other prisoners to understand and follow his lead. The soldiers couldn't believe their ears and again ordered Abu Jiab to state his name and repeat the insult. Abu Jiab refused. "Even if you tell me to say [then Israeli prime minister] Yitzhak Shamir is a son of a bitch, I won't do it," Abu Jiab told the soldiers. After years in jail he knew that the guards and the prison system always try to weaken prisoners by creating internal divisions, forcing each one to face the system's power alone. The soldiers, however, turned their backs on the other prisoners and set upon Abu Jiab, beating him. They continued long after he lost consciousness, until finally someone was able to run to the Shabak to call off the soldiers.

Unlike Abu Jiab and Mabhuh, Abu Mustafa needs little encouragement to talk about prison. He was arrested and interrogated several times before the *intifada* and was eventually tried for belonging to a Fatah military unit. "At every moment, there's something that reminds me of prison. A few days ago I was watching TV with my daughters and we saw a man hitting a donkey. I made a nervous movement and the girls asked me what was wrong. I was thinking about a time in 1973 when they hit me with a stick. Once they held me for three days and hit me with thick electrical wires. It happened twenty-three years ago but when I watched television the other day it all came back to me out of nowhere.

"Another time an interrogator spat in my mouth. That was in 1979. I don't like talking about these things. It was a Shabak guy, Abu Ishaq or Abu Ibrahim—they always go by Arabic names. They'd squeeze our testicles, too. They did it to everyone. But I didn't feel humiliated when they tortured me. It was only when this guy spat at me. I didn't know he was going to do it; my eyes were covered. He told me to open my mouth and when he spat I felt like vomiting. Someone had said I had a crate of hand grenades so they arrested me and kept up the interrogation for seventy-two days. But I never had those hand grenades."

Abu Mustafa believes the Shabak officers feel they are simply doing their job. "He's a person like us. He has children, a wife. He knows how to love people, how to get on with them. I see him as a big animal, but to others he's a person. He's just doing a job and it's a disgusting job. That's how I see it." Years later, Abu Mustafa learned the Shabak officer had been killed in an explosion in Lebanon. "The truth is that I was happy, very happy. I saw his picture on television and I remember jumping for joy. He was the only one who humiliated me that painfully."

Another Fatah member, Abu Majed, was detained for six months when he was fifteen and later, during the *intifada*, arrested for involvement in the Unified National Leadership. "One Friday," he told me, "the Shabak guy took me to the showers. He tied my hand to the showerhead, turned on the cold water, and then went home for the weekend. The whole time he was probably with his family, taking his kids on a trip or visiting their grandmother, while I was under the shower with my arm tied above my head. Before this they'd tied me up for an hour or two, maybe five hours. And the duty officer wouldn't take responsibility for freeing me so I stayed that way until Saturday night. Then I don't know what happened but I woke up in the clinic. My arm was paralyzed for a year before I began to move my fingers. My friends had to massage my hand. I still can't use it properly. Every winter it hurts. I can't lift anything."

The cramped conditions in Abu Majed's cell could only have exacerbated the pain in his arm. "We were thirty-four people in a twenty-foot cell," he said. "Twenty-four of us slept on beds and the others on the floor. Can you imagine how hard that is, even at night? This one can't sleep, that one tosses and turns, someone else is having a nightmare. People screamed and sighed in the night. I used to sleep during the day and read at night. It was forbidden to turn the light on, but my bed was near the hallway, where there was light."

Family visits, the prisoners concur, were their salvation. A prisoner's only link to the outside world is through his family, yet since Israel began sealing off the Strip in the early nineties families have been largely unable to visit relatives still held in Israeli jails. "That's the hardest thing," Abu Mustafa said, "when visiting hour is over and no one's come to see you. When I was angry with someone or I had a problem in my cell or knew that something bad was about to happen, I'd tell my family. We'd tell them in great detail just how we were being treated."

It was indeed common for prisoners to seek to create solidarity between themselves and those on the outside by sharing their experience. "The family are partners in everything," Abu Majed said. "They'd prepare for their visits; they were our mail service. Even the little children learned how to take mail without the guards' noticing."

Unlike many wives, though, Um Mustafa never felt cut off or excluded from her husband's prison life. "Ask her what I used to eat every day," Abu Mustafa urged me. "She can tell you everything." And Um Mustafa did: "In the morning they'd have tomatoes and share a container of yogurt among three or four people. It wasn't even enough for a child. They'd get a little soup with vegetables—not much to chew on and a lot of water."

"We had one chicken a week for eight people," Abu Mustafa continued. "And there was no end of lentils. There were lentils every day."

At first, Abu Mustafa and others were forbidden food from the outside. After a lengthy struggle with the prison authorities, they were allowed to bring some in. "We brought mint, sunflower seeds, tea, all at our own expense," Um Mustafa said. "You'd think it was a hotel that we had to pay for."

"Sooner or later," Abu Mustafa added, "the Israelis will probably charge us for bed and board."

The prisoners were allowed to watch television, which was one way to follow the *intifada* and learn about developments outside. Once Abu Mustafa even saw his son being arrested. "I saw Mustafa in an army jeep but I wasn't sure it was him. Then I saw my mother-in-law pounce on the soldiers, so I knew. After they told me what he'd done, that he'd thrown stones at a Shabak car, I felt proud, but at first I was just worried about what they'd do to him. The soldiers kept him in custody for a few hours. A young kid. But they let him go."

Tens of thousands of Palestinians came to know Israelis through the experience of prisons and detention camps. They all have stories about the good jailers and the bad ones, those who were humane and those who were full of hate. Abu Shamalla was hospitalized several times during his prison term and says he will never forget Ella, a nurse in Ramle who tended to him. Thus for many prisoners, the stereotypes of Israelis were shattered. Indeed, those I spoke to were quick to remember the good guards.

"I was teaching my friends Hebrew," Abu Mustafa told me, "and one of the guards stood by the door listening. When I was finished he asked where I had learned the language and we started talking. He was from India, a guy of twenty-six or twenty-seven, different from the others. He treated us all fairly. Soon he was telling me about his little boy and I showed him pictures of my family. The next day he brought in a cake his wife had made me. It was forbidden but he did it. We were never really friends, but I was fond of him and learned that there were other kinds of Israelis. They moved him somewhere else when they found out."

Abu Majed spoke of guards who already received danger pay but made additional money by smuggling forbidden goods to prisoners for a price. "The Israeli I met cares about his wallet. He doesn't give a damn about the rest of Israel." Still, he remembers unexpected moments of contact. One of his interrogators was rather overweight. As the man was jumping on him and squeezing his testicles, trying to get him to squeal on his comrades, Abu Majed managed to gasp, "They must be paying you double for your fat ass." Incredibly, the interrogator bent over with laughter and left the room. For Abu Majed, too, the good guards stand out. "My brother and I were detained in the same prison for a long time in 1980. We sat in solitary, in neighboring cells, but they wouldn't let us talk to each other. We were allowed out of our cells once a day, to go to the bathroom—although there was a pot to use the rest of the time—and there was one guard from Soviet Georgia who'd let us talk whenever I went to the toilet. And he told me why: he and his brother had been prisoners in the same place in Siberia but they never saw each other. After eight years he found out that his brother had died in prison, right next to him. I'll never forget that man. He was human."

The guards Abu Jiab remembers well were also Soviet Georgians, many of whom had come to Israel in a wave of immigration in the mid-1970s. "They behaved differently from the Israelis—they were very emotional. During one of our first hunger strikes, they couldn't look at us. They'd see the feeding tubes shoved down our throats and start crying and running away. They got worked up easily, like us Arabs. Once I was arguing with a guard and I spat in his face. I had a reputation for being self-controlled, so he was shocked. He took the cell keys, threw them on the floor, and walked out. Can you imagine? Leaving the keys? There's no greater crime. I was sorry that I'd hurt him and another guard intervened to patch things up." Abu Jiab recalled guards who would help get the prisoners all kinds of necessities—food, cigarettes, even hot water. "It was really something to be able to ask a guard to turn on the boiler so we could drink coffee at midnight or in the morning before roll call. I still appreciate it, even today." Eventually, according to Abu Jiab, the helpful Georgian guards got corrupted. "They got to be like the Israelis."

"What makes a good soldier?" I asked Rafat al-Najjar, who was released from Ansar shortly before our conversation. Every morning at six the Ansar prisoners would be made to gather in the square near their tents for roll call; they would wait, kneeling on the ground, their bodies bent over their knees, until every prisoner in all the sections and blocks had been accounted for. "A good soldier doesn't deliberately drag out roll call to make it harder for us," Najar said. "A good soldier doesn't point his rifle down our throats; he lowers the barrel." One good soldier pinched cigarettes and coffee from the supply room and threw them into the prisoners' compound when their supplies ran out. The soldier was eventually tried and jailed, but the inmates who were called to testify denied that he had ever done any such thing, Najar recalled fondly.

Some soldiers and prisoners developed friendships, and their stories have become occupation folklore. There is the soldier who wanted an ex-prisoner from Gaza to attend his wedding, but the Strip was under curfew. So the soldier recruited other soldiers, his friends, on a mission. They stole into Gaza in an army jeep, collected the Palestinian friend from his home in the Khan Yunis camp, and covered his head with a blanket as they approached the checkpoint. "Where are you going with him?" the checkpoint guards asked, indicating the Palestinian. The soldiers in the jeep said in whispers, "It's okay. We're taking him in for interrogation."

Over time, I heard the same story with slight variations from diverse sources. It had left the realm of historical truth, I believe, and become a symbol of something greater than a friendship between any one particular soldier and prisoner. The story and the way it spread reveal something about a fantasy and a wish to put aside national enmity. In prison, there were opportunities to see the Israeli not as a two-dimensional monster but as a complex human being. This seismic shift required a new approach, not only between individuals, but also politically.

In those jails where Palestinians were locked up together with criminal, that is, Jewish prisoners, they came to have an even more nuanced view. "I like Israeli criminals," my lawyer friend Raji Sourani once declared. "They have style." He waved away my skepticism. "In 1985 I was in Beersheba prison. We were separated from the criminal inmates by a partition between our two wings, but we could hear each other and pass things back and forth. I heard someone calling, asking for a few cigarettes and I threw over a couple of packages. He asked my name, thanked me, and that was that. The next day he said, 'Hey, friend, tell me what you guys need.' I told him: 'Women.' But he persisted. He wanted to know whether we had a radio, and then newspapers and a radio appeared out of nowhere. A week or two later I had an argument with a jailer who really infuriated me and I was about to hit him, a serious offense. The criminal guy called over and calmed me down. The next thing I knew the guard's face had been slashed."

It was this kind of firsthand knowledge of Israelis that began to undermine some Palestinians' belief in liberating all of Palestine through armed struggle. In prison, Abu Shamalla discovered what he calls "a people that wants to live." Until then he had thought that Israeli and Palestinian existence were irreconcilable. A.I. began to distinguish between Israeli qualities and flaws: "In Israel, talented people are given the opportunity to develop their abilities. That's how Israel has progressed so far in such a short time. But the Israelis talk about democracy and human rights when they don't respect them. A democratic person treats other people democratically too, even his enemies."

Others, like Abu Mustafa, reached understanding through the many books they read in prison. "I gained knowledge and came to the conclusion we needed to do things differently. I hadn't known that Israel had an atomic reactor, for example. I didn't know that Israel had the best weapons in the world. I didn't know that the whole world was helping Israel, even our own Arabs."

If prison produced a more nuanced, complex understanding of the enemy, it was also responsible, to some degree, for forging a new Palestinian sensibility, a cohesion between different parties and political groups that had been deeply factionalized. Fatah and Communist political prisoners were locked up with Popular Front, Democratic Front, and union activists, along with militants indicted for shooting at soldiers, planting bombs, and killing Palestinian collaborators. It is true that until the late 1980s, prison was predominantly a PLO experience; Hamas had not yet been established, and the Islamic Jihad and Muslim Brotherhood were sparsely represented. Nevertheless, Palestinians were united in their support of the prisoners as pioneers and heroes, soldiers who had responded to the call and to their inner convictions.

Prison is an island where the normative social structure breaks down and prisoners have little choice but to create a new structure out of whatever materials come to hand. The urge to make contact with anyone—guard or prisoner, criminal or political—plays its part in the new structure. And people are judged not by their standing or achievements on the outside but by their behavior behind bars, toward other prisoners. When Palestinians began fighting the occupation, Israel conceived of prison not just as a means of punishing individuals but also as a deterrent to others, a way to destroy unity, undermine self-worth, and, cumulatively, crush the resistance. In spite of the continuing trauma to scores of prisoners, Israel clearly failed in its goals. For one thing, none of the people I spoke to abandoned the fight against the occupation; many served multiple prison sentences. Moreover, prison produced some decisive Palestinian victories: during the early years of the prison experience—the 1970s and early 1980s—the inmates insisted, again and again, on better conditions and humane treatment. They fought for their rights collectively, and their battles ultimately enhanced Palestinian unity and pride, playing no small part in the history of Palestinian national identity.

In the early days of the occupation, prison represented something of a microcosm of Israeli-Palestinian relations. On the one side, there was an effort to divide and humiliate; on the other, resistance and confrontation that eventually led to a kind of conciliation, a change in Israel's attitude, and improved conditions. After the 1967 war, the first Palestinians to strike at the occupation were sent to Ashkelon prison, where Israel attempted a kind of reeducation. According to Ghazi Abu Jiab, imprisoned in 1969, Israel believed that crushing the first wave of prisoners was the key to eradicating armed opposition entirely. Abu Jiab remembers the first warden, who had a reputation for being inflexible and cruel. His deputy was no less callous. The prisoners called him a Nazi "because he was an Ashkenazi and had a German look about him," Abu Jiab said. Breaking the prisoners' spirits began immediately. On arrival, their hair was shaved and they were sprayed with DDT. "The guards thought that we Arabs considered our mustaches a symbol of manliness and that we'd feel humiliated when they shaved them off," Abu Jiab recalled. "I didn't care about my hair, I was only seventeen. I just didn't want them to hit me." Prisoners were also obliged to address the guards as *sidi*, "sir" or "my master" in Arabic. Conditions were tough. There were no pillows or mattresses and the inmates slept on the floor. They were allowed four blankets each and made pillows of their shoes. During the day a mat was spread out, but it was rolled up at night and placed where the guard could see it. Food was served in bowls and the prisoners had to pile the bowls in a pyramid against the wall when they were finished eating. During the day they wore high-topped army boots and were forbidden to remove them except for praying.

Pens, paper, and books were forbidden; a pen refill was supplied for writing letters home. "There was one man who knew all about the Bolshevik revolution," Abu Jiab remembers. "He wrote out the history of the Bolsheviks on wrapping paper from packets of margarine, and I

hid it inside my shoes. That's how we created reading material that
was passed from one prisoner to another. We learned these things from
men who'd been in Egyptian prisons." Inmates had to keep their
hands behind their backs whenever they left their cells—during exercise time, family visits, trips to the shower. If for any reason a prisoner
had to wait outside his cell, he was required to stand facing the wall.
"We couldn't even take a shower like human beings," Abu Jiab told
me. "There was one asshole of a guard, Giorno, a real son of a bitch,
who'd count to ten. We had to finish while he was counting—undress,
shower, and get dressed again before he got to ten." The food was poor
and in 1970 a new regulation forbade families to bring food into the
prisons.

The first of dozens of hunger strikes took place in 1971, following
an outbreak of violence in Ashkelon in which all the inmates were
beaten in reprisal for some prisoners' having attacked a particularly
brutal guard. "Hunger strikes were legal," Abu Jiab explained, "and it
was a way to prevent individual prisoners from doing anything reck-
less. We had to take action together." In 1971, the prisoners' demands
included an end to calling the guards *sidi*, longer family visits, longer
exercise periods, and permission to use sponges during showers.
Demands for improved hygienic conditions were an integral part of
every strike.

"We were denied the most basic things," said Abu Jiab, "deliberately, to oppress us. Just like now with the closures, the excuse was
always security. When we demanded beds, they said we'd use the iron
bars to escape." In the first strikes, the authorities chose the inmates'
representatives, but the prisoners fought for the right to decide for
themselves. Once they were allowed to have books, they fought for the
right to choose which books and who would supply them. Prison officials objected to books sent by the prisoners' families, to books sent
from abroad, and to Marxist literature. There was also a battle over
newspapers; for a long time Hebrew newspapers were banned.

According to Abu Jiab, work was introduced in the prisons to cause
dissension among the inmates. "Half the people worked and half
refused, and relations between the two groups became hostile. The
ones who worked lost their organizational discipline. It weakened their
desire to study and fight the administration. They made a little money
and became complacent. Our emphasis was on unity and collective

action, but the administration could divide us by granting privileges to a small group of workers."

The long hunger strike of 1975 was the hardest trial of Abu Jiab's life. "It lasted forty-five days. We never dreamed it would go on for so long. Only fifty-five of the original four hundred and fifty strikers stayed the course. The authorities always talked as if the strikes were imported from abroad or from the territories, as if we were getting orders from outside. They treated us the way they treated the PLO—no recognition for our organization or for our leadership. But they gave in when they needed our intervention." A delegation of Gazan dignitaries was brought in to negotiate a compromise and the strike was halted in return for certain promises, but the prisoners had been duped. "They agreed to give us combs," Abu Jiab said. "The strike went on for seven weeks and in the end we each got a comb. So a month later, we decided to strike again and then they did everything they could to break us. The strikers were sent to different prisons. There were no windows; the lights were on all the time. There was no night and no day, and that was harder to bear than the hunger. They really tormented us. Once they said they'd found a needle in the cell, part of an escape attempt. Then they tied us up and sprayed us with tear gas. My friend R. tried to kill himself; he started banging his head on the iron bars.

"At a certain point they force-fed us milk with eggs. It was awful because the milk can get into your lungs. Some people died that way at Nafha prison a few years later. We were in a tiny cell and slept on top of one another. At some point, we decided to drink the milk and eggs because both sides, the Israelis and we prisoners, agreed that drinking the mixture wasn't breaking the strike. In the end, though, they beat us. We didn't get our demands and our morale was very low. When that happens everyone starts blaming their leaders and everyone else."

Nevertheless, whenever a new prison opened, its inmates immediately went on strike. In 1980 Nafha was set up to separate the Palestinian leaders from the rest of the prison population. No sooner were inmates transferred there than they began to strike. The same thing happened at the Ansar prison camp in the Negev, where thousands were held in clusters of tents. "Movement between the tents was forbidden," says Abu Jiab. "It was like one huge cage in the desert."

By the time of Abu Jiab's release in a prisoner exchange in 1985, 90 percent of the prisoners' initial demands had been met, and they had gained more than material improvements. Veterans taught the younger inmates how to withstand the hardships and still keep their minds alive and develop their talents. A.I. remembers spending time with a senior Democratic Front activist, Omar al-Qassem, who suffered from kidney disease and eventually died in prison. "He told me what to do, how to take care of my health and my mind: get plenty of exercise, stop smoking, and read a lot. I wasn't convinced about the smoking until he invited me to run with him. We ran in the yard and he kept going when I quickly got out of breath. I felt ashamed and quit smoking."

A.I. believes prison made him a quieter man, more reserved and serious. "The less you talk, the greater respect you earn. You have to watch yourself, keep your self-respect. It's impossible to live like we did in a tiny cell. If you really thought about how you couldn't go out, you'd go crazy. So you'd have to think about other things, like reading. I started getting interested in mosques and made models of them from cardboard and glue."

A whole range of stratagems helped the prisoners get through their sentences, many of which they refuse to talk about out of consideration for those still in jail. Before they were permitted in 1985, radios and batteries were smuggled in. One prisoner would secretly listen to the news, write it down, and distribute his notes throughout the cells. Prisoners would tap into the electricity supply and so manage to keep the lights and later televisions on after hours. A.I. recalls making films with the video camera smuggled into Nafha, which was kept hidden in holes burrowed into the floor or the walls. Prisoners usually took this contraband outside with them during exercise time, for fear of its being discovered in their cells.

In the early days, the conditions were not the only things that were hard on the prisoners. They were hard on themselves, setting up a series of stringent, self-imposed controls. "We were always thinking about women, but we didn't talk about them except in whispers," says A.I., referring to one of the prohibitions. "After we got radios, for example, we banned listening to certain kinds of songs because they would corrupt us. We were also forbidden to fraternize with the guards, as if to do so meant breaking bread with the enemy. All these prohibitions ignored our human needs, and they gradually eased."

The cell was a forum for ideological discussion. A.I. argued against the concept of family honor. Abu Jiab opposed airplane hijackings whose object was ransom money rather than the release of prisoners. The inmates compiled monthly publications of articles, poems, and stories, which they copied into notebooks and distributed in the different prison wings. Forbidden texts were smuggled in, copied, and used in study groups. Diab al-Luh, also freed in the 1985 prisoner exchange, believes that his generation of prisoners was particularly well educated because of their extensive reading, a practice that fell off after televisions were introduced in the prisons in 1985. Official lending libraries sanctioned by the authorities were augmented by the texts of each political organization. Luh remembers that Fatah forbade its members to borrow Marxist books put out by the Popular Front. Fatah was not opposed to texts on national revolutions, only those with an anticapitalist message that conflicted with its view of itself as a government in the making. Each organization, according to Abu Jiab, refused to lend its books to the others. Speaking to me ten years later, he called the policy stupid, typical of the rivalries and sectarianism.

Factionalism was only one source of friction. "The day was full of countless problems between prisoners. They quarreled over insignificant things—over a slice of bread, over cleaning the cell, over their place in line for a shower, over cigarettes," recalled Abu Jiab. But the worst source of tension, one that consumed much of the prisoners' time and energy, was their suspicion of stool pigeons. The issue of traitors in jail provoked much cruelty; prison is a microcosm of the Palestinian world and the question of traitors in jail and the cruelty it provoked mirrors that society's inability to respond to the phenomenon of collaboration. Abu Jiab was among the first to speak out against killing collaborators. He recoiled from the savagery and was concerned about its long-term implications for Palestinian society. "Long ago, I concluded that the Shabak wasn't recruiting all those informers just to gain information—it's easy to get the information since everybody always talks so much. Rather, it's a way of corrupting and dividing our people. The Israelis managed to convince us that the Shabak knows everything and is deeply involved in our lives. The Shabak's success was that we began to doubt ourselves and suspect one another."

There is no accurate estimate of the number of collaborators Israel succeeded in enticing. The incentives were substantial: travel permits, building permits, business licenses, and the ability to arrange these perks for others. The Palestinians were painfully aware of their own impotence in this contest. Until the *intifada*, collaborators were able to act quite openly, protected by the privileges they enjoyed and spread around. But when the uprising was met with intensified Israeli oppression, people unleashed their anger, despair, and frustration on the targets closest at hand: Palestinians under suspicion of helping the enemy.

Suspected collaborators were captured by small groups of militants and often subjected to brutal torture. Frequently, the inquisitor was also judge and hangman. In many cases the suspicions were proven groundless, but usually too late. For years, people have refused to confront Israel's success at recruiting considerable numbers into its service; at the same time, they prefer to close their eyes to the guilt some Palestinians bear in the ruthless murder of compatriots who were denied the opportunity to defend themselves.

A.I. has admitted to murdering a collaborator in prison and expresses no regret. The informer had spent years disguised as a PLO student activist and had betrayed countless trusting students. A.I. insists that the man's cruelty far outweighed that involved in killing him. Under interrogation, the man admitted that he had been imprisoned as a way of shoring up his militant credentials. A.I. claims he murdered the man on orders from outside, but others said A.I. did not carry out the killing himself but rather took responsibility as the highest-ranking member of his organization in the jail. A killer's identity is often obscured to prevent the victim's family from seeking revenge. In this case, A.I. tells me, the man's father investigated his son's background, found the suspicions were justified, and denounced his son. "That's another good thing about prison," A.I. says. "It's easy to expose the informers."

The strain of being under suspicion as traitors and being constantly watched drove some men out of their minds, Abu Jiab argues. A.I. counters that inmates always know who the informers are: "You know the other prisoners better than you know your wife; you never spend as much time with anyone as you do with your cellmates."

In the end, the hope of getting out helped surmount the griefs of prison. Unlike criminal prisoners, who are buoyed by the promise of time off for good behavior, political prisoners must depend on external developments, but these were not entirely lacking. "There was always something going on, some reason for hope," says Abu Jiab. "Early on, our organizations were at the height of their military activity—hijackings, hostage seizures, other armed operations—so there was the prospect of being freed in a prisoner exchange. That's what kept us going, the thought that something—the October war in 1973, the Lebanon war—would lead to our release. The hope kept us sane, that and the family visits."

Um Muhammad, her head wrapped in a large white scarf and her hands red from henna, dropped heavily into the chair. She felt inside her blouse and retrieved what looked like a handful of pills. It turned out that the little capsules contained letters sent from prison, tiny strips of thin paper covered with cramped writing, then folded over and wrapped in plastic film. Um Muhammad had just returned from visiting her son, jailed in Israel since 1991, and had smuggled out a letter of protest from all the prisoners condemning the death of a Fatah militant detained by the Palestinian Authority. But Um Muhammad's concern was the infrequency of her visits to her son—this was the first in seven months. As long as the closures continued, she was unable to enter Israel to see him.

"This would never have happened before. All during the *intifada*, even during curfews, I could see him every fifteen days. Now I can't. There's always a problem. Why?" she asked. "My son says that everything's okay, and the prisoners are always smiling when we come. They don't want to worry us, but I know how hard it is for them."

Incredibly, the fate of the prisoners was ignored in 1993, in the Declaration of Principles. The Palestinian negotiators—PLO members living abroad—had not seen to the inclusion of any reference to the 11,000 Palestinians held in Israeli prisons for the crime, as the prisoners saw it, of opposing the occupation. This glaring omission was one more expression of the gulf between the leadership abroad and the people who lived under occupation. Given the oversight, the Israelis themselves could hardly be expected to acknowledge the argument that Palestinian prisoners were soldiers who had obeyed orders in time of war, that is, POWs.

Following a series of demonstrations, the omission was partially rectified in the Cairo agreement signed in May 1994, which laid out the terms of the first stage of Palestinian self-rule. The section of the agreement devoted to "confidence-building measures" allowed for the release of 5,000 prisoners from the Gaza Strip and the West Bank under a series of conditions and constraints (many of the men were prohibited from leaving the Gaza Strip or Jericho). After the agreement was signed, the two sides were to continue negotiating the release of additional prisoners.

Hisham Abed al-Razeq of Fatah led the Palestinian representatives in these talks. He had spent twenty-one years in prison and then became a member of the Legislative Council. By December 1994 he felt deep disappointment with the way Israel was handling the release of prisoners. The first 5,000 had been set free, including several hundred Hamas and Islamic Jihad prisoners who had signed a statement renouncing terrorism, but Abed al-Razeq complained that the piecemeal release schedule had prevented the kind of public celebration that would have strengthened the status of the Palestinian Authority and the agreement's supporters. But the worst blow was the fact that Israel had a free hand in choosing who would be set free.

"Our representatives left the decision up to the Israelis, who didn't release a single person who had taken an active part in the war against them." Even those who now accepted the peace agreement stayed in jail if they had killed or shot or injured Israelis, Abed al-Razeq explained. "The ones who were freed were people who'd been active in the *intifada* or had killed Palestinian collaborators." As head of the prisoners' committee Abed al-Razeq continues paying weekly visits to his comrades in prison. "I have no explanation to give them as to why they are still being held. The prisoners feel as if their commanders abandoned them on the battlefield."

Abed al-Razeq includes among those commanders everyone from Yassir Arafat down. "The prisoners can't believe that Palestinian cabinet ministers are paying them visits in Israeli jails. They feel betrayed. They weren't mentioned in the Declaration of Principles and when it came to the Cairo negotiations the Palestinian leadership didn't succeed in fixing a mutually acceptable timetable for their release." If the negotiators had sons in prison, the prisoners say, they would have worked something out.

Of the 6,000 prisoners still in jail in 1995, 650 participated directly in killing Israelis or, as Abed al-Razeq puts it, in the war against the Israelis. I pointed out that Israel views those prisoners as having blood on their hands, Jewish blood. "Both Rabin and Arafat have blood on their hands, yet they shook hands" is Abed al-Razeq's rejoinder. "The prisoners are soldiers who received orders, just as the IDF soldiers received orders to arrest them, beat them, break their arms and legs. To shoot. To kill. To torture them. To seal off the territories for weeks at a time. To grab land and transfer it to Jewish settlers. To close schools and spray the students with tear gas."

In the time that has passed since my conversation with Abed al-Razeq, another 3,000 prisoners have been released in dribs and drabs as a result of the interim agreement—Oslo 2—signed in Washington in September 1995. Those still in prison attempted a hunger strike in June of that year; the Palestinian Authority and other political organizations held demonstrations within the self-rule area. At the same time, the Authority's representatives begged the prisoners to end the strike. According to many, the Authority was afraid some inmates might die as martyrs in the hunger strike, causing widespread unrest among Palestinians and the Authority would be blamed.

Sooner or later, Abed al-Razeq believed, Palestinians would take to the streets over the prisoner issue. "This is a volcano," he said at the time. "If it erupts, heaven knows how far it'll go. I meet the prisoners' families and I can feel the eruption."* But the explosion did not come, not even when Israel's president, Ezer Weizmann, and Brigadier General Ilan Biran of the IDF Central Command refused to pardon five Palestinian women prisoners who were Jerusalem residents and thus subject to Israeli law. (It should be noted that the 1995 Washington agreement clearly stated that all women detainees and prisoners were to be freed in the first stage of releases.) Twenty-six other women prisoners refused to be released until their comrades were also freed. Several hundred male prisoners, however, did not join the act of solidarity and agreed to leave prison on schedule.

Negotiations over the prisoners have been at an impasse since the

---

*Abed al-Razeq's words proved prophetic. In December 1998, the remaining prisoners went on a hunger strike and massive demonstrations in support of the strike took place near several Israeli checkpoints. Five demonstrators were killed by IDF troops. The demonstrators were protesting against Israel's insistence on releasing common criminals rather than prisoners who had fought the occupation.

Palestinian Legislative Council elections in 1996 and a series of suicide bombings that year. The right to regular family visits has not been
honored and Palestinian prisoners have never been so divided among
themselves. "There's one man who's been in for twenty-three years,"
A.I. told me. "He was part of a unit that killed a police officer in Gaza,
and they refuse to let him go, even though it was twenty-three years
ago. It's not fair. There are Israeli officers who've killed plenty of
Palestinians but they're sitting at the negotiating table. Why is someone who killed a Jewish officer being punished for so long?"

Part IV

Gaza Prison

Chapter 10

Yesterday's Permit

"The only thing that's missing here in Gaza is the morning roll call," said Abu Majed. We were sitting on thin mattresses—the sole furniture in the room—drinking tea and nibbling cookies, a special treat for the Id al-Fitr holiday, which marks the end of the month-long Ramadan fast. Abu Majed's past reads like the saga of a Fatah everyman: occasional menial jobs in Israel, arrests and interrogations as a teenager, ten years in Israeli jails, eventual work as a Palestinian police officer. I can see him, a skinny boy mixing cement in Beersheba or hauling crates in Tel Aviv's Carmel market, making the most of his few Hebrew sentences, awed at first by the tall buildings and wide city streets, stealing glances at the women, then chiding himself for his weakness. I imagine him coming home to Gaza in the evenings with some cash for his family and a small present for his sister. And then the *intifada* and joining a UNL cell, arrests and more arrests, trial, and prison.

It was Abu Majed who made the connection between Gaza, prison, and peppers, the hot little red and green variety that, chopped up fine with garlic and tomatoes, gives Gazan salad its fierce reputation. "We missed those peppers in prison," he said, "the way they'd bring tears to your eyes. We could have pretended it was the sting that was making us cry and not our longing for home." Abu Majed went on to tell a story he had heard from some Israeli—a guard or one of his bosses, he couldn't remember which. Investigating a series of attacks on northern Israeli farms on the Lebanese border in the 1970s, the IDF concluded the infiltrators originated from Gaza, even though they had come by way of Lebanon. They had broken water pipes, smashed greenhouses, and ruined the fields, but one crop, though somewhat plundered, had escaped serious harm—the bushes of little green and red peppers. At least now, Abu Majed concluded ruefully, Gazans have plenty of peppers. "It's just the roll call that's missing." That and the constant presence of Israelis. "It's been so long since I've spoken Hebrew," Abu Majed said. "You're the first Israeli I've met in two years, since I got out of prison. You're a real museum piece."

After our meeting, I repeated Abu Majed's quip about the morning roll call at every opportunity. Gazans—ex-prisoners and others—reacted with peals of laughter. "Why didn't we think of that?" I heard more than once. Israelis, however, usually needed an explanation and even then I am not sure they thought the joke was funny. For the most part, Israelis continue to believe that the closures, sealing off the Strip—in effect locking up Gaza's entire population—are simply a response to terror and a means to prevent it, that they are in fact the only way to avoid having buses blown up. For many, the Oslo Accords evoke only the horrifying, bloody spectacles that Israel has experienced with such frightening regularity. But what is seen as a remedy by Israelis has become collective punishment in Palestinian eyes. For Gazans, the siege of the Strip serves only to provoke the anger that produced the suicide bombings and perpetuate the circumstances that, to some extent, explain them. In Gaza, "Oslo" and the "peace process" are now synonymous with mass internment and suffocating constriction. It is impossible to understand developments in Gaza since the beginning of Palestinian self-rule in 1994 without considering the grinding daily ramifications of keeping the Strip closed.

On and off since 1991—but for increasingly longer periods since 1994—some one million people have been confined to the 147-square mile Strip. Twenty percent of that land is restricted to Jewish settlements and barred to Palestinians. For most Gazans, most of the time, there is no exit, not to Israel, not to Egypt, and not to the West Bank.

"You can get an exit permit if you're about to die," Gazans observe wryly. According to the Israeli Coordination and Liaison Office (CLO)—the post-Oslo incarnation of the civil administration, responsible for issuing exit permits—there are several categories of people who may ask to enter Israel, at least when the checkpoints are open:

workers with steady jobs in Israel, truck owners importing or exporting goods (but only with an Israeli military escort), businessmen, sick people, those with special permits for "personal reasons" (to visit a sick relative or to catch a flight abroad, for example), and high-ranking Palestinian officials and police. In June 1996, 17,000 workers were allowed to leave the Strip; 300 of Gaza's 2,000 trucks, some 20 to 40 taxis daily of a fleet of 1,200, 28 businessmen, and between 10 and 20 sick people each day. (Before 1991, there were no figures because no records were kept—Gazans needed no permits and moved freely between the Strip, Israel, and the West Bank. However, even conservative estimates would put the pre-1991 number of Gazans working in Israel at 80,000.)

"Once I used to dream of a state," a Palestinian cameraman told me. "Now I dream of getting to the other side of the Erez checkpoint." Article 4 of the Declaration of Principles states clearly: "Both sides regard the West Bank and the Gaza Strip as one territorial unit whose geographical integrity will be preserved during the interim period." Yet the Strip has been cut off from the West Bank since the agreements were signed. To implement the principle of territorial integrity, the Cairo agreement, signed in May 1994, confirms that a "safe passage" will connect the Strip with the territory under Palestinian autonomous rule in the West Bank. To date, negotiations over the safe passage—who will control it and who will be entitled to use it—have come to nothing. Palestinians who must reach the West Bank have, in some cases, traveled via Egypt to Jordan, where they crossed the Allenby Bridge, all because they could not get a permit to make a two-hour journey across Israel.

One cannot leave Gaza on a sudden impulse to visit friends in Ramalla, take care of some bit of business that can be done only in East Jerusalem (Palestinians' religious, commercial, and cultural capital), or see one's family in Israel. Even in the rare instance when permission is granted, it never includes an overnight stay. There is little point in traveling several hours to one's destination, only to turn right around and come back home—and few Gazans can afford the cost, anyway. These restrictions on movement are not imposed only after a terrorist attack; they are in force all the time.

Sometimes it is impossible to leave even for an officially sanctioned "objective" reason. One Gazan doctor, for example, could not get permission to accompany his terminally ill mother to the hospital in Tel Aviv; she died alone. The doctor's brother, a well-known Palestinian writer, was not allowed to leave the West Bank to attend his mother's funeral in Gaza. A Palestinian journalist invited to teach part of a course in the United States was refused permission to pick up her visa at the American Embassy in Tel Aviv. A young man from the Meghazi refugee camp got engaged to a woman from the Jelazun camp in the West Bank and was unable to visit her for five months. Another young man, whose fiancée was in Jordan, was denied a travel permit for security reasons. When I wrote about his case he received a permit, but he was turned down two months later when he needed to travel again. One woman was unable to fly to England to defend her doctoral thesis, even though her husband was director general of a Palestinian ministry. A group of physicians employed by the Palestinian health ministry were not allowed to attend a ministry conference in Ramallah. A couple undergoing fertility treatment in Israel received one permit for the day of their appointment—for the wife only.

Whole categories of people are unable to leave the Strip. Men under forty, for example, are rarely granted exit permits; unmarried men, even those over forty, are also not allowed to leave. Many Gazan students enrolled in West Bank colleges and universities have now lost at least three years of their education. Even when students have been granted exit permits, they have been forbidden to stay in the West Bank. Sometimes students who have ignored the prohibition and stayed in the West Bank anyway have returned home for holidays and been refused new permits.

The all-important exit permit, the restrictions and refusals and contradictory, unfathomable logic behind its issue, has come to dominate life in the Strip. In most cases security reasons are cited. In most cases—including all those above—this excuse makes no sense.

"What do you want? We're actually making progress," one Fatah activist told a gathering of bitter Gazans. The man had been imprisoned in Ketziot, the mass-detention camp in the Negev desert, also known as Ansar. "There were seven blocks of tents in Ketziot and we weren't allowed to move between one block and another. Now we're down to three blocks—Gaza, the north West Bank, and the south West Bank. In Ketziot there were just us men. Here at least we've got our children and wives and parents. In Ketziot we weren't allowed to go anywhere. Here we can drive around Gaza." He went on: "And it's a good thing the roads are in such bad shape—it takes a whole hour to get from one end of the Strip to the other and you don't notice how small it all is. If you drive really slowly, say fifteen miles an hour, you can pretend that you're actually going a very long way."

Since 1994 and the beginning of Palestinian self-rule, leaving Gaza has entailed the following:

First, a person must submit a written request to the appropriate Palestinian ministry: someone seeking medical treatment to the health ministry, a worker to the labor ministry, a businessperson to the ministry of commerce and industry, a driver to the transportation ministry, a student to the ministry of education. (In 1996 responsibility for students was transferred to the Palestinian Civilian Liaison Committee, the body that represents Palestinian interests directly to the Israeli CLO.) One may request a one-day exit permit to Israel or the West Bank, a permit of several days' or weeks' duration, or a permit to enter Egypt via the Rafah border or Jordan via the Allenby Bridge in the West Bank.

Second, Palestinian officials transfer the exit requests to the CLO headquarters located near the Erez checkpoint, in the northern part of the Strip. The CLO is staffed by Israelis, both military officials and civilians; most worked in the old civil administration and many rank high in the Israeli military bureaucratic hierarchy. Some have been at their jobs—governing the Palestinian population—for five, ten, or even twenty years; since 1994 only their titles have changed. The former staff officer, for example, is now called the "coordinator." Anyone who needs to leave the Strip on a regular basis, like workers, has to carry the magnetic card mentioned earlier, an additional form of identification introduced early in the *intifada* to increase control over the population. The magnetic card is the only document Palestinians must procure directly from the CLO, without the mediation of Palestinian representatives; the Israelis who issue magnetic cards are either Shabak officers or soldiers subject to their oversight.

Next, the CLO officials examine and evaluate the Palestinian applications, reviewing, among other data, Shabak records. Exit permits are usually granted to sick people within a day. In especially urgent cases, permission may be granted by telephone or fax. But many requests are turned down; some are answered too late and the applicant simply misses his or her course or flight or meeting. Over the last few years, most Gazans have simply gotten used to the idea that they cannot leave the Strip. They curb needs and desires that the rest of the world takes for granted. They do not even try to test the system and demand the basic human right of freedom of movement.

When Israel imposes its most extreme measure, sealing Gaza "hermetically," all exit permits are automatically canceled. A permit holder may well have been waiting six months for an appointment with a specialist in Jerusalem; indeed, she may be scheduled for an operation. Another person may be booked on a flight abroad. Nevertheless, no one can leave or enter the Strip. The word "hermetic" is applied literally: no one comes in and no one goes out. As the closure gradually begins to ease, those same permit holders must submit their applications all over again.

The rumor quickly spread through Gaza that I, an Israeli, could help. In fact, my ability to intervene was limited, and I did not believe that I should get involved in individual cases. Still, people placed their hopes in me, overwhelmed as they were by the jumble of prohibitions and procedures and criteria, by the hidden workings of an arbitrary system that could, they believed, yield the elusive piece of paper if only handled correctly. People clutched at any possibility and told their stories to any receptive ear. Most Gazans have the mistaken idea, gained during the years of direct contact with the occupation and all its capricious rulings, that any Israeli can "work something out" with the authorities. "Can't you speak to someone there?" they would ask me. Wasn't there something I could do at the CLO or the Shabak or the IDF? Usually I rejected the entreaties—which presumed I had links with the military authorities—and I soon earned a reputation for being short-tempered. "Okay, okay, now you're upset," Gazans would say. "Don't worry, we'll just forget the whole thing."

Nevertheless, a fairly typical day would bring a string of appeals. At 8:00 A.M. the phone would ring (when the phone was working): the anonymous worker who called faithfully once a week, wanting to understand why he was not allowed to stay overnight in Jericho, in the West Bank. He worked in Jerusalem and was obliged to return each night to Gaza, a three-hour journey. There is no direct bus and he spent half his wages on transportation. "It would make so much more sense for me to sleep with friends in the West Bank and come home to Gaza once a week, with more money," he says (as he did before the Israeli redeployment in 1994). He hopes I can perform a miracle. Once again, he politely expresses his disappointment.

At 11:00 my friend Abu Basel might call: some workers had been turned back at the Erez checkpoint, forbidden to leave the Strip. All the men had been employed in Israel for at least fifteen years; only the day before, they had gone to work as usual. Now they were considered a security risk. Why? Who had made the decision? Was there anything they could do?

An hour later, Abu Naji, who owns a sewing workshop, would be on the phone. He had twenty-five truckloads of clothing ready to send to Tel Aviv and had scheduled an Israeli military escort to accompany the shipment, but the trucks had stood idle at the Erez checkpoint for eight hours. No one knew why. On their return trip, the trucks were going to bring back cloth for Abu Naji's next order. Now he was stuck with his merchandise and he had neither cloth nor buttons to give his workers. What should he do?

In the afternoon I might hear from Dr. P., who had been attending a course at a Palestinian hospital in East Jerusalem when Israel sealed the Strip hermetically. He had stayed in Jerusalem to help at the hospital, which the closure had deprived of most of its medical and nursing staff. Now it was time for him to return to Gaza but his exit permit had expired. He knew he would be detained at the Erez checkpoint for having stayed in Jerusalem illegally. "I heard you could help," he says.

Sometimes people called just to pour out their hearts; also, they knew that as a journalist I needed information. So I collected stories, about a truck filled with flowers that was kept waiting at the checkpoint for a full day in the searing heat, about an ambulance that was held up for two hours, about a Palestinian policeman coming back from the West Bank who violated the terms of his exit permit and found himself in detention in Israel. Without these stories, one cannot understand the Gaza Strip.

Sometimes I was actually able to advise people. When the permit was health-related, I sent them to the Association of Israeli and Palestinian Physicians for Human Rights (PHR), located in Tel Aviv; in other civil matters I referred people to Tamar Peleg, a human rights lawyer, who handled, among many other similar cases, those of West Bank residents stranded in the Strip for two months when the checkpoints were sealed. Only very rarely, though, was I able to alter the current by writing an article or requesting an official response to some arbitrary ruling. In a few instances I appealed directly to Israelis with political clout to intervene in situations that were glaringly unreasonable, especially where health was concerned; usually I turned to Knesset members Yossi Sarid, Naomi Hazan, or Yael Dayan. In time, I began to get a bad name at the CLO and even with some low-level negotiators. "She helps people and that's not right," they complained to my fellow journalists. "It's a conflict of interest." I even heard that I had opened an office in Gaza City to dispense advise—a far cry from accepting telephone calls in my rented apartment.

I departed from my self-imposed rule only once, when a friend's mother was dying of heart disease in a Tel Aviv hospital. On and off, hermetic closures had been imposed for several weeks, most recently following a suicide bombing in Jerusalem that had killed four people. Only those deemed "humanitarian cases" by the IDF and the CLO could leave. Three days after the bombing it turned out that the perpetrator had come from Dahariya in the West Bank, but Gaza stayed sealed off.

It was during this time that my friend A. called, asking me to take some X rays, medical reports, and two sets of pajamas to her mother in a Tel Aviv hospital. In the urgent rush of moving her from Gaza, these items had been forgotten. The doctors in Gaza had decided some two days earlier that A.'s mother needed immediate treatment in Tel Aviv, but it had taken a day to procure exit permits for the woman and one daughter, R. The following day at 6:00 A.M., mother and daughter had left for the Erez checkpoint in an ambulance, only to be held up there for almost three hours while soldiers insisted that no one could cross. Eventually R. lost her temper, the Palestinian officer who liaised at the border was called, and, after a security check, the ambulance was allowed to leave. R.'s permit did not include permission to spend the night in Israel, and violating the restriction could mean arrest or even being barred from receiving future permits. So R. had decided to return to Gaza the same night, reassured that her mother's condition was stable.

The next day, a Thursday, R. applied for a new permit, which ended up being granted three days later. A., her sister, who works in Israel, had a one-month permit but that day a new regulation was announced: people with long-term permits were now required to register with the Palestinian Liaison Committee each night prior to their departure from the Strip; the list would then be transferred to the Israeli CLO. (The regulation was quickly revoked; people were simply unable to comply.) In the meantime, A.'s father and a third sister had applied for their own permits and were awaiting approval. The family's only son was under thirty, below the minimum age for men to leave the Strip at that time, so there seemed little point in trying to obtain a permit for him at this stage.

That same Thursday evening I visited the mother, bringing the documents, the pajamas, and a kiss from her daughter. I was shocked to see her looking so frail and thin, while her legs were badly swollen. "When will my children come?" she whispered. "What about my son? I want to see my children." I brought her a little water and plumped up her pillows. Two days later, on Saturday, I returned at the request of the daughters. The mother had been moved to a different room and I found her connected to various tubes. A team of doctors surrounded her bed. "Where's the family?" one doctor asked me. "This woman won't live through the day."

I called the daughters, telling them to run to the Civilian Liaison Committee office and demand permits immediately, even though the Israeli CLO was closed on Saturdays. Next, I contacted the regional IDF spokesperson and was put through to a CLO representative, who took the family's particulars and promised that the permits would be delivered to the Erez checkpoint right away. So the father and daughters were allowed to leave but not to stay overnight. Still, the father spent several hours with his wife and hurried back to Gaza before his permit expired (all this by taxi, since cars bearing Gaza license plates are not allowed out of the Strip). A. decided to risk staying the night; the eldest daughter, M., who lives in the West Bank, had no exit permit but found a way to "steal across the border." I offered these illegals my apartment in Tel Aviv to sleep, or at least rest for a few hours during the day. That evening the mother showed signs of improvement; there is no doubt her family's visit gave her strength.

Over the next few days, the family fought for permits and ferried back and forth between Gaza and Tel Aviv. The eldest daughter stayed at her mother's bedside, an enemy infiltrator breaking the law. One week after entering the hospital, the mother slipped into a coma and the whole family—save the son, G.—simply ignored regulations and spent the night at her side. A relative with connections and influence—in Palestinian intelligence, I believe—managed to arrange retroactive permits, including permission to stay in Israel overnight. Then G. began his odyssey to leave the Strip; surprisingly he was able to receive a magnetic card, a prerequisite for a single man of his age, without trouble. He submitted a request to enter Israel, attaching a letter from the hospital describing his mother's condition, but was told he already had a permit—the CLO had confused his name with his father's. When the mistake was cleared up, he was promised a permit for the following day. But before G. could reach the hospital, his mother died.

Bringing her body directly back to Gaza for burial meant securing a driver's permit and supplying the registration number of the Gaza municipal vehicle that transports the dead and is allowed to enter Israel for that purpose. A driver was located, but he was denied permission to cross into Israel. Until a second driver was found several hours had passed and the family decided to wait no longer. The body was brought back to Gaza in an Israeli ambulance for transfer to a local Palestinian vehicle, a procedure people preferred to avoid if they could. When the ambulance reached the Erez checkpoint, a Palestinian policeman approached the IDF soldier on duty and explained the circumstances. Special permission was required for the two ambulances to meet on one side of the checkpoint. The soldier called his superiors at the CLO and asked for the green light, using a common Erez phrase to describe shifting goods from an Israeli truck to a Palestinian one. "I need to transfer a body back to back," he said. Mercifully, permission was granted, but yet more prohibitions prevented the family from being together at the funeral and during the mourning period. M., the eldest daughter, was allowed to cross from the West Bank into Gaza; her husband, also a native of Gaza, wanted to attend the burial and stay with his wife's family during the mourning period but his request was turned down. He was denied permission to leave the West Bank for "security reasons," but no one knew what those were. The man had never been arrested and was still living in an area directly controlled by the Israeli army, which could long since have detained him had he truly posed a security threat.

Within a few months of Palestinian autonomy, it was clear that this family's trial was not an exception. Many people fared worse. Of the numerous cases that came to my attention, however, I wrote about only a fraction; these stories quickly became old news and readers grew tired of them unless there was some newly shocking element. Nor did anyone want to read a meticulous breakdown of the heartless bureaucratic procedures that were becoming increasingly entrenched. So I found myself caught in a contradiction: I had hoped that my reports would wake Israelis up to what was happening in the Strip, but while readers have a right to know they do not have an obligation, nor are they required to translate knowledge into action. In time, this contradiction began to influence the style and frequency with which I wrote about the closures, which were so central to life in Gaza but so remote from Israeli concerns. I was caught in the journalist's dilemma: should I write about the things that interest readers or about what is actually happening? While I carried on writing about what I saw, my reports did not seem to convey a coherent picture of what was taking place at the Erez checkpoint, nor did they force the necessary conclusions, published as they were in a scattershot and fragmentary way. The occasional human interest story, one journalistic device, would only reinforce the sense that such incidents were regrettable isolated instances, and not—as I hoped to show—a constant occurrence. Rather than sounding a warning bell, each new report seemed to dissolve into the last, received with indifference and denial even by those most poised to care—the peace advocates and human rights organizations such as Peace Now, the Association for Civil Rights in Israel (which warily attempted legal action in a few select cases), the International Center for Peace, and the Israeli human rights organization B'tselem (which procrastinated for a long time before beginning to deal with the issue of closure in a comprehensive manner). Supposedly, peace had come, and the sound of congratulatory backslapping drowned out the evidence that the spirit of occupation was alive and well and basic human rights were being violated even more than before. Erstwhile militant peace activists now made regular pilgrimages to Palestinian and Fatah leaders, paying homage to the Oslo process and ignoring the lessons of the past: that the human distress of a million people is a sea of nitrogylcerin.

I would be lying, of course, if I said my concern with the closures was just that of a journalist. Unlike my Palestinian friends, I was free to leave Gaza at will. Who better than I could testify to the need to get out of the Strip? One's soul and one's sanity cry out for the open horizons beyond the Erez checkpoint, for conversation about something other than exit permits and magnetic cards, for the freedom to drive for miles without barbed wire and concrete roadblocks. I more than anyone knew the urge to escape and the destructive consequences of the inability to do so. Day by day, I saw my friends lose their spontaneity and the impulse, even the desire, to do something, go somewhere, for no good reason except the fun of it.

I began to learn something about us Israelis too, something not quite obvious in the cafés and parks of Tel Aviv. Large numbers of my compatriots, I came to realize, were hard at work devising ways to stop people from leaving the Strip and spinning sophisticated security arguments to justify their actions. And many more—those who paid daily lip service to the transformations of peace—preferred not to disturb the status quo by challenging the siege of Gaza. It was hard not to think of a remark I once heard from Ihab al-Ashqar. "The trouble with you Israelis," he said, "is that you think we just weren't made the same way you were."

And then, too, I was a student of history given that rare chance to watch a process taking place that would one day be summed up in a few paragraphs. I was able to track the evolving relationship between those who give the orders and those ordinary individuals who either carry them out or have to live with their consequences. I wanted to understand whether Israeli soldiers and officials were executing explicit instructions or interpreting unstated policy. Moving between Tel Aviv and Gaza, between the Israeli and Palestinian perceptions of what was taking place, I needed to know whether security concerns were an adequate explanation for imposing closures or whether some other political motive was at work.

Thus every request for an exit permit also served as raw historical material, providing clues to the real cause for this Palestinian experience. For one thing, I came to learn just how limited Palestinian power is, and how one issue like health care, for example, reflected the larger scheme of things. The Israeli occupation's harsh legacy included a stunted, underfunded health care system that trailed far behind the general standard of medical care in Israel. Although the Palestinian health ministry drew up a greatly increased budget, no one expected an immediate leap in the level of services. Thus many sick Gazans continued to seek treatment in Israel or in Palestinian hospitals in East Jerusalem even after the Authority ostensibly took over responsibility. Gazan patients clearly benefited from the high level of care received in Israel, but the practice also served to perpetuate the local system's inferiority, keeping Gaza's doctors from expanding their skills and knowledge, from developing long-term commitments to their patients, and from gaining the confidence of those patients. The situation would best be remedied by sending local doctors to professional courses at superior facilities like al-Maqassed Hospital in East Jerusalem or those elsewhere in Israel or abroad, but the closures crippled that effort.

The Israeli soldiers and civil administration officials in the occupied territories were accountable only to the IDF and the government, not to the people under their control. By its very nature, a nonelected administration acts on arbitrary regulations; without doubt, a cumulative cause of the *intifada* was Israel's changeable, whimsical decisions, which were never open to review and which Palestinians encountered daily in one form or another, from the soldier at the roadblock to the civil administration clerk who inexplicably denied a business license or a trip abroad or permission to add a second story to one's house. When civil and policing responsibilities were transferred to the Palestinians, there was hope that people's everyday lives would finally be free of the control of an alienated power acting in the interests of a foreign occupation. Such a change would not only improve the quality of people's lives, but reinforce their support for the negotiating process leading to a peaceful settlement with Israel.

The post-Oslo reality, however, proved terribly disappointing; in many ways, the accords made life even more difficult. The Palestinian economy and institutions were still dependent on Israel, which continued to hold ultimate sovereignty over the occupied territories. The interim agreements state that various responsibilities and documents—among them population registries, tax rolls, maps, and records of commercial agreements with Israeli firms, regulations governing import and export procedures, payments from the Palestinian Authority to Israeli institutions, and tax transfers—would devolve to the Authority through an ongoing process of negotiation and Israeli oversight even as economic and legal committees ("coordination and liaison committees") were hammering out permanent new arrangements. As it turned out, Palestinian reliance on Israel in just about every sphere of activity, including passage between Gaza and the West Bank, meant that these committees devoted most of their time to issuing exit permits.

Whereas the two sides' intelligence branches have shared information and the two police forces have joined in patrols, there has been no common effort to decide, through cooperation and with established criteria, who will be prevented from leaving Gaza. Logic would dictate that in a new system of coordination between equals, the act of denying an individual's freedom of movement would be subject to review and control by both sides. Rationally, setting exit quotas for workers, merchants, and medical personnel should involve consideration both of Israel's security needs and of the Palestinians' economic and civil requirements. In reality, though, the Palestinian Authority's representatives were little more than what they themselves called mailmen, merely delivering responses from the CLO, which, in turn, took its lead from the Israeli government.

In addition to the usual administrative roles, the Authority became responsible for mediating between the Israeli authorities and individual Palestinians. A test of the Authority's power has been its ability not only to improve people's lives but also to demand that Israel change its behavior toward civilians. The Israeli establishment was not unaware of the demands of the new age; the army and the former civil administration even gave courses to their staffs aimed at instilling new standards of conduct. "Changing the disk" was the military jargon for the switch: now, the message was, Palestinians had to be treated with respect.

But the series of hideous suicide bombings that began after the Baruch Goldstein massacre in Hebron in February 1994 overshadowed all other considerations. A number of Gazans were directly involved in attacks in October 1994 and January 1995 and in a later attempt using explosives smuggled out of the Strip in a truck filled with chickens; indeed, Israeli sources believe that a significant share of the explosives used in the various bombings were smuggled out of the Strip and that some of the masterminds were based there too. Two suicide bombers reportedly crossed the Erez checkpoint disguised as blind men, and the CLO claimed that some forged medical referrals had also been used by militants to gain entry into Israel.[1] Even the most vigilant systems, it seemed, had not succeeded in completely preventing people without permits from leaving Gaza.

Nevertheless, security measures were tightened considerably in the spring of 1995, in direct response to the possibility of terrorist infiltration: the Strip was circled by an electrified fence; Palestinians were denied access to Jewish settlements in Gaza; only three hundred trucks were allowed out daily, and only to collect or deliver goods. These trucks now required Israeli military escorts and were thoroughly examined over inspection pits for explosives. Ambulances were also inspected, and only patients in critical condition were exempted from a body search. No longer permitted to leave in Gazan vehicles, workers were ferried by Israeli buses. Only a very few merchants, and even those extremely rarely, were allowed to travel in their own cars.

Every Gazan, regardless of religion, sex, or age, became suspect, a person capable of committing an act of terror. But like every occupation force before it, Israel—despite having controlled the territories since 1967—had still not learned that resistance and terror are responses to occupation itself and to the form of terror embodied by the foreign ruler. Nor had it learned to distinguish between such acts of resistance as throwing stones or shooting at soldiers within the occupied territories and killing citizens inside Israel's international borders. Both sets of manifestations were seen as one virus that could infect the Palestinian population indiscriminately. Although the PLO had pledged in 1994 to renounce violence and only a small segment of Palestinians continued to carry out random acts, Israel persisted in ignoring the distinction.

Clearly, though, a policy of wholesale siege—in violation of the spirit of the Oslo process—could only strengthen the virus rather than isolate it. Nevertheless, as in the past, the Israeli political establishment closed its eyes and plugged its ears. Moreover, the decision has been translated into practice not by high-ranking officials but by those lowest on the chain of command, the soldier at the checkpoint and the

CLO clerk, who will inevitably give the policy its harshest interpretation: they will view each individual who crosses or submits a request to cross the border as a potential terrorist, so as not to risk responsibility for a possible attack.

I had paid little attention to the health crisis occasioned by the closures until I met Ziad S. at the Fatah office in Gaza City weeks before the transfer of authority to the Palestinians. The place was a hub of excitement just then, a magnet for journalists and activists buoyed by the anticipation of change. At the end of a blisteringly hot afternoon, Ziad S., a man of forty-five, trudged into the courtyard, looking for assistance. He had spent an exhausting day waiting outside the civil administration office and was sweating heavily. As he mopped his brow with tissues he pulled from his pocket, Ziad told me he needed an exit permit to accompany his wife, Samira, to her radiation treatments in Israel. As her doctor explained in a letter, the therapy was supposed to continue for two months, five days a week. The doctor asked that Ziad be allowed to accompany his wife; Samira did not speak Hebrew or know her way around Israel. In any case, she simply wanted her husband with her. Just as the treatments were to begin, the Strip was sealed hermetically following Baruch Goldstein's Hebron massacre, although Hamas had not yet carried out its retaliatory attacks.

At first Ziad was able to get his wife an exit permit, but only for the first two days of treatment. He himself was issued a one-day permit. Through persistence he managed to reach two senior Israeli officials, one a Soviet immigrant who spoke good Arabic and the other an Israeli Druze, and was given a one-month permit for himself and his wife. The officials essentially acted on their own; there were no real guidelines for easing the situation of people like Ziad and Samira, and in any case it had taken his entreaties to secure the obvious humane response.

But all permits were canceled following a suicide bombing carried out by a West Bank resident in the Israeli town of Afula, and Samira missed her treatment. It was back to the civil administration for Ziad, who was able to acquire a new one-day permit, for his wife alone, which he attached to the now-invalid monthly one. The next day the couple decided to take a risk and send Samira into Israel using the one-day permit after it expired. Luckily, the checkpoint was being manned by older soldiers on reserve duty, who generally tended to be less zealous than younger conscripts. A sick woman in an ambulance, a doctor's letter, and an old permit—these were enough for the soldier on duty to wave the vehicle through. The reservist had exercised the human prerogative the civil administration had abdicated, but he could not go so far as to uphold a man's right to accompany his wife to the hospital. Samira was forced to go to her radiation treatment alone.

By the time I met Ziad he was in despair. He had finally been granted a two-day permit—but the piece of paper bore the previous day's expiration date. "I miss work to wait all day like an idiot, my wife is on her own, and then they give me a permit that was good for yesterday," he said on the verge of tears. It was not the last time I was to see "new" permits that had already expired. Casting professional impartiality aside, I referred Ziad to the PHR, the Association of Physicians for Human Rights.

The next morning I ran into him again in the long line outside the civil administration. With him were retailers trying to get into Tel Aviv to stock up on supplies, physicians who worked in East Jerusalem and could not return to their jobs, truck drivers, taxi drivers, a woman who wanted to see her family in Jordan, someone else who needed to be in Nablus. The office opened at 8:00 A.M. but people came at 6:00 to get a place in line. Standing there for several hours as applicants struggled to fill out the Hebrew forms, I began to learn the chaotic, Kafkaesque dance of the exit permit.

"For every case we handle," PHR workers told me, "there are dozens of despairing people who don't know where to turn." As I began to write about these cases, I turned to the civil administration for an explanation. Among the questions I asked was why there was no separate line for medical exit permits. The response was courteous:

> The civil administration understands the difficulties presented by the closures, and therefore most of our staff and resources are devoted to dealing with them. But at the same time, the pressure exerted on our district offices is extreme. Most of the requests that reach us are

important and urgent and the civil administration cannot allocate a separate line for each sector that turns to us for help. Every resident sees his problem as urgent, and it is not always possible for our staff to set priorities. In principle, the closure should not prevent people from receiving medical care or entering Israel in humanitarian cases. The various civil rights organizations and PHR have brought exceptions—decisions contrary to accepted procedures—to our attention, and we act to find an immediate solution.

The civil administration's response followed a long tradition of dismissing all such cases as exceptions, then blaming them on the forces on the ground, begging the question of responsibility. The soldiers and officials who are charged with turning policy into practice usually represent the lowest level of the Israeli regime yet the most tangible. They are the most frequent target of Palestinian anger—for their contempt, their arrogance, and their lack of compassion. Many column inches in the Israeli press have been devoted to the cumulative damage of such behavior. To me, this focus diverts attention away from the system. The policies of the Israeli occupation would have been no fairer had they been implemented politely, patiently, and with a smile. After all, the soldier's job is to execute policies that are by nature discriminatory and that define the people of the occupied territories as threatening. His contempt, it occurred to me, is surely a defense against the dissonance between the moral code of his own society and the terms of the occupation, which he is entrusted to enforce. On the other hand, perhaps the soldier has grown accustomed to exercising power and has simply internalized the hostile and immoral policies.

In any case, the one immediate blessing of Palestinian self-rule was the end of direct contact between Israeli officialdom and the local population. As each Palestinian ministry would be responsible for the relevant exit permits, different categories would no longer be lumped together, nor would there be any more long lines: people would file their applications in the morning and return to pick up the answers in the evening. But in 1994 two even more fundamental qualitative improvements were expected—economic recovery based on more workers being able to leave the Strip and a general relaxation of border policies. In other words, Palestinians anticipated a resumption of their freedom of movement, at the very least between Gaza and the

West Bank via the much-anticipated safe passage. Beyond that, every-one hoped that Israeli officials and soldiers who continued to deal with the occupied territories would reflect the spirit of the new cir-cumstances. Indeed, support for the Oslo process was predicated upon such changes. But almost immediately, four hundred students were denied exit permits for the summer semester in the West Bank; even the permit of a Palestinian human rights activist was revoked. Inexora-bly, the air of optimism evaporated. My questions about Israeli policy and its implementation were as valid after Palestinian self-rule as they had been before.

In Gaza there is no facility for cancer radiation treatment. The government-run hospitals have no equipment for conducting CAT scans or mammograms. Biopsy-analysis skills are wanting and rehabili-tation facilities for physical disabilities and head injuries have been completely neglected. Cardiac surgery and the treatment of kidney disease are nonexistent. Anyone with needs in any of these areas has to make sure his condition is designated "urgent"; otherwise there is no leaving Gaza when the Strip is sealed. Eighteen-year-old A.K. was not considered an urgent case. Several years earlier, during the *intifada*, he had been hit by an IDF bullet and left completely paralyzed; his family was suing the army for compensation. The counsel for the defendant—the Israeli attorney general's office—had summoned A.K. for a medical examination in Jerusalem but for security reasons he and his father were denied exit permits. Happening to meet the father at the home of friends as he was scurrying back and forth between Palestinian Authority ministries and lawyers, I wrote to the CLO spokesman about his son's case. I also urged the father to contact Knesset member Naomi Hazan, who had helped advance similar appeals in the past. She and I both received the same CLO reply: "There has been some kind of mistake." Fortunately, A.K.'s appoint-ment took place one day before the borders were sealed again. Twenty-four hours later and a nonurgent case like his would have made departure from the Strip impossible "until further notice."

During 1995 the distinction between urgent and nonurgent cases evolved and became fixed. "Only cancer patients can get exit permits," I was told at the Palestinian health ministry. According to the CLO, "urgent" meant "every medical situation—cancer, cardiology, dialysis, and surgery—that the PA is unable to treat in the hospitals within its jurisdictional boundaries." All exit permits requested in connection with such conditions were approved, the CLO maintained. Nonetheless, I ran into a furious man whose relative, a cancer patient, was not allowed to leave the Strip. The request, along with those of six other cancer and two cardiology patients, had indeed been rejected—on the grounds that the condition was not urgent. One day later, the ministry submitted all nine requests again and this time the seven cancer cases were approved but not the cardiology patients. The CLO responded to my query thus: "We are not aware of cases that have been unequivocally rejected and then later approved without explanation." I was given to understand that the applications had been filed incorrectly and were later approved once the error was fixed. In any case, the CLO's explanation contradicted the version I had heard from the Palestinian Authority. Since then I have come across no end of irreconcilable accounts.

For example, Palestinians claimed that their officials were ordered to weed out all requests not submitted by cancer patients. In response to my query, the CLO denied the accusation: "The PA can submit any sort of request it chooses; the CLO has not given the PA any specific criteria for the submission of applications. On the contrary, each request that is submitted in accordance with all the procedures is considered and our answer is relayed to the PA."

The medical interpretation of "urgent," however, has never been quite as clear as the CLO presented it. A one-year-old baby girl who had undergone eye surgery in Tel Aviv was scheduled for a checkup. Her mother's request to enter Israel was denied. Exit permits were also denied to a paraplegic who had an appointment for routine treatment, and to a heart patient who needed the battery in his pacemaker replaced. One cardiology patient with an appointment for a catherization procedure never even received a reply from the CLO. (Another category of sick people was routinely rejected: private patients, willing to pay for their own care. After the transfer of responsibilities to the Palestinian Authority, the health ministry determined who required treatment outside the Strip and pledged to cover the cost of care. For some reason that no one was able to determine, private patients were almost never allowed to leave the Strip.)

Speaking of Gaza's "urgent" cases, Marwan al-Zaim, the head of public relations for the health ministry, noted that "the time factor in treating these people is critical to prevent deterioration of their condition. Postponing medical care doesn't make sense." He complained of a second by-product of Israel's policy: "Rejecting patients whose cases are not considered urgent creates tension and bitterness. The people come to us, not to the Israelis who set the policy, and hold us responsible."

The health ministry's liaison division sits on a small hillside in the Shifa government hospital compound, right on the seam between Gaza City's green and leafy Rimaal neighborhood and the concrete sea of al-Shatti refugee camp. Palestinians bring their applications to a narrow prefabricated structure that resembles a railroad car; a newly planted lawn and whitewashed concrete blocks set the building apart from the hospital. The room itself is furnished with three tables, two cupboards—one marked "Property of the Civil Administration"—and, in the summer, a creaky old fan. For the first few months after the office opened, people were required to pass their papers through a barred window placed too high to reach; later, a concrete block was added for them to stand on.

Members of the ministry staff checked each application for the relevant documentation—a letter from a doctor or a hospital in Israel, the Authority's commitment to cover the costs—and took down the person's particulars in Hebrew. A doctor looked over the forms, signed them, then added the papers to the daily stack conveyed to the CLO each afternoon. The pile of documents returned the same evening, approved or denied. In time, people were allowed to enter the office; the door was even left open and supplicants could bring their questions directly to the administrators' desks: "My daughter has an eye operation scheduled for the day after tomorrow. Why hasn't the permit come?" "I've got an appointment with the doctor who did my operation in Ashkelon. They already gave me two rejections. Why?" A cloud of humiliation and bewilderment hung over the room. Some people raised their voices in frustration. The Palestinian staff were impatient on occasion, throwing their arms up in the air, as if the sick person were to blame. "It's not in our hands," was the only answer they had to offer.

Fathi Z. was allowed to bypass the window and come directly into the office. Everyone there knew Fathi. Thirty-nine years old, he had been through nine operations for cancer in the past six years—exploratory surgery, partial amputations, excision of affected areas—as well as chemotherapy. In September 1995 his right kidney had been removed at Hadassah Hospital in Jerusalem and he was to report for a checkup at the urology clinic within the month. He also needed regular oncological examinations and was instructed to present himself at the emergency ward in the event of any deterioration in his condition. It was October and the Strip had been sealed for all but the most urgent medical cases for one period after another. The restrictions were now easing gradually, but most prohibitions affecting sick people were still in force.

At all times, Fathi Z. carried his various permits and doctors' letters; his scars sufficed as identification. His case was also well known to the Israeli authorities, as the old civil administration had initially approved his transfer to Israel for treatment. Even so, the CLO refused to give him a long-term permit that October, compelling him to apply anew for each separate appointment. In mid-October he attached two appointment slips from the Hadassah clinic to his application, one for October 22 and the second for October 30, and the Palestinian health ministry requested a nine-day permit to cover both dates. The CLO responded with a one-day permit and wrote on the second slip: "Resubmit at the end of the month." No sooner had Fathi come back from his first trip to Jerusalem than he needed to drag himself back to Shifa Hospital to submit his new application and return the next day to pick up the reply. His right leg was swollen due to "insufficient blood supply and the postoperative condition," according to his medical records, and he limped slightly. On occasion, Fathi had gone to Hadassah for his appointment and been told to come back the following morning because his condition had worsened. But he had no exit permit. True, one can leave in emergencies, but each extra effort only aggravated Fathi's bad health.

Fatma G., three years old, was also a cancer patient. That same October the Palestinian health ministry referred her to Tel Aviv for treatment and her father was to accompany her. It is customary for the man of the family to accompany the sick person—he usually speaks reasonably good Hebrew and knows his way around while the women rarely speak Hebrew and years of staying at home have made them timid and fearful when dealing with a profoundly foreign society.

The CLO returned Fatma G.'s and her father's applications, verifying the need for medical treatment but denying permission for the father to accompany his daughter. No explanation was given, but Palestinian officials surmised that the same regulation regarding work in Israel—that men under forty could not take jobs—was being applied. By the time Fatma's request was resubmitted, naming a female escort, the child had missed her appointment. Over time, the officials began to anticipate the Israeli response, and families knew to send older women along with their sick children.

Seventy-year-old Z.S.'s cataract operation was postponed twice and S.R.'s eye operation was also deferred. N.A. and her husband waited a long time for an appointment coordinated with N.A.'s ovulation at Yosef Shenkar's renowned infertility department at Hadassah Hospital, but they were denied exit permits as their need was not considered urgent. Six-year-old Muhammad Barud's case was also judged not urgent. He had lost the use of his right hand and was due to be examined by a Tel Aviv neurosurgeon but his and his mother's requests were denied. Twenty-year-old Hussein Abed al-Hamid Shehadeh was blind in one eye and losing sight in the second as the result of having had no proper diagnosis or treatment. He too was denied a permit.

The Association of Israeli and Palestinian Physicians for Human Rights, headed by Ruhama Marton, worked tirelessly on behalf of these and other patients, among them a sixteen-year-old boy who had lost a leg and the use of one arm in an accident and an eighteen-year-old woman with severe hearing problems. Despite PHR's efforts, the CLO dismissed these conditions as not life-threatening, although they continued to deteriorate.

In the case of Muhammad Barud, a PHR activist, Hadas Ziv, wrote to Prime Minister and Defense Minister Yitzhak Rabin: "While it is true that the child's life is not in danger, his quality of life is adversely affected every day that treatment is withheld." She wrote Rabin that impaired health was a widespread consequence of the closures. "Many times an appointment is made long before the Strip is sealed and is then postponed time after time as the closures are imposed anew. Even if the patient's life is not threatened, the delay of treatment results in continuous suffering and sometimes reduced chances for a full recovery." Ziv did not mention how hard it was to keep making new appointments and badgering the doctors. (Nor did she point out that when appointments are rescheduled, it is at the expense of other waiting patients.) In any case, neither Rabin nor his spokespeople replied to the letter.

The damage does not stop with the patients; these restrictions deprive medical staff of free movement as well and perpetuate Gaza's dependence on outside medical care. Riyad al-Zaanun, the Palestinian health minister, took part in a festive ceremony at Tel Aviv's Ichilov Hospital marking the enrollment of several Gazan doctors in an intensive professional course underwritten for them by a foreign charitable fund. The next day, when the course began, the doctors appeared in Zaanun's Gaza office: they had been turned back at the Erez checkpoint as their permits were invalid. Ron Pundak, an Israeli academic who had taken part in the early secret Oslo talks in 1993 and who had initiated the Ichilov course, exercised high-level *wasta* on their behalf. Only his intervention allowed the doctors to leave the Strip, but it could not keep them in Tel Aviv: one month later Gaza was sealed again and the doctors missed their training.

With every new hermetic closure, Gazans who work in hospitals and treatment centers in the West Bank cannot get to their jobs and medical equipment in the Strip lies idle for want of technicians. Scores of doctors, nurses, and physiotherapists find themselves stranded in one part of the occupied territories or another for months at a time. Several institutions in the West Bank and East Jerusalem have been on the verge of firing personnel from Gaza, unable to cope with these workers' frequent absences. Even senior health ministry staff members, whose authority extends to the West Bank, have often been marooned in the Strip.

The Association for Civil Rights in Israel (ACRI) has protested as illegal the restrictions preventing medical personnel from moving between the Strip, the West Bank, and East Jerusalem. In an appeal to Brigadier General Oren Shahor, the IDF coordinator in the territories, and Lieutenant Colonel Amos Giora, a military legal adviser in Gaza, ACRI cited East Jerusalem's al-Maqassed Hospital, the most advanced in the occupied territories, which employs 700 people, 428 of whom live in the West Bank and 48 in the Strip; the rest live in East Jerusalem. When a hermetic closure is imposed the hospital operates with a significantly reduced staff. ACRI asked that soldiers at the border crossings be instructed "to allow all medical personnel to pass freely from Gaza and the West Bank to East Jerusalem and back." As a result, some medical workers were allowed back to work in East Jerusalem, but they were forced to break the law: their permits did not include overnight stays, even though health care professionals are obliged to work night shifts.

Throughout the territories, Palestinian health care institutions have suffered the long-term effects of ruinous restrictions and unreliable staffing. West Bank doctors have been barred from traveling to the Strip to perform surgery, causing the delay of medical treatment within Gaza as well. And while al-Maqassed Hospital treats gallstones, for example, using an advanced method that avoids surgery, Gazan doctors have neither the requisite equipment nor the skills and continue to use older, more dangerous techniques. Gaza's two pathologists prefer to send biopsy samples to al-Maqassed for analysis, but when the checkpoint is sealed, these have, on occasion, been stranded on their way to the labs.

The chief radiologist at the Radiological Center for Medical Diagnosis, a new private facility in Gaza City, is a resident of East Jerusalem and has sometimes been unable to get to work. On top of that, the center's sophisticated equipment requires regular maintenance and there is no qualified technician in Gaza. Thus the mammography apparatus—the only one of its kind in the Strip—has sat unused for weeks because the technician, an Israeli Palestinian, could not enter Gaza.

In some instances David Levanon, the CLO's health coordinator who reviews the medical information attached to exit applications, has advised treatment at a local hospital, even though the Palestinian physician has recommended sending the patient elsewhere. Samir H., for example, had orthopedic surgery at al-Maqassed and his doctors in Gaza felt unable to provide appropriate follow-up care; the CLO deemed that local attention would suffice. On the same grounds, patients have been prevented from continuing treatments in the West Bank. In essence, this means that Israeli CLO health officials retain the right to dictate where Palestinian physicians may send their patients, even as responsibility for health care has ostensibly been transferred to the Palestinian Authority.

In October 1995 I published a long article on the health crisis. Once again, the CLO responded courteously:

> The actions of the health department of the Coordination and Liaison Office derive from the Cairo and Oslo 2 agreements and from agreements arrived at in cooperation with the Palestinian Authority in the framework of frequently convened joint medical subcommittees. Each agreement addresses security concerns as well. The CLO health department is very attentive and responsive to the matter of sick people who need to leave the autonomous territories, and the case of any person requiring treatment in Israel receives prompt attention, in accordance with the procedures agreed on in the joint committees. It should be noted that the Palestinian health ministry alone defines the degree of urgency of the treatment each patient requires. Even during closures, on its own initiative and out of a sense of commitment, the CLO operates at all possible levels to expedite the departure of sick people whose cases are defined as urgent, without undue delay. Patients whose cases are not deemed urgent are those whose lives are not in danger and for whom prevention of routine treatment will not cause a deterioration in health. During periods of closure, representatives of the CLO health section wait at the checkpoints so as to facilitate the efficient and speedy transfer of the sick, even though Israel is not obligated to do so under the agreements. In most of the cases that we have examined, we have uncovered no errors of judgment on the part of any one body. In certain instances the patient was in error. For example, one man who had been denied permission to leave the Strip for tests at an Israeli hospital had not provided a financial guarantee. . . . Channels of communication between the Palestinian Authority's ministry of health and the various sections of the CLO are open twenty-four hours a day. All requests referred via these channels receive affirmative responses even after regular working hours. . . . Many requests, unfortunately, reach us late, after some delay caused by the Palestinian Authority's officials due to their own bureaucratic problems.

The CLO did not answer each of my many detailed questions, explaining that I had submitted them only four days before the article was to go to press. In the months that followed, I sent more questions to the CLO well ahead of my deadlines but was told that to respond to queries on individual cases would be a breach of medical confidentiality.

But my general questions went unanswered as well. I was unable to learn who had established the distinction between urgent and non-urgent cases—the Israeli government, the IDF general staff, the coordinator of government activities in the territories, or the CLO itself. I could not find out whether the distinction had been informed by physicians, either military or civilian, or who determined how long it would remain in force. I wanted to know which officials decided that medical technicians could not enter the Strip and that a father could not accompany his sick daughter. Would those same officials support the wisdom of their policies if they had to send their own children off to a hospital alone?

Less than three months after the CLO's letter, things took a turn for the worse. Without warning, at the end of 1995, the CLO stopped providing the written explanations, albeit brief, that had previously accompanied denials of requests. The original application forms had included a space for the Israeli reply; now that reply was torn off and retained by the CLO and its decision conveyed orally to the Palestinian liaison person. The lack of a written response did nothing to improve efficiency or promote bureaucratic transparency. What it did, apart from making it impossible to understand what criteria had been used in individual decisions, was render it easier for applicants to blame Palestinian officials and their carelessness. It created an impression of disdain for the Palestinian population. In addition to the reply, the photocopies of applicants' identity cards that accompanied requests were no longer returned.

Then reports appeared of high-ranking Palestinian functionaries and doctors who had issued false medical documents—for pay—to help people leave the Strip. A rise in the number of young people with eye diseases deemed untreatable in the Strip (conditions usually confined to older patients) had alerted soldiers to the scam.[2] As the few cases of fraudulent medical papers were repeatedly invoked to justify the high level of suspicion directed at all sick applicants, I wanted to know whether action had been taken—whether the Palestinians responsible had been removed from their positions—and whether the real extent of the practice was known. So I tried again to elicit a detailed response from the CLO. Among other questions, I asked whether there had been more attempted bombings or attacks as a consequence of the phony medical permits. I wanted to know whether an Israeli eye specialist had determined that the cases in question were fraudulent or whether the assessment was based on the blanket assertion that such medical problems are not found in young people.

I raised the problem of people who wanted to visit sick relatives hospitalized in Israel, East Jerusalem, or the West Bank: they did not know where to send their applications. When their requests were submitted via the health ministry, the CLO insisted they should come through the Civilian Liaison Committee. But when the committee transmitted the requests, applicants were told to go through the health ministry. Which was the correct channel?

I asked why many patients referred to East Jerusalem's al-Maqassed Hospital were denied exit permits, among them a four-year-old girl needing an orthopedic procedure and a fifty-four-year-old heart patient. Was the person who turned down these permits a physician? Was the physician a specialist? Had a political decision been made not to send Gazans to a Palestinian institution in East Jerusalem? Why were a large majority of patients referred to St. John's ophthalmological hospital in East Jerusalem refused permits? Were there restrictions on the age of male escorts for sick children? If so, what was the minimum age? Who ordered the restrictions? Was there a general policy regarding private patients? Why were so many private patients denied exit permits? A sick person leaving to meet with his doctor for the first time could not yet establish conditions of payment; in such instances, what documents would satisfy the CLO?

I concluded my letter with the case of Ibrahim Sarsawi, who died in the emergency ward of an Israeli hospital. According to Palestinian officials, his ambulance had been detained at the Erez checkpoint for a lengthy search while his condition deteriorated fatally. (Even in extreme emergencies, doctors are never allowed to accompany their patients out of the Strip.) The CLO denied the claim. Why, then, did the transfer take so long after approval of the exit permit?

This time, the CLO's answer was short, handwritten, and not quite as courteous as before:

1. The entire matter of sick people entering Israel is coordinated jointly by the CLO and the Palestinian Authority. The procedure is as

follows: the PA submits the application to the CLO and, after the request has been reviewed, the permit is issued immediately. According to the agreement, we approve entry of a sick person within twenty-four hours of receiving the request; in practice, we approve requests within a shorter period of time and in urgent cases immediately!

2. In some instances the Palestinian Authority does not transfer requests for exit permits to the CLO because, in its view, the sick person can obtain treatment in the Strip and has no reason to leave for treatment in Israel. In many cases, a patient's departure is delayed after the CLO has approved the permit, and the ambulance reaches the checkpoint too late.

3. Israel's security checks are meticulous since, in the past, hostile elements have attempted to leave the Strip by using falsified referrals. It should be remembered that Israel allows sick people to leave Gaza as long as their departure does not adversely affect the security of Israeli citizens.

Attached to the handwritten answer, I found a typed letter from the CLO spokesman:

To: Ms. Amira Hass
Re: Reply to your query on health care
1. I would be happy to have the accompanying response published in full.
2. We have chosen not to reply to each question individually, even though we are quite certain that most of the Palestinian claims are completely baseless.
3. All the complaints against Israel, the CLO, and the coordinating office of Israeli government activities in the territories are intended to stop the closures, which, as you know, were imposed following brutal attacks inside Israel.
4. To my regret, we do not consider you an objective journalist who is guided by the truth and we do not see our way clear to respond to you in detail in the future either, given our bitter experience with your negative attitude, an approach that even Palestinian journalists have not adopted in their work.

I had not been singled out for special treatment. Palestinian officials have also been unable to discern a uniform set of criteria for the CLO's actions, despite Israel's insistence that all matters are coordinated with the Palestinian Authority. Nor have Palestinians been able to learn why people wishing to pay for private medical care in Israel have been denied exit permits. In principle, Palestinians are entitled to appeal rejected requests and resubmit their applications, either by telephone or through meetings between high-ranking health ministry officials and their CLO counterparts. Sometimes a negative response is reversed or an answer is received after a long delay. Usually, though, reversals occur only after the PHR applies pressure or someone goes over the heads of the CLO and uses *wasta*, or pull. So much for clear guidelines. . . . Again and again I saw that high-level Israeli intervention could alter a mid-level decision.

M.B. was the liaison officer between the health ministry and the CLO; like most Palestinians in similar positions, he had worked as a clerk in the civil administration, under Israeli command. So the Israelis knew him well, and they also knew that he and his wife had long been unable to have children. In one of my articles about medical treatment, I quoted M.B., using his full name, with the agreement of Marwan al-Zaim, the head of public relations for the ministry. Several months later I learned that M.B.'s exit permits had been revoked and he was no longer allowed in CLO headquarters—all for security reasons. As a result, the Palestinian health ministry was obliged to replace him with someone else.

Efforts to secure new exit permits proved fruitless, and the Palestinian liaison committee members were convinced that M.B. had been blacklisted both because he was quoted in my article and because he tended to argue with the CLO when permits were refused. After this incident, I decided to quote no one by name other than Arafat, Allah, and M.B., whose cover was already blown. The CLO refused to explain the security threat posed by M.B., nor did it act as if there were a threat by asking the Palestinian Authority to question or arrest him or terminate his employment. Nevertheless, the risk seemed to reach international proportions when he and his wife were turned back at the Rafah crossing, forbidden to travel to Jordan via Egypt. At this point I asked a Knesset member, Yossi Sarid, to intervene. The next day, Sarid's parliamentary assistant confirmed that M.B. was indeed considered a "serious" security risk but would be allowed, just this once, to cross into Jordan.

The IDF and the CLO use the term *humanitarian* to describe their intervention in the cases they are willing to review. The word, which has become deeply lodged in military discourse about Palestinians, allows the authorities to beg the more rigorous questions surrounding the suppression of human rights. True, the number of medical applicants is small compared with the sea of workers, businesspeople, and drivers who are unable to leave the Strip every day. But these are precisely the people the Israeli authorities promised would not suffer from the closure policy. And it is precisely with regard to the sick that greater consideration and more compassion could have signaled a profound change in the Israeli attitude.

If anything, however, there is less consideration in evidence than ever before. I appreciate officials' fear of responsibility for attacks in Israel, but I am convinced that none of the refusals I have documented—withholding surgery from a three-year-old, denying a man fertility treatment, preventing a son from being with his dying mother—have anything to do with security. It will fall to historians to unearth who, if anyone, issued instructions to prevent medical treatment in these cases or whether forces on the ground were free to interpret broad orders in whatever way they saw fit. The same historians may well ask why the peace camp, the "pro-peace" Labor-led coalition, failed to set up a civilian oversight committee, for example. Certainly a monitoring body of civilians who have not served for years as the omnipotent rulers of the Palestinian population would be in a better position to decide, with greater objectivity and self-confidence, free of the lust for control, whether a fifty-four-year-old woman with advanced coronary disease is likely to be planning a terrorist attack when she asks to leave the Strip.

Chapter 11

Waiting to Turn Forty

It is the summer of 1996 and the liveliest place in the Strip, if not in the whole country, is the Erez checkpoint between two and six every morning. While their families sleep, fifteen to twenty thousand people, blessed with precious exit permits, make their way through the security checks and onto the buses that will take them to their jobs in Israel.

At the entrance to a large parking lot surrounded by several Palestinian police lookout posts, the workers alight from taxis or park their cars and vans—always filled to overflowing with coworkers and neighbors. Then they begin a half-mile trek across the lot to the border checkpoint. "There are two stretches near the beginning where the sand is very deep," says Ahmad, a forty-five-year-old engineer from Rafah. "It's not so bad when there's time to spare—you just go a little slower and stop to shake the pebbles and sand out of your sandals. But it's harder when you're late, and you always have to leave at least half an hour for the security inspection."

At its northern tip, the parking lot tapers, funnel-like, into a narrow path fenced in on both sides by two layers of tall chain-link fence and covered with an asbestos roof. The path itself is not visible from the outside, where foreign diplomats and Palestinian VIPs cross the border. On one side, the path is hidden by a row of whitewashed concrete slabs; on the other, there are large bails of barbed wire to prevent anyone from sneaking out. All around is the debris left behind: piles of rusty soda cans and yellowing newspaper pages that blow in the wind. The thousands of people fed through the funnel every morning call the path the "dairy" or the "cow shed," and they themselves are the cows.

The Israelis developed this passage of asbestos and barbed wire during the winter of 1994, after the advent of Palestinian self-rule. The path, which runs for some 275 yards, is only wide enough for three men, so progress is slow. Every ten or fifteen minutes the Israeli soldiers stop the stream of men (and the small number of women) to avoid creating pressure near the exit points at the end of the line. The air thickens and it becomes hard to breathe; crammed in, back to belly, people begin coughing and flapping their hands to ward off the heat and claustrophobia. Then the signal goes up to begin walking again and people press forward, murmuring their relief. "Thank God for this and every other situation," three or four older men say in chorus. It could be worse; they could be stuck at home. Once, in the pouring rain, I heard a different tune: "Let the devil take the lot of us, the Jews and the Arabs."

The peddlers who fill the parking lot outside arrive early, just after midnight, spreading their wares out on the ground or wheeling them on carts. They sell cartons of yogurt and sour cream, hot falafel straight from the frying pan, halvah and cookies and rugelah, American-style visors and the floppy kibbutznik hats. Every few minutes a taxi driver pulls up: the incoming passengers needing a ride to Gaza City won't arrive before 8:00 A.M., but the drivers come early to get a place in line. Most of the cabs come from the nearby village of Beit Hanun. A few drivers bring their small children or nieces and nephews, seven- or eight-year-olds who stand with boxes slung from their necks, peddling wafers for a shekel a piece. Much later, after all the workers have gone, an entire family from Beit Hanun, a father and all his children, comes to clean up the lot for twenty shekels—to pick up the soda cans, fruit peels, and other garbage strewn around.

Between 1:00 and 3:00 A.M. the first of the workers show up, those employed farthest away, north of Tel Aviv. The Israeli checkpoint does not open until 3:00 but the workers take their place on the narrow path, several thousand of them, resigned to a long wait in order to avoid the crowds and reach their buses on time. After 3:00, getting through the checkpoint can take more than half an hour, depending on how the searches go, and following that year's six-month hermetic closure, every hour of work is precious.

The parking lot and passageway are lit by powerful floodlights that give off a flickering yellow glow. Mist and dew make glue of the sand, but at dawn the dust begins to rise in spirals from beneath the workers' tramping feet, blurring the floodlight and creeping into the men's mouths, eyes, and noses. "It's not so bad in the morning," says Fawzi, "when we're still fresh from sleep. But coming back after a day's work when you're lugging something home, the heat and the dust in your throat are just terrible." (At work Fawzi's employers call him by a Hebrew name, Uzi, to prevent any problems with the customers.)

After 3:00 A.M. the tide of workers builds to a torrent. Aouni from Rafah shows up an hour and a half later, although he left his home at 3:20. As always he is immaculately dressed and smiling. (Sometimes I see Aouni at home in Shabura, returning from work at five or six in the evening, looking as well-groomed as he did at the beginning of the day and still with a spring in his step. An hour later, his daughters whispering so as not to wake him, I remember that his workday began at 2:30 A.M. and ended some fifteen hours later.) Fortunately, Aouni's wages are relatively high for a Gazan, NIS 150 per day; some people make only 60 to 80 shekels for just as many hours. But they are all glad for their jobs in Israel—inside the Strip, a day's pay ranges from 20 to 50 shekels. Aouni arrives with Muhammad, a sub-contractor from Rafah's Brazil neighborhood. Muhammad's droopy eyes make him look permanently tired; he too leaves the house buttoned up and well-ironed, but by the time he reaches the Erez checkpoint, his shirttail is hanging out of his trousers and one sleeve dips longer than the other.

Aouni stops, smiles, says shalom, and asks in his quiet voice when I'll come to his house for another visit. Without slowing his pace, Muhammad thunders at me in Hebrew. "How you doing?" he calls. "You must be out of your mind! It's four o'clock in the morning!" He is washed along with the human current down to the mouth of the funnel. Some men stride in threes and fours, exchanging a word or two, some walk by themselves. All greet the Palestinian police warmly or with a nod of their heads and are greeted affably in return. Someone jokes with a policeman from the same refugee camp. One man carries a basket, another a sack, but most come empty-handed to save time going through the Israeli inspection.

The men are all middle-aged or older; in order to leave the Strip, they must be married. Each time a hermetic closure begins to ease, the first workers allowed out are those who are forty and over. In time, the age limit gradually drops, but since spring 1995 it has never fallen below thirty.* I remember a barbecue on the beach organized by Fathi, who was lucky enough to work at a supermarket in Kastina (Kiryat Malakhi), a mere twenty minutes from the checkpoint. His whole family had been employed there for years, but now, at twenty-eight and thirty, his brothers were barred from leaving the Strip. Sometimes Fathi came home with frozen meat his boss sold him at a discount; he and a bunch of unemployed friends from Jabalia would hang out at the beach grilling the meat, celebrating nothing in particular. One friend used to own a small tailoring shop but was forced to shut down by the closures; another was an ex-prisoner who refuses to work in the various Palestinian security forces. A third, lucky friend was a math teacher, earning NIS 1,000 a month. But Fathi's brother Fawzi was too young to leave the Strip. "So what are you doing?" I asked, and Fawzi answered without missing a beat. "We're waiting to turn forty," he said.

Workers entering Israel have to pass through five screening stations. The first is a roadblock at Beit Lahia junction, where a Palestinian policeman stops each vehicle, peers inside, and looks over the passengers. The second is at the entrance to the parking lot at the Erez checkpoint, where uniformed or plainclothes Palestinian police dispense parking slips and glance at the men, assessing their ages. "Hey you, how old are you? Eighteen? Get out of here, there's no way you've got a permit." No amount of pleading will help the young man here.

The final Palestinian inspection point is just before the dairy path. As the workers pass, they flash their sheaf of papers—ID, magnetic card, work permit—at two Palestinian policemen. Every so often the police stop some woman loaded down with baskets, check her belongings, and look over her documents; occasionally they pull someone out of line who has failed to display his permits. At the fourth screening station Israeli soldiers wait, standing at the end of the fenced-off pathway behind concrete blocks and a few sandbags, rifles at the ready. As the Palestinians approach the front of the line they stop talking and a familiar cloud of anxiety settles on the crowd. The people wait, uncertain, afraid of an unexpected blow—a disdainful word from

---

*The age limit fluctuated for several years, but in 1998 it remained steady, at twenty-five. Unmarried men were still barred, however.

a baby-faced soldier or the computer beeping its rejection of someone's
magnetic card. "This is the third time you've tried to sneak through," a
soldier yells at a boy who cannot be more than fifteen years old. "Do
you want to be arrested?" Several Israeli border police scrutinize the
silent crowd passing through the first turnstile. One man is plucked
from the throng—he, too, looks suspiciously young. His papers confirm that he is old enough but the border police keep looking at him
skeptically.

The fifth screening station is a row of nineteen turnstiles that open
onto what is called the "Israeli square," the Israeli zone. Here, the
computer monitors, metal detectors, and electronic gates enforce efficient and relentless security—anyone who has slipped through this far
will go no further. One older man, approximately sixty, is no stranger
to the soldiers; he has turned up at the checkpoint without an exit permit several times in the past. He managed to get as far as the fifth station only by dint of his age: the Palestinian police would not think to
question a man that old. Every so often the man tries his luck this way,
hoping to arouse some soldier's pity, hoping that in the faint light
of dawn the sleepy border guard will overlook the absence of a magnetic card and exit permit. But the soldier on duty—himself only
twenty-one—takes the man's ID and locks him in a tiny, airless prefabricated cell, one of several such cells behind the turnstiles. The man
calls out through the bars of the small cell window: "Soldier, come
here for a minute, please. Let me out."

"You tried to slip through," says the soldier. "Why didn't you listen
when they told you to leave?"

"Just give me my ID and let me go. I won't come back," the man
replies. "I'm sick. I feel bad."

"I told you to leave before, but you still tried to sneak in," the soldier
says again.

"Once I caught him wandering around in Ashkelon," another soldier joins in. "He said someone there owed him a hundred shekels."

"Believe me, my children are all under thirty. They can't go out to
work," the man calls out. "What am I supposed to do? I have to work,
we've got no bread in the house."

"Sorry," the first soldier calls back. "I'm not the right person for that;
I can't give you permission to enter Israel."

"Just be quiet," the second one adds. "For the time being you have
to stay in the cell."

"Please call the officer. I'm old enough to be your father. I'm not a thief."

"Yes, you are," says the first soldier. "You stole across the border. That's exactly what we call you in Hebrew."

In their scolding, patronizing tone the young soldiers speak to the man as if to a child who needs to learn better behavior through punishment and education. In the end, perhaps, this is the soldiers' only defense, their only way of blocking out the true meaning of their difficult job: to prevent infiltration, not just of terrorists, but of old men hoping for a day's work, hoping for a hundred shekels, enough to keep the family going for three or four days.

Soon after the transfer of authorities, the frustrations of the workers at the Erez checkpoint reached breaking point. On July 17, 1994, only three months after the beginning of Palestinian self-rule, tensions there boiled over in an event that came to be known as the "bread *intifada*." Workers were tired of starting their days at the crack of dawn and standing in excessively long lines for inspection; they were always worried about being held up and losing a day's pay; they chafed at the humiliating treatment they received at the hands of the soldiers; they were worn down by the severe poverty at home and the cumulation of emotional strain. When several permitless Gazans tried to sneak through the checkpoint, causing guards to halt the line, the men had had enough. Some shoved the guards and, when the soldiers prepared to open fire, began throwing stones. A riot ensued—the asbestos roof was smashed, the fences were torn down, and anything that would burn was set alight. By the end of the day, four men were dead: three Gazans shot by an IDF soldier, and one Israeli guard killed by the Palestinian police.

Aouni and Muhammad and the delinquent sixty-year-old are all living out the economic politics of Israel's occupation. Like thousands of others, Muhammad began supplementing his family's income at thirteen—darting among the Carmel market stalls as a porter or picking tomatoes during summer vacation on one of the moshavim bordering the Strip. He learned a few dozen Hebrew words and quickly grasped the syntax. Later he took a brother and a neighbor boy along with him. At seventeen they all found work in construction in Ramat Gan, learning to read Hebrew by slowly sounding out the names of shops and streets. They worked overtime, washing dishes in a restaurant, and returned home once a week with money for the whole family, another few Hebrew sentences, and tales of some forbidden escapade. All this because after 1967 Defense Minister Moshe Dayan advocated an integrated Israeli-Palestinian economy and open borders. His vision—designed to rule out future territorial separation— won out over the opposition of Finance Minister Pinhas Sapir, who was inclined to encourage independent and separate development.

Immediately following the Six-Day War, Dayan began to argue for the West Bank and Gaza's economic integration—in effect the subjugation of their economies to Israel's. As a result, in 1972 the IDF, the ultimate authority in the occupied territories, issued all West Bank Palestinians a blanket entry permit into Israel. A similar permit was issued to Gaza Strip residents only in 1985, but the policy had effectively been in place many years earlier. The instant consequence was that Palestinian laborers were co-opted into the Israeli workforce, first in construction, agriculture, and garbage collection, then in restaurants, factories, and auto shops. At the same time, Palestinian markets were opened to Israeli produce.

Until 1967, the great majority of Gazans—mostly refugees and their children—were unemployed, living off support from the United Nations Relief and Works Agency (UNRWA), occasional temporary jobs, seasonal work in agriculture, or money sent by relatives in the Persian Gulf. Moshe Dayan believed that relative prosperity would weaken nationalist fervor and diminish the Palestinian preoccupation with independence. A second aspect of this political logic involved stifling the economic and industrial development of the territories themselves by means of meager budgets, heavy taxes, and a tangle of rigid bureaucratic restrictions and procedures that discouraged investment and enterprise.

From the beginning there was a marked discrepancy between the generally improved standard of living for many (as well as the substantial improvement for a few) and the efforts to block economic development of the Palestinians as a community. In Gaza especially, one motive for the obstruction of development was the none-too-secret political objective of encouraging a mass exodus: Gazans who left the Strip would subsequently lose their residence rights.[1] Israel's control over the Palestinians' right to work was a blatant political device whose calculated long-term aim was their ultimate economic, national, and geographic displacement. The construction of Jewish settlements, which began very quickly and used valuable land and water resources, was another aspect of the same stratagem.

Said Medallal, the director general of the Palestinian labor ministry, keeps a large chart (table 2) hanging in his office that sums up the history of the occupation economy, the gradual chronic dependence on Israel, and the evolution of ties that bind almost every Gazan family to the Israeli colonial power. The chart shows the number of Palestinian laborers from Gaza who have registered with the Israeli government employment bureau, a procedure that became law in 1970. Thousands of other Gazans have worked as unregistered day laborers and many more have worked for years, especially in agriculture and restaurants, for employers who have never declared their workers to the Israeli tax authorities. Thus, the chart does not give an accurate figure for all the Gazans working in Israel but it does show the trends in their employment.

An international UNRWA document from February 1995 puts the number of Gazans, registered and otherwise, working inside Israel before the *intifada* at about 80,000, out of a workforce of 120,000. On the eve of the 1991 gulf war, the figure was 56,000, according to the same UNRWA document. Other sources, especially Gazan trade unions, quote higher figures, estimating that as many as 100,000 Gazans were employed in Israel prior to the gulf war. In either case, before Palestinian self-rule in 1994 the lion's share of the Strip's GNP—40 to 50 percent—was earned in Israel. The remaining income came from within the Strip and abroad. In addition, the income from Israel was the indirect source of a further 10 to 20 percent of GDP; that is, it had a direct impact on commerce and cash flow within the Strip.[2]

The most striking changes in Medallal's chart take place in 1989 and 1991—years that left their mark on Aouni, Muhammad, Fawzi, and thousands of others, watershed years in the occupation and in the history of Gaza's devastating dependence on Israel. In 1989, Israel imposed its first restriction on the freedom of movement that Moshe Dayan had bestowed on the Palestinians in 1970: in June of that year—through the use of the magnetic cards—the civil administration began to deny certain groups the right of entry into Israel. Those with criminal records (as defined by Israel) or a history of security offenses (also defined by Israel) were forbidden entry outright.[3] All other men up to age fifty

TABLE 2. EMPLOYMENT AMONG REGISTERED GAZAN WORKERS

YEAR	REGISTERED WORKERS	REGISTERED WORKERS HIRED IN ISRAEL
1967	4,840	2,665
1968	14,256	4,412
1969	12,618	8,795
1970	16,908	10,685
1971	18,715	14,001
1972	19,862	13,350
1973	12,932	11,860
1974	15,995	10,839
1975	14,349	11,273
1976	16,137	11,046
1977	23,323	13,599
1978	24,019	15,939
1979	25,469	14,469
1980	23,204	14,377
1981	22,944	13,279
1982	19,447	11,619
1983	18,726	11,877
1984	20,082	13,258
1985	23,424	13,537
1986	21,184	12,490
1987	23,298	13,745
1988	22,571	14,398
1989	21,009	9,826
1990	24,467	20,656
1991	60,520	44,531
1992	62,765	37,134
1993	58,368	29,138
1994	59,824	21,294

were to receive magnetic cards valid for one year. The civil administration announced its intention to issue 150,000 magnetic cards, while 30,000 people would be barred from leaving the Strip.

The *intifada* leaders denounced the magnetic cards as one more instrument of oppression and means of increasing Israeli control, forcing Gazans into greater dependence on the civil administration. Since the early days of the uprising, the Unified National Leadership (UNL) had urged people to refrain from paying taxes and to boycott all bureaucratic services supplied by the civil administration. But people were unable to comply with the UNL's boycott and attempts to disrupt distribution of the cards by confiscating them, burning them, and otherwise frustrating the Israeli authorities came to nothing.

As it was still possible to sneak out of Gaza without a magnetic card (the Strip was not yet tightly sealed), many Gazans continued to work "illegally." But the Palestinians' message to the *intifada* leadership was clear. Muhammad remembers several Rafah youths who tried to dissuade him from standing in line at the civil administration building. The nationalist credentials of his family were beyond question: his two brothers, both *intifada* activists, had been killed by the IDF. "Are you crazy?" he recalls saying. "How are we supposed to manage without working? Can you give me work so that my kids and my brothers' kids can have a decent life? We can't just live on heroic slogans and memories." By October 1989 the civil administration had succeeded in distributing 73,000 magnetic cards, a figure the security establishment considered a great triumph.[4] By January 1990 the number had risen to 120,000.

The *intifada* had proved to Israel that even some degree of personal economic well-being had not served to dampen national aspirations. But the number of registered workers hired in Israel jumped from 9,826 in 1989 to 20,656 in 1990, a leap that signified the failure of Palestinian organizations to dislodge the pattern set in place by Israeli policy since the 1970s. The occupied territories could no longer survive without work in Israel.

The second extraordinary piece of data (the 1991 jump in registered workers in Israel) demonstrates Israel's power—and its intention—to unilaterally change its relations with the Palestinians at a stroke. In early 1991, during the Gulf war, Israel imposed a lengthy curfew, paralyzing the Palestinian economy. Also, the general exit permit was rescinded and Palestinians were now obliged to carry personal permits allowing entry into Israel. Initially the regulation applied only to males over sixteen, then it was gradually extended to everyone. At the same time, Israel began to enforce a twenty-one-year-old ruling that Palestinians could only be hired through the official employment bureau. Thus the chart's leap that year did not reflect so much an increase in workers leaving the Strip as the greater number who registered. In theory, workers would benefit from registration, as Israeli employers would less easily be able to evade minimum-wage laws and other obligations, such as sick pay, clothing allowance, and paid vacation. Registration could have served to eliminate the more exploitative practices that Palestinians had suffered in the workplace.

In practice, however, there was simply a drastic reduction in the percentage of registered Palestinians employed in Israel, and since 1992 the gap between the number of registered job seekers and those who find work in Israel has continued to widen. Indeed, the reason for canceling the general exit permit was Israel's desire not only to keep closer tabs on Palestinians' movements but also to cut down on the number of Palestinians "wandering about" in Israel, as some politicians put it. In October 1990, twenty Palestinian worshipers were killed at the al-Aqsa mosque by Israeli police trying to control stone throwing directed at Jews praying at the Western Wall below. In response to the twenty deaths, there was a wave of fatal stabbings within Israel by Palestinians and in November—long before anyone had conceived of the nightmarish attacks on buses in Israel—the IDF imposed the first closure on the occupied territories. The measure paralyzed many workplaces in Israel but was hailed by some key figures who believed shrinking the Palestinian presence in Israel was the way to ensure safety.

The call for imposing closures as part of permanent policy would never have found a sympathetic ear had it not been for massive immigration from the former Soviet Union and the assumption that these newcomers would need the many positions being filled by Palestinians. When the assumption proved wrong, however, Palestinians were still not allowed to go back to work: Israel simply imported foreign labor from Africa, Eastern Europe, and the Philippines. Indeed, Israel had begun to bring in guest workers earlier that year, demonstrating its intention even then to reduce the number of Palestinian workers.

Closure as permanent policy had begun to take hold after the Gulf war. During the war, the closures were seen as an emergency measure, prompted by Yassir Arafat's support for Saddam Hussein and by the sympathy many Palestinians expressed for Iraq. The blanket exit permit was not reinstated after the war, however, indicating Israel's long-term intentions. Overall, revoking the general exit permit became a means of enforcing demographic separation between Israelis and Palestinians without geographic or political division. This demographic segregation, though, has always been blatantly one-way: Jewish settlers continue to move freely in the occupied territories. And although the closures had become policy long before the suicide bombings on Israeli buses, when the attacks started, Israelis, who perceived them as an "all-out Islamic war" on the Jews, felt they justified abrogating the freedom of movement of hundreds of thousands of people, denying them employment and access to food and other commodities for days and weeks at a time.

Back in 1992, the stage had already been set for removing Palestinians from the Israeli landscape. That year, employing Palestinians stopped being as easy and profitable as it once had been: red tape, fines, and new restrictions all contributed. Employers were no longer allowed to keep Palestinian workers on the night shift, for example. The police began systematic searches for Palestinians violating the terms of their permits (walking in the street even a short distance from one's workplace was considered a "violation"); offenders received heavy fines and had their papers confiscated. More and more employers simply stopped hiring Palestinians.

When the Israeli government revoked the general exit permit, it instructed the civil administration to ease its policies blocking development within the territories and also launched a series of concessions and incentives for entrepreneurs, to promote job creation. On the recommendation of an economist, Ezra Sadan, the government began to plan for industrial parks in the Strip. There was a clear and well-founded concern that mass unemployment in the Strip would create unbearable pressure and consequently threaten Israel's security.

Still, at the end of the *intifada*, Palestinians were reluctant to invest, given the Strip's limited freedom of movement, economic downswing, and fickle military occupation. Only an economic miracle could generate within a year the 40,000 to 50,000 jobs necessary to replace the ones lost in Israel. In the three years between 1991, when Israel began imposing longer and longer closures, and the installation of the Palestinian Authority in 1994, optimistic estimates put the number of new jobs created in the Strip at 3,000. Closing the borders had a direct and immediate effect on the size of Gaza's workforce. Before the long closure in 1993, the workforce constituted 18 percent of the Strip's population; after the borders reopened, the number fell to 13 percent.[5]

After May 1994, Israel left the Palestinian Authority with the formidable task of reversing its legacy of economic neglect and responding to the army of unemployed people. But the mammoth challenge was predicated on an economic arrangement with Israel, stipulated in the Cairo agreement, which guaranteed workers freedom of movement and the flow of merchandise between the two areas (in exchange for retaining the customs union between Israel and the occupied territories). The ability of Gazans to work in Israel was especially beneficial as Israeli wages have always been at least three times as high as those in the Strip, even at the bottom of the wage scale (while prices in the Strip have been on a par with those in Israel).

Ironically, the policy of closure enforced by the Likud government before Yitzhak Rabin's election in 1992 was less draconian than the measures taken later by the Labor-led "peace" coalition. Only declassified cabinet minutes and documents will reveal the thinking process and decision making that resulted in the closure policy. But it is a fair assumption that ill-considered, knee-jerk responses to Israeli distress and the sense of urgency created by waves of Soviet immigration helped shape the policy. Over time, though, denying the right to work and free movement became a way to attain a set of political goals, just as, in the past, the blanket exit permit and making work available had been a way to secure a different political objective.

The Labor government imposed its first hermetic closure in March 1993, preventing anyone's departure from the Strip rather than "sifting" the population as before. Palestinian-Israeli negotiations had become mired in disagreements on fundamental issues, especially concerning the status of Jewish settlements. At issue was the nature of any future solution: whether it should be "functional," entailing the demographic separation and self-administration outlined by Shimon Peres and Moshe Dayan in the 1970s, or "separation in principle," which involved acknowledging Palestinian rights to the country's land and water resources as the basis for Palestinian self-determination.

Consequently Palestinians saw the hermetic closure, and the economic and mental anguish that came with it, as a form of political pressure applied by the Labor coalition—their negotiating partner—intended to weaken their demands. And right or wrong, Palestinians still view the closure policy as a kind of Israeli arm twisting. Indeed, since the Oslo Accords, the negotiation teams have spent much of their time arguing over the number of exit permits and who should receive them, and each additional permit is now regarded as a gesture of Israeli goodwill.

In the past few years, restrictions on movement have undergone some refinements: not only has the West Bank been cut off from the Gaza Strip but it has been divided into north and south, separated by Jerusalem, and a special permit is required to enter the city. East Jerusalem, with all its cultural, medical, religious, and national institutions, has been effectively isolated from the other Palestinian territories. Thus the Palestinian world has been split into three distinct pales of settlement, a state of fragmentation quickly consolidated under the Labor-led government precisely during the implementation of the Oslo Accords.

Between May 1994 and October 1996, hermetic closures were imposed eighteen times. Despite this, my friends in Gaza and their Israeli employers stayed loyal to each other. "My poor boss," Aouni said to me once. "When I don't come, his work just doesn't get done." Aouni is a master metalworker who can repair any household appliance or children's toy. No wonder it's impossible to manage without him. His employer tried hiring Russian immigrants and Romanian guest workers during the closures, but he always takes Aouni back and sends him advances on his salary, too.

The long-standing relationships with employers in Israel have been invaluable. When restrictions were first placed on work, Palestinians were still able to find jobs through the employment bureau or by obtaining temporary exit permits to go to Israel and look around, but since May 1994, these options have no longer been available. The only way a worker can find a job is if an employer asks for him by name through the bureau in Israel. In most cases, this happens when worker and boss have known each other for years, although occasionally a worker recommends a friend. But being asked for is only the beginning. Next comes vetting by the CLO, which also checks the Shabak files, a complicated process that has diminished the chances of finding work even when the government relaxes its restrictions. In the summer of 1994, for example, Yitzhak Rabin agreed to raise the quota of workers' exit permits to 30,000 as a gesture of goodwill. But six months later, only 23,000 people had been able to find work.

The personal relationship between worker and employer is considered a security measure, a way to minimize the risk of potential terrorists crossing into Israel and "just wandering around," in the words of one CLO official. But a long relationship with his boss was of no help to Aouni's friend Abu Ibrahim. I remember sitting on a mattress in Aouni's family room one evening in 1995 while Abu Ibrahim reeled off a list of all the places he had worked in Israel since he was fourteen. In his eyes shone the clear glint of nostalgia. "I worked in agriculture from the age of sixteen, even before I had an ID card. Then I was a housepainter in Jerusalem and from there I went to a plastics factory in Or Yehuda. Afterward, I worked fixing tractors and then in a gas station in Savyon," he said, referring to an exclusive suburb of Tel Aviv. In 1982 he took a job in a small factory in south Tel Aviv, where he remained for thirteen years, enjoying a relationship of trust and respect with his employers. Then in August 1995, a soldier at the Erez checkpoint suddenly confiscated his magnetic card and barred him from leaving Gaza.

The Strip had been sealed hermetically following threats of terrorist attacks. Several days into the closure, the CLO announced a plan to replace all the magnetic cards in circulation with new, updated cards. Abu Ibrahim was among the 16,500 workers who received new cards and work permits, which, they came to realize, were equipped, through a sophisticated bar code, to store more information than before. Unlike the old cards, these recorded the bearer's dates of departure from the Strip, putting an end to Abu Ibrahim's practice of spending the night at his workplace, like many other Palestinians. Although staying overnight entailed the risk of a trial and a fine, it was preferable to the long, oppressive journey back to Gaza each night and helped the men work overtime and save money.

When Abu Ibrahim received his new card, the CLO and the Shabak were essentially granting him a clean bill of health. He was, in any case, delighted to return to work and his employers were equally happy to have him back, but he managed to put in only seven days before he was stopped at Erez. Most soldiers do not actually look at the men's work permits, satisfying themselves by checking the magnetic card only. But that eighth morning the soldier asked to see Abu Ibrahim's work permit and ID card before calling on another soldier to take him away. Abu Ibrahim was handcuffed and locked up in a pre-fabricated detention room, which gradually filled with other suspects. The youngest among them were, like Abu Ibrahim, thirty-five years old. Later that morning they were released but their documents were withheld. Abu Ibrahim asked for a slip of paper confirming that his magnetic card had been confiscated. "Go to your people at the labor ministry," he was told. There Abu Ibrahim found dozens of workers with the same problem; some of them had received their new magnetic cards only the day before. Eventually, the CLO informed Abu Ibrahim that he was considered a security risk and that his magnetic card would not be returned. With obvious envy, Abu Ibrahim told me about a neighbor who had thrown a big party when he finally got his new card, inviting all his friends and neighbors, even slaughtering a sheep. The man still has his precious card and still goes to work.

Seven hundred new cards were confiscated the same month as Abu Ibrahim's was, according to Said Medallal, all from men deemed security risks. Married men of thirty-five or older, with five or six children apiece and large extended families who relied on their wages, they had all worked in Israel for more than ten years. It hardly seemed likely that they had decided, en masse, in the few days between receiving their new cards and losing them, to join in hostile militant activities. And despite their being security risks, their names were never passed on to the Palestine Authority for appropriate action, although Israel sends the Authority a regular flow of information about Hamas and Islamic Jihad suspects, requesting their arrest.

Medallal called the CLO and questioned the logic in the whole situation. At his urging, eighty-five magnetic cards were returned but not Abu Ibrahim's. In the year following the loss of his card, he managed to find occasional work as a porter for the Preventive Security Force. D., Abu Ibrahim's longtime Israeli boss, was "very surprised" to hear that the man he knew had suddenly become dangerous. "I don't believe it. He's never been arrested, he didn't even throw stones during the *intifada*. He's a good man, honest and reliable. I got in touch with the people at the CLO, all the way up to the legal adviser, but they told me not to interfere, that it was none of my business." Thus Abu Ibrahim, like thousands of others, was tried and convicted in the court where Shabak data are both prosecutor and judge. He never got the right to defend himself, but then again, he never learned the charge.

All Gazans working in Israel have come to dread the sudden and unexplained cancelation of their magnetic cards and work permits. After years of steady work in Israel, Muhammad, Aouni's friend from Rafah, fell into the same net. As a respected and successful subcontractor, he was able until 1994 to arrange permits that allowed him to move about freely even during curfews, when he sometimes helped me get around Gaza and its deserted streets. After a four-month closure in 1996 he was one of the 7,258 happy men allowed back to work—for a month, until the Erez computer beeped, barring him "for security reasons."

Through his connections in the Palestinian Preventive Security Force and through their connections with the Shabak, Muhammad was able to go back to work. But two days later the computer beeped again. So back to Preventive Security, who once again clarified Muhammad's case with the Shabak, who yet again gave him the green light. But the computer would have none of it. "There are a lot of people in the same boat," Muhammad told me. "We sit together in the evenings, smoke a narghila, and try to understand why. I used to think that it was because I had spoken out against the closure on the radio. But I spoke against Hamas, too. Now we think that anyone who had any kind of connection with the *intifada* is barred. My two brothers were killed. My assistant's brother was imprisoned. His little sister was shot. When they check the Shabak records they see all that and maybe they think we're going to take revenge—now, of all times." Muhammad is a stubborn man and after badgering Preventive Security ceaselessly, he received an exit permit but no explanation. "What about all the poor people who don't have *wasta*, without connections, who don't know how to make pests of themselves? They can't prove that they're not dangerous."

Medallal puts forward a number of conjectures to explain the large-scale, illogical confiscation of cards. For one, some employers, tired of workers who cannot be relied on to show up regularly, have reported them to the Israeli authorities as dangerous in order to avoid paying severance and outstanding wages. But Medallal is quick to point out that for every such employer, there are many others who phone him and curse each day of closure.

Simple human or computer errors account for some confiscations. For example, there is the soldier who demanded the card of a worker who was trying to leave the Strip at nine in the morning, two hours later than usual. After confiscation, the computer automatically registers that the card bearer is barred from leaving, regardless of the reason. "You have to leave the Strip by seven," the soldier insisted, although the worker's permit entitled him to depart for Israel between 4:00 A.M. and 7:00 P.M. Only the intervention of Palestinian Authority officials recovered the card. There are some reports of police confiscating permits and saying only that the conditions have been violated, without giving any details at all.

Palestinian security sources have confirmed that confiscating cards is a way of recruiting collaborators and informers. In exchange for work permits, people promise to report on events inside the Strip. Indeed, receiving a magnetic card is now the only bureaucratic procedure that brings Palestinians from the occupied territories in direct contact with CLO and Shabak officials. I have heard from numerous workers who, having gone to renew or pick up their cards, were told by the Shabak, "You help us and we'll help you."

In theory, one can appeal a permit's cancelation. Said Medallal passes the barred workers' names to the Palestinian Civilian Liaison Committee's chairman, Freij al-Hiri, who brings the list to his discussions with the CLO head, Colonel Dov Zedaka. The CLO, however, only reviews and updates its list once every six months, and the Palestinians have no say in the review process.

As in the case of sick people, the Israeli government has chosen not to set up an efficient, permanent joint monitoring committee that could challenge exclusions on a daily basis, demand a detailed explanation of the CLO's decisions, and perhaps prevent arbitrary or nonsensical rulings. But there should be little surprise in that: the lower ranks of the occupation—the ultimate sovereign power—are implementing a political strategy of manipulating the number of Palestinian workers allowed into Israel or, more precisely, the Strip's unemployment rate. Once again, the Palestinian Authority is placed in the position of supplicant pleading with the Israeli authorities even as it desperately strives for material and political legitimacy in the eyes of its people. The Labor government that brought Israel to Oslo proved itself unable to shake off the imperious, supremacist style of rule enforced since 1948.

In turn, Palestinian negotiators at all levels have been unable to defend the interests of thousands of "refuseniks," to get them back to work or at least to obtain an honest explanation for their exclusion. And Palestinian public sentiment swings between anger, suspicion, and pity for the representatives' impotence.

"My next-door neighbor has a fantasy of kidnapping an Israeli soldier," says Abu Jamil from Jabalia. " 'What will you demand in exchange?' we ask him. 'The release of all Palestinian prisoners?' 'The prisoners can go to hell,' he says. 'So what do you want?' we ask. 'More leverage for Arafat in the negotiations?' 'To hell with the negotiations,' he says. 'I just want my work permit back.' "

Chapter 12

The Engine Has Stalled

The high-rise building opposite my rented apartment in Gaza City threatened to make a mockery of my journalist's credentials. When I moved into the apartment in 1995, the imposing ten-story structure was just a concrete skeleton with its front wall missing. From my window, I could see into the apartments—open-faced like the rooms of a dollhouse—and admire the skill of the architect and workmen who had tempered the square design with molded archways and wrought ironwork. Visitors from Israel or abroad marveled at the building. "Look at that! What more do you want? The construction that's going on here is unbelievable!" For a while I tried to set them straight—the building had in fact been left in the same state for four or five months; the work had only just resumed. Then I gave up being a killjoy. When winter came, I wondered how the sole occupants felt; the one family that had moved into the top floor was perched ten stories above an empty, still-exposed building with no outer wall or elevator. Clearly, there were no buyers. But I stopped trying to deflate my impressionable guests, stopped asking them what would happen to the unplastered walls when the rains came. I simply nodded my agreement—the balconies were lovely. Fifteen months after I moved in, only three apartments were occupied. The rest were still under construction, with two or three men working lethargically, as if they had all the time in the world.

Hundreds of other buildings in various stages of construction dot the roads of Gaza, creating the image of a booming, bustling economy. Add to this picture a few paved roads, restaurants by the beach, seafront hotels, the new shops and display windows in the center of town, a couple of small amusement parks, and a lively bazaar that now fills an old IDF helicopter landing pad, and you will perceive a Gaza that is profoundly different from the place that emerges from my articles in *Ha'aretz*. Advertisements in the Palestinian press that bolster this vision of a recovering economy catch the attention of, and provide proof of success for, people who have never actually visited Gaza. The buildings, the shops, and the advertisements all fulfill the expectations of the Oslo Accords, and were indeed seen as the necessary condition for the accords' success, signals of an even greater economic revival yet to come: new businesses, more jobs, new industries, opportunities for the thousands of Palestinians who had returned from abroad, and expanding markets locally, in Israel, and overseas. Faced with the flood of articles written by twenty-four-hour-stopover journalists, I, like most Palestinians who are in business, have learned that hopes and assumptions are far more powerful than hard facts in changing people's impressions.

Every so often even I walk around the center of Gaza and begin to doubt the reliability of my own reporting. The streets radiate normalcy, economic progress, ease. The city center reminds me of busy streets in Jerusalem or Tel Aviv: with every step I meet someone I know, who greets me smiling broadly and whose hearty laughter belies his troubles. Indeed, Gazans joke and grin quite a bit, and the drop-in visitor is convinced that everything is just fine. Why else would they be smiling?

Many things about Gaza City's center reinforce the sense that one is in a genuine city: the sidewalks have been paved with new ornamental tiles; traffic lights have been installed at two busy intersections; stores selling toys and electrical appliances attract curious window-shoppers; an eye-catching sign in Arabic and English directs one to a dazzling, whitewashed renovated building that houses the Ministry of Welfare; throngs of people are milling about the Ministry of Education, which is preparing for the new school year. But my doubts are banished when I see groups of young men sitting in a café at eleven in the morning or sucking on narghilas, staring blankly at the world outside, lost in thought. And then I notice that the shops are empty and the storekeepers are reading newspapers or watching the passersby. By the Nasser movie theater—closed since the *intifada* began—I turn down an alleyway and find that the sewing workshop that stood there is gone, as if it never existed, with all its sewing machines and bolts of cloth, its cutting tables and children at work.

Only a year earlier I had visited the workshop with an Israeli TV reporter. "What more do you want?" he asked, echoing the guests in my apartment. "Look how much work they've got," he went on, revealing the optimist's deep need to believe that the Oslo Accords were succeeding. Even then, Gaza's small sewing shops were in trouble. Since 1970, they had evolved into the second-most-productive industry in the Strip after agriculture, in terms both of the employment they provided and their share of the GDP.[1] The endless new restrictions on exports and transportation as well as the closures and their constantly changing procedures, however, had inflicted heavy losses; many workshops had closed, while others had laid off workers. The long closure of February and March 1996, following the series of suicide bombings in Israel, had dealt the industry a fatal blow.

Z.A.'s sewing shop in Beit Lahia is both a testament to the complex link between Israel and the Strip's economy and a victim of the Israeli ingratitude that has been much in evidence since the advent of Palestinian self-rule in 1994. Z.A. and his workers have been making clothes for an Israeli fashion chain for over twenty years. In 1977 he received a certificate of honor from Haim Bar Lev, Israel's minister of trade and commerce. Under the heading "The Challenge—Export," Z.A.'s document reads: "Dear Worker, this certificate of honor is awarded to you in appreciation of your enterprise's achievements and contributions to the development of Israeli exports during 1976. Once again, we have learned this year that our export achievements are the fruit of all our combined efforts. I have no doubt that your work and that of your colleagues has played an important part in the advancement and growth of exports. Please accept this certificate as an expression of our appreciation for your part in furthering Israel's economy. Sincerely, Haim Bar Lev."

Z.A. continued to further Israel's economy. The jeans, shirts, and overalls he manufactured were considered Israeli products and sold in Israel and abroad. Z.A. estimates that most Israeli-manufactured jeans are still sewn in the West Bank and Gaza, "because it's particularly hard work." Most other kinds of clothes are cut in Israel ("cutting is easier and more profitable") and then stitched in the occupied territories, but Z.A.'s workshop does the whole job, from cutting to finishing. He receives the bolts of cloth from the Israeli buyer—even during the long curfews and closures of the Gulf war, he had a permit to drive to the Erez checkpoint to pick up the cloth and deliver the finished product.

Just before the Israeli redeployment, Z.A. added extra stories to his house in Beit Lahia, believing that now he would begin to contribute to the Palestinian economy and increase his business in the process. The unfinished staircase and unfurnished rooms stand as a reminder of Z.A.'s frustrated aspirations. His lauded contributions to the Israeli economy, like those of his coworkers, have brought him no benefits; nor is he exempt from the general suspicion that hangs over every Gazan, manifested in Israel's policy of closure. Every time Israel seals the Strip's borders, the sewing shops shut down for longer stretches than before. Since the summer of 1994, Z.A. has been unable to meet with the Israeli supplier and buyer in the Erez industrial zone, which is under Israeli control. The costs of transportation have doubled and tripled. Each hermetic closure has made it harder to receive the cloth, deliver the finished garments to Israel, honor the workshop's commitments and schedules, and hold on to Israeli customers. To avoid losing his remaining clients, Z.A., like many other workshop owners, has agreed to work for prices that are almost below cost, the same prices he received years earlier.

According to Gaza's tailors union, some two hundred of the eight hundred remaining registered workshops shut down in the summer of 1996. Close to three hundred small workshops had already closed during 1995. Traditionally, they had always been able to market their goods in the West Bank as well. But despite Israel's affirmation in the 1993 Declaration of Principles that the West Bank and Gaza Strip constituted a single territorial unit, the West Bank markets, which used to absorb more than 50 percent of Gaza's manufactured products, had been made inaccessible by the restrictions on movement. The workshops that still functioned had laid off a third of their employees, and the remainder were working only a few days a month. Salary increases to match the rise in the cost of living were out of the question, as were benefits such as vacation, severance pay, and unemployment compensation. Before the transfer of authority, the tailoring industry had constituted fully one-third of the Strip's industrial concerns; now it was in a state of collapse. Workshop owners were selling their homes to repay loans and cover their employees' paychecks. Meanwhile, the buyers in Israel were looking for new workshops in the Galilee, the West Bank, and Jordan. So much for free enterprise.

One wet day in April 1996 I went to visit Z.A. The heavy rain beat down on the workshop's roof and drummed against the windows. Every drop echoed in the big empty room where the sewing machines stood silent. Piled up were quantities of jeans destined for Israel but stuck in Gaza because of the lengthy closure. This was my first visit but the sight was familiar. Since early 1995 I had seen similar scenes over and over again—stilled factories that made cinder blocks or cosmetics, silent carpentry shops that once filled orders from the West Bank, a closed citrus-processing plant, a factory that, unable to ship the water containers it made to customers in other Arab countries, was left with one-tenth of its workers. In every place I saw the same empty chairs, the same couple of workers filing down some part or greasing a machine, the same mounds of ready-to-ship products in a corner: cartons full of new telephone receivers, pretty floor tiles wrapped in plastic, empty cans gathering dust. For weeks or even months at a time, it is impossible to move goods out of the Strip; there is nowhere to sell them: not in Israel, not in the West Bank, not in Jordan, not in Egypt.

The machines stand idle because raw materials cannot be ferried into the Strip (concentrate for making juice, for example), because a container is stuck in the port of Ashdod or because a spare part is available only in Tel Aviv and the factory owner who needs it has no exit permit and cannot afford to hire a truck to bring it in. There are always a few laid-off workers who come around to inquire, hopefully and respectfully, whether the owner has, by some miracle, managed to obtain the missing part or the buttons or the cloth, whether he has done the impossible and gotten the shipment through the roadblocks to the West Bank, whether he has been paid for his goods and has settled his mounting electric and phone bills. And just to make sure that I really get the picture, the owner always whips out his bank statement and points to his vast overdraft, swelling from month to month. And there is always a phone ringing in the background whose strident clang shatters the silence and this forced industrial inertia.

The patrons of the Oslo process—the donor nations, the International Monetary Fund, the World Bank—and its two principal players, Israel (which escaped punishment for its antidevelopment policies) and the PLO (which was handed the job of reversing the legacy of the occupation) shared a number of simple economic assumptions. The world's contributions and loans to the Palestinian Authority would be used to rehabilitate the economy and install infrastructure (roads, sewers, water and electricity, telephone lines), refurbish and construct government buildings and schools, improve people's quality of life, and prepare the ground for functioning factories and businesses. Building the infrastructure immediately generated jobs in the public sector. Money was earmarked to guarantee these public-sector salaries for a year or two, in the belief that this extensive investment would stimulate initiative and investment in the private sector, in commerce and manufacturing.

Two groups of people were targeted for the mission of reviving the Gazan economy and creating jobs for the army of unemployed workers. The first was local Palestinian entrepreneurs—the weak but ambitious mainstay of the Palestinian economy, made up of *muwataneen* families with considerable property and savings and of those who had managed to build up subcontracting businesses and accumulate a little capital during the occupation. The second group was Palestinian entrepreneurs living abroad, who were eager to invest in their homeland, and other foreign investors.

These assumptions were predicated on the belief that a growing number of Gazans working in Israel would generate the cash flow to nourish the Strip's developing domestic market and the expansion of exports to Israel, the West Bank, and overseas. Altogether, the money in circulation would increase the Palestinian Authority's volume of taxes to create a sound treasury. Within Gaza, the cost of creating a new job in the manufacturing-industrial sector ranges from $8,000–$10,000 to $25,000. Every year, between 5,000 and 10,000 people join the labor force, not counting the thousands of Palestinians returning from the diaspora. The continued employment of Gazans in Israel—indeed, an increase in their numbers—was crucial for the private sector to flourish, so crucial as to be encoded in the 1994 Paris Protocols, which address the economic aspects of the Oslo process and stipulate the free movement of goods and workers between the Authority-administered territories and Israel. Foreign dignitaries—from the U.S. secretary of commerce, who visited the Strip several times, to various national commercial attachés and World Bank officials—have all emphasized the importance of the private sector's development as the engine of the entire Oslo process, economically *and* politically.

"But this engine has stalled," I was told as early as November 1995 by a senior official acting for the donor nations. For whatever reason, he preferred not to be quoted by name, although many others in high positions have agreed with his assessment. Their criticisms were heard in internal forums and delivered to Israel officially but were muted in public because they might scare off potential investors and because all these people continued to believe in the necessity and feasibility of the Oslo process.

Three Israeli forces, representing three levels of authority, have been directly responsible for the ongoing systematic strangulation of Gaza's economy. They are the same forces that have impeded every Palestinian who has ever wanted to invest in a business venture that would profit himself and his community: first, the Israeli government's decision makers, who have clung to their policy of sealing the Strip; second, the anonymous individuals who implement that policy, the military commanders and senior officials in the civil administration, now the CLO; last, the soldiers and CLO bureaucrats in direct contact with the Palestinian population.

Since January 1995, the mechanics of closure, as they pertain to business, have been refined. Random security inspections of vehicles have been replaced by mandatory and systematic inspections and the number of vehicles permitted to leave the Strip has been reduced. After the owner of a sewing workshop from Jabalia, a member of the Islamic Jihad, assisted with a suicide bombing in January 1995, the authorities, persuaded that the Islamic organizations had justified the need for more meticulous inspections, extended their suspicions to every last Gazan businessman or plastics manufacturer. Two months later, a truck belonging to a Gazan poultry merchant was found in the Negev, in Israel, carrying explosives. By that point the repetitive cycle of hermetic closure had taken on its final character.

In the first stage, following an attack or warning of an attack, or during Israeli holidays or elections, or at particularly sensitive times, such as after Yitzhak Rabin's assassination, the standing restrictions on movement are intensified, and the entry and exit of all goods, including flour, medicine, fruit, and milk products, comes to a complete halt for days at a time. In the second stage, the closure begins to ease and food and raw materials are allowed in. Gradually, and only after much pleading, Palestinian products start to trickle out of the Strip. The final stage is the resumption of the standing restrictions—regular closure—

which became significantly harsher after early 1995, when Israel's Labor-led coalition drastically restricted the number of people still allowed to leave the Strip, including entrepreneurs from the private sector—the "backbone" of Gaza's recovery—and businesspeople traveling to the West Bank, a major market for Palestinian manufacture and agriculture. The number of vehicles permitted beyond the Erez checkpoint was cut to a bare minimum. The quantity of businesspeople allowed out has since fluctuated according to the number of permits the Palestinian Civilian Liaison Committee manages to negotiate with its Israeli counterpart: at one time 150, on another occasion 300. During one brief, happy period, following endless entreaties to Israeli ministers, some 1,000 permits were granted—although 3,000 requests were pending. (Unlike other permits, those granted to businesses are given en bloc to the Palestinian industry and trade ministry.) Age limits apply here too: men under thirty and single men need not apply. I met a twenty-eight-year-old Gazan, a partner in a West Bank quarry, who twice managed to outwit the system: he bought tickets to fly abroad and was therefore granted one-time permits for the airport, but after leaving the Erez checkpoint he drove an hour east instead, to the West Bank, to see how his business was doing.

As with medical permits, business permits are canceled when the Strip is sealed hermetically, and the entire process begins again: merchants submit their applications and sometimes wait for months. Again, as the closure starts to ease, twenty or so lucky men receive permission and then the number increases to, say, fifty as the various coordination committees meet and agree on more "concessions." The very privileged few, a mere handful, are allowed out with their cars, and only under exceptional circumstances.

Businesspeople are first screened by the Palestinian Preventive Security Force, which is responsible for border crossings and sifts out people associated with the opposition organizations. The Palestinian industry and trade ministry runs a second check on the applicants and decides how to distribute the precious permits, taking into consideration each business's size, capital, turnover, and number of employees. People at the ministry admit that, contrary to the logic of a developing free economy, the prospects for a start-up enterprise to expand its market, find clients, and attract investors and partners—in the West Bank, if not in Israel—are sabotaged at the outset by a system that, of necessity, favors the well-established. "The system leaves itself open to corruption and influence peddling," I was told by the official from the donor nations who preferred to remain nameless.

Every so often the Israeli government decides to make a show of easing the closure by handing out a sudden bonus of several hundred business permits and thousands of work permits. Inevitably, Israeli analysts and politicians, Palestinian officials, and even former U.S. Secretary of State Warren Christopher (who has occasionally displayed first-hand knowledge of these gestures) proudly point to the windfall as if it were a miracle, a sacred act proving great strides in mutual trust and economic growth. At such moments, the Israeli government appoints the anonymous forces of the CLO and the army—the second level of authority—to implement these concessions. But in the occupation's long tradition of foot dragging, activity at this level always seems to take at least a month. The delay plays right into the hands of certain branches of Israeli business, which quickly act to improve their penetration into the Palestinian market. Trucking companies, for example, have succeeded in forcing out their Gazan competitors in the West Bank.

The procrastination might be due to the army and the CLO, to the government, to a simple inability to behave otherwise, or to the problem of too many cooks in the kitchen (the army, the CLO, the office coordinating government activities in the territories, the police, the Shabak). But there is a new element, too, a combination of mistakes, misunderstandings, unscheduled delays, and disagreements on the Palestinian side. And corruption as well: a Palestinian official might sit on a permit while he waits for *baksheesh* or just not pass on a request for any number of personal or political reasons. Israel learned to manipulate the many accusations leveled at Authority officials, claiming that the PA had simply not passed on the request. Distrust and anger have poisoned the atmosphere.

In addition, the number of permits allocated might suddenly turn out to be a hundred, instead of three hundred as promised. The CLO might decide to hand out some of those permits directly, bypassing the Palestinian Civilian Liaison Committee. Ignoring the Palestinian bureaucracy always provokes anger and suspicion toward the Israelis and raises questions about those who receive these permits and their relationship with the CLO. Under direct Israeli rule, there were always some businessmen who maintained particularly good relations with the civil administration and its officials and were able to move about with an unusual degree of freedom.

"What do you mean, collaborators?" said one furious businessman who had received such a permit, when I asked about the suspicions raised by his direct dealings. "Despite all the promises, our trade ministry just can't get the permits from the Israelis," he explained. "So an Israeli executive calls the CLO and arranges a permit for an old friend or former partner." Again, as in matters of health care, an Israeli's intervention can often untangle the bureaucratic knot. Sometimes, however, people from the Preventive Security Force confiscate permits issued directly. Inevitably, the Palestinians' fury—their long wait for requests to be answered, the large gap between promises made and commitments fulfilled—is, in the end, deflected from the CLO to Palestinian ministry employees, who are accused of laziness, corruption, indifference, and incompetence.

The Strip's commercial and industrial life depends on a two-way passage of goods: access to Israel's markets, on the one hand, and the free passage of products and supplies into Gaza, on the other. Some 90 percent of the Strip's raw materials, construction supplies, basic food products, gasoline, and electric appliances come either from or via Israel; the occupied territories are a major market for Israeli trade.[2] According to the Paris Protocols, Israel allows limited passage of goods from Egypt and Jordan through its territory, although most of these commodities are subject to a customs union with Israel, which means that they are no cheaper for Gazans than Israeli products.[3]

The principle of a customs union for Israel and the Palestinian territories was predicated on the "free passage of goods and labor" stipulated in the agreements, but the union has remained unchanged even though the permanent closure has rendered the notion of free passage meaningless. A reciprocal flow of goods and the assumption that a large segment of the Palestinian workforce would be bringing home Israeli salaries (usually the minimum wage in the case of Gazans), however, were the only justifications for the Israeli demand to hold prices in the territories at the same high level as those in Tel Aviv or Jerusalem—in order to prevent a black market in cheap goods. But in practice, Gazans are paying Israeli prices for gasoline, flour, cement, water, electricity, electrical appliances, and meat, while they are unable to generate income from their own products, are severely restricted in their right to work, and take home a quarter to a third of a low Israeli salary if they have the good fortune to hold a job inside the Strip.[4]

Prior to the Oslo agreements, the civil administration believed that the expected recovery would provide a boon to Gaza's considerable haulage and transportation branch, and incentives were offered for investment in this sector.[5] However, the number of trucks and taxis allowed out of the Strip (there is no system of public transportation in Gaza; shared taxis provide that service) has gradually dwindled since 1994. Of a thousand-strong taxi fleet that once plied the route between Gaza, the West Bank, and Israel, only two or three dozen cabs are permitted to cross the Erez checkpoint, and only during periods of grace. On a good day, 500 of Gaza's 2,700 trucks make their way into Israel, but usually no more than 200 or 300. (Trucks from Gaza are not allowed to enter the West Bank, nor those from the West Bank Gaza.) In the past, drivers' wages were high, as a single truck was able to make three or four round-trips daily; since early 1995, though, the restrictions on movement and lengthy security checks have reduced that number: anyone who manages to make one round-trip in twenty-four hours is considered lucky. Accordingly, the income of drivers has plummeted by two-thirds or more, even though they now work longer days. Of course, drivers under thirty cannot leave. "You get your license at eighteen," one trucker told me, "and then you have to wait until you're thirty to start driving."

There are two methods of transporting goods in and out of the Strip. Haulage trucks leave the Erez checkpoint in convoys, always accompanied by an Israeli military escort. Until the suicide bombings in February and March 1996, the escorted trucks were allowed to make several stops in Israel before picking up loads, usually at a central location, to take back to Gaza. Each industry was designated a different point of collection; clothing manufacturers, for example, received their supplies at Jaffa's Bloomfield sports stadium. Now, however, trucks are allowed to make one stop only, which generally means that truckers can no longer both deliver and collect goods.

The second method of transportation, and the one most commonly used, is the "back-to-back" system, which evolved after a period of several months in 1995 when no trucks were allowed out of the Strip and exports had come to a complete standstill. The system is in operation at the two cargo terminals in the eastern part of the Strip, Karni and Sufa, and at a smaller cargo terminal at Erez. In the beginning, Gazan trucks would bring goods destined for Israel and the West Bank as far as the terminal and the cargo would be transferred directly to an Israeli truck, which would complete the delivery. The same system was used for carrying goods into the Strip. But when, in March 1996, it turned out that a suicide bomber had been smuggled out of the Strip in an Israeli cargo truck, an additional stage was introduced to make the system foolproof: direct contact between Israeli and Palestinian drivers was eliminated by the installation of an inspection platform at the terminals, where goods from Gaza would be unloaded before being transferred to Israeli trucks (at some terminals the goods are unloaded onto the ground). After the unloading, the area is cleared of Palestinians and an Israeli crew arrives to complete the work. Of course, large quantities of merchandise are ruined this way. In the process of being moved from truck to platform to truck, glass jars and floor tiles break, ice cream melts, and carefully pressed clothes, whose finished appearance partly determines the price the Israeli buyer will pay, get wrinkled and dirty.

"Look at these trucks just standing here," one haulage company owner complained bitterly. "Each one is worth about $100,000 and together about three billion, and they're all turning into scrap metal. On top of that, we have to absorb the extra costs of the Israeli truckers who haul the goods to and from the borders. It's the Israelis who make money from the whole arrangement," he went on. "The Israeli trucking firms, the drivers, and the government, which gets their taxes. A Palestinian manufacturer used to pay fifteen shekels per ton of haulage; now it costs thirty-five shekels or more."

It is the CLO's responsibility to arrange escorts, while inspection at the checkpoints falls to the IDF and the Israeli police. The few hundred Gazan truck drivers allowed to leave the Strip begin their workday at eight in the evening, waiting in line to pass the Palestinian police roadblock. At the next stop—the IDF inspection pits where soldiers check each vehicle's engine, undercarriage, doors, and cabin—drivers have sometimes had to wait for as long as ten or eleven hours. The waiting time is a matter of luck, depending on the number of soldiers working the shift and the length of their meal breaks. The truck drivers may manage to catch a few hours of sleep in their cabins but they have no alternative except to be patient, sometimes starting their journeys after ten, twelve, or fourteen hours of standing in line. Frequently, the Palestinian in charge suddenly gets a phone call telling him that the military escort has been canceled; after hours of hanging around, the drivers are simply told to turn back and return home. No reason is ever given.

Sometimes the truckers get as far as their destination, one of the Israeli quarries, for example, where they plan to load up with gravel, but the convoy arrives just as the quarry's shift is changing. The military escort, acting on instructions from the CLO, orders the trucks to return to Gaza rather than wait the half hour for the quarry's work to resume. The CLO has told me that these occasional lapses are caused by a lack of coordination on the Palestinian side, but I have heard of many similar incidents. On one occasion, a shipment of flowers arrived late at the Israeli packing plant after soldiers at the Erez checkpoint had held up the convoy, waiting for a green light from their superiors even though the drivers had all the necessary permits. At the plant (where goods are checked a second time), the inspectors took a break after going over two trucks' worth of flowers. Instead of waiting, the escort sent the remaining trucks back to Gaza still loaded with flowers. In the end, the growers fed flowers to herds of goats and sold the rest for a shekel a bunch on every Gaza City street corner.

Another time a convoy of citrus was held up on its way to the port of Ashdod and the ship meant to carry the fruit back to the buyer in Eastern Europe was forced to sail without it. No doubt the buyer will prefer in future to deal with a Spanish or Israeli company rather than rely on Palestinians.

Imported goods on their way to the Strip, such as electrical appliances and building supplies, are sometimes stranded at Ashdod for months when the Gazan importer is unable to arrange their release. The result is a fortune in storage fees, money that could otherwise be used for investment and job creation. Instead of building new factories, Gaza's entrepreneurs count the number of days their plants and factories have been closed during the past year: 50 days, 90 days, and for one as many as 180.

These incidents only begin to suggest the magnitude of the problem. Ali al-Hayeq's story is typical. A manufacturer of floor tiles in his early thirties, he is a key financial supporter of the Palestinian Youth Association for Peace, which, among other things, organizes Israeli-Palestinian encounters. Early on, he put his faith in the Oslo process and prepared himself for the new prosperity he believed was at hand, signing contracts with Israeli companies before the Palestinian Authority was installed.

Al-Hayeq's father was one of Gaza City's veteran manufacturers of floor tiles, but Ali, a financial whiz kid, transformed the family business, increasing the daily output from 2,000 square feet of floor tiles to 19,000. He reasoned that, post-Oslo, private and public construction would boom, following the large demand for new apartments and office buildings. By mid-1995, however, he had reason to regret his decision. Production at the al-Hayeq factory was down to 5,000 square feet a day and falling. Another floor-tile factory in Gaza, Matar Dormush, which had opened in 1985 and employed twenty people, shut down in late 1995. The al-Shawwa factory, which had been in operation for thirty-five years and gave jobs to thirty people, closed its doors at the same time.

"You can't imagine how easy it is to lose 30,000 shekels a day in Gaza," al-Hayeq told me dejectedly. He had just ordered 1,200 tons of Turkish cement, which was now stuck in Ashdod. The day after his cement had docked, al-Hayeq had sent fifteen trucks, hired in advance, escort in tow, to pick up his delivery. However, the dock workers only got around to his cargo on the third shift, late in the afternoon, and by then the military escort forced the trucks to return to Gaza empty. Al-Hayeq had no choice but to store the cement overnight, at a cost of NIS 24,000, on top of the NIS 6,000 he had to pay the haulage company. "If this was a one-time thing, it might not be so upsetting," he said. "But every week something similar happens to one Gazan manufacturer or another."

Al-Hayeq stopped selling floor tiles in Israel and the West Bank—his principal markets—after the long period of hermetic closure in early 1996. Several months later, the system of transporting tiles in convoys was scrapped altogether, leaving only the back-to-back method. The inspections and loading were taking so long, however, that an average of only five trucks were able to leave each day. According to Israeli security sources, floor tiles are simply not conducive to thorough inspection. No wonder al-Hayeq lost his customers; even companies in Bethlehem were compelled to desert him and begin to buy from Israel.

Under the circumstances, foreign investors, the second group expected to jump-start the post-Oslo economy, were in no hurry to put their money into the Strip. One acquaintance of al-Hayeq's had come from the gulf states with deep pockets and good intentions. Like many other Palestinians, he bought a plot of land and planned to build a house. As the foundations were being dug and the concrete poured, the enthusiastic investor began to get the picture: the borders were closed, any potential partners and markets were cut off, and the double or even triple cost of transportation would make any venture unprofitable. He filled the new foundations with earth and flew back to the gulf. "I prefer to lose 80,000 shekels now rather than a million dollars tomorrow," he said. Foreign consuls all know of investors who came to look around with neither political nor altruistic motives, only economic interests, in mind but failed to see any reason to put their money on such a loser.

The silent factory floors and dusty time cards are reflected in the statistics: according to economists and officials of the donor nations, losses to the Palestinian economy caused by closures amounted to some $600 million in 1995—about the same amount pledged in donations that year, as it happened. A significant share of the money donated was transferred from long-range projects to pay for short-term employment in menial and Sisyphean public works, such as clearing streets of sand that only returns the next day. The statistics for real GNP in the West Bank and the Gaza Strip between 1992 and 1996 show it plummeting 22.7 percent; the per capita GNP plunged 38.8 percent.[6]

The Palestinian Ministry of Finance and the IMF based the Palestinian Authority's 1996 budget on an assumed 6 percent annual growth rate in the GDP but predicated their estimate on the renewed movement of workers and goods. In mid-1996, after an unprecedented five months of hermetic closure, the World Bank warned that the Palestinian GNP would nosedive by another whopping 17 percent if 30,000 breadwinners, at least, did not go back to work in Israel. The fall was averted because workers did begin returning to their jobs in June that year, and by August their combined numbers from Gaza and the West Bank stood at 50,000. From September on, though, the situation started to deteriorate again.

The Palestinians who were able to go back to their jobs that year rescued the Palestinian economy—and within a very short period of time. This turnaround reflects three dismal facts: first, two years after the transfer of authority, the inability of Gazans to work in Israel was still able to harm all branches of the Strip's economy; second, the level of subsistence had reached such a low point that it rose visibly with each blessed day that people were allowed to work, creating an illusion of improvement; last, in the two years since the Palestinian Authority was installed, the number of Gazans employed in civilian, that is, nonsecurity, sectors had dropped, according to figures posted by the Palestinian Ministry of Labor.

At the end of 1994, the Gazan workforce numbered 136,290, including those registered as employed and those listed as job seekers with the employment bureau. In truth, however, the size of the labor force and the number of unemployed were both much larger. For one thing, the security establishment was not included in the figures. For another, the number of Gazans working inside Israel was based on peak figures for that year and did not reflect the actual numbers, which were much lower because of the long hermetic closure. Moreover, the labor ministry's data do not include unregistered workers, such as children or other family members employed in small family businesses. So while the figures do not represent accurate statistics, they do illustrate some crucial changes.[7]

TABLE 3. GAZAN WORKFORCE, 1994–95

	1994	1995
WORKING IN ISRAEL	21,294	21,213
SEEKING JOBS	31,896	60,578
WORKING IN THE STRIP	83,100	65,168
PUBLIC SECTOR	13,700	18,664
TRANSPORTATION	12,600	3,740
COMMERCE AND FOOD	16,400	9,472
CONSTRUCTION	15,100	16,048
INDUSTRY	9,900	5,596
AGRICULTURE	15,400	11,648
TOTAL	136,290	146,959

The table shows a considerable yet predicted upswing in public-sector employment, but in the private sector the story was different: not only were there no new jobs, there was a sharp drop in the number of existing jobs. The consequences of closure are directly represented in the figures for the transport industry and agriculture. (The price of vegetables had fallen as a result of a glut caused by the inability to export them.)

Since Israel imposed the harsh closure of 1993, an economic cycle has been established, its consequences becoming more severe over time: first, workers are unable to reach their jobs in Israel; then they cut down on all purchases other than food and essential commodities, hurting retailers, importers, and manufacturers. Across the Strip, people fall behind on their electricity and water bills and so the municipalities, with their diminishing incomes, pay their employees late and the Palestinian treasury is unable to collect taxes; people stop traveling inside the Strip, so taxi drivers suffer, as do auto repair shops; they stop paying their minimal health care and school fees and start dipping into savings earmarked for their children's education or for expanding their houses; gradually they buy cheaper food and less of it, scouring the markets for low-quality leftovers. Fruit and meat are out of the question. "Fruit?" said my friend Yusuf, a doctor from the Rafah refugee camp. "Fruit is like a drug—you don't even dare think about it. Who can pay seven shekels for two pounds of peaches?"

The people of the Strip have long suffered from widespread ill health triggered by emotional tension: high blood pressure, respiratory infections, headaches. With each new hermetic closure these conditions worsen, according to Rabah Mohana, the head of the Union of Health Work Committees, a network of nongovernmental clinics set up by the DFLP and PFLP before the *intifada*. As many as 60 percent of Gaza's children suffer from anemia and 90 percent from intestinal parasites. Treating parasites involves treating the whole family, but when the borders are sealed the family cannot afford to buy the medicine.

It doesn't take an economist or an intelligence expert to trace the chain of damage caused by the closures and grasp the long-term consequences. And it doesn't take a scientist to make the connection between general privation and other troubling health findings:

approximately 15 percent of children under five show signs of malnutrition, reflected in subnormal weight and retarded growth. A study conducted by Terre des Hommes, a Swiss organization, reveals that 28,576 children under five (out of an estimated 188,000) need urgent treatment for malnutrition, which is most prevalent in the southern Strip and the refugee camps, where 20 percent of the children are underweight and 22 percent show retarded growth, compared with 8.9 percent and 10.2 percent in Gaza City. According to Terre des Hommes, 9 percent of Egyptian and Jordanian children of the same age are underweight, compared with 2.5 percent in healthy, well-nourished populations.

The study finds that the malnutrition is not caused by a shortage of food. "More than anything else, [it] apparently reflects a continual decline in purchasing power as a result of the economic ramifications of the *intifada*, the gulf war, and the closure, as well as pollution, unsanitary conditions, and poor distribution of existing resources." The use of polluted water in milk substitutes (that is, baby formula) is also a factor. In 1995, the study shows, 41.6 percent of Gazan families had to sell possessions in order to buy food; 53.8 percent borrowed money to buy food; only 5 percent had savings. A change in diet was reported by 56 percent, and of these, 86.2 percent said the change had been for the worse. Even so, "only" 10.3 percent of those families said they had depended on welfare assistance during the second half of 1995. This relatively low percentage is the result of the Palestinian family's network of mutual support and does not indicate the real sweep of poverty.[8] In fact 36.3 percent of Gazans were living below the poverty line ($650 per person expenditure yearly) by 1995.*

In the various coordinating committees, Palestinian representatives pleaded repeatedly with their Israeli counterparts on behalf of the private sector—the so-called backbone, cornerstone, motor of the Gazan economy. One World Bank official told me that it turned his stomach to see the best Palestinian brains wasting their energy and talents on one entreaty after another, instead of devoting their time to devising a real economic program with clear and viable guidelines for potential investors.

---

*At the end of 1997, 40.4 percent of Gazans were living below the poverty line, as were 11.1 percent of people in the West Bank, according to United Nations reports.

. . .

Top-level Palestinian leaders also took part in the criticism and pleading, making occasional declarations threatening to bar Israeli goods
from the areas under Sulta control. But these were idle threats, given
the Palestinian economy's overwhelming dependence on Israel. In the
end, there was a clear discrepancy between the Palestinian Authority's
periodic sharp statements and its impotence, its inability to effect
change and to generate ways of dealing with Israel's security concerns
that would neither push the Strip into further economic decline nor
punish the whole Palestinian population.

I have questioned whether Arafat, his ministers, and his close advisers have fully exercised their bargaining power and common sense to
expose the practice of closure for what it is: a policy with long-term
disastrous effects that sabotages the explicit intent of the Oslo Accords.
One day the negotiating proceedings, when open to public scrutiny,
might provide a definitive answer. Until then, the shiny king-size cars
parked outside Gaza City's gleaming new apartment buildings and lavish hotels offer something of a clue. These symbols of riches have
sparked waves of rumor and conjecture about the growth and consoli-
dation of Gaza's wealthy; their sudden and conspicuous rise to afflu-
ence contrasts starkly with the economy's general deterioration yet
does not represent the fruits of productive enterprise.

After the Palestinian Authority was installed, its elite immediately
set up a series of extensive monopolistic arrangements with several
Israeli firms. The first two agreements were concluded with Nesher,
which has the exclusive right to supply black cement to all Authority
territory, and Dor Energy, which has the monopoly on gasoline, diesel
fuel, and cooking and heating gas. These transactions not only shut
out Israeli competitors and violated the free-market principles to
which the Authority had committed itself but also eliminated hundreds of Palestinian retailers, importers, and truck drivers, who had
sold these products directly in the occupied territories. Consumers
were also affected, because prices rose even though the Authority was
buying the supplies at a discount.

Frozen meat, flour, paint, and wood are also sold in Authority territory through similar monopolistic arrangements with Israeli firms, and
the right to market these goods has been awarded to just a handful of
Palestinian agents. All these gigantic transactions have been brokered

by al-Bahar, a Palestinian parent company set up right after the Authority's establishment, which operates in a gray area, part private concern, part government company. According to various credible reports, al-Bahar's anonymous owners are senior officials in the Palestinian executive and security branches who have a hand in all aspects of the political negotiations. Therefore they also carry VIP permits exempting them from the restrictions related to the closures that hobble other businesses.

Al-Bahar has the authority to set up subsidiaries, each run by some dozen local businessmen, whose role is to distribute the merchandise throughout the self-rule territory. The firm that facilitated several of these start-up subsidiaries was the Palestinian Company for Commercial Services, whose guiding spirit is Arafat's economic adviser, Muhammad Rashid, also known as Khalid Salaam. Of Kurdish origin, he has worked closely with Arafat in various capacities since the PLO's days in Lebanon and even heads the Palestinian committee for economic negotiations with Israel. He operates with Arafat's full endorsement and blessing.

None of the details of these monopolies have been reported in the Palestinian press, but Palestinian sources (who insist on anonymity) do discuss the companies' business practices, which were described in a February 1996 investigation by the biweekly *Jerusalem Report* and by *Globes*, an Israeli financial daily. Both reports mention Yossi Ginossar, a former Shabak senior official who works alongside Khalid Salaam as Israeli liaison. The general manager of Amidar, a massive Israeli government housing company, and the owner of several private concerns, Ginossar also served as political liaison between Rabin and Arafat. Both reports allege that a string of lucrative deals yielded huge commissions for Ginossar and Salaam. Ginossar never responded to the articles; Salaam agreed to meet with the *Jerusalem Report* but canceled at the last minute.

Among other involvements, Salaam's Company for Commercial Services holds a significant number of shares in the private Palestinian telephone company, Paltel. Al-Bahar, the Palestinian Authority–controlled company, owns a 30 percent share in Team International, a computing, engineering, construction, and consulting firm owned by Palestinians, and a 30 percent share in Sidata, a computer company owned by Palestinians in Germany. Thus al-Bahar and Commercial

Services now control a major segment of the computer and communications industry in the Authority's territory. Authority bigwigs, mostly returnees from the diaspora or their family members, are partners in these companies or are involved in some other way.

In spring 1996, the new Palestinian Legislative Council discussed the al-Bahar company, which had just been commissioned to conduct a census. The Council demanded that Arafat's office cancel the contract, arguing that responsibility for a census clearly lay with the Palestinian Central Bureau of Statistics. Responding to protests by building contractors and importers of construction materials, the Council also demanded the termination of an al-Bahar subsidiary's monopoly on importing gravel. On both counts, the Council achieved success: the census was halted and the gravel monopoly was prevented, proving once again that the Legislative Council is the only body within the Palestinian Authority that dares to stand up against improper PLO practices. The Council failed in its bid, however, to dismantle al-Bahar: legally the company is privately owned and therefore immune to rulings on government monopolies.

Aside from the personal profit that accrued from these deals, eliminating competition has assured the Authority of increased income, greater control over its share of the profits, and the ability to set prices. The Authority's interests are safeguarded by the Preventive Security Force's police, who control the checkpoints, not only sifting through merchants' and truckers' security records but also making sure their cargos do not compete with goods handled by the monopolies. There is even a special unit of the force, called Economic Security, responsible for checking goods and the people bringing them in. The force gives first approval to businesspeople requesting permits to leave the Strip or to load merchandise at the freight terminals; it employs the army of cargo handlers who work there and controls the central gasoline terminal where Dor Energy deposits the Authority's petroleum products.

(Businesspeople are prey to various other extraministerial operations as well. For example, a unit of the General Security Force modeled on a similar outfit in Syria slaps arbitrary "taxes" on businesspeople in transit. The special operations unit of Force 17—Arafat's presidential guard—is authorized to collect fines from businessmen suspected of tax evasion or swindling their Israeli partners. Altogether, these activities take place outside the official jurisdiction of the various ministries.)

A considerable portion, if not all, of the Palestinian Authority's profits from these transactions never reach the finance ministry and therefore do not appear as income in the Authority's budget. It is widely assumed that some of the profits are siphoned off to bank accounts in Israel and earmarked for various extrabudgetary purposes set by Authority leaders, Arafat first and foremost. Part of the profits are used to supplement the security apparatus's budget and pay the salaries of both registered police and undercover agents, many more than are actually listed in the official records.

When the independent Palestinian newspaper *Al-Bilad* published the *Globes*'s report on monopolies in Arabic translation, its editor, Asad al-Asad, was detained for three days. The paper's Gaza correspondent went on to write his own report, which included accusations of *baksheesh* finding its way to Preventive Security Force people in exchange for driver's exit permits. He, too, was detained, for a week, and pressed to reveal his sources. The message got out to all reporters in Sulta territory: the subject was taboo.

But no secret is safe in Gaza, and what the papers don't print people pass on by word of mouth. True, laws were passed to encourage private investment and development. And true, the Authority did commit itself to observing impartiality, keeping its affairs transparent and accountable, and putting contracts up for bid. Nevertheless, all too many entrepreneurs have complained that government incentives have not come their way; worse, they are often charged fees or asked to pay bribes for business permits, and frequently they have to rely on *wasta*. One man confided that he helped finance a new police building. Another was made to understand that in exchange for a construction permit, he would have to donate an apartment to a nameless VIP. Someone else, who tried to ignore veiled demands for *baksheesh*, suddenly ran into a wall of bureaucratic impediments. A foreign Palestinian entrepreneur came to promote a commercial idea and found that he would have to set up a partnership with one of the monopoly front companies. There is no body empowered to review these complaints and so paranoia and rumors meet and feed off each other, compounding the deep-seated alienation between the governing elite and the rest of the population.

The collusion of the Authority's elite—its political, security, and economic leaders—should be familiar to anyone acquainted with the history of Jewish settlement in pre-1948 Palestine and of the Mapai party's years in power. But the system evolving in the Palestinian self-rule territories is unique in that it receives reinforcement and inspiration from Israel's closure policy. Sealing off the Strip has enabled the rapid rise of monopolies, needing as they do maximum control over the borders and the people within them. The Strip's near-absolute dependence on Israeli imports and the Palestinians' forced acquiescence to customs union, along with their meager tax income, provided the preliminary justification for signing broad contracts that would lower the cost of products at source. The reasoning was that instead of relying on income from taxes on manufacture—which, against all predictions, was continuing to shrink—the Authority could increase its profits from imports, at least theoretically, and thus quickly stand on its own two feet as the donor nations were demanding.

Connected umbilically to Israel, the Gazan business class long enjoyed privileges bestowed by the Israeli military government. But it had no political role to play in Palestinian society. Now, says economist Salah abd al-Shafi, this once-favored group has been displaced by people who do have a political role to play. Yet many of those Palestinian political leaders who are supposed to be arguing against the closure policy in their sessions with Israeli negotiators have also learned to profit from and exploit it for personal gain and the benefit of their immediate circle. Without doubt, this dual involvement has limited the politicians' ability, suitability, and perhaps even desire to propose reasonable alternatives to closure, which continues its systematic destruction of Gaza's economy and its stranglehold on every business-person's freedom of action.

The World Bank, the IMF, and the donor nations—the first to notice Gaza's monopolistic practice and those involved in it—have never sought to impose effective sanctions to restrain it, even though it runs counter to their demands for competition and a free market. At the same time, all the foreign observers are aware of the closure policy and its consequences and have warned the Israelis more than once of the damage being done to Gaza's economy, social fabric, and general health. Moreover, they have all expressed concern that their donations have, in effect, been used to subsidize the closure. Thus, despite their criticism of monopolies and the Authority's business affairs, they well understand that these practices are not the sole cause of the Strip's economic decline.

In private, foreign representatives do not dispute Israel's security concerns but doubt whether sealing off the strip, with all the attendant restrictions, is motivated by security considerations alone. Every development in the private sector has completely upended the expected economic recovery: the loss of the West Bank markets to Israeli companies; the Palestinian manufacturers' neutralized competitive edge over their Israeli counterparts; vanishing incentives for new investments; factories unable to meet their customers' timetables; limited opportunities for entrepreneurs; a stagnant cash flow; everyone eating into their savings.

The IMF, the World Bank, and foreign observers all see that a crippling political system, in which the Palestinian Authority and Palestinian business have no control over the conditions in which they operate, will surely undermine any national strategy. No economic plan can sustain a factory owner when he cannot fill his orders on time, hold down his transportation costs, meet his West Bank partners, obtain a driver's exit permit, or guarantee that a shipment of oranges will reach its boat when its military escort has been canceled.

Chapter 13

A *People Up in Arms*

The rumor spread through Gaza like wildfire. I first heard it from a Hamas man, so I did not take it too seriously: people were saying that any Palestinian policeman who left the force to go and work in Israel would be punished by the Palestinian Authority with a four-year sentence. It was May 1996, the week after Benjamin Netanyahu's election, and the rumor meant that, like everyone else in Gaza, the Palestinian Authority believed Netanyahu, the Likud leader, was about to reverse the Labor Party's policy and allow large numbers of workers back into Israel. Sealing off the Strip and the West Bank actually reinforced the 1967 borders, separating the occupied territories from Israel; the Likud was firmly against any territorial separation and so was expected to reintegrate the Palestinian workforce—at least partially. Hope was in the air. Young men began talking about the Israeli construction sites waiting for them; others contacted former employers and told them to submit their hiring requests. Middle-aged men sighed with relief: now their sons and younger brothers would help support the family. Children were excited, chattering about the new clothes and books they would have for the coming school year.

Another story had it that Yassir Arafat had sent a personal memorandum to all senior security men, ordering them to prevent a mass exodus of police. But three months after Netanyahu's election, closure was still in force and the police had not shed their uniforms for shovels and pruning shears. Arafat's supposed order was never put to the test, but it conveyed a sociligical truth evident to everyone in the Strip: the horrific bloating of the Palestinian police and security forces was a direct result of Gaza's chronic unemployment.

Time and time again I bump into people I met early on—Fatah

militants, exiled men who have returned home, young prisoners just released—now wearing uniforms. One is directing traffic, another is the driver for a high-ranking police officer, a third escorts the armored car carrying money from the bank, yet another is a guard at the labor ministry, armed with a Kalashnikov. I ran into the ministry guard just before the January 1996 Palestinian elections. We talked about the campaign, about Tel Aviv, about Arafat and the woman, Samiha Khalil, who was running against him. The guard left me in no doubt as to his loyalty to Yassir Arafat. Nevertheless, when we began to talk about the closure, he took me by surprise. "If they let twenty-five-year-olds go back to work, I'll leave the police force," he said.

Hope follows its own cycles; at every political turn, in every event, Gazans saw some logical reason for lifting the closure. Everyone believed that the Palestinian elections would stabilize the Strip and more work permits would be issued. Then there were the unlikely interpretations of Netanyahu's intentions. And with each fresh disappointment, people looked to the police force as a source of employment. I remember a hot summer evening with my friends from the Shabura camp. As was their habit, they took a few stools out to the sandy alley and seated themselves between the tin fence and concrete walls, placing a teapot on a charcoal burner. The flames threw up fuzzy shadows that danced on the walls; a muezzin called out in the distance, then a second muezzin, closer. Several children asked for permission to join us, and the adults gave them jobs to do—bringing out more tea, fetching water, running down to the kiosk to buy a pack of cigarettes. Bored youths wandered around the houses, and from the end of the alley came the clickety-clack of dice hitting a wooden backgammon board. An uncle's wife, bold enough to sit outside with the men (I don't count), joined the group with her eighteen-year-old son, settling onto one of the stools and extending her hand for a glass of tea. "Just look at him," she said to me, jabbing her finger at her son, making sure I knew whom she meant. "What do you think, is there any way he can work in Israel? He finished school, he needs to work. It doesn't make sense." Today that son is a policeman.

According to the May 1994 Cairo agreement, the police force in Gaza and Jericho was to comprise four security branches employing 9,000 people, 7,000 of whom were to be Palestine Liberation Army members returning to the territories from the Palestinian diaspora.

Article 9 of the agreement states: "The Palestinian Authority shall establish a strong police force. Outside the Palestinian police force referred to in this article, and the Israeli military forces, no other armed force will be established or operate in the Gaza Strip and Jericho." I understood quickly that the 2,000 people to be recruited locally was a flexible figure; after all, I personally knew about 76 recruits and my fellow journalists knew 304. The various branches of the Palestinian police soon became the largest employer in the Strip and the most successful income-generating project. By the eve of the IDF's redeployment in the West Bank in late 1995, the police branch alone had mushroomed to 21,000 (according to various reports) and was still growing. The other branches of the force were flourishing too.

As described in the Cairo agreement, the force was broken down into police, general security, intelligence (the Mukhabarat), and civil defense, with the coast guard a unit within the police force but operating as an independent outfit. But in practice, there are more security branches: preventive security (responsible for the checkpoints and crossing into Israel, among other things), military intelligence, the presidential guard, or Force 17, as it is known, and a unit for special missions within Force 17, which some people call Force 87 after the number of men serving in it who were once wanted by Israel. People distinguish between the General Security Force and the Border Patrol, although they are both generally referred to as "the Army." Each security branch maintains its own jails—by 1996 there were twenty-four in the narrow Strip—its own interrogators, and its own esprit de corps, and no Gazan is immune from recurrent arrests by the different branches of the security apparatus. As the Palestinian Authority's detractors have been quick to point out, there is one policeman for every fifty people in Gaza.

Curiously, Israel did not protest this blatant violation of the Cairo agreement. Indeed, Muhammad Dahlan, head of the Strip's Preventive Security Force, was a much sought-after partner for talks with Israel on security coordination. Ultimately, in fact, the violation of article 9 received Israel's blessing: the 1995 Taba agreement provides for 30,000 police to be stationed in the West Bank and Gaza Strip, and increases the number of security branches to six. By the summer of 1996, approximately 40,000 men were serving in the various forces.

For the first month or two after the Palestinian Authority was installed, *police* was a synonym for the men who had returned from abroad. The Cairo agreement stipulated that those coming back to fill the ranks of the police force would bring their wives and children. Thus the provision for 7,000 policemen from the Palestinian diaspora was seen as a kind of distant cousin of the right of Palestinian refugees to return to their homeland—a holy grail for all Palestinians that was put on hold until the final-status negotiations. Rejoicing Gazans greeted the crowds of confused, exhausted men, just arrived from Yemen, Libya, and Egypt, who filled the newly vacated IDF buildings. "They purposely chose older men who would bring their families," a police cadet from Beit Lahia told me. "The intention was that later they could step aside to make room for our younger men from Gaza." Still, there were some young returnees, who mostly looked lost. Until dozens of simple homes were erected throughout the Strip, they were housed in tents and in several public buildings. A few slept out in the open. In an outpouring of national joy, hundreds of people came to visit them, bringing food and demonstrating human concern for the homeless. And six months after their return, the policemen were bound to the people of Gaza after a shooting incident in which three returnees were killed by the IDF. The event is still unexplained: the IDF maintained that an Israeli patrol had been fired on; the Palestinian police denied it. Palestinians argued that, even if the report was accurate, IDF soldiers had no right to enter the territory of the Authority and open fire on the local police. Soon after the killings, some men from the border unit, still in shock, said, "It was a black day when we came to the Strip."

In time, disenchantment affected both the returnees and the Gazans. Following the bread *intifada* in July 1994, when Gazan workers waiting at the Erez checkpoint erupted in anger, Palestinian police were assigned the job of sifting the workers approaching the checkpoint at a series of roadblocks placed along the way to the border. Israeli soldiers stationed at the checkpoint had admitted how hard it was for them to withstand the pleas of permitless workers trying to get through. The logistical conclusion was not to increase the number of workers allowed across the border but instead to spare Israeli soldiers the painful job of weeding out permitless Gazans by leaving it to the Palestinian police force. In addition to the new series of roadblocks, Border Patrol units (made up largely of returnees from Libya) were deployed along the northern end of the Strip to keep a close eye on the citrus groves of Beit Hanun, where people would take ladders and scale the stone fence (until an electrified fence was installed) or bring donkeys, stand on their backs, and leap toward the hope of work.

Soon the workers in Rafah were cracking bitter jokes about the "seven" Palestinian stations they had to pass before reaching the Israeli checkpoint and the "foreigners" who were posted at them. "It's still dark when I get to the last Palestinian checkpoint, where they go through the papers very carefully," A. told me. "Sometimes they put someone there from Egypt or Yemen, black as the night, who can't read a single letter of Hebrew. He shines a flashlight on my work permit and holds it upside down and he's supposed to decide whether the permit is fake. Then we go on to the Israeli checkpoint, where a new immigrant from Ethiopia, also black as the night, looks at my permit for half an hour because he can't read Hebrew, either. He peers at the photograph and then up at me and I feel like the biggest criminal in the world." Once, Muhammad Dahlan himself came to Erez to check on the procedure and an Ethiopian soldier asked for his documents. The soldier wasn't satisfied, according to Dahlan, and he had to call over some big Israeli officer to explain to the new immigrant who he was. "Why don't you stick them in prison for a while?" he suggested. "Then they'll learn Hebrew like we did."

Before long Gazans saw trucks driving around the Strip transporting grim-faced men in uniform with their machine guns bolted to the trucks' floors, barrels up, and the newcomers acquired a nickname: "Look, the Arabs are coming," one friend said to me as a truck drove by. (Nevertheless, the same friend invited me back to his house to meet a beloved newly returned uncle, now a high-ranking general security officer.) Another friend spoke nostalgically of his days in the Israeli police force, where he served until the *intifada* broke out and all the Palestinian policemen quit. "Inspection used to last fifteen minutes at most," he quipped. "Now, with all these commanders from the Arab states, we have to stand at attention for hours."

When Hani Aabed, the Islamic Jihad member assassinated in 1994, was released from detention in a Palestinian jail, I asked whether he had demanded to see his lawyer. "It didn't occur to me," he answered. Nor did he insist on seeing his detention order. "I know the Arabs," he said, by way of explanation. His comment was not racist; he was referring to the style of governing and policing that prevailed among his neighbors.

Gazans carry with them a deep sense of the vast Muslim space in which all of us, Israelis and Palestinians, live; their sense of belonging did not begin with the arrival of their "brothers from the diaspora." I first encountered this palpable connection to the broader Muslim world in poetic, even romantic circumstances. It was during 1993, when the IDF still patrolled the streets of Gaza and the night curfew was in force. I had been invited to spend Id al-Fitr, the holiday marking the end of Ramadan, with friends in Rafah, but they could not tell me exactly when the three-day feast would begin. That date, I learned, is determined by a sighting of the new moon in the skies of the Islamic world. The first person who sees the new moon at sunset conveys the information under oath to the local *qadi*, or Islamic judge, who in turn relays the news up the chain of the religious hierarchy. Theoretically, my friends said as they skimmed over a map, it is enough that one small child standing by the Gaza seashore see the new moon for the news to spread instantly throughout the Muslim world. My friends remembered going down to the seashore when they were young and searching for the moon together.

Now, during the *intifada*, children could no longer wander the beaches at twilight. Instead, my friends wandered the radio stations of Cairo, Amman, Jerusalem, even Saudi Arabia, to hear whether and where the moon had been sighted. There, inside the tiny room, I could almost touch the soothing sense of connection to the region in this display of Islamic unity.

Sometimes the moon is sighted in one country but not in another — often for political reasons and not because of cloudy skies. In Rafah, people have chosen to follow Egypt and its imams, while those in Gaza City have gone with the West Bank, which has followed Jordan. In 1993, Gaza's imams proclaimed the new moon in tandem with Saudi Arabia, while the West Bank devout adhered to Israeli state radio and Jordan, waiting an extra day to break the fast and unite with the rest of the world's Muslims.

Work in the Persian Gulf states, studies in Egypt, Libya, and Iraq, family in Jordan, books imported from Lebanon and Syria, common Islamic holidays — all these extend the boundaries of the Gaza Strip, adding a broader cultural and conceptual map, an Islamic map, to the three others etched in the Palestinian consciousness: the first is the pre-1948 map, the original paradise lost and the source of both passivity and discontent; the second is the map of greater Israel, of Jewish supremacy, in which arrogance and state-sponsored discrimination against Palestinians have fostered deep wells of frustration and rebellion. The third map in the Palestinian mind is a refined and idealized image of the State of Israel as a model of an open, argumentative society that knows how to challenge its own myths when necessary, one in which the individual and the community readily pit themselves against the authorities. But for those who maintain that the encounter with Israel exposed Palestinians in the occupied territories to the workings of a democracy, the truth is more complex. With growing self-assurance, Palestinians learned to measure the standards of the democratic State of Israel against the repressive rule of greater Israel. The Palestinians' adoption of democratic values in their struggle for free speech, a free press, freedom of protest, assembly, and association, as well as in their national struggle, has never been a wholesale imitation of the Israeli model. Instead it has entailed relentless and critical review of Israel's other, antidemocratic aspect. In fact, Palestinians have gained firsthand knowledge of the strains and contradictions between the laws and principles applied to Israeli citizens, particularly the Jewish citizens, on the one hand, and those applied to Palestinian subjects of an occupying Israeli power, on the other. By the same token, Palestinians have compelled Israelis to examine this contradiction, too.

In any case, while setting up self-rule, Gazans were able to draw on a wealth of examples of government and of relations between government and society, and they rejected the "Arab model" of authoritarian regimes. At the same time, Gazans assumed that Yassir Arafat and his top men would start out by introducing an "Arab-style" regime, since that was the only form of rule they had known during their exile in the Arab states and was the model they had developed during years of controling Palestinian enclaves, especially in Lebanon.

"They'll solve the refugee problem by putting us all in very tall buildings," one wisecracking refugee friend told me two months before the transfer of authority. "They'll cover the Strip with tall buildings and won't leave a speck of green. Then they'll put a policeman in the entrance to each building who'll watch everyone and report on all our comings and goings," he went on. "That way they'll solve all their other problems, too." He envisaged the whole Strip under the control of a multiplicity of police and their spies.

In May 1994, another sharp refugee, M., told me to start getting used to a new word, *waziz*, or squealer. "You'll be hearing it all the time. The *waziz* will be the man standing on the street corner, pretending to read a newspaper, thinking he hasn't been noticed and that we don't know that his job is to report on our every little twitch." Two years later I asked Z., a critical-minded Fatah member, whether the police force included the *wazizeen*. "Not at all," he said. "The *wazizeen* are separate. There's one in every household, in every family." Over time people learned which *waziz* was attached to which security branch and to recognize them in the hospitals, the schools, the universities, and the mosques.

Once N., a Popular Front man and former prisoner, told me, "I see your right-wingers demonstrating against the accords, and I know we won't be allowed to demonstrate like that." He continued, "We always knew that the IDF had a red line it wouldn't cross. The Arab rulers have none. Assad killed twenty thousand people without batting an eyelid." A senior police officer, a friend of N.'s, agreed to talk to me when it was still unclear which police were allowed to talk and what they were allowed to say. A few weeks later, I saw him in town, dressed in uniform, with his revolver and his hat. Very loudly, within earshot of any passerby, he acted the part of the tough officer. "Enough, that's it. Go! Get out of here! There'll be no more press roaming about, writing anything they please."

Sadly, his performance proved all too prophetic. Gradually, in what seemed in retrospect a remarkably calculated process, freedom of the press was curtailed. First, *Al-Nahar*, a pro-Jordanian publication, was denied a publication permit. Then the editor of *Falastin*, a new weekly, was held in deluxe detention for two weeks and the publication was shut down. Even the fact that he also worked for a foreign news organization did not prevent his arrest when he received a Hamas leaflet at his office. Then came the crackdown on the distribution of *Al-Nahar* and another East Jerusalem daily, *Al-Quds*, for publishing high estimates of the number of participants at Hamas and Jihad rallies.

The measures became ever more harsh. Reporters who dared transmit critical news were detained for longer periods of time (upon release, some reporters published letters of thanks to Arafat for letting them go). One editor was arrested for translating an article from Hebrew on the economic monopolies owned by senior figures in the

Palestinian Authority; another editor was arrested for not printing a news item flattering to Arafat on his front page. The offices of an opposition newspaper in East Jerusalem were broken into and new machinery destroyed; an Islamic Jihad paper was shut down after it published an article exposing corruption. Journalists were pressed to reveal their sources. It was never clear when these actions were ordered from above and when they were initiated spontaneously. Either way, the economic threat to the newspapers' management and the reporters' constant fear of detention achieved their objective: most editors stopped taking risks and their reporters avoided news items liable to cause controversy. They hoped that the prominent figures who wrote critical articles would occasionally confirm troublesome information the public already knew but was not allowed to read, or that Israeli television would broadcast information that Palestinians were forbidden to report.

At first I wanted to believe that Gazans' great sense of self-irony would help curb the development that people had begun to predict: a Palestinian society in which the security establishment dictated the limits of speech and action. I was buoyed by early conversations with Fatah activists who indicated that autocratic rule was not inevitable. I hoped that people aware of the dangers would shape the new Palestinian government.

I met with I. and T. before Arafat's arrival in Gaza. They were waiting—for the IDF's redeployment, to take over from the civil administration, for Arafat to take up his place. In their words I heard the familiar blend: a sense of self-worth, criticism of their rivals—in this case the Fatah commanders arriving from "outside," who would be assigned higher ranks—affection for Arafat, misgivings about him, confidence in their personal futures yet a feeling of responsibility for their people. Asking to speak off the record, the two men spoke candidly.

"We were the commanders here—we had to give answers to whoever had questions," T. explained. "The ones from outside don't know the situation here. It's as if someone told me to go to Brazil and deal with the drug cartel. They close one ear and the other one hears only what Arafat says. He pulls all the strings. In the end we'll set up some form of state, but it's better for us if that state is democratic. That's what we learned struggling against the occupation. Most of the people are with Fatah, and Fatah is the only organization that can make decisions, so Arafat knows that without a strong Fatah behind him the accords will fail. And when he comes, those of us in Fatah will convince him to change the way he operates. Up to now, people would see him in Tunis and tell him only what he wanted to hear. When he comes to Gaza, he's also going to hear things he won't like. He'll see things, too. Every Fatah supporter has an inner voice saying the same thing. I'm from Isdud, for example, but I've stopped talking about Isdud. We've lost Palestine, Haifa, Acre, and Safed. We've accepted this rotten agreement because we want the war to end. Our children have never known anything but stones and bullets and leaflets. We want them to live differently. I see your people on the left, our old friends, ditch all their principles once they're in power. And people say the same about Fatah, that we'll sacrifice our principles for the sake of power. But you know, the throne may be permanent but the person sitting on it can be replaced. Most Fatah people don't want to be in the government. They know this is a time for dirty politics, and they don't want to be part of it. Up to now, we were clean; what we did was for our people, not for ourselves."

Today, I. and T., in their mid-thirties, have jobs in the intelligence and police forces. They still talk, off the record, of an independent state and a free society, but they are driven by concerns for their children's education and well-being. Their hopes for a different governing style have gone and their movement, Fatah, failed to shape the system that is in place. Nor has Fatah's standing been strengthened by an improved economy and quality of life. As individuals, they feel unable to take openly critical positions, which would jeopardize their livelihoods and their children's futures, if not more. They feel helpless against the growing power of PLO and Fatah bigwigs from abroad, many of whom were immediately given jobs, apartments, cars, permits to travel to the West Bank and overseas. Prejudice and scorn marked these new officials' attitude toward local Gazans.

"I remember some high-level forum," said A.N., who was deeply offended. "One person said of us, 'They are the fruit of the occupation.' He meant that we were damaged because of living under the Israelis and that we deserved contempt." Abu Saber also suffered the disdain of Palestinian returnees. "You can only control this society by keeping them down," was one of the remarks he heard. "They see our carts and donkeys, our ruined towns, the garbage in the streets, and equate that with our culture and our thinking," Abu Saber told me.

I needed no persuading, having heard as much from the Palestinian newcomers, especially those in high places. A senior PLO figure widely considered an intellectual explained: "It's a backward society, not yet ripe for democracy." I remarked that he and others like him found it convenient to construct this distorted image of Gazans in order to preserve their privileged status as PLO leaders and the governing elite. I was idealizing the Gazans, he replied in a conciliatory tone.

Here and there, people did hear of Fatah members trying to raise unpleasant issues in their sessions with Abu Amar. One was placed under house arrest for two days, another was reprimanded, someone else was scolded personally by Arafat, and one man was subjected to a "court martial." "You have to find the right time, the right moment to tell him something he doesn't want to hear," several Fatah people said, explaining the gap between their generous criticism, which flowed freely in private, and their tight-lipped stance toward the outside world, not to mention their defense of positions and behavior they opposed. All these people had been awarded various positions in the civil and police establishments.

About the time I was talking to I. and T., just as the Palestinian Authority was taking over its responsibilities in Gaza, Fatah was busy assigning ranks to its members. The different designations were based on the extent of one's military record, years served in prison, and duration of membership in the movement. The degree of seniority would, in the future, determine the salaries of Fatah members working in the public sector. Simultaneously, the most prominent opposition movements, Hamas and the Popular Front, were being forced to decide whether to permit their activists to join the new police force. Thousands of Palestinians would soon be returning from abroad, people who would need work and salaries, people who would most likely receive preferential treatment given their long standing in Fatah. To many Gazans it seemed that the present opportunity could not be ignored. "If you folks from the Popular Front don't join the police force now, in three months you'll find there's no room for you," I heard one man say as he sat with a group of friends in a sun-drenched courtyard in Beit Lahia, around a tray heaped with strawberries from the family greenhouse.

Fatah supporters received instructions not to come out as a movement to welcome the policemen arriving from "outside": "This is the people's army, not Fatah's. We can't let the two become synonymous."

But the impression of identity was created nonetheless and became increasingly entrenched over time, even though members of all the PLO constituent organizations eventually joined the various branches of the security apparatus. And as with any other open secret, it was well known that certain Fatah people in essentially civilian jobs had begun receiving salaries from the security forces. For others, the opposite was true: they received civilian salaries but had been "lent" to the security establishment. Everyone treated these cases as a natural phenomenon unworthy of comment.

In February and March of 1995 I suddenly began hearing in the unemployment-plagued alleys about fourteen hundred new police jobs for young Fatah supporters. It was a time of particularly tight closure following a suicide bombing inside Israel. Young men were being told to sign up with one of the forces and begin collecting a salary. And the work? "Not yet, there's still nothing to do; just sign up and you'll get paid." However, at meetings with representatives of the countries giving money to the PA, the donor nations, the Palestinian Authority had promised to freeze the number of jobs in the public sector because of its budget deficit. This contradiction confirmed the rumor that the budget for the "excess" policemen was coming from unidentified sources.

One of the men in that sunny courtyard in Beit Lahia was a Fatah member who had completed a training course in Egypt before joining the police force. He tried to convince his brother and his friend S.— both from the Popular Front—to join as well. Around that time, S. was approached by friends from Fatah with another tempting offer: to take a course in Germany, become a high-ranking officer, and join the Palestinian intelligence; later there would be other courses in other countries. (All of Rafah was abuzz with tales of local youths who had taken a very secret CIA or FBI course in the States. One of them had never been beyond the Rafah camp's alleyways, jail cells, and interrogation rooms; a second was a fugitive who had been on the run from the IDF for many long months; a third had grown up in a family without enough money to buy shoes for the children.)

G. from the Popular Front and several of his friends had been invited to join Force 17, Arafat's presidential guard. The Front eventually decided to allow its members to join the civilian police and the General Security Force but not the intelligence branch, which "works very closely with the Israeli interests that are instruments of oppression," as someone explained to me. For similar reasons, Hamas people were allowed to join the civilian police, although some of them had their weapons confiscated after a Hamas-affiliated policeman perpetrated an attack in Jerusalem.

The opposition organizations had no answers for their unemployed young members in the refugee camps, all former prisoners, who saw their counterparts in Fatah receiving salaries and some kind of future for themselves. Members argued that joining the police force, like working at administrative jobs in Palestinian Authority ministries, did not mean support for Oslo. "I understand you. When it's a matter of milk for the children, no other consideration takes precedence," a senior Popular Front official told G., who had joined Force 17 and been ousted from the organization.

"On the one hand, I know that it's almost the only opportunity I'll ever have for a permanent job with the possibility of advancement and a higher salary," said thirty-year-old S., sharing his private misgivings—and, essentially, the ideological and practical misgivings of his organization—with me. "But on the other hand, I know that Arafat is interested in our joining his apparatus in order to gradually silence us as an opposition. He wants us to undergo the same process as everyone else: to gradually come to identify ourselves with the regime. And I'm not at all sure that those of us in the opposition have the strength to withstand what we know is going to happen."

B., too, is thirty years old, but he had fewer reservations. A member of Fatah and a university graduate unable to find a job in the social sciences, he regarded the suggestion that he serve in the Palestinian security forces as natural. His family supported the idea, B. told me. His father saw it as an opportunity for secure, permanent work; those who serve in preventive security, moreover, are treated with respect. In the top ranks of preventive security, unlike the other security forces, his father argued, there were only "our own"—that is, Gazans and, most especially importantly, refugees. Other members of the family hoped he'd acquire *wasta*, the pull that would make it easier for them to avoid the usual red tape.

In the end, neither S. nor B. joined the security forces, for which they both thank their lucky stars, especially when they hear about the behavior of those shielded by uniform and rank. At first there was the

delusion that those police who were "our own" and who had themselves undergone interrogations and imprisonment would unswerv-
ingly uphold the law and mete out fair treatment to prisoners and to
people in general. Very quickly this belief was proved wrong, and
everyone learned that the role shapes the person. In June 1994 came
the shocking news that a detainee suspected of collaborating with
Israel had died under torture in an interrogation cell. His interrogators
were familiar with Israeli methods. The press was informed that those
responsible would stand trial, but to the best of my knowledge, at least
some of them are still at their jobs. I recalled then what A., a human
rights activist, had said to me in December 1993: "The victim will
become the hangman."

While still in Israeli jails, Palestinian prisoners had discussed this
eventuality and ways of countering it. "Among ourselves we said that
under no circumstances would we become interrogators or work in
prisons," a number of newly released prisoners told me. But reality
proved more powerful. Even though the death of the suspected collaborator was presented as an "error," such errors would recur again and
again in prisons in Gaza and the West Bank. Despite attempts to por-
tray the incident as an exception, it was clear that former torture
victims were now participating in interrogations, using homegrown
methods of torture and humiliation.

These were at first employed primarily against suspected collaborators, small fry with whose fate Israel did not concern itself. (The most
important collaborators had always been brought into Israel and
issued Israeli identity cards when things got too hot for them.) Very
soon torture was being used on Hamas and Islamic Jihad people as
well. In the first three years after the Palestinian Authority was set up,
at least twenty men died in Palestinian cells.

Young men in their twenties were never able to afford the luxury of
indecision about joining the Palestinian police. Since 1994 it had
been clear that Israel would not allow people their age—or any single
men, for that matter—to leave the Strip. Gradually, the minimum age
worked its way up, from twenty-two to twenty-six to twenty-eight, thirty,
and finally forty. About 9 percent of Gaza's men are now in their thirties.[1] The educations of many of these men have been disrupted, and
what opportunities they might have had for study vanished with the

intifada and with closed schools, curfews, and strike days. Their hopes of finding work in the Strip vanished, as well, with the failure of the much-touted industrial boom to materialize; indeed, workshops and factories began to shut down. The owner of a new hotel placed a want ad to fill 11 jobs. Within a day or two he had received 617 applications.

Given such high unemployment, Arafat was able to create a local police force whose members felt a sense of loyalty and personal debt to him for their guaranteed monthly paychecks. Within a short time, a very large group of families also came to owe their (relative) deliverance from the cycle of poverty to the security establishment and the man at its helm. The distance from personal gratitude to total identification with and subservience to the forces of government and police is rather short. The youth of most of the recruits ensured that a fairly brief period of conditioning was all that was needed. Who knows? It is even possible that the large-scale recruitment of police will curb the contentious Gazan spirit of criticism and skepticism and stifle open debate. Meanwhile there are uniformed young men everywhere—in the riot police, in the unit that guards nongovernmental institutions, at the entrances to officials' homes, outside universities and hospitals, sometimes near mosques. They are at every roadblock—whether to direct traffic or to report on people's comings and goings is not clear, but at least they are bringing home $264 a month and can start thinking about getting married.

And they feel important, as well, like the two plainclothes policemen, barely old enough to shave, who insisted on checking my papers when I innocently stopped alongside a man selling grapes on the road along the shore. Giving the order to "show your ID" was a delicate issue in Gaza for the first few months after May 1994. People had long entertained the fantasy of leaving their IDs at home, something they could never do when the Israeli army patroled the streets. Going out without an identity card was for many the epitome of freedom, but the fantasy was soon dispelled when worshipers on their way to early-morning prayers in the mosques were detained for not carrying their documents.

I never forget my papers, and the easiest thing would have been to show them to the young policemen. But they had touched a nerve. First, I'd done nothing to make them stop me. Second, how did I know they were authorized to check my documents? My irritation was one more sign that I had absorbed Gazan ways. "First, you show me *your* identification," I said, knowing this was how some of my Gazan friends would have reacted. My anger was defused by the confusion on the young men's faces: for them, it was clear, the epitome of freedom was having the power to ask other people to show their papers. These were men whose first sight had been that of army uniforms, their first sound that of gunfire. From the time they could talk they had watched soldiers stopping their parents and demanding to see IDs.

My friend H.S. is less forgiving. "It's hard to think in sociological terms when someone in uniform talks to you as if you're dirt," he said. "What is it with these guys in their uniforms that makes them so rude? First the Israelis and now our own." Another friend, I., carries a revolver in the glove compartment of his car, and his papers—which testify to his high status and his many years in Israeli prisons—would humble any young policeman, although I. never flashes them around. "A policeman stopped me at one of the roadblocks and barked something at me," I. recalled. "I asked him to speak politely but he barked at me again and demanded to search my car. 'Go ahead,' I said, 'you're welcome.' He opened the glove compartment, saw the revolver, and apologized immediately." Another time, it was the papers that made the policeman change his tune. "I always ask these children," I. said of grown men eight years his junior, at most, "why they hold some papers and a gun in higher esteem than the person. It's not logical."

A.D., a high-ranking officer who went in civilian clothes to arrange a personal matter at the Palestinian interior ministry one day, was obliged to wait for hours. "I wasn't pleased with myself, but the next day I came back in my uniform and was immediately greeted with cries of 'Welcome' and 'What can I do for you, sir?'" Another senior man, whose son swallowed a coin late one evening, called the hospital to have his boy admitted. The physician on duty was busy with a more urgent case and said that the coin would no doubt come out in the boy's feces. The department head echoed the physician's opinion, but an irate call from Abu Amar's office demanded immediate hospitalization and treatment. The doctor stuck to his position that the coin would be expelled without any outside intervention and, in response, Arafat's office ordered that the physicians involved be docked two weeks' pay.

Some people attribute the growing reverence for uniforms and high military rank to the Strip's "Arabization," but they tend to forget that another kind of favoritism—toward fawning subordinates and small-time collaborators—was the rule in the days of the Israeli civil administration. H.S., though, accepts no excuses. "Under occupation we could live with some things as inevitable. But they're far more obnoxious when we do them to ourselves."

"Uniforms come first" was the message in Gaza, and complaints about the perks and privileges of policemen were a voluble part of the 1996 election campaign. There is always some explanation in the street why one particular neighborhood has merited large-scale renewal projects, improved roads, new sewers, and water pipes. "We're lucky," someone tells me. "We've got a couple of big officers and some senior Fatah people living in our neighborhood." Through the grapevine one hears of this minister's expensive new furniture and that police officer's large, airy apartment, both paid for by the PLO. People speculate openly about the VIP who has just bought himself a penthouse by the sea.

One sign of the times is that the police now poke their noses into everything—this in a society known for breeding resistance to authority. I experienced the change firsthand when a policeman was called in to solve a problem that could easily have been resolved without him. Right after the Legislative Council elections in 1996, I was on my way out of Gaza, needing a rest and wanting to escape Ramadan, which had just begun. The long month of fasting makes a normal life impossible: the men stop smoking, making most of them irritable. They pace about distractedly, unable to focus on anything for longer than a minute or two. Anyone who isn't fasting sneaks about, looking for a corner where he can light up a cigarette or sip some coffee. Around noon, everyone begins to shop for the big evening meal and the narrow streets fill up with crowds and cars, pushing and honking, and the whole mass moves in a kind of collective frenzy.

That day I set out in my car and immediately knew I had made a mistake. If only I had waited until 5:00 P.M., when everyone is at home breaking their fast with the meal the women have been toiling over all day, I could have spared myself the traffic jams and the shouts to get moving. Serene Israeli music was wafting from my radio when I felt a powerful thump and my car and I were propelled forward, into the back end of the Subaru just ahead. Its bumper was bent a little, mine was bent a lot, and my taillight was smashed to smithereens. The poor driver behind me, preoccupied with thoughts of the meal await-ing him, couldn't even get his ancient Peugeot to start again.

We all got out of our cars and sized up the damage; the shopkeepers in the vicinity came to offer advice. Someone, of course, concluded from my accent that I was an Israeli and started speaking Hebrew; some men helped the Peugeot owner roll his piece of junk off to the side so that it wouldn't block the road. An old neighbor recognized me and got out of his car to help and make sure I was being treated prop-erly. Some time later we reached a decision to go to a garage where the Peugeot owner would pay for my repairs.

"And what about me?" Mr. Subaru said. "You hit me, too." The Peugeot driver was ready to pay for his small repair as well, but Mr. Subaru wasn't convinced that this indigent-looking person had the means to do so. Clearly he did not have the proper insurance papers for his car. One man raised his voice, another lost his temper, and Mr. Subaru demanded that we call the police. "Once upon a time," a shopkeeper whispered to me, "they would've worked things out with-out police or anything. Now, anyone with a brother or cousin in the police force runs over there and makes a mountain of a molehill." (The shopkeeper had forgotten for a moment that once upon a time the police had been Israelis or working for Israelis, and people were not inclined to turn to them for help.)

I tried to protest the waste of time, and Mr. Subaru said threaten-ingly, "I'll know where to find you." Now it was my turn to get angry, and because I was so upset, I'm sorry to say that I even shed a few tears; I phoned my own private *wasta*, Ihab al-Ashqar, the former UNL leader and now a partner in an insurance company, and asked him to come help me at the police station, where everyone knows and respects him. Ihab sent his brother over right away.

Once at the police station, everyone began to shout and talk about suing for damages and going to court. Several stern-looking policemen pulled out pens and paper and I could not follow who wanted to sue whom, but one stickler in uniform started to write down my particu-lars; after all, he was obliged to report any incidents involving Israelis to the district Coordination and Liaison Office. I could see days slip-ping away from me, hours wasted on bureaucracy, one of the hall-marks of the Oslo era. I was afraid the Israelis would see the incident as a deliberate attack (they would at least want to check out the possibility) and decide that it was too dangerous for me to drive my car. My broken taillight, a simple Ramadan accident, would escalate into a "nationalist incident."

I shared my fears with the police, exaggerating a little, and tried to soften them up: "Look, I've become a Gazan; I eat hot peppers just like you." In the end, we all came to an understanding, which we could have done on our own from the start. I reminded myself that I had met some pleasant policemen and that anger toward them is not always justified, because it diverts criticism from the system to the individual.

One quiet Friday morning two months after the transfer of authority in 1994, a phalanx of police was stationed on the corners of al-Wahda Street. They were actually very courteous, checking people's IDs and telling them not to get too close to the YMCA building on al-Jalaa Street. That morning the Gaza branch of the Democratic Front for the Liberation of Palestine (DFLP) was opening its annual convention; the Front had a tiny following in the Strip, but some leaders had recently returned from the diaspora and come to settle in Gaza. The convention was closed to the public, although representatives of other organizations had been invited to the opening. The DFLP had adopted unbending opposition to the Oslo Accords, although it continued to advocate a two-state solution. Unlike the Popular Front (PFLP), which had ordered the members of its military wing to turn in their weapons, the DFLP had allowed its own group, the Red Star, to remain armed. Over the months there had been reports of roadside time bombs and of shots fired at Israeli soldiers in the Strip, for which the mysterious Red Star had accepted responsibility, pledging its resistance to the ongoing occupation and its determination to continue the struggle until an independent state was established. But in Gaza everyone knew that the Democratic Front was virtually nonexistent, politically and militarily.

The day of the DFLP convention, Police Commissioner Ghazi al-Jabali declared the YMCA a closed military area, having first complained that the Front had not requested a permit for its meeting. He contacted the YMCA's director and forbade him to open the auditorium to the Front members. All protestations—that the number of participants was very small, that the sessions were being held in a closed room—were to no avail. Only days earlier, the police had ordered that everyone required a permit for a political gathering—not just the organizers but also the owners of the hall where it was to be held and the bus company conveying participants to the event. A Palestinian legal expert explained that Jabali was acting in accordance with the Cairo agreement, which directed the Palestinian police to comply with British mandatory emergency regulations that had been in force since the days of Egyptian rule.

But Palestinians weren't thinking about the Cairo agreement; they were thinking about their experiences of the past year. One sign of change, even before self-rule, was that most organizations hardly bothered to request such permits (political assemblies had been forbidden altogether until the start of the Oslo process), either from the Israeli civil administration or, later, from the Palestinian police. Free assembly was a true taste of freedom, of which everyone was proud. In June 1994, for example, the PFLP had organized a week of demonstrations in support of Palestinian prisoners, without applying for a permit. So the DFLP people reasoned that their little convention could not possibly disrupt public order, with fifty or sixty participants at most sitting in a closed room on a Friday morning. In the end, though, the formal opening was canceled, and the several dozen Front members held their closed conference elsewhere. Perhaps the incident was merely an attempt by the police to enforce a legal demand. Some interpreted it, however, as a sign of political control of a sort that easily gave rise to arbitrary refusals and the imposition of constraints.

Since then, many public meetings, as well as demonstrations by all the organizations, have been allowed in the Strip, and their participants have usually enjoyed relative freedom of speech, although criticism is generally not directed at Chairman Arafat. The election campaign also saw a flurry of public meetings. Altogether, only a small fraction of applications for permits to hold meetings were turned down. The refusals, though, were clearly political and not for the sake of preserving public order: once Hamas was denied a permit to commemorate Land Day; another time, the Gaza Center for Rights and Law was not allowed to host a meeting of legal experts on the subject of the State Security Court; a vigil in memory of a PFLP activist who had been murdered as vengeance for the death of a collaborator was forbidden.

Usually the prohibitions were accompanied by flimsy excuses, and most came at politically sensitive times—but what is democracy if not the possibility of meeting precisely during sensitive periods? Little by little, people came to realize that the police could prohibit the holding of this or that conference without reference to any consistent overriding criterion—such as the law. From then on, people had a hard time knowing whether a given directive had come straight from Arafat or simply from a local commander claiming instructions from on high. The presence of police and intelligence agents—both known and incognito—at all kinds of political meetings dictated caution from the outset and resulted in formulations that were more restrained and circumspect than had been the intent. All these symptoms are the ways that limits are set on civil society, either through clear orders from above or through ambiguous signals that are interpretated farther down the line.

Such signals became more frequent and ominous. During a beachside walk with H., I learned of more creeping encroachments on Palestinian freedom. A DFLP member, H. had been detained for some fifty days with several dozen of his comrades. They had been arrested after an anonymous phone call to a news agency in Jerusalem had claimed that the Red Star was responsible for the murder of an Israeli security escort on his way to a gas station at the northern end of the Strip. Usually when the Democratic Front was involved, leaflets with a red star were found at the scene. This time there were no such leaflets, and several Front activists said the attack's precision ruled out the Red Star, about whose operational capabilities no one had any illusions. The IDF spokesman's office assumed that a Hamas cell was responsible for the attack. In any case, dozens of DFLP activists were arrested: old men, young men, people who had been abroad for years, some who had been in Israeli prisons. Others went into semihiding.

By the time he was released, H. had lost about twenty pounds. "I was jailed here at home, in one of Arafat's prisons, you know," he said. The Front detainees were not tortured, though two senior activists, both about fifty years old, were held in solitary confinement despite their delicate health. They were all interrogated about the Front, its political positions, and their roles in the organization. It was clear that the interrogators knew that most, if not all, the detainees had absolutely no connection with military actions. Several of those who were interrogated told family members that they had been enticed to leave the Front and accept work with the Sulta. They had all been detained for weeks, in violation of the Palestinian law requiring that any extension of the period of detention be decided by a judge within forty-eight hours of arrest. Several extensions are allowed, but at the end of a reasonable period of time (two weeks, sometimes eighteen days), the law calls for either release or submission of a charge sheet and presentation of evidence.

On one occasion the detainees' families tried to hold a demonstration outside Arafat's office and were forcibly dispersed. There were also behind-the-scenes deliberations with senior Palestinian Authority figures to obtain the detainees' release. One Fatah activist said a few things to placate the petitioners, and a second activist promised that the men would be released right away. An acquaintance of mine from the PLO abroad smiled broadly when he heard of the arrests. "In Lebanon, Arafat used to put Fatah people who annoyed him under house arrest," he said, obviously not bothered by the notion. "Apparently that's how he thinks of people in the Strip, as if they're all members of Fatah who owe him personal allegiance."

Throughout the entire long detention period, hints were tossed around about a "political rapprochement," an admission that the detentions were intended to intimidate and were a flagrant (and eventually successful) attempt to impose ideological unity or, at the very least, to silence political criticism. The main signal communicated was that the judiciary was not independent. People obtained their releases solely by means of *wasta*, not through legal channels. And indeed, the releases of many members of Hamas and the Islamic Jihad—especially senior figures—often took place in the presence of none other than representatives from Arafat's office.

Lawyers who had always denounced Israel's violations of the law and its compliance with the Shabak now nodded their heads at one another knowingly, but no one was willing to go on record. "Now is the time to be silent," one of them told me. "Public protests aren't helpful." And indeed, none of the organizations whose younger members had in the past come out in droves, baring their chests to Israeli rifles, dared to mount even one protest outside the prison.

Nor did they mobilize their dignitaries to lobby behind closed doors or publicly demand that the Authority's executive branch obey the law. Nor did they appeal to the public to think about the arrests and take action: not the Popular Front, not Hamas, not the Jihad, and certainly not Fatah, even though many of its supporters were deeply concerned.

The bloody clash at the Falastin mosque in which thirteen Palestinians were killed had succeeded in inducing fear, although no one will ever know whether that was the objective. People were now afraid to risk a confrontation with the Palestinian police, with their brothers in uniform. They did not want to test the widely held assumption that there were no lines the Palestinian police were not prepared to cross. The threat of civil war hovered over Gaza like a cloud, constraining the population's behavior and even its thinking and desire to act. People's silence confirmed what many had already noted: in the age of self-rule, the underground political organizations of the past were disintegrating.

The opposition as a whole was unable to adapt to the new reality and to pose a civilian—political rather than military—challenge to Israel. It was hamstrung by its assumption that what was taking place was the continuation of the Israeli occupation in a different form. Unlike in the past, however, the opposition was separated from the occupation by a thick buffer of Palestinian police and officials. In fact, the opposition's scathing critique of Palestinian institutions—that they were, in effect, acting in the service of Israel—along with its compassion for the Palestinian Authority's weakness in the face of Israeli strength, undermined its ability (especially that of the secular left, small as it was) and its willingness to attempt public action that would openly focus on the autonomous aspects of the Authority's exercise of power. The Islamic opposition had proven its power to mobilize the masses only when the direct target was Israel and only behind suicidal slogans invoking blood and martyrs. And Fatah itself—despite its diversity of opinions and strata and analyses—was conflated in people's minds with power and the Authority. Fatah was unable to cope with the growing alienation between its rank and file and the governing elite. Moreover, many of its key activists had gotten drawn into the overattachment to privilege that proximity to power invites and clung to the perks of their position.

. . .

Raji Sourani, the head of the Gaza Center for Rights and Law, adopted the open, direct approach: in April 1995 he petitioned the Palestinian Supreme Court to end the illegal detention of a member of the Islamic Jihad, Abdallah al-Shami. Several weeks passed before the appeal was heard and the court reached its decision to release Shami. He remained in prison for several more days, in spite of the court order. The decision was proof that the judges were trying to adhere to the spirit of the law and to the principle of separation of powers. The procrastination in releasing Shami, on the other hand, proved that the executive authority was contemptuous of these very principles, as it would continue to be in the future. When the Supreme Court in Ramallah ordered the release of ten students, supporters of the Islamic opposition who had been detained for a number of months with no charges and no trial, the students remained in jail. They constituted but one percent of the thousand Palestinians in the West Bank and Gaza Strip who—as of summer 1996—had been detained for five or six months without being charged. Most of the students had not met with lawyers or appealed their detention, although some of them had endured weeks of harsh and humiliating interrogation that failed to produce the evidence needed to bring them to trial. Several students would later be released as a goodwill gesture, but the Supreme Court justice responsible for the decision would himself be dismissed.

"We have to maintain a certain number of prisoners to satisfy the Israelis," a report by the Palestinian Society for the Protection of Human Rights and the Environment quoted a prison guard as saying.[2] "Of course, there are those that the Authority wants in jail, but most of these guys are here to fill a quota."

The terror attacks of February and March 1996 eroded the chances of carrying on a serious debate in Israel on the goals and legality of mass arrests and on their implications for Israeli-Palestinian relations. The horror put an end to any interest Israelis might have had in trying to understand the causes of the arbitrary arrests, which are, in many ways, simply a variation on Israel's own use of administrative detention. For the Palestinians who dream of living in a free society, however, these are fundamental questions: Are such arbitrary actions simply part of the Palestinian Authority's imported style of government? Are these arrests intended to force people's political and ideological capitulation? Are they an efficient way to fight terror or simply a response to Israeli pressure?

There is a blurry line where the "natural" tendencies of Arafat's regime and Israel's expectations converge. A wave of detentions in July 1995 demonstrated just how hard it is to distinguish between those two factors. That month, two young Israelis were murdered while hiking in Wadi Qelt in the West Bank. Certain pieces of evidence led to the PFLP in Jericho (which was under Palestinian jurisdiction), and several days later Arafat assured Israel's foreign minister, Shimon Peres, that he had "arrested the leaders of the Popular Front." Arafat's declaration sent several journalists, myself included, and a large number of Popular Front supporters running to various offices to see who had been arrested. No one had, as it happened. Without really believing there would in fact be arrests, everyone laid bets on who should be standing ready with his toothbrush. "Don't they know that there isn't any Popular Front?" one activist said comically. By the next day five rank-and-file members had been arrested, four from Jericho and one from Jabalia, a seventeen-year-old caught spraying a wall with graffiti proclaiming the PFLP's responsibility for the murders. "The idiot deserves to be arrested if he's proud of the killings," said my neighbor and friend Marwan Kafarna, who had represented the Popular Front in the first UNL of the *intifada*.

Events moved quickly. The same day, the Israeli culture and communications minister, Shulamit Aloni, met with Yassir Arafat in Gaza City. Israeli journalists expected to hear him condemn the murder and one even asked a direct question, something along the lines of "What do you intend to do about the Popular Front?" or "When will you take action?" The journalist's questions clearly reflected the interests of the Israeli security sources with whom he was in regular contact. Arafat assured him that he had ordered the Palestinian intelligence agency, the Mukhabarat, to act quickly in Jericho and Gaza to find the killers. That night he had no choice but to do what he claimed had already been done: sometime after midnight, ten prominent PFLP men were arrested at their homes in Gaza, toothbrushes in hand.

Anyone familiar with Gaza knew that arresting the PFLP leadership

was absurd—an obvious step of appeasement, taken, not coinciden-
tally, precisely during negotiations over the extension of the Oslo
Accords to the West Bank. Both the Israeli and the Palestinian intelligence services were fully aware of the truth.

First, as early as the *intifada*, Gaza's Popular Front leaders had
developed a moderate program free of influence from forces in the
West Bank and abroad. The program—articulated more in de facto
positions than in written statements—included acceptance of a "two
state" solution, general support of the Madrid negotiations, reluctance
to cooperate with Hamas, and a readiness—in contrast to the Front's
West Bank leaders—to participate in local municipal councils, even
before the Palestinian Authority was installed.

Second, the PFLP's independent stance in Gaza (which had
caused a prolonged rift with its West Bank affiliates) had been most
forcefully expressed on the eve of the Palestinian Authority's forma-
tion, when the movement's leaders ordered its military wing, the
Red Eagle, to disarm. The Popular Front had opposed the Oslo Accords
but concluded that the new circumstances demanded a change of
approach: henceforth its actions would be political only. The Front's
Gazan members complied with the policy and have since refrained
from armed activity. (The Palestinian State Security Court had already
tried two PFLP members, one of them a minor, for terrorist acts, but
there was little credibility to the charges.)

Third, the murder of the two hikers did not "require" an order from
above, and certainly not one from the Gaza Strip. Given the severe
conditions of the closure and the Front's organizational rupture, it was
unlikely that members in Gaza would possess any information about
decisions taken by the inner circles in the West Bank, especially when
they involved using weapons.

Finally, some of the men detained in the ludicrous midnight raid
had played a pivotal role in the Front's decision to disarm. Those same
members had for years driven the movement's realistic trend; Muhammad Yihye Salman, one of the men detained, was in fact the director
general of the transport ministry. Indeed, when the Palestinian intelligence officers came to arrest Fathi al-Bawab, the oldest of the group,
they had tears in their eyes: he had been released from an Israeli
prison only a few months earlier and had been severely tortured by the
Shabak during the *intifada*. Fatah members who had been with him

in prison shook their heads sadly and privately called his arrest a disgrace. Marwan Kafarna was also arrested, although he had left the Front and was now a senior staff member for Terje Larsen, the United Nations envoy in the occupied territories and a principal proponent of the Oslo Accords.

Of course, after ritual lobbying at Arafat's office and the exercise of all kinds of *wasta*, the detainees were released within a day or two. None had been interrogated; the whole farce had patently been designed to satisfy Israel's demand for quick action. Without doubt, the Israeli security forces knew everything: who had been detained, what the men had done in the past, how they were being held, and just how idiotic the entire event really was. But the pressure to act was meant to elicit the Authority's obedient response, even when Israel's demand was illogical. And the Palestinian public got the message: there were no guarantees against arbitrary arrest, if that was Arafat's, and Israel's, desire.

A month after this episode I watched amazed as, once again, Israel's media eagerly and unquestioningly countenanced injustice among its Palestinian neighbors. Three Hamas people in Gaza suspected of planning terror attacks had been arrested by Palestinian police acting on specific information and a clear demand from Shabak. At the time, an ongoing closure was intensifying pressure within both the Strip and the Authority. Simultaneously, an Israeli radio newsman reported that Israeli security forces were displeased that Arafat had halted the State Security Court's proceedings in recent months. (The State Security Court, which held secret summary trials in the dead of night, had been set up by Arafat in February 1995 at Israel's urging.) The newsman asked Diab al-Luh, the head of public relations for Fatah, why the Hamas members just arrested in Gaza were not being tried in the State Security Court. Discomfited by the question, Luh nevertheless had the good sense to answer that the matter rested with the Palestinian legal system.

What he could not say was that the State Security Court was seen as the greatest threat to the future of democracy for Palestinians; people loathed waking up to the news that someone had been tried in the middle of the night in a hearing lasting all of five minutes—and been convicted of charges that his court-appointed lawyer would have learned only moments before the trial. The newsman's question displayed a deep Israeli assumption that dictatorial methods alone would succeed in preventing terror and that Arafat would know how to use them better than anyone else.

Israeli security's spilling information to the press was successful: two days later Gazans heard (on Israeli radio) that the State Security Court was up and running again. Three PFLP activists had been convicted of planning armed attacks and of throwing a hand grenade at an IDF patrol in the Strip.

An Amnesty International report published in June 1995, *Trial at Midnight*, attacked the State Security Court and its procedures in sharp and unequivocal language.[3] Its purpose, according to Arafat's original decree, was to "adjudicate crimes affecting internal and external security . . . and other crimes affecting the safety of the military forces." Palestinian sources consistently emphasize Arafat's direct and significant involvement in the court's decisions. Arafat himself has, since its inception, refused to tolerate any criticism of the court from either Palestinian or international sources, although critics maintain that the Strip's existing criminal and civil judicial system is sufficient and able to contend with any crime. When the Gaza Center for Rights and Law published a statement criticizing the State Security Court, Raji Sourani was detained for several hours, then, a few weeks later, relieved of the center's directorship, evidently following high-level intervention.

Although the court was set up in February 1995, it began operating only in April, after terror attacks by the Islamic Jihad and Hamas near Jewish settlements in the Gaza Strip. The court functions outside the regular criminal justice system and is also not part of the military legal system by which members of the security forces are tried. The Amnesty International report describes the court's trials thus:

> The State Security Court trials in Gaza have been held secretly. All trials except one reportedly took place in the middle of the night. Many started around midnight. Some reportedly lasted only minutes. Those appointed to serve as judges in this court are active officers in the security forces who apparently have never before served as judges.
>
> The authorities gave no advance notice of these trials. People tried by the court have reportedly stated that they did not know they

were to be tried until they were taken from their cell at night—or even until they set foot in the courtroom. Families of those tried, including those who visited their relative days or even hours before the trial took place, were not even aware of any charges or trial until they heard on the radio that their relative had been convicted the night before. Some of those tried by the court were tried, sentenced, and convicted within one or two days of their arrest. . . . Defendants have been represented by court-appointed lawyers; none have been defended by independent lawyers of their choice. At least some of the court-appointed lawyers are reportedly employees in the security forces. The lawyer of one defendant was not informed of the charges against his client and did not receive any notice of the trial—he was not aware that any trial had taken place until he heard on the radio that his client had been tried the previous night and sentenced to seven years' imprisonment. . . .

State Security Court trials in Gaza are grossly unfair, violating minimum standards of international law, including:

- the right to a fair and public trial by a competent, independent, and impartial tribunal;
- the right to have adequate time to prepare one's defense;
- the right to be defended by a lawyer of one's choice;
- the right to appeal to a higher court. . . .

Amnesty International has strongly condemned and opposed abuses by armed opposition groups in Gaza, including the deliberate killing of citizens in armed attacks and [with] suicide bombs. Authorities have the right and responsibility to bring to justice those responsible for crimes.

But no government authority, under any circumstances, at any time, should assign security force officers to try citizens in secret proceedings in the middle of the night, without a defense lawyer of their choice, without having time to prepare their defense.

The report also takes Israeli and American officials to task for their open support of the State Security Court: "Representatives of both the Israeli and U.S. governments welcomed the first sentences handed down by the court at trials which so clearly violated international human rights norms." The trials "took place after Israel pressed the Palestinian Authority to take action against those suspected of carrying out or of supporting acts of violence against Israelis." Indeed, both the Americans and the Israelis predicated progress in negotiations on the Authority's taking quick action against suspects. According to an April 12, 1995, *Jerusalem Post* article, Yossi Sarid, the environment minister of the liberal Citizen's Rights Party, is quoted in the Amnesty report as saying, "We had specific demands, one of which was to bring terrorists to trial and that was done yesterday, and this is how it should be." Vice President Al Gore of the United States was full of praise for the court even before it began operating. "I know there has been some controversy over the security courts," he said. "I personally believe that the accusations are misplaced and that [the Palestinians] are doing the right thing." Amnesty International notes dryly that, at the same time, "Gore announced a package of U.S. economic aid for projects designed to create jobs in the Gaza Strip."

The day after the court began operating, an American State Department spokesman declared at a press briefing, "We expect the Palestinian Authority to take this type of concrete action against those within its jurisdiction who seek to destroy the peace process through acts of violence and terror." After the court's second trial, a U.S. spokesman commented in the same spirit: "We've called upon the Palestinian Authority to take concrete steps to effectively pre-empt and to prevent terrorist acts by arresting and trying and prosecuting. . . . The Palestinian Authority obviously has taken action over the last twenty-four hours to do that. Chairman Arafat has expressed his commitment to addressing the security concerns of Israel, and we very much expect and hope that the Palestinian Authority will continue these efforts."

The Amnesty report reminds Palestinians and Israelis that the court contravenes international conventions and certain articles in the May 1994 Cairo agreement. Article 14, for example, reads: "Israel and the Palestinian Authority shall exercise their powers and responsibilities pursuant to this agreement with due regard to internationally accepted norms and principles of human rights and the rule of law."

One of the defendants in the midnight court was Sayyed Abu Musameh. He was tried in his capacity as editor of the Hamas-affiliated weekly *al-Watan* several days after it published an article equating the behavior of Palestinian police with that of the IDF. Abu Musameh was sentenced for a series of offenses: writing seditious articles, libeling the PA and its security forces, inciting action against the PA. At his trial, Abu Musameh was immediately sentenced to three years in prison, but he was one of eleven men released on Arafat's authorization seven months later—none of the group served full terms—to join a Hamas delegation in Cairo that was renegotiating its relationship with the Authority.

Despite the circumstances of his conviction, Abu Musameh's name appeared on a list of released prisoners issued by the Israeli nongovernmental organization Peace Watch as evidence of Arafat's laxness in fighting terror.[4] In a press release, the organization wrote of "serious lapses in the Palestinian Authority's policy concerning the punishment of terrorists" and noted that the Authority had not complied with Israel's demand that it extradite fourteen people suspected of terrorist activity. In reference to the State Security Court, it stated:

> The special court has thus far indicted thirty-nine people for direct or indirect involvement in carrying out terrorist acts against Israelis, and of these, thirty-seven have been sentenced to prison terms ranging from six months to life. Peace Watch has discovered that the court has put suspects on trial only when pressure on the Authority has been great or in circumstances where the trial has been intended to prevent Israel from demanding their extradition. Furthermore, the Authority has consistently avoided trying key leaders and activists who constitute the nucleus of those involved in terrorist activity.[5]

In its critique of the Authority's elusive intentions, the press release cited the names of all those granted early release, including Abu Musameh, lumping together suspected and convicted murderers with a man who was guilty of nothing more than speaking out against the Palestinian Authority. The press release contained not one word about the nature of the court, which is in itself a violation of the Cairo agreement. Peace Watch's attitude mirrored the widespread Israeli notion (which conveyed more than a little encouragement) that the Authority was not expected to choose its methods selectively, or uphold rigorous standards of justice and international law, or distinguish between murder and "incitement," between terror and speech. The Peace Watch report noted rightly that some trials were intended to prevent extradition to Israel. Thus the court, which functions outside the law, has also been used to circumvent Israeli demands.

In this aspect, the report reflected another flaw in Israeli logic: as long as arbitrary force, legal obfuscation, and the undemocratic merging of executive and judicial powers serve Israeli interests, they are welcomed; when they are used to dupe the Israelis or, in particular, to contain and quell Palestinian resentment and prevent a public outburst, they are held up as proof of Arafat's sins. But a regime that adopts arbitrary behavior and deliberate obfuscation is necessarily uncontrollable and unpredictable. The same court would later extend the detentions of two human rights activists who had criticized the Palestinian Authority — Eyad al-Sarraj and Muhammad Dahman.

The State Security Court's murky workings had two clear objectives. First, the mass arrests and extended periods of detention equipped Arafat's regime with an immediate deterrent to opposition. Second, the court was able to sever the individual's link to his community: the prisoner stands alone, without family or organization at his trial, in his cell, and in solitary confinement. The court's purpose was, in a word, intimidation, the most effective weapon against mass public action. As long as the rift continues to grow between a ruling Palestinian elite that has not kept its promises and a people whose elementary hopes have been crushed, the leadership will continue to depend on such intimidation. Its long-term efficacy in preventing acts of terror, however, is questionable, especially when those acts are carried out by individuals bent on suicide.

I raised these kinds of issues during the early days of the State Security Court and repeated them in an interview on Israeli television news. Several hours after the news broadcast, I was summoned to the Palestinian intelligence agency's press office and was brought to the department head, a native of Gaza who had returned from Damascus after the Israeli redeployment. He started out warmly, saying that he was simply interested in meeting me; all the while he was leafing through a pile of articles published in the Israeli press and translated into Arabic, probably including some of mine. The conversation then moved quickly from ingratiating compliments on my "fame" in Gaza to my "lack of discipline" for not having a press card from the Palestinian Ministry of Information. Then came the current "state of emergency" in Gaza, which brought him swiftly to his point. "Because of the state of emergency and because you don't have a press card," he declared, "you are requested to leave the Strip today and come back when the card is ready."

I couldn't fathom how a press card would protect me. In any case, I had never been threatened, never been attacked, never felt any fear, even during the *intifada*. The department head explained that the Palestinian police would be unable to look out for my safety during this difficult time. "Who knows if we can guarantee, for example, that something won't happen to your car—or to you?" For the first time in all my years in the Strip I felt threatened. The whole thrust of our conversation became unclear, and without noticing, I began to raise my voice. "Don't get upset," he said. In the end we agreed I would put in my application for a press card and then leave Gaza within three days, returning only when the card arrived—which clearly meant never.

I had three days' grace to apply everything I had learned about *wasta*, and I pulled out all the stops. I turned to Fatah insiders, to a businessman friend with connections in the Preventive Security Force (which competed with the Mukhabarat), to a Palestinian minister, to close friends of the Mukhabarat department head who had called me in, to all sorts of contacts from the *intifada* days who were now working in various branches of Palestinian bureaucracy and security, and to one very senior foreign diplomat. My campaign gave me a small taste of the difference between outside people—those who had returned from the Palestinian diaspora—and Gazan "insiders." As it turned out, all the people who worked to overturn the order were locals; especially helpful were the Fatah members who, among other things, wisely advised me not to leave Gaza under any circumstances until the whole thing was settled.

And when my three days were up I got a reassuring phone call: there had simply been a misunderstanding. "Just make sure you get a press card," I was told. Ever since, a few influential Fatah and preventive security men like to joke when they run into me. "How come you're not in detention?" they say. "Write what I just said and they'll arrest you." And even, "How's your car?" So there are always balances, I discovered, people who redress the capricious, unfathomable workings of authoritarian rule.*

My misgivings about the use of intimidation in the war against

---

*In September 1998, I received a call from police headquarters, this time in Ramalla in the West Bank. "Your life is in danger," I was told. The officer did not ask me to leave but did advise me to take care. The threat was thinly veiled: a day earlier I had published an article about the overnight trial and execution of two young men in the security force who were convicted of murder and I had been highly critical of the Authority. One day later, I went to police headquarters with high-level *wasta* and the threats gave way to flattery. I did learn, however, that the initiative had come from Arafat's office.

terror were confirmed by the suicide bombings that occurred in Israel and the occupied territories after the State Security Court began operating in April 1995. These reinforced my view that stopping terror involves recognizing its social, economic, and historical context, and alleviating human suffering. The three attacks in February and March 1996, which killed fifty-seven Israelis, have not changed my opinion or that of the minority of Israelis who share this view.

The suicide attacks convinced the Israeli government that Arafat's methods of combating terrorism were ineffective, that he had essentially failed to deliver his share of the deal. After two attacks on February 26, 1996, Foreign Minister Ehud Barak, the former IDF chief of staff, articulated a widely held position. At a meeting with representatives of the donor nations, Barak listed a series of steps that Arafat should take: house searches, arrests, trials, imprisonment. Then, after a slight pause, he declared, "Arafat can do what the leaders in the other Arab countries do." There was no opportunity to ask Barak to clarify his remark, because after three questions he quickly rushed back to the Knesset.

The foreign ministry insisted that, contrary to the impression that a few listeners might have received, it had been an aside. Just a hint, I was told. The main message was that the donor nations should put pressure on Arafat—"political pressure, not economic"—so that he would understand how grave the complications arising from such attacks could be. "He has to take action for his own good," the spokesperson said. "He has to realize that all that he's accomplished is being threatened."

But what did the hint mean? What was it that Arafat was supposed to do like the other Arab leaders? "Well, it doesn't mean flattening the Sheikh Radwan neighborhood, not like Hafaz al-Assad did in Hama," the foreign ministry said. "More like Jordan." The ministry insisted that Barak hadn't been advocating random violence. On television afterward, it pointed out, he had said that Arafat was taking vigorous action against some individuals, just not against organizations. Having won the election, Arafat had some responsibilities. "The Israeli claim is that he isn't standing up to terror to the best of his ability. . . . Fundamentalism is a threat to him, not us. He doesn't seem to grasp that it has the potential to destroy the whole process if he doesn't deal with the Islamic infrastructure—not just its military part but also the education and welfare parts. To dry up the swamp, that's the intention."

If more Israelis with good intentions would actually come to Gaza and talk to people directly, I am convinced that they would have a better understanding of this "fundamentalism" and a better grasp of the true face of the Oslo Accords. But Israelis are not allowed into Gaza unless they come to meet with Palestinian Authority leaders as part of an official delegation.

On May 17, 1994—the advent of Palestinian self-rule—the chief of the IDF Southern Command prohibited the entry of Israelis into territory under Authority jurisdiction, except by special permission (settlers are excluded from this prohibition, of course). During 1995 the order was enforced with increasing rigidity; ordinary people with friends, work contacts, or family in the Strip found it harder to receive permission and impossible to fathom what criteria the IDF were applying. In May 1995, Tamar Peleg, a human rights lawyer, petitioned the High Court of Justice, complaining about the absence of clear and consistent procedures for receiving entry permits into Gaza. Several weeks later, the IDF announced new guidelines. The Israeli Coordination and Liaison Office would maintain "exclusive and comprehensive responsibility for issuing permits," according to the IDF's statement. In a letter to Peleg, the IDF's Gaza legal adviser, Amos Giora, outlined the new regulations: "An Israeli who requests entry for personal or humanitarian reasons, such as family gatherings, meetings with residents of the Palestinian Authority–administered territories, etc., shall be issued a one-day permit." Thus, Israelis were barred from spending the night in the Strip. Moreover, it was necessary to "coordinate a security escort with the Palestinian police"; Israeli Arabs were exempt from this requirement. The meaning: Jews needed to equip themselves with a Palestinian policeman.

Despite the IDF's guidelines, most Israelis—Palestinian citizens of Israel, Palestinian residents of East Jerusalem, and Jewish Israelis alike—have found it almost impossible to enter the Strip, and just as hard to put their finger on what or who is stopping them: the government, the army, the CLO, the police, letters that go astray, fax machines that do not work, CLO telephones that go unanswered.

Felicia Langer, a well-known Israeli attorney who has represented thousands of Palestinians, including many senior figures in the Palestinian Authority, was also denied entry into Gaza. Her odyssey began when she faxed her request to the CLO. In clear contravention of the IDF's statement, Langer was told that the CLO did not issue entry permits. She was instructed to apply to the Palestinian Authority or to the Erez checkpoint. On Langer's behalf Tamar Peleg appealed directly to Amos Giora but a permit was again denied. She turned to the High Court of Justice department in the state attorney's office and received the following response: "If Ms. Langer were to be invited by the Palestinian Authority according to standard procedures, it would be possible to arrange her entry tomorrow." The Authority promptly informed the Palestinian Center for Human Rights, which was hosting Langer, that she would be welcome and that a representative would come meet her at the checkpoint and arrange for an escort.

After a week of feverish correspondence and telephone calls to all possible levels of officialdom, Langer finally arrived at the CLO office in Gaza expecting to receive her permit. A Palestinian military liaison officer permanently stationed at the Erez checkpoint indeed came to the CLO to welcome her and ensure her safety. Both of them had wasted their time: after five hours of waiting, Langer returned to Tel Aviv. The CLO claimed that Langer had not applied to the right office, had not been invited by the Palestinian Authority, and had appeared at the Erez checkpoint with Tamar Peleg but without having arranged for an escort.

But Tamar Peleg had not gone to the checkpoint; she had been at home in Tel Aviv. And the Palestinian Authority escort, bearing an invitation, had waited faithfully with Langer at the CLO office.

Naama Havkin, an Israeli psychologist, has been visiting her friend, Hayder abd al-Shafi, in Gaza since 1967. She was told that a direct request from Sufian Abu Zaide, the head of the Palestinian Authority's Israel desk, would procure her the coveted permit. The request was made but she did not obtain a definitive response. Her phone calls were simply shunted from one CLO clerk to another. "Madam," they said, "you just don't know what it's like in the Strip."[6]

The Gaza Strip has thus become terra incognita for Israelis and easier now to demonize as a breeding ground for terrorist intrigue and fundamentalism. No wonder every Jew is regarded as needing a police escort in such a place; no wonder closure, sealing up the Strip hermetically, is widely accepted as the only way to deal with Gaza; no wonder security is a sacred justification, accepted without question, for denied health care and the right to work. By barring Israelis from entering Gaza, the CLO—either following orders from above or giving its own extreme interpretation to deliberately vague instructions—is taking a step that even the evolving authoritarian Palestinian regime has refrained from taking: deciding which Israelis may enter Palestinian territory and, in effect, permitting official delegations only, approved people making courtesy calls on Arafat, Fatah leaders, and the upper reaches of the Palestinian police and intelligence—hardly those who represent the true face of the Strip.

Epilogue

There is no better backdrop than the Erez checkpoint for the Orwellian drama being played out in the Gaza Strip since the advent of Palestinian self-rule. At a quick glance it looks like a perfectly ordinary border crossing with a clean, bright, international terminal, bold signs welcoming visitors, policemen at their posts checking passports and other documents, and an efficient freight area off to one side. The throng of traffic carries foreign delegations on their way to call on Yassir Arafat, Israeli officials, overseas diplomats, Palestinian ministers, Fatah leaders, and police off to meet with colleagues in Israel or the West Bank.

A high embankment, raised with cinder blocks, spares these dignitaries the sight of the narrow, fenced-in pen where, on ordinary days of standard closure, 20,000 lucky men with exit permits stir up the dust on their way to work inside Israel. What they do see, though, is a long line of trucks inching over the inspection pits, waiting for the signal to head into Israel and collect food and raw materials or deliver Palestinian produce. There is, it seems, a brisk, nonstop flow of goods and people back and forth.

Visitors aware of the bustle may well not realize that the legions of trucks and hordes of workers represent twenty-seven years of direct military rule and economic standstill, during which Israel and its products have become the Strip's lifeline. They may not understand that, even now, Israel controls down to the very last detail the kinds of cargo the trucks may carry, the amounts, the destinations, and the frequency—who will leave and how often, and how many hours they will waste waiting to do so. The economists, diplomats, and army brass, all of whom are charged with shepherding the fledgling Palestinian Authority toward some goal unspecified in the Oslo Accords, draw on a lexicon of military and commercial jargon to obscure the misery of one million individuals trapped behind Gaza's electrified fence. Easing of restrictions. Upping the quota of workers. Job creation. Growth. Positive GNP.

We know that the jargon conceals the truth: by 1996 Gaza's per capita GNP had fallen by 37 percent since 1992; the total GNP had declined by 18.5 percent. In six months, unemployment had risen by 8.2 percent to reach 39.2 percent. Gazans fortunate enough to hold jobs in the Strip saw a 9.6 percent drop in real wages in 1995. Those who worked in Israel lost 16 percent of their salaries.[1] Beyond a doubt, Israel's policy of closure bears responsibility for the appalling figures. One can hardly imagine that Israel's decision makers did not realize the inevitable consequences of imposing what is, in effect, a siege of years' duration. As we have seen, Israel explains the closures solely as an inevitable response to terrorism and as the only way to prevent more attacks. But careful analysis of the policy and its consequences—along with other Israeli steps taken in the context of the Oslo Accords, such as blocking the safe passage route between Gaza and the West Bank— suggests a different understanding of closures.

To grasp their significance, we need only consider that the Oslo Accords do not define the last step in the process. The ultimate goal was meant to emerge through negotiations. During the discussions, however, Israel's Labor-led coalition never declared its ultimate intention, while the Palestinians have always stated their aim clearly: an independent state in the West Bank and the Gaza Strip. The Palestinians' bargaining chips are primarily the various UN resolutions concerning their refugee status and their right to the land (including the "right of return" and the designation of the Jewish settlements as illegal), as well as the universal principles of self-determination and independence. An additional source of Palestinian leverage is the Israeli promise that all fundamental issues will be resolved in the final-status negotiations— the refugee question, the Jewish settlements, the borders, Jerusalem, and access to water sources. One way or another, Palestinians, or at least those who support the process and their leaders, understand the accords to mean that the Israeli occupation will gradually fade away. In exchange, Yassir Arafat and Palestinian negotiators agreed to give up a key bargaining chip of their own: armed opposition or any other act of resistance that the occupation regards as "violence," historically the one form of leverage available to people in occupied territory.

As stated, Israel did not disclose its intentions although it did hold on to its prerogative, as the ruling power, to shape the future. And it has shaped it with a vengeance: between the peak years of the Oslo negotiations and implementation of the agreements, 1992 to 1996, the Labor-led government allowed a 50 percent increase in the number of Jewish settlers in Gaza and the West Bank, from 100,000 to 150,000 (which does not include the settlements in East Jerusalem). Furthermore, with Arafat's consent, the government began to carry out an old plan to link the West Bank settlements to Israel through a network of expressways. In the new parlance of Oslo, these have become "bypass roads"—broad, high-speed slashes of asphalt that will, Israel argues, ensure safety and freedom of movement for the Jewish settlers. This massive construction project has involved confiscating and destroying thousands of acres of cultivated Palestinian land and has forever altered the natural weave connecting West Bank towns and villages. Palestinian consent was easily obtained— ostensibly, the bypass roads were designed to boost the success of the interim stage by protecting the Jewish settlers and thereby enabling all parties to reach the final-status negotiations without too much acrimony.

Built at a cost of billions of shekels, solely for the needs of the tiny Jewish minority, the network of bypass roads will play no small part in Israel's negotiations over retaining territory. Anyone who invests a fortune in roads does not intend to dismantle the communities that use them. Moreover, this network, which guarantees Jewish settlers in the West Bank and Gaza Strip a safe and speedy lifeline to Israel, was put in place at exactly the same time as even greater constraints were imposed on Palestinian freedom of movement. It is true that since 1994, more land has come under the jurisdiction of the Authority, but the blocs of Jewish settlements and the patchwork of new roads are in effect the nail in the coffin of a contiguous Palestinian state, whatever form it might take. The new geography means that Palestinian society will be splintered, fragmented into isolated enclaves; the size and proximity of these enclaves are yet to be fixed and will be determined by the strength of the Palestinians' bargaining position, but movement between the enclaves will always involve passing roadblocks and checkpoints manned by Israeli soldiers. In the West Bank, social, cultural, and economic life have already been harmed by the region's fragmentation, and especially by the separation of north and south into two distinct areas. But for the real model of the future, one need only look to the 147-square-mile enclave of the Gaza Strip.

Israel has been able to shape the outcome of negotiations in another way as well: its bargaining position has been immeasurably improved by being able to exert economic pressure on its Palestinian partner, creating a sense of material urgency and managing to postpone crucial decisions in order to wrestle over immediate practical needs. A few more work permits, another convoy of trucks—these are presented as Palestinian achievements and evidence of Israeli goodwill. In this way, the occupation's balance of power between ruler and petitioner has been redoubled, leaving the Palestinians even more dependent. And it is the policy of closure that has proved to be the most effective means of control and leverage.

The decaying economy has also undermined the Palestinian Authority's standing among its people. The Authority has proved weak at the negotiating table yet hungry to maintain its power—a combination that guarantees submission and compromise. Under other circumstances a more resolute Authority might have rejected the concessions it has made. Furthermore, the economic decline has narrowed many Palestinians' expectations and demands. The same people who hoped and struggled at the beginning of the *intifada*, who fought to push back the limits of their freedom, are now more weighed down by everyday material concerns than ever before. Workers' rights for Palestinians—in Gaza as in Israel—are considered luxuries that no one even bothers to protect. The growing economic despair has brought Palestinians to the point where they are willing to accept a new arrangement: closed industrial zones along the borders, à la Mexico.

Palestinians suspect that the real purpose behind the closures, the bypass roads, and the separation of the West Bank, Gaza, and Jerusalem—ostensibly for security reasons—is to carve up the occupied territories permanently, keep them under different political systems, and complete the destruction of the Palestinian social structure that began in 1948.[2] In mid-1993 Shimon Peres unveiled his notion of separation in a closed meeting with Jews from America and Europe. He floated the idea of an "independent" ministate in Gaza and an autonomous West Bank linked to Jordan, where a local parliament would resolve matters jointly with the Jewish settlers.[3] Palestinian leaders rejected a similar proposal in the spring of 1995, but practical measures subsequently implemented by the Rabin-Peres government indicate that the idea had not been abandoned.

That such separation contravenes the Declaration of Principles is not in dispute, but Palestinians cite several restrictions that, they believe, prove that separation has little to do with security concerns either: relatives are not allowed to move freely between the two territories to visit immediate family members; Gazans who are allowed into the West Bank are always forbidden to spend the night there; people who enter Egypt via the Rafah border are not permitted to return to Gaza via Jordan and the Allenby Bridge; trucks from the Strip and the West Bank are not allowed to transport goods between the two areas. Crucial negotiations over a "safe passage" corridor between Gaza and the West Bank have been dragging on since 1994. For many long months, the Israelis refused to include in any safe-passage agreement a specific citation of the Declaration of Principles' confirmation that the two territories form one integral unit. Precious time was squandered on this point. Although both sides finally agreed to simply cite the relevant article number without the explicit words, Israel's resistance speaks volumes.

The most painful and symbolic example of the separation is provided by the 1,300 Gazan students enrolled in West Bank universities who are not allowed to attend classes. The continuous interruption of their studies began in 1991, when Israel revoked the general exit permit enabling Palestinian residents to move about freely. After the 1994 transfer of authorities, Israel withheld the students' travel permits until long after the semester began and sometimes indefinitely. Some West Bank academic institutions no longer accept students from Gaza because of their erratic attendance. The uncertainty and difficulties have discouraged the many students who would prefer to study at West Bank universities, which are known to be superior. The students represent a small group compared with the millions who suffer the effects of Gaza's separation from the West Bank, but their treatment is significant for the future of Palestinian society and emblematic of the post-Oslo reality: the students' freedom of choice, so vital for the whole community's intellectual and professional development, has been narrowed to an unprecedented degree.

By 1990, the Israeli goal of demographic separation—that is, keeping Israelis and Palestinians apart—had been quite clearly articulated. Mass participation in the *intifada* had fallen off; the uprising continued, however, more as a series of armed activities by discrete groups, and still with the support of the majority despite the growing oppression and collective punishment meted out by Israel. For its part, Israel was caught at an impasse: while unwilling to address the core demand of the *intifada*—independence—there were limits to the instruments of suppression at its disposal. Bombing refugee camps (as in Lebanon) or mass deportations were out of the question. The physical proximity of the two peoples, Israelis and Palestinians, and the inevitable condemnation by an international community that had just ended the Cold War ruled out such overt and brutal action. Instead, Israel devised an administrative policy as a way out of the impasse, carried out under the guise of "security measures."

In 1970, opening up the Israeli labor market to the occupied territories was intended to weaken Palestinian nationalism and preclude territorial separation; in the 1990s, shutting off the source of labor became a means of quashing the drive to independence. For Israelis, the immediate consequence of demographic separation was that Palestinians disappeared from their streets, thereby quelling their increasing fears of Palestinians "just roaming around," in the words of a CLO official. (Their fear contained an intuitive understanding of the frustation building in Gaza and the West Bank, and Israelis seemed to know that such frustration would inevitably lead to a reaction, one that might not pose a strategic threat to the State of Israel but would instead endanger individual civilians.) For the Palestinian political elite and the Israeli peace camp segregation was seen as a harbinger of political and territorial separation. With hindsight, this was clearly wishful thinking.

The expansion of Jewish settlement in the occupied territories during the Oslo years revealed that Israel continued to consider the land as a resource for Jews alone: a Palestinian presence is tolerated but Palestinian needs have no claim. Israel continues to deprive Palestinians of access to most of the undeveloped land in the occupied territories even as it designates those areas for future Jewish development. Effectively, Israel has declared that Palestinian prospects will always be subjugated to Jewish needs, desires, and strength. And it has done so under the watchful eye of the Oslo Accords, which explicity upheld Israel's position as the sovereign power.

But ultimately, land remains negotiable—a resource that isn't going away. Time, on the other hand, is another matter. Palestinians have lost precious years shut up in their enclaves, unable even to travel to other Palestinian cities. The ability to visit friends, look for work, or attend university is no less a human right than freedom of speech or religion. For Palestinians, though, freedom of movement is no longer a right but a privilege, alloted to an entitled few. Israel awards the privilege incrementally, by means of a pass system that has carved up Palestinian society in much the same way as the new geography has carved up the land. Each segment is defined by its access to movement: there are workers allowed into Israel with sleeping permits and workers restricted to one-day permits only; some businessmen may enter with their cars, others may not; one class of manufacturers is permitted to enter the West Bank, another allowed only into Israel; VIP 1 status is awarded to the most senior Authority officials, VIP 3 status to lesser functionaries. The quota of those who are privileged is fluid; the principle is not: it is Israel that sets the criteria and controls the benefits.

Most people's livelihoods depend on this system. Protesting the injustice of it may mean losing one's meager portion of the benefits. And for the Palestinian leadership, which enjoys the lion's share even as it continues to negotiate with Israel, freedom of movement has translated into power, business opportunities, and great material comfort. By creating such divisions and dependency, Israel has ensured Palestinian complicity with separation, an extremely sophisticated method of restraint reminiscent of apartheid. To sum up: the Oslo Accords have ensured Palestinian segregation from the Jewish-Israeli population, which elects the sovereign power, enjoys geographic and economic domination, commands all natural resources, and controls a pass system limiting the Palestinians' movements.

In the meantime, Palestinians in the Strip find ways to go on—or to escape. Students have been prevented from returning to the universities for some three years, yet an unknown number have developed complicated ways of leaving Gaza and going "underground" in the West Bank. They cannot see their families for months at a time and live in constant danger of being caught at one of the many IDF roadblocks. A Western consul reports that his country's embassy has seen a drastic increase in Palestinians applying to emigrate. Others migrate inward, closing their eyes and ears, stifling their fury and sense of indignity, trying not to dwell on the shortfall between the words in an agreement and the absence of an exit permit. Most people live in a narrowly proscribed space: friends, weddings, courses, books, although some cannot endure the claustrophobia—police statistics show a persistent increase in suicides.

In September 1996, the pressure exploded in violence. For several days, masses of demonstrators poured out their wrath on settlers and soldiers after the Israeli government opened an entrance to an ancient Jewish tunnel that happened to face the holy Islamic sites in Jerusalem's Old City. The demonstrations—organized, according to rumors, primarily by Fatah on Arafat's instructions—spilled over into the Strip, where young men hurled rocks at a Jewish settlement, an IDF outpost, and the Rafah border. (They also set out for the Erez checkpoint but were stopped by the Palestinian police.) Thirty-one Gazans and three Israelis were killed in the Strip alone, and some five hundred Palestinians were wounded. Israel blamed Arafat for orchestrating the demonstrations but to people in the occupied territories, and in Gaza in particular, the outbreak seemed inevitable. People responded to the call out of a need to communicate their frustration to the world.

At the time, my friend Abu Basel was on his way to Gaza City. When he saw the clusters of men outside Kfar Darom, the Jewish settlement, he stopped his taxi and walked toward the clash. As Israeli soldiers opened fire, Abu Basel, a thirty-five-year-old father, a man who saw little point in throwing stones, found himself running toward the guns. Like others at that moment, he felt the urge to die.

One could have predicted that the demonstrators would find their way to the settlements and checkpoints, sites of friction with Israeli power and emblems of the intractable view that the country's Jews are more deserving than its Palestinians. Even more, these are the sites that expose the Orwellian language of what is applauded as a peace process. When, in the heat of their rage, the young Palestinians shook the fences at Kfar Darom and Rafah, they were pounding on the walls that are closing in on their people and their future, that deny their freedom as if they were animals in a cage.

In their hearts Palestinians will persist in seeing all the land as theirs; they will not renounce their longing for the fields that now bear Hebrew names; they will not forget the pain of expulsion, the very first link in a chain of loss that goes on. But from living in Gaza I learned that its people have the ability and an honest desire to separate their heartfelt wishes from the need for a peaceful political solution. "We are, after all, the mother of the child," they say, alluding to King Solomon's judgment to explain their readiness to share the country. On condition, of course, that any solution treat the Palestinians with dignity, as a people with elemental rights and a claim equal to that of the others who live in this land and call it home.

Acknowledgments

The list of people to whom I owe thanks is endless. It includes all the people in Gaza and in its refugee camps who taught me about the Strip, hosted me, accepted me as I am, and helped me with my work and with the writing of this book. More than anything else, they gave me the opportunity to experience the humanity that can flourish under harsh and humiliating conditions. Unfortunately I cannot mention all their names, mostly because space is limited but also because to do so might jeopardize their well-being. Those whom I cannot mention by name know that I am forever grateful to them.

My special and open thanks, then, to Huda and Dr. Hayder abd al-Shafi, to Bassam al-Agra, Kawthar Ne'irab, Mustafa Ibrahim, Mirwat and Marwan Kafarna, Rick Hooper, John Inhat, Amal and Raji Sourani, Ihab al-Ashqar, Faher and Fatma Awad, Marwa Kassem, Ismail Saleh, Diab al-Luh, Sufyan Abu Azida, and Hisham Abed al-Razek; to the editor in chief of *Ha'aretz*, Hanoch Marmari, and the news editor, Moshe Gal, who suggested that I be the paper's correspondent in the Gaza Strip; to Ada Ushpiz and David Landau, the feature editors, who always took an interest in my writing and encouraged me; to the desk editors at *Ha'aretz*; to the staff of the paper's archives; to the IDF Southern Command spokesman, the civil administration, and the CLO spokespeople; to the staff of the Palestinian ministry of information; and to the Workers' Hotline.

There is a special place in my heart for my friend Michal Levine, who understands so well. And for Tamar Peleg, another Gaza addict, who, more than anyone else, always knew the good experiences and the difficulties and helped in times of inevitable frustration and pain.

Finally, no words of thanks suffice to express my gratitude to Riva Hocherman at Metropolitan Books, whose sensitivity to the subject and rigorous concern for its integrity allowed my book to live in translation.

Notes

Introduction

1. Hanna Levy-Hass, *Inside Belsen* (Sussex, Eng.: The Harvester Sussex Press, 1982). The diary was published after the war in several languages.

1. The Military Governor Has Moved Buildings

1. Shaul Bibi, *Ha'ir*, November 10, 1995.
2. Joel Singer, *Justice*, December 1995. International Association of Jewish Lawyers and Jurists, Tel Aviv.
3. In October 1997, Hayder abd al-Shafi resigned from the Legislative Council. He had reached the conclusion that despite the separation of powers, the Palestinian executive branch, headed by Arafat, had marginalized the Council and ignored its resolutions, especially those concerning the financial conduct of those in leadership positions and calls to uphold human rights. "The Council's first mission was to establish a democratic process, and there has been no progress toward this goal, I fear," he said.

3. Bougainvillea and a Pile of Rubble

1. This is the official figure presented by the Palestinian Bureau of Statistics, the result of its 1997 population census.
2. Association of Israeli-Palestinian Physicians for Human Rights (PHR-Israel), *Intifada-Related Head Injuries and Rehabilitation of the Head-Injured*, Tel Aviv, July 1995.
3. After a lengthy legal battle conducted by Dan Assan, an attorney for PHR-Israel, an Israeli court ruled that the state must pay 75% of the costs of treatment, for as long as Lulu lives. The court ruled that the family must pay 25% of the costs, arguing that it was responsible for failing to prevent the injury.

4. Khalid Switches Parties

1. In the summer of 1997 a special committee of the Legislative Council that reviewed allegations of corruption in the Authority denounced Nabil Shaath and Jamil al-Tarifi and demanded that Arafat fire them and put them on trial for embezzlement. The two remained in their positions and dismissed the accusations as populist and amateur behavior on the part of the Council. They claimed that any mistakes were the result of an inexperienced administration.

5. As It Is Written in the Quran

1. N.J. Dawood, tr., *The Quran* (London: Penguin Classics, rev. ed. 1990), p.18.
2. Ibid., p.19.
3. Ibid., p.82.
4. Nadav Shragai, *Ha'aretz*, May 23, 1994.
5. After reading the book in Hebrew, my friend Nihad Sheikh Khalil, an observant Muslim, wished to offer a correction. According to Islamic texts, it was not Muhammad who violated the treaty. In response to a call from Bnei Bekar, a Jewish community, the Quraysh joined in an attack on the Muslim Huz'a community. Thus the prophet considered himself released from the treaty.
6. When this joke was circulating in early 1994, before the transfer of responsibilities to the Authority, men over forty were allowed through the Israeli checkpoint that marked the northern entrance to "greater Jerusalem" (an area annexed by Israel that includes East Jerusalem and the Old City). Two years later, even older men were barred from entering.
7. This translation appears in Hillel Schenker, ed., *After Lebanon: The Israeli-Palestinian Connection* (New York: The Pilgrim Press, 1983), pp. 441–43.
8. Ibid., p. 445.

6. A Tax on Being Alive

1. World Bank, *Developing the Occupied Territories: An Investment in Peace* (Washington, D.C., 1993), vol. 2, p. 113.
2. E. A. Sadan, *Policy for Immediate Economic Industrial Development in the Gaza Strip* (Jerusalem, 1991), p. 65.
3. Ibid., p. 41.
4. Ibid.
5. World Bank, *Occupied Territories*, vol. 5, p. 1.
6. Palestine Economic Policy Research Institute, *The Palestinian-Israeli Trade Arrangements: Searching for Fair Revenue Sharing*, Dec. 1995, p. ix. Quoted in O. Hamed and R. A. Shaban, "One-Sided Customs and Monetary Union: The Case of the West Bank and Gaza Strip under Israeli Occupation," in

G. S. Fisher, D. Rodrick, E. Tuma, eds., *The Economics of the Middle East Peace* (Cambridge: MIT Press, 1993).

7. World Bank, *Occupied Territories*, vol. 2, pp. 107–10. The quotations in the paragraphs that follow are from these pages as well.

8. *Ha'aretz*, March 3, 1993.

9. Sadan, *Policy*, p. 6.

10. Samir Hazboun et al., Possibilities for Industrial and Entrepreneurial Development in the West Bank and Gaza Strip, p. 25

11. World Bank, *Occupied Territories*, vol. 5, p. 7.

12. Ibid., 68.

13. Sadan, *Policy*, p. 6.

14. World Bank, *Occupied Territories*, vol. 5, p. 1.

15. Ibid., p.5

16. Municipality of Gaza, *Priority Projects Program for Gaza City, 1996–2000*, prepared by the Large Project Team, Technical Department, and Welfare Association Consultants, Nov. 1995.

17. World Bank, *Occupied Territories*, vol. 5, p. 7.

18. Sara Roy, *Gaza Strip* (Washington, D.C.: Institute for Palestine Studies, 1995), p. 166.

19. The high figure for the combined supply is estimated by Palestinian sources. World Bank, *Occupied Territories*, vol. 5, pp. 49–50.

20. In permanent settlement negotiations Israel has maintained that the division of water must be based on the status quo regarding consumption and on historical rights to the use of the mountain aquifer. These rights were determined seventy years ago, before Palestinians began to make wide use of water from this aquifer. The Palestinians are now demanding equal access to and use of the common resources, while rejecting the argument that the present difference in consumption stems from a difference in "mentality."

21. Peace Now, *Demographic and Geographic Analysis of the Population in the West Bank and the Gaza Strip*, Nov. 1992, p. 33. According to data from the spokesman of the IDF Southern Command, July 1996.

7. We Are from the Same Village

1. Benny Morris, *The Birth of the Palestinian Refugee Problem, 1947–1949* (Cambridge, Eng.: Cambridge University Press, 1987), pp. 9–10.

2. Sara Roy, *Gaza Strip* (Washington, D.C.: Institute for Palestine Studies, 1995), p. 269.

3. Albert Hourani, *A History of the Arab Peoples* (Cambridge, Mass.: Belknap Press of Harvard University Press, 1991), p. 17.

4. Central Bureau of Statistics, Palestinian Ministry of Planning and International Economic Cooperation, *Statistical Abstract of 1995*, March 1996.

5. Roy, *Gaza Strip*, pp. 182–86.

6. Ibid., p. 205, marginal comment 83.

8. Missing in Action

1. Central Bureau of Statistics, Palestinian Ministry of Planning and International Economic Cooperation, *Statistical Abstract of 1995*, March 1996, p. 23.
2. M. Heiberg and G. Ovensen, eds., *Palestinian Society, 1993* (Oslo: Falch Hurtigtrykk, 1993), p. 185.
3. Palestinian Ministry of Planning, *Statistical Abstract of 1995*, p. 14.
4. *Requirements for Gender Development in Palestinian Society* (Jerusalem: Jerusalem Media and Communication Centre, 1995), pp. 10–11.
5. Rima Hammami, "Women in Palestinian Society," in Heiberg and Ovensen, *Palestinian Society*, pp. 307–08.

10. Yesterday's Permit

1. A B'tselem report on the border closings attributes the claim about the blind men to the coordinator for activities in the territories, Jerusalem, April 1996.
2. Eiten Rabin, *Ha'aretz*, June 20, 1996.

11. Waiting to Turn Forty

1. Ephraim Kleiman, an economist, more than hinted as much in a roundtable discussion with Yitzhak Segev, a journalist; Benyamin Begin and Haim Ramon, members of the Knesset; and Mordechai Gur, the former IDF chief of staff, in April 1996. The discussion was moderated by Ze'ev Schiff, a senior military correspondent for *Ha'aretz*.
2. E. A. Sadan, *Policy for Immediate Economic Industrial Development in the Gaza Strip* (Jerusalem, 1991), p. 11.
3. Collaborators and employees of the civil administration were exempt from the ruling on criminal records, even though some of them had been involved in narcotics dealings.
4. *Ha'aretz*, Oct. 22, 1989.
5. Geir Ovenson, *Responding to Change*, FAFO Report 166, Oslo, 1994, p. 69.

12. The Engine Has Stalled

1. At the beginning of 1995, the tailors' union estimated that 30,000 people were employed in this sector, including many children and undeclared family members working in family-owned businesses. Other official figures put the number of industry workers at approximately 10,000.
2. In 1995, imports to the Strip amounted to $524.1 million. Of that, Israeli goods accounted for $470 million, those from the West Bank $25.7 million, and those from abroad $28.4 million. The same year, Gaza sold goods worth $77.8 million, primarily agricultural produce and clothing. Four years earlier,

the Strip imported $355.4 million of merchandise and exported $70.7 million. Thus the Strip barely managed to export more in 1995 than it had in 1991, despite the flood of contributions, investments, and promises. (Palestinian Ministry of Planning and International Economic Cooperation, *Statistical Abstract of 1995, Gaza*, March 1996), p. 94.

3. The negotiations of the Israeli-Palestinian Committee on the Principles and Procedures for the Transfer of Goods through the Rafah Terminal and via the Allenby Bridge continued until summer 1995, about one year after the transfer of authority, when the Palestinians agreed to the Israeli demand that the goods be transferred by the back-to-back system at the border crossings. Only then did very limited commerce begin via the Rafah Terminal (to Egypt) and the Allenby Bridge (to Jordan).

4. In 1995, the average daily wage of a factory worker in Gaza was the equivalent of $8.88. For someone working in Gaza in the food industry it was $9.60 and in the sewing industry $8.70. Monthly salaries in the public sector ranged from $320 to $780 (*Statistical Abstract*, p. 72).

5. Sara Roy, *Gaza Strip* (Washington, D.C.: Institute for Palestine Studies), p. 269.

6. Office of the UN Special Coordinator for the Occupied Territories (UNSCO), *Economic and Social Conditions in the West Bank and Gaza Strip*, Gaza, Oct. 1996.

7. The Ministry of Planning and International Economic Cooperation published data, gathered in cooperation with the Palestinian Bureau of Statistics, which are very different from the Ministry of Labor's. According to the planning ministry, the size of the workforce in 1995 averaged only 113,400. Of these workers, 19,000 were in agriculture, 11,000 in industry, 23,000 in construction and public works, 16,800 in commerce, 29,800 in the public sector (it is unclear whether the police are included here), and 13,400 in a variety of other occupations (*Statistical Abstract*, p. 13). The disparity between the two sets of figures is rooted in the competition that exists between the various ministries and their inability to cooperate in carrying out tasks such as gathering statistics. I have chosen the Ministry of Labor's data, since they are broken out into more categories. I therefore believe them to be more accurate and thus likely to produce a more realistic estimate of the size of the workforce.

8. Palestinian Economic Policy Research Institute (MAS), *Poverty in the West Bank and the Gaza Strip*, Nov. 1995, p. 31. In total, 19.1% of Palestinians had a per capita expenditure of less than $650 per year—the estimated poverty line.

13. A People Up in Arms

1. M. Heiberg and G. Ovensen, eds., *Palestinian Society, 1993* (Oslo: Falch Hurtigtrykk, 1993), p. 44.

2. *News from Within* (Jerusalem: Alternative Information Center, Aug. 1996).

3. Amnesty International, *Trial at Midnight: Secret, Summary, Unfair Trials in Gaza*, London, June 1995.

4. Set up as a voluntary nonaffiliated body to document violations of the Oslo Accords, Peace Watch published detailed reports, and was especially meticulous in monitoring the activity of the Palestinian Authority in areas related to security but also to the economy. Its founders included political figures and scholars from the center of the Israeli political spectrum, that is, from the Labor Party and farther right, including settlers in the occupied territories and Minister of Commerce and Industry Natan Sharansky. Peace Watch was dissolved after Benjamin Netanyahu's election in 1996.

5. As an instance of an attempt to avoid extradition, the press release cited the trial of two Qalqilya residents discovered in Jericho and accused of murdering the two Israeli hikers in Wadi Qelt. Instead of being extradited to Israel they were tried by the Palestinians for other crimes and sentenced to ten years at hard labor. The information concerning them had come from another suspect in the murders, who had been interrogated by the Shabak. He was eventually released for lack of evidence and maintained that the information he had provided was untrue and had been given under duress. Meanwhile, the two imprisoned men have demanded a retrial and in 1998 went on a three-week hunger strike.

6. I asked the CLO for a copy of the clear procedures that would enable the entry of Israelis into the Strip. My request was attached to the list of questions on health matters that I submitted in July 1996 (see chapter 9, "Yesterday's Permit"). The CLO's refusal to provide answers to specific questions—because I am not an "objective journalist who is guided by the truth"—extended to this request as well.

Epilogue

1. UN Special Coordinator for the Occupied Territories (UNSCO), *Economic and Social Conditions in the West Bank and Gaza Strip*, Gaza, Oct. 1996.

2. This thesis was presented at Tel Aviv University in June 1995 by Saleh abd al-Jawwad of Bir Zeit University. He was the first to analyze the ongoing process, from 1948 to the Oslo Accords, and to term it sociocide.

3. Amnon Barzilai, *Ha'aretz*, Nov. 28, 1994.

Index